The
BERKSHIRE
Book
A Complete Guide

THE
BERKSHIRE
BOOK
A Complete Guide

THIRD EDITION

Jonathan Sternfield

With Linda Glick Conway and Sarah Novak

**Berkshire House Publishers
Stockbridge, Massachusetts**

On the Cover and Frontispiece:
Front Cover: Background — *Mauserts Pond, Clarksburg State Forest, Clarksburg,* by A. Blake Gardner. Insets — *Cross-country skiing at Canyon Ranch, Lenox,* by Jonathan Sternfield; *Lawn Crowd at Tanglewood, Lenox,* by William McCoy; *Gallery in the Clark Art Institute, Williamstown,* by Bill Binzen.
Frontispiece: *Looking over the Monument Mountain Valley;* Arthur Palme, courtesy of the Berkshire County Historical Society.
Back cover: *Hancock Shaker Village, Hancock,* by Bill Binzen; *Norman Rockwell's studio, Stockbridge,* by Paul J. Rocheleau, photo courtesy of The Norman Rockwell Museum at Stockbridge; *Porch at the Red Lion Inn, Stockbridge,* by Bill Binzen.

ISBN: 0-936399-60-0
ISSN: 1056-7968 (series)

Editors: Virginia Rowe, Constance Oxley. Managing Editor: Philip Rich. Original design for Great Destinations™ series: Janice Lindstrom. Cover design: Jane McWhorter. Map revisions and new Berkshire County area maps by Ron Toelke Associates. Production services by Ripinsky & Company, Connecticut.

Berkshire House books are available at substantial discounts for bulk purchases by corporations and other organizations for promotions and premiums. Special personalized editions can also be produced in large quantities. For more information, contact:

Berkshire House Publishers
Box 297, Stockbridge MA 01262
800-321-8526

Manufactured in the United States of America
First printing 1994
10 9 8 7 6 5 4 3 2 1

No complimentary meals or lodgings were accepted by the author and reviewers in gathering information for this work.

The <u>GREAT DESTINATIONS</u> Series

The Berkshire Book: A Complete Guide
The Santa Fe & Taos Book: A Complete Guide
The Napa & Sonoma Book: A Complete Guide
The Chesapeake Bay Book: A Complete Guide
The Coast of Maine Book: A Complete Guide
The Adirondack Book: A Complete Guide
The Aspen Book: A Complete Guide
The Charleston, Savannah & Coastal Islands Book:
  A Complete Guide
The Gulf Coast of Florida Book: A Complete Guide
The Central Coast of California Book : A Complete Guide
The Newport & Narragansett Bay Book: A Complete Guide
The Hamptons Book: A Complete Guide

The Great Destinations™ series features regions in the United States rich in natural beauty and culture. Each Great Destinations™ guidebook reviews an extensive selection of lodgings, restaurants, cultural events, historic sites, shops, and recreational opportunities, and outlines the region's natural and social history. Written by resident authors, the guides are a resource for visitor and resident alike. Maps, photographs, directions to and around the region, lists of helpful phone numbers and addresses, and indexes.

Contents

CHAPTER ONE
From the Glaciers to the Present
HISTORY
1

CHAPTER TWO
Getting Here, Getting Around
TRANSPORTATION
16

CHAPTER THREE
The Keys to Your Room
LODGING
28

CHAPTER FOUR
What to See, What to Do
CULTURE
88

CHAPTER FIVE
Pleasing the Palate
RESTAURANTS & FOOD PURVEYORS
155

CHAPTER SIX
For the Fun of It
RECREATION
230

CHAPTER SEVEN
Fancy Goods
SHOPPING
284

CHAPTER EIGHT
Practical Matters
INFORMATION
320

Acknowledgments

"The company is very good and a lot of fine minds live here," Tina Packard, artistic director of Shakespeare & Company, has said of Berkshire County.

So many fine minds and so rich a culture that Berkshire presents a cultural quilt in need of some firm stitching. Fortunately, many exceptional Berkshire friends and colleagues contributed their efforts to this third edition. Linda Glick Conway, author of several published cookbooks and an experienced editor and North County resident, undertook the *Lodging* chapter, updating and recasting every old inn entry and adding many new ones. Sarah Novak, Berkshire native and Berkshire House editor, put aside editing long enough to write the "Food Purveyors" section of the *Restaurants* chapter and the complete *Shopping* chapter. For the latter she had the help of Marcia Perry, an antiques expert who was her indefatigable shopping companion, and Gae Elfenbein, another antiques expert. Sarah also reviewed three of the inns in the *Lodging* chapter. Virginia Rowe, researcher, spent many hours keeping me in line with fresh facts and new insights, and she brought her experience with past editions to edit sections of the book, as did Constance Oxley, whose culinary expertise in particular contributed enormously to the *Restaurants* chapter. Ron Toelke brought a fresh eye to the maps for this book, and with his associate, Michael Martin, revised some maps while bringing others firmly into the electronic age.

Finally, thanks to Jean Rousseau, president and publisher of Berkshire House, and his staff — Mary Osak, tireless bookkeeper and moral support, Madeleine Gruen, enthusiastic and gifted marketing director; and Philip Rich, managing editor. Their guidance throughout helped bring the project to fruition. Thanks, too, to David Emblidge, with whom the idea for this book was first developed.

Introduction

*Lenox has had its usual tonic effect on me, and I feel
like a new edition, revised and corrected. . . .*

This was Berkshire's revitalizing influence on Edith Wharton, in 1902, and
we feel that tonic effect, too, nearly a century later, coming around again in a
third edition, revised and corrected.

We feel encouraged. The first two editions of *The Berkshire Book* were well
received, our judgments confirmed, our candor praised. There was a call for
more. So, here we go again.

"In olden times, authors were proud of the privilege of dedicating their
works to majesty," wrote Berkshire author Herman Melville in the 1850s to the
nearby Sophia, wife of Berkshire author Nathaniel Hawthorne. Melville continued, calling such a dedication "a right noble custom, which we of Berkshire
must revive. For whether we will or no, Majesty is all around us here in
Berkshire, sitting as in a grand Congress of Vienna of majestic hilltops. . . ."

Pure nature is a Berkshire tradition, but so is the careful grooming and tend-
ing of nature. A village improvement speaker at the Laurel Hill Society meeting in Stockbridge put it this way: "We mean to work till every street shall be
graded, every sidewalk shaded, every noxious weed eradicated, every water-
course laid and perfected, and every nook and corner beautiful — in short, till
Art combined with Nature shall have rendered our town the most beautiful
and attractive spot in our ancient commonwealth."

The original Berkshire is in England, south of Oxford, and there it's pronounced
"Bark-sheer." "Berk" derives from "bark," related, of course, to trees or forest;
"shire" means "hilly country town."

"Art combined with Nature," that is the essence of Berkshire life, an essence
that led novelist Henry James to write of his visits to Lenox novelist Edith
Wharton: "This renews the vision of the Massachusetts Berkshire, land
beyond any other in America today. . . ." Ever since the 19th-century influx of
artists and art patrons, Berkshire culture has had a ripe medium in which to
flourish. The legacy for us today is an almost unbelievably rich cultural life,
from soaring symphonies at Tanglewood to breathtaking dance artistry at
Jacob's Pillow; from the folksy characters of Norman Rockwell's paintings to
the elegant austerity of Shaker ways and means; from the dramatic heights of
acclaimed theatrical stars at Williamstown Theatre Festival and Berkshire
Theatre Festival in Stockbridge to the great theatrical moments at Shakespeare

& Co. in Lenox and at the Berkshire Public Theatre in Pittsfield. Berkshire is home to great museums, too, like the Clark and the Williams College museums in Williamstown, the Berkshire Museum in Pittsfield, and the new Norman Rockwell Museum outside Stockbridge.

The cultural brilliance doesn't set with the sun. Pop music comes to life after dark, from guitar-strumming folksingers to blues and jazz groups, from hard rockers to new wavers, all playing at a variety of pubs, clubs, taverns, bars, restaurants, and boogie joints.

There is lodging to suit every taste here, from the baronial "cottages" such as Wheatleigh and Blantyre, to the rusticity of dozens of quaint houses offering a simple bed and breakfast. For those who prefer to sleep closer to nature, the county's state parks are a camper's delight. Berkshire has its own restaurants, too — hundreds of them — from haute cuisine to home cookin', with true winners in every category.

In recreation the region gets its greatest attention from skiers, drawn by the county's fine downhill and cross-country ski runs. For hikers, the Appalachian Trail traverses the entire county. And in warmer weather, Berkshire golf courses, tennis courts, and lakes come alive with sportspeople, eager to play.

Berkshire, by common consent, is not only a good place to be born in, but a good place to live in, and a good place to die in, as well. It is also prominently recognized as a good place to go out from, and an equally good place to come back to. A Berkshire birth is something to be proud of, a Berkshire sojourn a delight, a rest, a recreation, a circumstance of pleasant memory, ever after; and a Berkshire residence a rich and enjoyable life experience.

The Book of Berkshire, 1887

As in previous editions, the *Culture* chapter, "What to See and What to Do," is based on the events themselves; on insider's information; on personal interviews with public relations and artistic directors; art gallery owners, and artists; and finally on book research, including histories, biographies, and letters. For the third edition, all of Berkshire's perennial cultural attractions, and some new ones, were visited and reviewed. Where space permitted, comments about performances or shows occurring since the second edition were included.

For the *Restaurants* chapter, every restaurant reviewed in the last edition was revisited, many newly opened establishments sampled for the first time. The editorial budget paid for all meals; we were in no way indebted to any restaurant, and we never announced our visit or our intention. During the meals, we often had extensive conversations with waiters, managers, and sometimes the chefs themselves.

Recreational opportunities were studied again, and transportation alternatives reviewed. And the *Information* chapter has been brought up to date.

From start to finish, we have aimed to create a comprehensive, reliable guide for one of America's premier places to live or vacation. We wish you every pleasure as you come to know the Berkshires better, and we hope our *Berkshire Book* continues to serve you as a trusted friend.

Jonathan Sternfield
Stockbridge, Massachusetts

THE WAY THIS BOOK WORKS

ORGANIZATION

Entries are located by subject in the appropriate chapters. Among the chapters, arrangements vary to suit the needs of subject matter. Most material is arranged in three geographical groupings, with ***South County*** offerings first, followed by those in ***Central County***, and finally ***North County*** A few nearby listings that are located ***Outside the County*** are given, as well.

Within these geographic groupings, listings are arranged alphabetically — first by town or topic, and then by establishments' names. Some entries, such as those in *Shopping*, are arranged by type; hence all the crafts shops appear together. Each chapter has its own introduction, and the specific arrangement of that chapter is spelled out there.

Factual information was researched at the latest possible time before publication, but be advised that many of these "facts" are subject to change. Chefs and innkeepers come and go, hours change, shops appear and disappear. When in doubt, phone ahead.

Specific information (such as address and location, telephone number, hours of business, and a summary of special features or restrictions) is presented in the lefthand column or is otherwise shown separately, adjacent to descriptions of various entries throughout the book.

LIST OF MAPS

Berkshire Towns
Berkshire County
Berkshire Topography
Berkshire Access
Berkshire Recreational Sites
Town maps: Great Barrington, Stockbridge, Lenox, Pittsfield, Williamstown, North Adams

PRICES

With few exceptions, specific prices are not given. Because pricing is constantly changing, we have noted price ranges in two key chapters, the ones on lodging and dining.

Lodging prices are on a per-room rate, double occupancy, in the high season (summer, fall foliage, and ski months). Low-season rates are likely to be 20–40% less. We urge you always to phone ahead for updated prices and other information and for reservations.

Restaurant prices indicate the cost of an individual's meal, which includes appetizer, entrée, and dessert but does not include cocktails, wine, tax, or tip. Restaurants with a prix fixe menu are noted accordingly.

Price Codes

	Lodging	*Dining*
Inexpensive	Up to $65	Up to $10
Moderate	$65 to $100	$10 to $20
Expensive	$100 to $175	$20 to $35
Very Expensive	Over $175	Over $35

Credit Cards are abbreviated as follows:

AE — American Express	DC — Diner's Club
CB — Carte Blanche	MC — Master Card
D — Discover Card	V — Visa

AREA CODE

There is one telephone area code for all of Berkshire County: **413.**

INFORMATION BOOTHS

In warmer weather, many Berkshire towns feature tourist Information Booths, usually manned by volunteers. Year-round tourist information can be obtained from the **Berkshire Visitors Bureau**, Berkshire Common, bottom level, Hilton Hotel, West St., Pittsfield (413-443-9186). The bureau is open Mon.–Fri., 8:30–4:30.

Great Barrington Information Booth: 362 Main St.; 413-528-1510. Open Mon.–Fri., 9:30–4:30; Sat., 11–4.

Lee Information Booth: Main St. at the park; 413-243-0852. Open Mon.–Thurs., 10–4, Fri.–Sat., 10–6; Sun. 10–2.

Lenox Chamber of Commerce Information Office: Lenox Academy, 75 Main St.; 413-637-3646. Open Mon.–Thurs, 10–4; Fri. & Sat., 10–6; Sun., 10–2.

Massachusetts Turnpike: at Burger King, Eastbound Mile Marker 8, Lee; 413-243-4929.

Northern Berkshire Chamber of Commerce: Main office, 40 Main St., Holiday Inn, N. Adams; 413-663-3735. Open Mon.–Fri., 9–5. Tour booth located on Union St.; open 7 days, 10–4.

Pittsfield Information Booth: Bank Row. Open Mon.–Thurs., 9–5; Fri.–Sat., 9–8; Sun. 10–2.

Stockbridge Information Booth: Main St. 413-298-5200; Self-service, open 7 days. Lodging information 413-298-5327.

West Stockbridge Information Booth: Rte. 102 at Berkshire Truck Plaza. Self-service, open 24 hrs.

Williamstown Information Booth: Rte 7; 413-458-4922. Open daily 10–6.

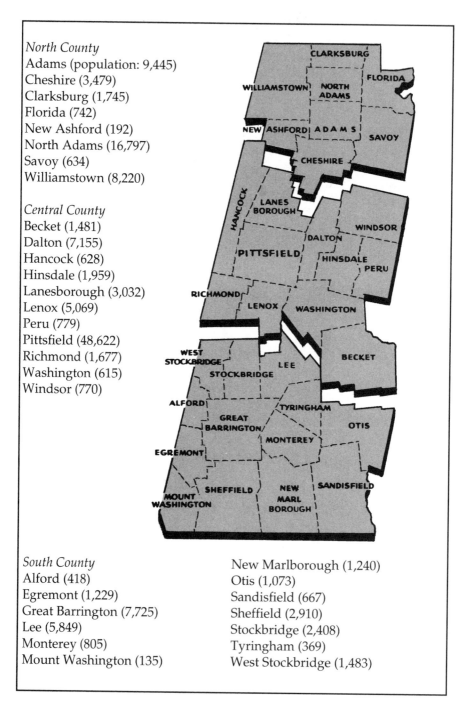

North County
Adams (population: 9,445)
Cheshire (3,479)
Clarksburg (1,745)
Florida (742)
New Ashford (192)
North Adams (16,797)
Savoy (634)
Williamstown (8,220)

Central County
Becket (1,481)
Dalton (7,155)
Hancock (628)
Hinsdale (1,959)
Lanesborough (3,032)
Lenox (5,069)
Peru (779)
Pittsfield (48,622)
Richmond (1,677)
Washington (615)
Windsor (770)

South County
Alford (418)
Egremont (1,229)
Great Barrington (7,725)
Lee (5,849)
Monterey (805)
Mount Washington (135)

New Marlborough (1,240)
Otis (1,073)
Sandisfield (667)
Sheffield (2,910)
Stockbridge (2,408)
Tyringham (369)
West Stockbridge (1,483)

Berkshire Towns

The
BERKSHIRE
Book

A Complete Guide

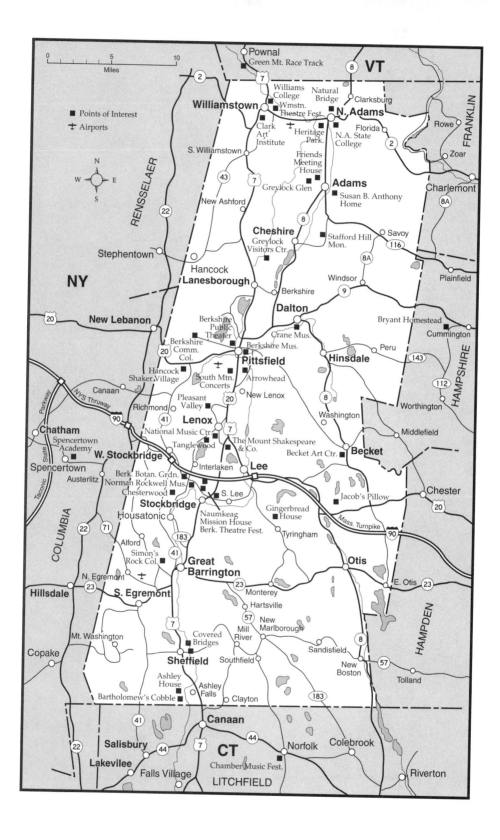

CHAPTER ONE
From the Glaciers to the Present
HISTORY

Shadowbrook, overlooking Stockbridge Bowl. One the largest and most extravagant homes ever built in America, the mansion was destroyed by fire in 1956.

Berkshire's early history is a story of water and ice, of mountains and wildlife forming a beautiful, but inaccessible "place apart." It is a story of hunters seeking game and eventually a refuge. Later, it becomes the story of religious pilgrims in search of sanctuary, of artists and art patrons coming to be inspired and renewed. It is a saga of industry tapping the region's waterways and cutting into its woodlands. And it is a tale of farmers and engineers, housewives, and schoolchildren, poets and actors, craftsmen and shopkeepers, dancers and dreamers.

There is also a new Berkshire history being written, one of restoration, revival, and recreation. Where once the old was regularly pushed aside to make way for the new, now it is again revered, and often revitalized. From historic estates, like Linwood, now transformed into the new Norman Rockwell Museum, to the majestic lawns of Highwood, now cradling Tanglewood's new Seiji Ozawa Hall, classic Berkshire experiences are being created in a marriage of old and new. Building on tremendous tradition, the arts in Berkshire are excelling and expanding — in their seasons, in variety and in sheer number of offerings.

Lively issues are at hand in the hills: how to balance year-round economic viability with overbearing commercialization of the villages; when to stop con-

dominium and time-sharing development. The county is still a haven for zeal-
ous religious groups, and though there are few Shakers left, there are several
popular groups in Berkshire whose members put their spirituality first, day in,
day out.

Being three-quarters covered with trees, today's Berkshire is more forested
than it has been in a hundred years. Its area of protected lands, nearly 15 percent, is on the rise. Industries come and go, without much overall growth, and
air pollution continues to be minimal. General Electric and now Martin Mari-
etta remain the backbone of the urban economy here, but it is an increasingly
high-tech operation, leaving some traditional assembly line workers behind.
Berkshire arts and recreational facilities have burgeoned; the county is now
fun during four seasons of the year, day or night. What was once wild and
hilly has been selectively cultivated, and now all of Berkshire is in bloom.

Note: Many of the cultural sites mentioned in this chapter are described at
greater length elsewhere in this book; see the Index for page references.

NATURAL HISTORY

> *Tell me your landscape and I will tell you who you are.*
> Ortega y Gasset

Berkshire's natural history starts over 500 million years ago, when the
region was probably flatter, covered with mud, sand, and the waters of an
inland sea. Just as underwater life was beginning, shifting continental plates
caused undersea upheavals, thrusting land masses upwards into the open air.
These first Berkshire hills were mountains, on the scale of the Rockies — lofty
peaks overlooking the waters. And on their upland slopes, limestone formed
from the decaying primitive sea life, while schist, gneiss, and quartz developed
from the sand and mud.

Then the glaciers came. From the north and northwest, vast tidal waves of
slow-moving ice crept into the region, smoothing and gouging, sculpting the
landscape. Gradually, the ice melted, leaving rushing rivers, and huge lakes in
areas like Great Barrington, Williamstown, and Tyringham. But the snows in
the northlands began to fall constantly again, and once more the oceans of ice
slowly swept into the region. Three more times this cycle repeated: glacial
dominance and melting. Without vegetation, this smooth-surfaced Berkshire
was a place of howling winds, sandblasting the landscape. As climatic conditions tempered in this latest melting period, vegetation began to grow again,
about 11,000 B.C. The grasses and bushes further tempered the climate, and
from the boggy marshland, trees such as spruce sprang up, then pine and
birch, and finally hardwoods such as oak and maple.

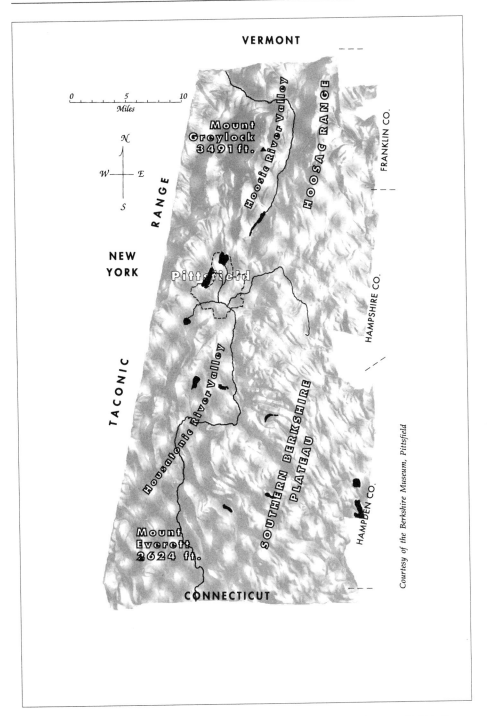

VERMONT

0   5   10
Miles

N

W —— E

S

Hoosic River Valley

HOOSAG RANGE

FRANKLIN CO.

Mount
Greylock
3491 ft.

RANGE

NEW
YORK

Pittsfield

HAMPSHIRE CO.

TACONIC

Housatonic River Valley

SOUTHERN BERKSHIRE
PLATEAU

HAMPDEN CO.

Mount
Everett
2624 ft.

CONNECTICUT

Courtesy of the Berkshire Museum, Pittsfield

From the relief map by Bartlett Hendricks, courtesy Berkshire Museum

As trees and other vegetation softened the landscape, and as the land itself began to dry out, animals from neighboring regions moved into Berkshire. And not long after that (between ten and twelve thousand years ago) came descendants of the Asians who first called this continent home. These original native Americans were foragers at first, but after developing tools, they then crafted weapons and became hunters. In South Egremont not long ago, the remains of a 12,000-year-old mastadon were found, and around it, arrowheads of the same age. Bow hunting came early to Berkshire.

What the native Americans and animals found back then in Berkshire is close to what we find today: a glacial landscape, with hills and mountains smoothed to a fraction of their former height, with lakes like Onota and Pontoosuc, whose basins were scoured by the ice, with steep bowl-shaped cirques like Greylock's "Hopper" (visible from Rte. 7) carved deep into mountainside, with massive rock slabs like those in Ice Glen and at the foot of Monument Mountain, and with widely strewn rocks and boulders almost everywhere. Every spring, a new harvest of rocks appears in the fields, brought up by frost and plow. And those old stone walls partitioning the pastures served not only as fencing, but as rock depositories for farmers attempting to keep their fertile fields free of glacial "pebbles."

The overall topography of Berkshire (see map p. 3) shows the glacial path clearly. Deep north-to-south furrows are bounded by two north-to-south mountain chains, with two major rivers running through the valleys. The contours of social and economic history in the region have always followed this lay of the land. On the east is the Hoosac Range — high, rugged country that came to be called "the Berkshire Barrier" because it blocked easy access for pioneers coming over from the Connecticut River valley. On the west, toward the New York border, is the Taconic Range, ruled over by Mt. Greylock (3,491 ft.) in the north and Mt. Everett (2,600 ft.) in the south.

The Housatonic River rises above Pittsfield and flows south through Berkshire, down to Stratford, Connecticut, and out into Long Island Sound. The Hoosic River, flowing northward from Hoosac Lake and tributaries, passes through the Adamses and into Vermont on its way to the Hudson River, above Albany. Because the rivers provided power for mills and generators and because the adjoining land was so fertile, Berkshire history became very much a "waterwheel" — sculpted by glacier and erosion, driven in our time by industry and recreation.

People who visit the Berkshires today only for high culture or fine food, or even for robust skiing, and who don't walk the trails or sit still on the hilltops, miss what is perhaps the better half of the local entertainment. The sheer variety of Berkshire habitats and animal families is staggering. Though wildlife in Berkshire was undoubtedly richer before the arrival of people, there are still herds of deer, the occasional moose (sometimes appearing in an urban backyard), and black bear, red and gray fox, a few coyotes, bobcats, even eastern cougars, as well as more common beaver and mink. Berkshire has rare salamanders, extant only in these wetlands because the area's naturally high lime content counteracts the effects of acid rain, allowing the fragile creatures one last safe habitat. Giant blue heron, with wings six feet across, can be seen here on isolated ponds, and ruffed grouse, quail, and wild turkey occupy the woods. Though formal gardens at historic homes are beautiful, not to be missed are the delicate alpine flowers on the tops of the tallest mountains, like Greylock, above the tree line.

In this geologically momentary melt between glacial flows, Berkshire is green, welcoming and beautiful.

Want to know more about Berkshire natural history? Lauren Stevens' *Hikes & Walks in the Berkshire Hills* has a nice overview, informed by the author's extensive trail experience, and consultation with Williams College geologist, Paul Karabinos. The pamphlet *A Canoe Guide to the Housatonic* provides some good color commentary on the local ecology. A nifty new natural history is provided by Berkshire Sanctuaries director, René Laubach, in his *Guide to Natural Places in the Berkshire Hills*. Laubach's deep familiarity with Berkshire's flora, fauna, geology, and ecology, together with his enthusiastic teaching style make this book a must for all Berkshire naturalists. The Berkshire Museum is the county's center for natural history study. For field trips, try any of the "Nature Preserves" (see Chapter Six, *Recreation*). And in the summer, the Appalachian Mountain Club runs excellent nature study programs at sky-high Bascom Lodge atop Mt. Greylock.

SOCIAL HISTORY

History is to the community what memory is to the individual.
Shaker saying

From the outset, Berkshire's social history was greatly influenced by the effects of its natural history. Set off by imposing mountain ranges and beset by fierce winters, the area became home to migrant wildlife around 10,000 B.C., and shortly thereafter, was visited by roving bands of Amerindian hunters in search of game. Over the next 11,000 years, Berkshire was a summer hunting ground for many of these peoples, and for some, the area provided the materials to begin agriculture.

Among the woodland Indians, the Mahican lived along the Hudson River and ventured to Berkshire for the summer hunt. They called the major river here the Hooestonic ("the river beyond the mountains"), and from it, they fished shad, herring, and salmon in the springtime. The Mahican built weirs to trap fish in the Housatonic's tributaries and also fished with hand nets from dugout canoes on the river. They gathered mussels from the rocky river bottoms and smoke-cured them together with their surplus fish for winter storage. They hunted duck and geese; and they maintained gardens in the river's floodplain, which was fertilized annually by the spring flood.

After the Dutch established a fur-trading outpost at Fort Orange (now Albany, NY) in 1624, the Mahican fell into conflict with the neighboring Mohawk. The two tribes went to war over the valuable fur trade, and by 1628, the Mahican had been driven from the west bank of the Hudson, settling permanently in Berkshire.

In 1676, the first European of record set foot in Berkshire, when Major John Talcott overtook a raiding band of about 150 Indians "neare unto Ousatunick" (Great Barrington). It was the last significant battle of King Philip's War, and Major Talcott preserved both Colonial security and his perfect unbeaten battle record.

Fate did not smile upon the Mahican. Smallpox dramatically reduced their ranks in 1690. Not long after, Dutch farmers migrated east from the Hudson Valley and settled into Berkshire, near what is now the town of Mount Washington. There are still Dutch town names in South County, such as Van Deusenville (in Great Barrington).

In 1724, a small band of Mahican led by chiefs Konkapot and Umpachenee sold their lands along the Housatonic River (including what is now Sheffield, Great Barrington, Egremont, Mount Washington, Alford, and parts of Lee, Stockbridge, and West Stockbridge). The buyers were the Parsons, proprietors through the Colonial Commonwealth of Massachusetts; the price, "£460, 3 bbls. of cider, and 30 qts. of rum." In a matter of months, scores of English settlers moved into Berkshire, to the Sheffield grant known as Lower Housatonic Township. The earliest homesteads were built at some distance from the Housatonic, on the second river terrace. This allowed the fertile floodplain to be used for agriculture and kept the settlers away from the malarial lowlands.

In the mid-1730s, the Rev. John Sergeant came from Yale College to proselytize and educate the hundreds of Mahican who lived around *W-nahk-ta-kook* ("Great Meadow"), later called Indian Town and then Stockbridge. He learned their language and won the respect of the Indians. Ten years later (1744), Berkshire was opened to cross-country road travel for the first time, when the "Great Road" was laid out between Boston and Albany, crossing the county at Great Barrington. John Sergeant died in 1749; and gradually, the Mahican faded.

There seemed something of a renewal when the Rev. Jonathan Edwards came to Stockbridge two years later. With his fiery preaching style, Edwards had stirred up the "Great Awakening," a religious revival sweeping New England. His zeal, however, had offended parishioners at his previous pulpit in Northampton, and Edwards had been dismissed. Exiled, in effect, to Stockbridge, he now had a small but well-schooled congregation. One of America's earliest philosophers of religion, Edwards published *Freedom of the Will*, in 1754, Berkshire's first book.

With the conclusion of the French and Indian War, marked by the British victory over the French at Quebec (1759), Berkshire was no longer so vulnerable to invading Indian attack. With the British solidification of power in the area, the royal governor, Sir Francis Bernard, created the county. Striking off a section from the already-existing Hampshire County, the governor declared this one "Berkshire," after his home county in England. The date was July 1, 1761 — Berkshire was born, in America, in Massachusetts.

As his tribe dwindled to fewer than 400, Konkapot, at age 94, stepped down as chief of the rechristened "Stockbridge Indians." Two years later, in early 1773, a group of townspeople and lawyers met in the Sheffield study of Colonel John Ashley. There, in one of the earliest public assertions of American freedom, they drafted "The Sheffield Declaration," stating to Britain and all the world that "Mankind in a State of Nature are equal, free and independent of each other. . . . " By the following year, ferment in the county against the British was reaching fever pitch. In July, a county convention met under the chairmanship of Colonel Ashley; and from this meeting, the "Stockbridge Non-Intercourse Articles" of 1774 were drafted, complaining that "whereas the Parliament of Great Britain have of late undertaken to give and grant away our money without our knowledge or consent . . . , we will not import, purchase or consume. . . ." any British goods. By mid-August, British oppression had mounted, and on the 16th, the people of Berkshire would take it no longer. Fifteen hundred strong, they staged a peaceful sit-down strike around the Great Barrington Courthouse, preventing the royal judges from meeting. It was the first open resistance to British rule in America.

In April 1775, a regiment of Berkshire Minutemen under Colonel John Paterson of Lenox started out for Cambridge to aid in the Revolutionary effort. And in May, former Sheffield resident Ethan Allen led his Green Mountain Boys from Vermont and 57 Berkshire men in a successful surprise attack on Fort Ticonderoga. That following winter (1776), General Henry Knox led Continental troops and over 100 oxen, dragging captured Ticonderoga cannon, through Berkshire on the way to General George Washington in Cambridge. Aided by this additional weaponry, Washington was able to drive the British from Boston.

Once the United States was established, all sorts of religious, cultural, and industrial developments began to take place in Berkshire. In 1779, one Mrs. John Fisk was excommunicated from the church in Stockbridge for marrying a Revolutionary War officer accused of habitually using profane language. A cause célèbre in Massachusetts' Congregationalism, the case pitted Calvinist orthodoxy against church liberals, a regional division with parallels to the contours of the ongoing national debate between Federalists and Jeffersonians. At the county courthouse in Great Barrington in 1781, Theodore Sedgwick of Stockbridge — who brought distinction to the county by serving in both houses of Congress — won the freedom of Colonel John Ashley's slave, Mum

Bett, said to be the first American slave freed by law. By 1784, the Indian community in Berkshire was nearing its end, having collapsed socially and economically. Beginning that year, the Mahicans were forced into westward migration, leaving only their Housatonic legends behind them. In the 1790s, the Shakers established colonies in Hancock and Tyringham; Williams College opened; and marble quarrying started in West Stockbridge.

The farmers of Cheshire pooled the entire town's milk production for a day in 1801, and produced the Great Cheshire Cheese, a 1,235 pound, barrel-shaped cheddar that was hauled by oxen to Albany, and then by boat to Washington, for presentation to President Jefferson.

Cheshire Cheese and the President

In 1993, residents of the town of Cheshire again pooled their milk, or some of it anyway, and created another wheel of Cheshire Cheese for the president. Once again, the president of the United States, this time Bill Clinton, sent a thank-you note to this tiny Berkshire town for their wheel of Cheshire Cheese, this time 21 pounds.

"Please extend my thanks to everyone involved with this gift, especially the Cornstalkers 4-H Club," wrote President Clinton. "Your thoughtfulness and generosity are deeply appreciated."

The original communication between president and Berkshire cheesemakers was not only about a bigger cheese, but also about considerably weightier issues. Wrote the townspeople of Cheshire to President Jefferson:

> *We believe the Supreme Ruler of the Universe, who raises up men to achieve great events, has raised up a Jefferson at this critical day to defend Republicanism and baffle the arts of aristocracy . . . The cheese was procured by the personal labor of free-born farmers with the voluntary and cheerful aid of their wives and daughters, without the assistance of a single slave. It is not the last stone of the Bastille, nor is it an article of great pecuniary worth, but as a free-will offering, we hope it will be favorably received.*

It was. Jefferson delighted in his gargantuan Cheshire Cheese, personally eating the delicacy often and sharing it with his cabinet members and visiting dignitaries. Every White House servant got a wedge, and not to leave any significant party out, Jefferson cut a generous slab of the cheese and returned it to Berkshire, that the residents of Cheshire might enjoy the product of their own labor.

Along with the cheese, President Jefferson sent $200 to the town, in payment for the Great Cheese, at the going rate of 16 cents a pound. Accompanying his unsolicited payment, the president sent the following note:

> *I receive with particular pleasure the testimony of good will with which your citizens have been pleased to charge you. It presents an extraordinary proof of the skill with those domestic arts which contribute so much to our daily comfort . . . To myself, this mark of esteem from freeborn farmers, employed personally in the useful labors of life, is particularly grateful. . . .*

"Americans! Encourage your own manufactories and they will improve. Ladies, save your RAGS." The 1801 ad that started the Crane Paper empire.

Industry took a firm hold in Berkshire about the same time, when Zenas Crane began paper production in Dalton; and David Estes opened the first textile mill in North Adams. By the sides of Berkshire's rivers, plants of a new sort were sprouting.

Spanish merino sheep were introduced into Berkshire — the first in New England — and with their wool woven into fine worsted in the county's state-of-the-art mills, Berkshire broadcloth was fashioned into President Madison's inauguration suit in 1813. Shortly thereafter, the first stage route in the county was established, running from Greenfield to North Adams, Williamstown, and Albany.

And the writers began to come. First there was poet William Cullen Bryant in Great Barrington (1820). As he attempted to divine the art of poetry while earning his living as a lawyer, his new Stockbridge friend Catherine Sedgwick published her first novel, *A New England Tale,* to critcal acclaim. By stagecoach, Alexis de Tocqueville visited the Sedgwicks in Stockbridge in 1831. Not long after, trains came huffing into the hills, one of them bringing Henry Wadsworth Longfellow to honeymoon in Pittsfield. Dr. Oliver Wendell Holmes built a home on ancestral lands at Canoe Meadows and began to spend his summers in Berkshire. Then, in 1850, Herman Melville bought Arrowhead Farm in Pittsfield. Nathaniel Hawthorne moved from Salem to Lenox and took up residence at a property he called Tanglewood. Shortly thereafter, Dr. Holmes introduced Hawthorne to Melville on the occasion of a climb up Monument Mountain; the two great writers' imaginations were entwined thereafter.

In 1851, construction was begun on the Hoosac Tunnel (between the Berkshire towns of Florida and North Adams), a project that was to last decades — and tragically take hundreds of lives. It was a tunnel that was destined to be the longest in America and the one through which most tunneling technology was developed. Here nitroglycerin was used for the first time, speeding the work, but also the demise of many workers.

Hawthorne and Thoreau

Nathaniel Hawthorne was one of 19th-century Berkshire's greatest admirers. During his year-and-a-half residency in the "Red Cottage," at "Tanglewood," overlooking Stockbridge Bowl, he kept a journal, recording the fullness of his affection for the landscape.

October 16, 1850

A morning mist filling up the whole length and breadth of the valley, betwixt here and Monument Mountain; the summit of the mountain emerging. The mist reaches to perhaps a hundred yards of our house, so dense as to conceal everything, except that, near its hither boundary, a few ruddy or yellow tree-tops emerge, glorified by the early sunshine; as is likewise the whole mist cloud.

H. D. Thoreau shared Hawthorne's reverence for these hills, saying of Williams College's position at the foot of Greylock:

It would be no small advantage if every small college were thus located at the base of a mountain, as good at least as one well-endowed professorship . . . Some will remember, no doubt, not only that they went to college, but that they went to the mountain.

But before those essentially creative explosions were silenced, there were many totally destructive ones sounding in the Civil War. Five days after the Confederate forces opened fire on Fort Sumter, Berkshire militiamen were on their way south to defend the Republic. These first county recruits stayed three months and saw little action; other Berkshire regiments took their place, fighting often in the coming months, through 1865, as far south as the state of Florida. In that same year, President Lincoln was assassinated, and Berkshire mourned.

The wooden rake man, Lee, about 1865.

Courtesty Berkshire Historical Society

After two unsuccessful attempts, Cyrus Field of Stockbridge and his engineers finally laid a cable across the Atlantic, in 1866, connecting American communications with Europe. A year later, in America's leading paper town, Lee, paper fabrication from wood pulp rather than rags was demonstrated for the first time in the United States.

"Save Time and Distance: Take the Hoosac Tunnel."

Industry was now booming in Berkshire. Aided by plentiful water power, textile and paper plants lined the rivers. Fueled by the county's abundant forests, iron smelters and other heavy industries cut deep into the Berkshire woodland. It was not long before nearly 75% of the county's timber was gone, and the hills were nearly bald. In 1875, the Hoosac Tunnel was finally completed, opening North County to interstate commerce; and shortly thereafter, in 1879, Crane & Co. of Dalton, obtained an exclusive contract with the federal government to produce American currency paper, a contract involving a lot of money, both blank and printed.

In 1886, William Stanley installed the world's first commercial electric system, in the town of Great Barrington, where 25 shops along Main Street were lighted. The General Electric Company visited Stanley in his Pittsfield workshop, and soon after, moved in nearby. Five years later, an electric trolley system was introduced in Pittsfield, running from Park Square to Pontoosuc Lake. Soon, this quiet, reliable transport would interconnect most of the county.

The decade of the 1880s ushered in Berkshire's Gilded Age as well, the age in which millionaires came to the hills to play and build their dream "cottages." Mrs. Searles had just completed her $2.5 million castle in Great Barrington; Anson Phelps Stokes had spent nearly as much in completing the largest home in America just then, his 100-room Shadowbrook in Stockbridge. A mile away, the 33-room Italianate palazzo called Wheatleigh was being finished, a gift of H. H. Cook to his daughter on the occasion of her marriage to Count Carlos de Heredia. The 50-room Elm Court was nearby too, in Lenox, built by rug magnate W. D. Sloane; and across town, Giraud Foster had erected his multimillion-dollar likeness of the French Petit Trianon at his estate, Bellefontaine. In Stockbridge, there was also Naumkeag, Ambassador Choate's homey mansion; and sculptor Daniel Chester French's splendid Chesterwood. Soon in Lenox, Robert Paterson would have Blantyre built, and novelist Edith Wharton would oversee the design of the Mount. In all, some 75 extraordinary mansions had been added to the Berkshire landscape. The Berkshire community would never again be a cultural backwater: European and urban tastes had come to live in the hills.

Making even grander strokes in Berkshire land acquisition was William C. Whitney, secretary of the Navy under President Grover Cleveland. In 1896, in the Berkshire town of Washington, Whitney established an 11,000-acre game preserve and stocked it with buffalo, moose, Virginia deer, and elk. The estate was later to become October Mountain State Forest, a giant wilderness in county center.

In the fall of 1902, President Roosevelt visited Berkshire, but he barely escaped alive, sustaining minor injury after his coach overturned near the Pittsfield Country Club. That next summer, both ex-President Grover Cleveland

Railroad Street, Great Barrington, around the turn of the century.

Courtesy of the Snap Shop

and humorist Mark Twain summered in Tyringham. Eight years later, on July 4, 1911, as Pittsfield observed its gala 150th anniversary, President Taft spoke before a crowd of 50,000 at the railroad station. And later that same year, Edith Wharton's novella *Ethan Frome* was published, a critical and popular success that derived many of its dramatic and scenic details from life in the Berkshires.

Twentieth-century Berkshire has been marked with events principally in industry and the arts. Since 1903, General Electric has played a significant role in the county's industry, and all through this century, that role has developed as the industrial giant has diversified its product research and manufacturing. The huge electric transformers still produced in Pittsfield are descendants of the ones first demonstrated in Great Barrington by William Stanley. In 1914, GE established a high-voltage laboratory in Pittsfield, and seven years later, the lab made electrical history by producing a million-volt flash of artificial lightning.

In the arts, the Stockbridge Playhouse (later to become today's Berkshire Theatre Festival) opened in Stockbridge in 1928, with Eva LeGallienne in *Cradle Song*. Ted Shawn established his School of Dance at Jacob's Pillow in Becket in 1932. The 1930s also saw and heard the first Berkshire Symphony Festival concerts, preludes to Tanglewood.

Downhill skiing debuted in Berkshire in 1935, as Bousquet opened runs in Pittsfield and arranged for "ski trains" from New York. Other mountains soon had trails carved across them, and Berkshire became a winter recreational mecca.

The 1950s saw the arrival of famed artist Norman Rockwell in Stockbridge and the creation of the Sterling and Francine Clark Art Institute in Williamstown, a collection and facility of international import. The Williamstown Theatre Festival began performances, enlivening all of Berkshire with star-studded drama. In the 1960s, two colleges were opened: Berkshire Community College, in Pittsfield, the first in a projected series of state junior colleges; and Simon's Rock Early College, in Great Barrington, a progressive school that is now part of Bard College.

In the mid-'60s, General Electric made another breakthrough, this time in plastics, and the company subsequently developed a whole new family of

Symphonic music comes to Berkshire: The New York Philharmonic at Hanna Farm, Interlaken, in 1934, establishing the model for Tanglewood.

polymers that diversified the corporation still further and sent a regional invention to the Moon — from the Lexan laboratories in Pittsfield to Tranquility Crater. And in the last ten years, the arts have blossomed still more gloriously, with Shakespeare & Co. being born in Lenox, then ambitiously beginning the restoration and adaptation of the Mount, Edith Wharton's mansion. In Pittsfield, too, a company found its home when the Berkshire Public Theatre settled into restoring the old Union Square Theatre.

Culturally, Berkshire's rich smorgasbord has been further enriched by the offerings of the Berkshire Film Society, offering special screenings and lectures by cinema notables. And in the health-recreational arena, the county's stock went skyhigh with the successful establishment of Canyon Ranch at Bellefontaine, one of the most luxurious and sophisticated spas in the world.

Other great estates have been recycled as well, turning Berkshire's fiefdoms into public domain. In the Glendale section of Stockbridge, the gracious Linwood estate was transformed into the new home of the Norman Rockwell Museum. Looking back toward Tanglewood from this splendid site, the visitor gets a fresh view of unspoiled, 19th-century Berkshire. And the museum itself makes Rockwell's obvious genius more accessible than it's ever been. You get greater vision on more paintings, in a completely unhurried tour of America's greatest illustrator.

Just a few miles away, near the center of Lenox, the Springlawn or Bible Speaks property has found a new life, being the site selected by the National Music Foundation for its new National Music Center. Spearheaded by rock 'n' roll's godfather, Dick Clark, the facility is to include a residence for musicians and radio people, a performing arts center, museum, library and educational facility.

Tanglewood has expanded, creating Seiji Ozawa Hall, an arched concert hall, where 1,180 music lovers can enjoy both acoustic intimacy and fidelity. Tall sliding doors can be opened in warmer weather, allowing breezes in and also permitting about 700 additional concertgoers on the adjacent lawn to both see and hear the performers clearly. Set just back of Highwood, the estate adjoining Tanglewood, the Concert Hall is a welcome acoustic upgrade to New England's mecca for classical music.

Berkshire's current events still center around condo development, shopping malls, bypasses, and the proposed Greylock Glen recreational area. The Mass MoCA modern arts complex in North Adams, planned several years ago, still remains a possibility. The Wal-Marting of Berkshire has begun, first up in North Adams, and probably next in Central or South County. Once again the Berkshire Barrier has been broken, this time by the nitroglycerin of mass marketing. Some say Wal-Marts create jobs and bring low prices to the people; others say Wal-Marts are the kiss of death to any downtown area. Certainly, the successful Berkshire Mall has drained life away from downtown Pittsfield. We see Berkshire as capable of sustaining most of these new developments, in moderation. Bypasses, rerouting Route 7's truck traffic around Stockbridge and Pittsfield, are often discussed, and just as often bypassed.

Other environmental issues are being addressed head on. A variety of ecologically aware groups are mobilizing efforts to clean up Berkshire's principal river, the Housatonic. It will take countless millions of dollars and the ideas of some of the world's great minds to undo the damage inflicted by toxic sludge, but true success in this endeavor could restore Berkshire to a state of environmental purity it hasn't known for over a century.

Under the watchful eye of the Berkshire Natural Resources Council and other environmental protection groups, the splendor of the landscape is being guarded and preserved. With the gradual shrinking of industry here, and tourism among the most stable of Berkshire businesses, protecting the rolling hills seems to make good economic as well as aesthetic sense. Once, the hills were decimated, shaved bald by paper and lumber mills, and by charcoal manufacturers. Now the hills are once more alive, fully forested and soothing to the eye. In many respects, Berkshire seems to breathing easier, to be coming back to its senses.

With the Earth and Berkshire in the background, Stockbridge-raised astronaut F. Story Musgrave tends to a repair on the Hubble Space Telescope. This futuristic eye-in-the-sky is now so powerful and clear-sighted it can actually look back towards the beginnings of time.

Courtesy of NASA

CHAPTER TWO
Getting Here, Getting Around
TRANSPORTATION

From the author's collection

The astonishing Pittsfield Train Station, around 1905.

Traveling to the Berkshires can be fun these days, especially by car, but it wasn't always so. During Colonial times, when Berkshire County was a patchwork of farms, travel here was by horseback or stagecoach over rough dirt roads. Colonel Henry Knox found this out in 1776 when he had to cut his own trail across Berkshire while dragging cannon from Fort Ticonderoga to Cambridge.

Some passage towards Berkshire was afforded by both the Hudson and Connecticut rivers aboard sailing ships, but river travel did not become popular till 1825, when the steamboats began regular service. Both Albany and Hartford were connected to New York City by steamboat runs, the upper Connecticut River being outfitted with an elaborate system of locks to bypass the rapids.

With the harnessing of steam for riverboat power, it wasn't long before the iron horse came huffing into the Berkshire Hills. Rails were laid from New York to the Berkshires by the Housatonic Railroad; and two lines competed to the west: the Albany–West Stockbridge Line and the Hudson and Berkshire Line. From Boston, construction of the Western Railway up from Springfield was reportedly "delayed by competition between Stockbridge and Pittsfield for fixing of the route through their town. After surveys, Pittsfield won." During the summers of 1840–41, deep cuts in the hills were made and many bridges built. When the lines were completed, Berkshire was nine hours by train from Boston and about three hours from Albany. But many who had come to work on the railroads never took the train back. Hundreds of the Irish rail laborers from cities east and west grew to love the Berkshires and stayed on.

Perhaps sons of these rail workers influenced local transport too, for early in our own century, a remarkable system of electric trolley track was laid among hilltowns in the Berkshires, running from Williamstown south through North Adams and Adams, through Pittsfield, Lenox, Lee, Great Barrington, and Sheffield. Quiet and reliable, this Berkshire Street Railway grew so popular that opulent parlor cars were constructed and put into service, running till 1932. When automobiles and buses were refined, the possibilities for public transport changed; paved roads were improved, and unpaved ones were surfaced. Rail service to and within the Berkshires withered.

PRESENT POSSIBILITIES

Amtrak serves Pittsfield from Boston, but you'd better be on time for that one, because there's only one train a day in each direction!

So, if a car is available, by all means drive to the Berkshires. You'll want a car here to explore the back roads and byways, and by auto, the trip to the Berkshires can be enjoyed at your own pace. If an automobile is not your way, and you're not on the train east or west, bus is the next logical option, and these run regularly from New York, Hartford, Boston, and Albany. If you're in a hurry to get to these hills, you can fly in, but alas, now only by private or charter plane to Great Barrington, Pittsfield, or North Adams. Major airlines with regular service fly into both Bradley International near Hartford and to the Albany County Airport; from there, car rentals or limousine and bus service are available. For your convenience, a host of details about Berkshire transportation follows.

GETTING TO THESE HILLS

BY CAR

From Manhattan: Take the Major Deegan Expressway or the Henry Hudson Parkway to the Saw Mill River Parkway, then proceed north on one of the most beautiful roadways in the world, the Taconic State Parkway. For the southern Berkshires, exit the Taconic at "Hillsdale, Claverack, Rte. 23" and fol-

BERKSHIRE ACCESS

Using Tanglewood (on the Stockbridge–Lenox line) as the Berkshire reference point, the following cities are this close.

CITY	TIME	MILES
Albany	1 hr	50
Boston	2.5 hrs	135
Bridgeport	2 hrs	110
Danbury	1.75 hrs	85
Hartford	1.5 hrs	70
New Haven	2.5 hrs	115
Montreal	5 hrs	275
New York City	3 hrs	150
Philadelphia	4.5 hrs	230
Providence	2.5 hrs	125
Springfield	.75 hr	35
Waterbury	1.5 hrs	75
Washington, DC	7 hrs	350
Worcester	1.75 hrs	90

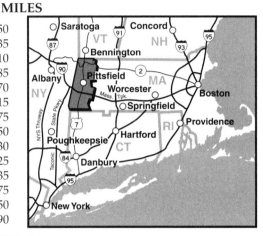

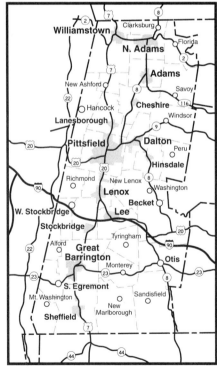

Berkshire County is 56 miles south to north, from Sheffield to Williamstown. Depending on the season and the weather, it's normally a two-hour leisurely drive up Rte. 7. Because of the mountain ranges that run along this route, east-west travel across the county remains much more difficult, with all the county's east-west routes (2 in the north; 9, midcounty; and 23 in the south) being tricky drives in freezing or snowy weather. Back roads in particular vary tremendously in condition and type, ranging from smooth macadam to rough dirt. On these back roads especially, drivers should keep an eye out for bicyclists, horseback riders, hikers, joggers, and deer.

low 23 east, towards Hillsdale and on to Great Barrington. For Stockbridge, Lee, and Lenox, (and all points in south and central county) proceed up Rte. 7. For Williamstown and all of northern Berkshire, you might want to proceed farther up the Taconic and exit at Rte. 295, leading to Stephentown, then follow Rte. 43 through Hancock.

From New Jersey, Pennsylvania and south: If local color is high on your list or you'd rather ramble northward, Rte. 22 north is a good choice, and you can pick it up as far south as Armonk or Bedford in Westchester County, New York. Rte. 22 is a road still proud of its diners: of particular note is the Red Rooster in Pawling, just north of I-684's end. Further upstate on Rte. 22, turn right at Hillsdale on Rte. 23 east toward Great Barrington. For the most direct route from New Jersey, Pennsylvania and south, take the New York Thruway to I-84 east; at the Taconic Parkway, go north to Rte. 23 for southern Berkshire, or drive on to Rte. 295 for northern Berkshire.

From Connecticut and/or the New York Metro Area: Rte. 7 north was an early stagecoach thoroughfare to Berkshire, and you join the same trail at Danbury, via I-684 and I-84. Driving up Rte. 7, you'll wend your way along the beautiful Housatonic River, north through New Milford, Kent, and Canaan and into Massachusetts through Ashley Falls (an especially good ride for picnics and antiques). To arrive in southeastern Berkshire, Rte. 8 is a quick and scenic drive as it follows the Farmington River north.

From Boston and east: The Massachusetts Turnpike is the quickest, easiest, and one of the more scenic routes west to the southern Berkshires, and from Boston, there's no better bet. West of the Connecticut River, you can get off the turnpike at Exit 3 and take Rte. 202 south to 20 west and pick up Rte. 23 west at Woronoco for the best route to Otis Ridge, Butternut Basin, and Catamount ski areas. Most people stay on the turnpike right into the Berkshires, exiting either at Lee or West Stockbridge.

A less rapid but more colorful route westward from Boston is Rte. 20, which cuts across southern Massachusetts, connecting with Lee. If you're coming west to the Berkshires from more northern latitudes, Rte. 9 from Northampton is a splendid drive, a high road, with long lovely vistas and few towns. Still farther to the north, eastern entry to Berkshire County can be gained by driving the original Mohawk Trail, an Indian byway. Also known as Rte. 2, this is the most direct way to Jiminy Peak and Brodie Mountain skiing.

From Hartford: The quickest route by far is I-91 north to the Massachusetts Turnpike west. Then proceed as in directions for Massachusetts Turnpike travel from Boston. A slower but more pleasant drive is Rte. 44 west, up through Avon, Norfolk, and Canaan, where you turn right and take Rte. 7 north into Berkshire County.

From Montreal or Albany: Leaving Canada, take I-87 (known as "the Northway") south to Albany, and exit at Rte. 7 to Rte. 2 toward Williamstown, or continue on I-87 south to I-90 east, connecting then to the Massachusetts Turnpike, which is the continuation of I-90 east. Exit at either Canaan, New York, or Lee.

BY BUS

Arriving at Lenox from New York, a Berkshire Bonanza.

Jonathan Sternfield

From Manhattan (3.5 hours): **Bonanza** (800-556-3815) serves the Berkshires out of New York City's **Port Authority Bus Terminal** (212-564-8484) at 40th St. between 8th and 9th Aves. Tickets may be purchased at the Greyhound ticket windows (212-971-6363), near 8th Ave. Boarding is down the escalators at the center of the terminal, and then to the right, usually at Gate 13. Bonanza runs three buses daily: 8:45 a.m., 2:15 p.m., and 5:15 p.m. There is also an additional Friday evening bus, leaving Port Authority at 7:30. Berkshire locales marked with an asterisk are Flag Stops, where you must wave to the bus driver in order to be picked up.

Berkshire Phone Numbers for New York Buses

Canaan, CT	Canaan Pharmacy, Main St.	203-824-5481
Gt. Barrington	Bill's Pharmacy, 362 Main St.	413-528-1590
Hillsdale, NY	*Junction Rtes. 22 & 23	800-556-3815
Lee	McClelland Drugs, 43 Main St.	413-243-0135
Lenox	Lenox News & Variety, 39 Housatonic St.	413-637-2815
New Ashford	*Entrance to Brodie Mt. Ski Area, Rte. 7	800-556-3815
Pittsfield	Bus Terminal, 57 S. Church St.	413-442-4451
Sheffield	Rte. 7, *First Agricultural Bank	800-556-3815

S. Egremont	*Gaslight Store	800-556-3815
Stockbridge	Chamber of Commerce Booth, Main St.	413-298-3344
Williamstown	Williams Inn, Main St.	413-458-2665

From Boston (3.5 hours): *Bonanza* and *Greyhound* serve the Berkshires from Boston out of the *Greyhound Terminal* at 10 St. James Ave. (617-423-5810). Peter Pan/Trailways runs two buses daily to Pittsfield out of the *Trailways Terminal* at 555 Atlantic Ave. Berkshire-bound passengers change buses at Springfield. Call 800-343-9999 for prices and schedules.

Berkshire Phone Numbers for Boston Buses

Lee	McClelland Drugs, 43 Main St.	413-243-0135
Lenox	Lenox News & Variety, 39 Housatonic St.	413-637-2815
Pittsfield	Bus Terminal, 57 S. Church St.	413-442-4451
Williamstown	Williams Inn, 1090 Main St.	413-458-9371

From Hartford (1.75 hours): The *Greyhound Line* runs two buses to Pittsfield daily, at 11:15 a.m. and 4:20 p.m., from the *Greyhound Terminal* at 409 Church St., Hartford (203-547-1500).

From Montreal (6 hours): *Greyhound* runs south to the Albany Greyhound Terminal. Connect to Pittsfield as noted below.

From Albany (1 hour): *Bonanza* runs two buses daily from Albany to Pittsfield. Greyhound runs one bus daily.

BY TRAIN

From Manhattan: Until World War II, the Housatonic Railroad ran ski trains from Manhattan to the Berkshires. And right up to 1971, Penn Central ran trains from New York City to the Berkshires, via Danbury. Since that time, however, rail service northward has no longer linked the Big Apple with the Berkshires. If you're inclined to ride the rails, *Amtrak* (800-USA-RAIL or 413-872-7245) can help you get to the Berkshires, but not all the way. Their turbo-liner from Grand Central Station runs frequently and smoothly along the Hudson River, a splendid ride. For southern Berkshire, stay aboard till Hudson, a river town recently restored; for northern Berkshire, carry on to Rensselaer. For travel connections from Hudson or Rensselaer to the Berkshires, see "By Taxi or Limousine."

From Boston: Amtrak runs a single train daily through the Berkshires, starting from Boston's South Station. The Pittsfield depot has no actual station; it's just a shelter. (To find the depot: take West St. westwards past the Hilton; at the first light, turn right onto Center St.; take the next right onto Depot St.; the shelter is on the left.) Anyone boarding the train in Pittsfield must purchase tickets on the train. The round-trip ticket prices vary, depending on time of travel and seat availability. Private compartments are available.

From Montreal: Amtrak runs one train daily from Montreal through Albany. There is no same-day train connection from this run to the Berkshires; to get here by hired car, see "By Limousine or Taxi"; or see "By Bus."

From Albany: Amtrak has a single Pittsfield-bound train daily from the Albany/Rensselaer Depot on East St. (2 miles from downtown Albany).

BY PLANE

If you own a small airplane or decide to charter one, you can fly directly to the Berkshires, landing at Gt. Barrington, Pittsfield or N. Adams airports.

From New York City: Feeling rich, traveling high with some friends or riding on the corporate account? There are several charter air companies in the metropolitan New York area that will fly you from La Guardia, JFK or other airports near New York to any of the Berkshire airports. Airlines currently flying these routes include:

Aircraft Charter Group	800-553-3590
Chester Air, Chester, CT	800-752-6371
Long Island Airways	800-645-9572

and from Westchester County:

Panorama (White Plains airport)	914-328-9800
if calling from New York City:	718-507-9800
Richmor Aviation	800-331-6101

From Boston: There are several charter flight companies that fly from Beantown to Berkshire. Some of those you can try are:

Bird Airfleet	508-372-6566
Wiggins Airways	617-762-5690 Ext. #251

From Hartford: Bradley Airport in Hartford handles numerous domestic and international airlines, so you can fly to Bradley from nearly anywhere. From there, charter air service to the Berkshires is available through any of the companies listed under "From Boston" or through the Berkshire County companies listed below.

From Albany: Albany is terminus for a substantial volume of domestic jet traffic and, being under an hour from the Berkshires by car, is the closest you can get to these hills by jet. Charter connector flights from Albany to the Berkshires are available through *Page Flight* (518-869-0253) or through the Berkshire County companies listed below.

In Berkshire County: There are three aviation companies in Berkshire County which operate air taxi service to just about any other northeastern airport.

Berkshire Aviation	Gt. Barrington Airport	413-528-1010
		or -528-1061
Lyon Aviation	Pittsfield Airport	413-443-6700
Esposito Flying Service	Harriman & West Airport	
	N. Adams	413-663-3330

BY LIMOUSINE OR TAXI

If you're with a group or want to pamper yourself, a limousine direct to Berkshire is the smoothest approach. There are many limousine services which will whisk you away from urban gridlock to the spaciousness of this hill country.

From New York and its Airports:

| Kabot | 718-545-2400 or 413-626-3700 |
| Esquire | 212-935-9700 or 413-737-7000 |

From Boston and Logan Airport:

| Cooper | 617-482-1000 or 800-342-2123 |
| Fifth Avenue | 617-286-0555 |

From Hartford and Bradley Airport:

Carey, Aster Madison Avenue	800-RE:LIMOS
Ambassador	203-633-7300 or 800-395-LIMO
Buckley	203-953-8787
Elite	203-223-4423

From Albany, Albany Airport and Rensselaer:

| AAA Limousine Service | 518-456-5030 |
| Diamond Limousine | 518-283-8000 |

To northern Berkshire (by reservation only):

| Norm's Limousine Service | 413-663-8300 or 413-663-6284 |

From Hudson, NY and its Amtrak Station:

| Star City Taxi | 518-828-3355 |

GETTING AROUND THE BERKSHIRES

Note: Individual town maps of Great Barrington, Stockbridge, Lenox, Pittsfield, North Adams, and Williamstown can be found at the back of the book.

> *You are entering
> God's country.
> Don't drive through
> like hell.*

Sign Near Otis.

Rte. 7 is Berkshire County's main roadway, connecting cities and towns from south to north. Driving in winter, you'll certainly need snow tires. In summer, the cruising is easy; but on certain weekends during Tanglewood season and fall foliage, temporary traffic delays in popular villages are likely. Whenever possible, park and walk. Friendly but firm traffic cops will suggest outlying parking areas. And motorists beware: several Berkshire towns have laws requiring a full stop for pedestrians in crosswalks.

BY BUS

Berkshire County is no longer served by the electrified Berkshire Street Railway, but the "*B*," a public bus system, has in some ways filled the gap. The buses run from early in the morning to early in the evening. A complete schedule can be obtained from the **Berkshire Regional Transit Authority** (413-499-2782 or 800-292-2782). Fares vary by distance. If you're visiting without a car, the "*B*" will provide plenty of access to other communities, but you will need to plan activities around the weekday (and slightly different weekend) bus schedules.

BY RENTED CAR

Car rental agencies abound in Berkshire. Most will not deliver cars — you must first go to their place of business to do the paperwork. One exception is **Ugly Duckling Rent-A-Car.** They will pick you up from the train, bus, or wherever, then drive you back to their office to complete the paperwork. Berkshire car rentals are available through the following agencies.

Canaan, CT	Ugly Duckling (new and used)	203-824-5204 or 800-843-3825
Cheshire	Bedard Brothers Auto	413-743-0014
Gt. Barrington	Caffrey Motors	413-528-0848 or 800-698-0848
	Condor Chevrolet	413-528-2260 or 800-328-5551
	Larkins Enterprises (used only)	413-528-2156 or 413-528-9190
Lee	R.W.'s, Inc.	413-243-0946
Pittsfield	AJMCC Rent-a-Car	413-499-7733
	Hertz	413-499-4153 or 800-654-3131
	Johnson Rent-A-Car	413-443-6437 or 800-825-FORD
	Pete's Rentals	413-443-1406 or 800-696-7383
	Rent-A-Wreck	413-447-8117
N. Adams	Mohawk Rentals	413-663-3729
	Scarafoni	413-663-6516
Williamstown	B & L Service Station	413-458-8269

BY TAXI OR LIMOUSINE

Numerous taxi and limo companies serve Berkshire County. The following is a listing by town, with notations indicating if they have only taxis (T), only limos (L), or both (B).

Gt. Barrington	Taxico	413-528-0911 (T)
Lee	Abbott's Limousine & Livery	413-243-1645 (B)
	Park Taxi	413-243-0020 (T)
Lenox	Aarow Taxi	413-499-8604 (T)
	Alston's	413-637-3676 (B)
	Lenox Taxi	413-637-4441 (T)
	Tobi's Limousine Service	413-637-1224 (L)
N. Adams	Berkshire Livery Service	413-662-2609 (L)
	Norm's Limousine Service	413-663-8300 or 413-663-6284(B)
Pittsfield	A Unique Transportation Service	413-447-9224 (L)
	Aarow Taxi	413-499-4860 (B)
	Airport & Limousine	413-443-7111 (L)
	Berkshire Limousine	413-499-3232 or 800-543-6776
	Rainbow Taxi	413-499-4300 (B)
Stockbridge	Stockbridge Livery	413-298-4848 (T)
Williamstown	Luxury Limo	413-458-9414 (L)

BY BICYCLE

Bicycling in the Berkshires gives an exciting intimacy with the rolling landscape. Though practical only in warmer weather, biking from town to town is still quite reasonable here. Bike rental prices vary widely, with bikes available through:

Ashley Falls	The Bike Doctor	413-229-2909
Lenox	Main Street Sports & Leisure	413-637-4407 or 800-952-9197
Pittsfield	Plaine's Ski & Cycle Center	413-499-0391
Williamstown	Spoke Bicycle & Repair	413-458-3456

ON FOOT

The Appalachian Trail enters southern Berkshire in the town of Mount Washington and runs over hill and dale, past Great Barrington, through Monterey, and down into Tyringham Valley, then up near the town of Washington, through Dalton and Cheshire, over Mt. Greylock, and toward Vermont, bypassing North Adams. If you've got the time, we've got the trail. See "Hiking" in Chapter Six, *Recreation*.

Many Berkshire towns are small enough for walking exploration, and three in particular are well suited to visiting without a vehicle: Stockbridge, Lenox and Williamstown. All are lovely villages, with good accommodations, fine dining, interesting shopping, and first-rate cultural attractions within easy walking distance.

NEIGHBORS ALL AROUND

Though one tends to think of the Berkshires as a place apart, the county and its people frequently have close ties with neighboring communities. Travelers will want to connect with the neighbors, too, for Berkshire is surrounded by areas of extensive natural beauty, and certain nearby towns are loaded with good restaurants, old inns, and cultural attractions.

TO THE SOUTH

The Litchfield Hills of northwest Connecticut are gentler than the Berkshire Hills, but still make for good hiking. There is lovely architecture in this area, with many stately homes in Salisbury, Lakeville, Sharon, Litchfield, and Norfolk. And there are music festivals as well, such as the ones at Norfolk and at Music Mountain in Falls Village. See "Music" in Chapter Four, *Culture*.

TO THE EAST

Halfway over the Berkshire highlands between the Housatonic River valley and the Connecticut River lies the jagged eastern county border, shared with Franklin County up north and Hampshire County down south. Besides this eastern area's natural splendor, an attractive array of cultural possibilities is located here. The "Five College Area" of Amherst, South Hadley, and Northampton offers all the aesthetic and academic action anyone could want with the presence of Amherst, Hampshire, Mt. Holyoke, and Smith Colleges, as well as the University of Massachusetts.

TO THE NORTH

The Green Mountains of Vermont offer great skiing, hiking and camping. The town of Bennington makes an interesting stopover, with its museum (featuring Grandma Moses paintings), a fine college (Bennington), and Robert Frost's grave. There is also the extraordinary Bennington Pottery, where you can both buy and dine on their handsome stoneware. Rte. 7 up here continues as the spine of most communities, and a ride to architecturally stunning Manchester is worth the time; but consider the slower, less traveled Rte. 100 (the continuation of Massachusetts Rte. 8) threading through the mountainous midstate.

TO THE WEST

An interesting neighboring area is Columbia County in New York State. This county of farms holds treasures for antiques and "untiques" hunters and those who like small, unpretentious, all-American towns. Berkshire is not far from the Hudson Valley, an area rich with history and with vineyards worth visiting. And then there's Albany, which offers big city, cultural entertainment such as the touring New York Metropolitan Opera, performing at the capital city's structurally unique theater, *The Egg.* A bit farther north is Saratoga with its spas, its springs, its own summer arts festival (known as *SPAC*), and its elegant and justly famous racecourse.

CHAPTER THREE
The Keys to Your Room
LODGING

Snoozing on the porch of the Red Lion Inn

As stagecoach travel through the Berkshires developed in the 18th century, the need for roadside lodgings grew; and of those original inns still welcoming wayfarers today, the *New Boston Inn*, in New Boston, was likely the first. Built in 1737, this recently restored inn is about as authentic an early American lodging experience as you can find in New England. Quite close in age and attention to period detail is the *Old Inn on the Green* (1760), also in New Marlborough. This inn served as a tavern, a store, and later as post office. Today it comforts travelers with a small number of authentically Colonial rooms and a superlative restaurant. Next came the *Red Lion Inn* (1773), in Stockbridge, which provided not only housing for sojourners but also a meeting place for pre-Revolutionary political activists eager to communicate their grievances to Britain. More than 200 years later, the Red Lion is still the best-known stopover on the Berkshire trail.

There are many other 18th-century Berkshire inns continuing to offer warmth and hospitality, with the invitation of a good night's sleep, often in a four-poster bed. There's the *Village Inn* in Lenox, built as a farmhouse in 1771; the *Egremont Inn* (1780) and the *Weathervane Inn* (1785) in South Egremont, the *Elm Court Inn* (1790) in North Egremont, and the *Williamsville Inn* in West Stockbridge, originally a farmhouse dating from 1797.

Is the 19th century's sumptuous Gilded Age more your cup of tea? For you, Berkshire offers, among other possibilities, an Italian palazzo called *Wheatleigh* and a Tudor castle called *Blantyre*, both in Lenox. Strikingly different in style, these palatial estates-turned-hotels share the ability to satisfy even the most refined of tastes and to do so with panache.

Of course, there are in Berkshire many lesser lodgings, shorter perhaps on romance but more reasonably priced. A great many are charmingly situated and competently run — entirely comfortable places where almost any traveler would be pleased to spend the night. There is an ever-growing number of guest houses, both in town and out, many offering bed and breakfast ("B&B"); there are the simpler inns where precious quiet is an everyday experience; and there are modern hotels and all grades of motels for those on a budget or with little concern for country charm.

To evaluate lodgings, we place a high value on hospitality, the personal attention and sincere care that can turn a visit into an unforgettable sojourn. We also assign value and significance to the architectural qualities of a property; to its historical renown and traditions; its care in furnishing and use of antiques or other art; to the views and the natural beauty right at its doorstep.

For reviews of inn dining rooms, see Chapter Five, *Restaurants*.

BERKSHIRE LODGING NOTES

Rates

Rate cards are generally printed early in the spring and will change slightly from year to year. Reminder: Price codes are based on a per-room rate, double occupancy, during the high seasons (summer, fall foliage, skiing). Off-season rates are usually 20–40% lower. Many establishments have midweek rates as well.

Inexpensive	Up to $65
Moderate	$65 to $100
Expensive	$100 to $175
Very Expensive	Over $175

These rates do not include room taxes or service charges. (Note: AP = breakfast and dinner included in room rate; MAP = all meals included.)

Minimum Stay

Many of the better lodgings require a minimum stay of two or three nights on high season weekends. For a single night's stay in Berkshire at such times, the B&Bs or motels are the best bet. During the off season, minimum-stay requirements relax and in most instances no longer apply.

Deposit/Cancellation

Deposits are usually required for a confirmed reservation. Policies regarding deposits, cancellations, and refunds vary. It is always wise to inquire about these in advance. In the high season, lodging demand occasionally exceeds supply, so reservations for the more popular places need to be made months ahead.

Special Features

Wherever pertinent, we mention special features of lodgings, along with any caveats, e.g. restrictions on smoking or pets. We also suggest the ages of children for whom the inn might be appropriate, based on information provided by the establishments themselves. This is intended as a general guide only, and it is always best to call and inquire, as policies are often flexible and subject to change according to the season.

Other Options

For last-minute or emergency lodging arrangements in Berkshire, here are some numbers to phone.

Berkshire Visitors Bureau: 413-443-9186
Bed & Breakfast USA: 413-528-2113
Berkshire Bed and Breakfast Connection: 413-268-7244

Information Booths

For single-night stays in the high season or spur-of-the-moment arrangements at other times, visit any of the tourist information booths listed in the Introduction.

LODGING SOUTH COUNTY

Egremont

North Egremont

BREAD & ROSES
Managers: Julie & Elliot Lowell.
413-528-1099.
Box 50, Star Rte. 65, Gt. Barrington, MA 01230.

A charming, 1800s farmhouse, featuring five bed-rooms, all with private bath, air-conditioning, telephones, and robes, far from the madding crowd. Curl up in front of the cheery fireplace in the living room, perhaps with a book from

On Rte. 71, 1.5 mi. from jct.
  with Rte. 23.
Price: Moderate.
Credit Cards: None.
Handicap Access: Limited.
Special Features: No smok-
  ing; No pets; Children
  over 9.

the extensive library, or sit out on the spacious porch and listen to the babbling brook. Breakfasts from Julie's kitchen feature French toast Grand Marnier and a soufflé of spinach and mushrooms. French is spoken here, too.

ELM COURT INN
Managers: U. & G. Bieri.
413-528-0325.
P.O. Box 95, N. Egremont,
  MA 01252.
227 Rte. 71, in the center of
  N. Egremont.
Price: Moderate.
Credit Cards: AE, MC, V.
Special Features: No pets.

Immaculate, comfortable rooms above one of the more popular restaurants in South Berkshire. One room has a private bath; the other two share a bath. At the center of a quaint, quiet hamlet.

**HIDDEN ACRES BED
  AND BREAKFAST**
Owners: Daniel & Lorraine
  Miller.
413-528-1028.
35 Tremont Dr., Alford,
  MA 01230.
From Great Barrington, Rte.
  71, N. 3 mi. to Rowe Rd.,
  then 0.9 mi. to Tremont
  Dr.
Price: Moderate.
Credit Cards: None.
Special Features: No smok-
  ing; No pets; Children
  over 11.

Perhaps the loudest noise you will hear at Hidden Acres is the sound of falling leaves. Stone walls, massive trees, and five secluded acres invite walks, picnics, and solitude. Full country breakfast is served in the large country kitchen.

South Egremont

**BALDWIN HILL FARM
  B&B**
Owners: Richard & Priscilla
  Burdsall.
413-528-4092.
RD3, Box 125, Gt. Barring-
  ton, MA 01230.
From Taconic Parkway,
  Rte. 23 E. to S. Egremont,

If you have a secret desire to live on a farm, you'll love Baldwin Hill. In a very rural setting and blessed with a 360-degree view of its magnificent surroundings, this establishment includes an 1820s farmhouse turned B&B and barns galore. Peace, quiet, and tranquillity abound on 500 acres perfect for hiking, cross-country skiing, or simply observing the wildlife. Guests enjoy reading by the field-

left on Baldwin Hill Rd.,
to inn on left.
Price: Moderate.
Credit Cards: MC, V.
Special Features: Pool; No
smoking; No pets; Children over 12.

stone fireplace in winter or on the screened porch in summer. Four rooms, two with private bath, have views across fields to the mountains beyond. Full breakfast, from a menu with numerous choices, is served by friendly innkeepers, who take pride in this farm that has been in the family since 1910.

THE EGREMONT INN
Manager: Jo-Ann Charde.
413-528-2111.
Old Sheffield Rd., S. Egremont, MA 01258.
Side street off Rte. 23 in center of village.
Price: Moderate to Expensive.
Credit Cards: AE, MC, V.
Special Features: Pool;
Tennis.

Coziness, low ceilings, fireplaces, broad porches, 22 delightful rooms furnished with antiques: these set the tone for this historic 1780 inn nestled on a quiet side street in the heart of a classic, old village. Scenery ranges from lovely to gorgeous. Pool and tennis courts for guests' use. Tavern and fine restaurant located on main floor.

TRAIL'S END GUESTS
Owners: Anne & Cory
Hines.
413-528-3995.
678 S. Egremont Rd., Gt.
Barrington, MA 01230.
On Rte. 23, just E. of S.
Egremont.
Closed: Nov.–Apr.
Price: Moderate.
Credit Cards: None.
Special Features: No smoking; No pets.

This large modern Colonial is neat and trim inside and out. Set back from Rte. 23, it has three rooms, all with private bath, air-conditioning, and TV. Look for the handsome sleigh on the porch or in the yard. In summer the spacious screened porch is a popular spot for reading. Children are welcome.

THE WEATHERVANE INN
Owners: Anne & Vincent
Murphy.
413-528-9580.
Box 388, S. Egremont, MA
01258.
Rte. 23, just E. of the village.
Closed: Dec. 1–27.
Price: Expensive; MAP on
weekends.
Credit Cards: AE, MC, V.
Handicap Access: Limited.
Special Features: Pool; No
Pets; Children over 7.

This is a comfortable, clean, and very well-run operation set within a 1785 farmhouse; all 12 rooms have private baths. Your hosts are skilled at their trade and provide their version of Colonial lodging and fine dining in their cheery restaurant. Location is convenient to some of the best antiques shopping in the Berkshires, including one shop just behind the inn. Note that weekends in July and August have a three-night minimum.

WINDFLOWER INN

Owners: Liebert & Ryan families.
413-528-2720.
684 S. Egremont Rd., Gt. Barrington, MA 01230.
Rte. 23, just E. of S. Egremont.
Price: Expensive (MAP).
Credit Cards: AE.
Handicap Access: Limited.
Special Features: Pool; No pets.

One of the prettiest locations in South Berkshire complements the soothing, comfortable interior of this gracious and respected inn. Antiques furnish the common rooms as well as the bedrooms. All 13 rooms have private bath and six have fireplaces. Excellent prix-fixe restaurant on main floor of this family-run inn. Please note that MAP price includes full breakfast and dinner for two.

Great Barrington

ARRAWOOD BED & BREAKFAST

Managers: Marilyn & Bill Newmark.
413-528-5868.
105 Taconic Ave., Gt. Barrington, MA 01230.
Corner of Taconic Ave. & Oak St.
Price: Inexpensive to Moderate.
Credit Cards: None.

This graciously restored Victorian home, is located on a lovely, residential street. Fireplaces in public rooms, a full, country breakfast, and canopy beds in guest rooms are special touches. Informal elegance. (**Note: closed as of Spring 1994.**)

COFFING-BOSTWICK HOUSE

Proprietors: Diana & William Harwood.
413-528-4511.
98 Division St., Gt. Barrington, MA 01230.
Corner of Rte. 41 & Division St. 2 mi. N. of Gt. Barrington.
Price: Moderate.
Credit Cards: None.
Special Features: No pets.

It's hard to imagine now, but the sleepy village of Van Deusenville was once a bustling town with mills, factories, and a train station. Little remains except this large 1825 mansion of the village founder, now a six-room bed and breakfast. The guest rooms are spacious and well appointed, as are the public rooms, although the exterior of the main house and the outbuildings need repair. Breakfasts prepared by the owner, a local caterer, are sumptuous. Just down the street is the church where Alice of "Alice's Restaurant" fame lived, now owned by Arlo Guthrie.

ELLING'S B & B

Hosts: Jo & Ray Elling.
413-528-4103.
RD3, Box 6, Gt. Barrington, MA 01230.

Your hosts here are seasoned, well-regarded veterans of the hospitality trade. The oldest house in Great Barrington, set on six pastoral acres high on a hill overlooking the valley, the guest house

On a hill above Rte. 23, between S. Egremont & Gt. Barrington.
Price: Inexpensive to Moderate.
Credit Cards: None.
Special Features: Badminton; Horseshoes; No smoking; No pets; Children over 9.

GREENMEADOWS
Owners: Frank Gioia & Susie Kaufman.
413-528-3897.
117 Division St., Gt. Barrington, MA 01230.
1.5 mi. N. of Gt. Barrington, 0.25 mi. W. of Rte. 41.
Closed: Mar. & Apr.
Price: Moderate.
Credit Cards: AE, MC, V.
Special Features: No pets.

LITTLEJOHN MANOR B&B
Managers: Herbert Littlejohn, Jr. & Paul A. DuFour.
413-528-2882.
Newsboy Monument Lane, Gt. Barrington, MA 01230.
On Rte. 23, W. of town, en route to S. Egremont.
Price: Moderate.
Credit Cards: None.
Special Features: No pets; Children over 12.

ROUND HILL FARM BED & BREAKFAST
Owners: Rebecca Tillinghast & Tony Blair.
413-528-6969.
17 Round Hill Rd., Gt. Barrington, MA 01230.
From Taconic Ave. (Alford Rd.), 0.25 mi. from Simon's Rock College, left on Seekonk Rd.,

has six bedrooms, four with private bath. The location is convenient to swimming, ski slopes, Tanglewood, and the best of southern Berkshire.

A rural setting on a quiet, country road. The rooms have had a recent face-lift and a new greenhouse/breakfast/sitting room is expected to be completed by late summer 1994. A suite in the former carriage house has a large deck overlooking pastoral fields, plus a full kitchen.

This turn-of-the-century Victorian home is run in a very friendly way and furnished partially with antiques. One of the four bedrooms has a working fireplace and all share two baths. A full English breakfast is complemented by afternoon tea served in the sitting room (to assure the freshest of homemade scones and shortbreads, reservations are necessary for tea). Delightful flower and herb gardens.

This hilltop country property has new owners since the spring of 1993, and guest accommodations are now located only in the spectacularly renovated 1820s Dairy Barn. A perfect place for families or groups of friends, the air-conditioned space consists of a spacious master suite, a studio suite, and a separate bedroom that shares a bath with one of the suites. The Master Suite has a living room, gourmet kitchen, bedroom, bath, deck, and

then next left on Round Hill Rd. to farm.
Price: Moderate to Expensive.
Credit Cards: AE, MC, V.
Special Features: Tennis; Swimming; Hiking Trails; No smoking; No pets; Children over 15.

laundry facilities, and the Studio Suite has a large bedroom, room-size dressing room, and equally large bath. Wicker, Laura Ashley fabrics, antiques, and a superb sense of style combine to make the interior spaces very special. A collection of sculpted cows adds a touch of humor. A full breakfast is served in the 1907 farmhouse, from a menu replete with choices. The outdoor space is equally special — panoramic views and access to 300 private acres of woodlands, fields, swimming holes, streams, and trails for hiking and cross-country skiing. *(Please note that in summer and fall 1994 the rooms will be available as a single apartment only, on a weekly — or longer — basis, without breakfast service.)*

SEEKONK PINES INN "BED & BREAKFAST"
Owners/Innkeepers: Linda & Chris Best.
413-528-4192; 800-292-4192.
142 Seekonk Crossroad, Gt. Barrington, MA 01230.
Rte. 23, between S. Egremont & Gt. Barrington.
Price: Moderate.
Credit Cards: MC, V.
Special Features: Pool; Bicycles; No smoking; No pets (except horses).

This 150-year-old house, originally the main house for a large estate, and surrounded by meadows and well-groomed acreage, keeps getting better and better. Furnished in Early American and just plain country, the inn is filled with personal touches. Linda is an artist, and her watercolors brighten many of the six guest rooms, as do her original stenciled floors and walls. Family quilts warm the beds. A recently added guest pantry has a refrigerator, hot water dispenser, and sink, with complimentary beverages available. There are a swimming pool for hot summer days and formal gardens for walking or reading. The healthful, hearty breakfast features home-grown berries and whole grains.

THORNEWOOD INN
Owners/Innkeepers: Terry & David Thorne.
413-528-3828; 800-854-1008.
453 Stockbridge Rd., Gt. Barrington, MA 01230.
Rte. 7, just N. of Gt. Barrington.
Price: Moderate to Expensive.
Credit Cards: AE, D, MC, V.
Handicap Access: Yes.
Special Features: Pool; No pets; Children over 11.

Creativity and imagination are evident throughout this marvelous inn. It all started several years ago with the purchase of an old, run-down, but handsome Dutch Colonial. The owners have restored and expanded to create 12 lovely guest rooms, all with private bath, and four delightful public rooms. The antiques used throughout include canopy beds, pier mirrors, and original sinks. The carriage house, refurbished in 1992, has two rooms, and is especially convenient for families. The restaurant has a view of the Berkshire hills, and the full breakfast might include strawberry-stuffed French toast or apple pancakes.

TURNING POINT INN
Managers: Jamie & Irving
  Yost.
413-528-4777.
RD2, Box 140, Gt. Barring-
  ton, MA 01230.
Rte. 23, E. of town.
Price: Moderate to Expen-
  sive.
Credit Cards: AE, MC, V.
Special Features: No smok-
  ing; No pets; Children
  welcome.

Very well-regarded lodging in a handsome brick and clapboard former stagecoach inn that's over 200 years old. Informal atmosphere. Full vegetarian breakfast served to inn guests (there are six inn rooms—four with private bath). A separate two-bedroom cottage is perfect for families. The popular Butternut Basin ski area is 1/3 mile down the road.

Housatonic

BROOK COVE
Managers: Clifford &
  Barbara Perreault.
413-274-6653.
30 Linda Lane, Housatonic,
  MA 01236.
Rte. 41, 5.7 mi. from Exit #1
  Mass. Pike.
Price: Moderate.
Credit Cards: None.
Handicap Access: Yes.
Special Features: No smok-
  ing.

Definitely not your typical guest house. The Perreaults have one large ground-floor apartment with full kitchen, which they rent by the night. The apartment sleeps four, with more beds available. Since the country property meanders down to the Williams River, the setting seems ideal for longer stays. The room price is for two, with an $8 charge for each additional person, and there is no breakfast served.

**CHRISTINE'S GUEST
  HOUSE B&B**
Hosts: Steve & Christine
  Kelsey.
413-274-6149.
325 N. Plain Rd.,
  Housatonic, MA 01236.
Rte. 41 about 4 mi. N. of Gt.
  Barrington.
Price: Expensive.
Credit Cards: MC, V.
Special Features: Putting
  green; Gift Shop; No
  smoking; No pets;
  Children over 11.

A little jewel (three rooms, all with private bath), off the beaten path between Great Barrington and West Stockbridge. The rooms and the innkeepers are delightful. One room is decorated in white wicker, one has a cannonball bed, and the other a four-poster. All are filled with handcrafted items. Cheese and crackers served in the afternoon. Full "surprise" breakfast. If you book for a holiday weekend, prepare for a bonus experience; there are always decorations, often a special rates package, and usually a favor (fathers take home a bag of homemade chocolate chip cookies on Father's Day and mothers a bouquet of flowers on Mother's Day).

Lee

(See also South Lee)

APPLEGATE
Owners: Nancy & Rick
  Cannata.
413-243-4451.
279 West Park St., Lee, MA
  01238.
Off Rte. 7, between Stock-
  bridge & Lenox.
Price: Expensive to Very
  Expensive.
Credit Cards: MC, V.
Special Features: Pool; No
  pets; Children over 12.

This magnificent white-pillared Colonial is special in every way. From the gracious and delightful hosts — he a pilot and she a flight attendant — to the detailed attention they have lavished on their inn, a stay at Applegate will be a cherished treat. Public rooms are large, with fireplaces and bay windows. Inn dolls Martha, Heather, and Claudia observe the activity from their antique rockers. Breakfast coffee is served from a collection of antique cups. Guests are greeted in their rooms by crystal decanters filled with brandy and Belgian chocolates selected in Brussels by the owners. Six large guest rooms all have private bath and several have a fireplace; one even boasts a sauna/shower. The house has central air-conditioning. From the screened-in porch filled with wicker furniture, the view across the pool, enclosed by a low rock wall, to the six landscaped acres beyond, is tranquility itself.

**BEST WESTERN BLACK
  SWAN INN**
Managers: Sallie Kate &
  George Kish.
413-243-2700 or 800-876-
  SWAN.
Rte. 20W, Lee, MA 01238.
On Laurel Lake, N. of Lee.
Price: Moderate to Very
  Expensive.
Credit Cards: AE, CB, D,
  DC, MC, V.
Handicap Access: Yes.
Special Features: Pool;
  Exercise room and sauna;
  No pets.

From the outside, this 52-room "inn" looks decidedly like a motel, but its location on placid Laurel Lake, its private balconies, Colonial decor, and friendly hospitality provide an innlike atmosphere. Lovely restaurant, swimming pool, and exercise room with sauna. There are boat rentals for boating on the lake. Close to Tanglewood, hiking trails, countless other Berkshire amenities. Conference facilities available.

CHAMBÉRY INN
Owners: Joe & Lynn Toole.
413-243-2221; 800-537-4321.
199 Main St., Lee, MA
  01238.
On Main St. (Rte. 20) in
  Lee.
Price: Moderate to Very
  Expensive.
Credit Cards: AE, D, MC,
  V.
Handicap Access: Yes.

Joe Toole is an unabashed romantic, and we all are allowed to benefit. The Chambéry Inn began life as a schoolhouse in 1885, when five nuns arrived from France to teach the youngsters of St. Mary's Parish in Lee. Joe's grandfather was in the first class. Concerned that it was scheduled for the wrecker's ball and enchanted by its remarkable history, Joe assumed the gargantuan task of moving the schoolhouse to its present location. He left the proportion of the rooms as they were, which is

Special Features: No smoking; No pets; Children over 15.

BIG, with 13-foot ceilings and massive windows. There are eight rooms (six are suites with fireplaces); all have large private baths with whirlpools, and king or queen beds. The furniture, including canopy beds, is Amish handcrafted cherry. All the rooms have central air-conditioning, telephones, and color cable TV. Breakfast is delivered to the room. A charming feature in the suites is the original blackboards. Joe invited former students and teachers to share their remembrances of school life at St. Mary's. Chambéry Inn is probably a "one-of-a-kind" in the United States.

THE DONAHOES
Owner: Mary Donahoe.
413-243-1496.
Box 231, Lee, MA 01238.
2 blocks off Rte. 102
  between Lee and
  Stockbridge; turn onto
  Davis St., go to Fairview
  (Donahoes is at 780
  Fairview St., facing
  Davis).
Closed: Dec–Mar.
Price: Moderate.
Credit Cards: None.
Special Features: No pets;
  Children over 11.

Country setting in a Shaker Colonial high on a hill, where only the birds will waken guests. Great location for theater and concert fans. The house and two guest rooms, both with private baths, are furnished with simple, authentic Shaker pieces.

HAUS ANDREAS
Owners/Managers:
  Benjamin & Sally Schenk.
413-243-3298.
85 Stockbridge Rd.,
  Lee, MA 01238.
Off Rte. 70 just outside
  village of Lee.
Price: Expensive to
  Very Expensive.
Credit Cards: MC, V.
Special Features: Heated
  pool; Tennis; Bicycles;
  No pets; Children over
  10.

No expense was spared in renovating this 1800s house, built by a Revolutionary War soldier and initially restored by George Westinghouse in the early 1900s. The small estate became the 1942 summer sanctuary for Queen Wilhelmina of the Netherlands, her daughter Princess Juliana, and granddaughters Beatrix and Irene. The house is secluded, with ten air-conditioned rooms, all with private bath. Breakfast is "continental plus." The Schenks took over the business in Spring 1994.

The gracious front doorway at Haus Andreas.

Jonathan Sternfield

INN ON LAUREL LAKE
Managers: Jean & Bernard
  Morris.
413-243-1436.
615 Laurel St., Lee, MA
  01238.
Rte. 20, 2 mi. W. of Lee.
Closed: Mar.–Apr.
Price: Moderate to Very
  Expensive.
Credit Cards: None.
Handicap Access: Limited.
Special Features: Private
  beach; Tennis; Sauna; No
  smoking; Children over 9.

On the shore of Laurel Lake, this 80-year-old country property has attracted a loyal following with its 20 comfortable bedrooms and two sitting rooms filled with an impressive collection of record albums, books, and games. The tennis court, sauna, and private beach add to guests' playtime possibilities. Proximity of major highway needs to be noted.

AUNTI M'S
Owner: Michelle Celen-
  tano.
413-243-3201.

Formerly Jirak's Guest House, Aunti M's (for Michelle) is a restored Victorian set above a busy thoroughfare. There are five comfortable

60 Laurel St., Lee, MA 01238.
Rte. 20, W. of Lee.
Price: Moderate to Expensive.
Credit Cards: None.
Special Features: No smoking; No pets; Children over 9.

rooms, all with period furnishings, floral wallpapers and borders, and oak floors. One has a private bath and the others share two baths. There is a homey feeling here, and Michelle Celentano says of her guests, "Whatever is ours is theirs." A piano in the foyer is the focal point for after-breakfast cameraderie. The full breakfasts always include a home-baked goodie, and picnics are available on request.

THE MORGAN HOUSE INN
Innkeepers: Lenora and Stuart Bowen.
413-243-0181 .
33 Main St., Lee, MA 01238.
Town center, .8 mi. from Exit 2, Mass. Pike.
Price: Moderate to Expensive.
Credit Cards: AE, D, DC, MC, V.
Special Features: No pets; Children welcome.

A full-service inn under new ownership since June 1993, with some changes in place and others underway. The Morgan House, built in 1817 and a stagecoach stop beginning in 1853, has a bustling and convenient in-town location and 13 comfortable rooms in a variety of shapes and sizes, some with private bath, some shared. The Bowens have 17 years' experience in the innkeeping and restaurant business, and Lenora has the distinction of being owner/chef. The dining room has been spruced up, and the new menu features New England cuisine with a contemporary flair; light fare is available in the tavern. Morgan House hospitality begins in the small lobby, where the "wallpaper" is actual pages from 19th-century guest registers — look for U.S. Grant and George Bernard Shaw.

PARSONAGE ON THE GREEN
Owners: David Renner & Michelle Moore.
413-243-4364.
20 Park Pl., Lee, MA 01238.
Just off the village green, beside Congregational Church.
Price: Inexpensive to Expensive.
Credit Cards: MC, V.
Handicap Access: Limited.
Special Features: No smoking; Children welcome.

This white, center-hall Colonial houses three guest rooms, one with private bath. Cozy, attractive decor and furnishings. The public rooms include both living room and parlor with fireplaces. Wine and cheese are served Friday and Saturday nights. David is an accomplished chef at one of the most highly respected local restaurants. Prepare for a *surprise* continental breakfast.

PROSPECT HILL HOUSE
Owners: Marge & Chuck
  Driscoll.
413-243-3460.
100 S. Prospect St., Lee, MA
  01238.
Just off Park St.
Closed: Nov.–May.
Price: Moderate
Credit Cards: None.

This Cape Colonial on one acre at the end of a street, offers a quiet setting, near the golf course. Three rooms, most with shared bath. An apartment may also be available; call for information. Common room has fireplace. Full breakfast served.

RAMSEY HOUSE
Managers: Mickey & Dick
  Ramsey.
413-243-1598.
203 W. Park St., Lee, MA
  01238.
Up hill W. of town center.
Price: Moderate to Expensive.
Credit Cards: MC, V.

An 1895 Colonial in residential area above town. Antique-furnished rooms are quite special, some with canopied or four-poster beds and private bath. Golf and tennis across the street at small club. Congenial hosts pay particular attention to their guests. Modified continental breakfast includes freshly baked breads and perhaps a baked apple. (**Note: closed as of Spring 1994.**)

South Lee

Federal House: the ambiance of classic Americana.

Jonathan Sternfield

THE FEDERAL HOUSE
Owners: Robin &
  Kenneth Almgren.
413-243-1824; 800-243-1824.
Rte. 102, S. Lee, MA 01260.
Just E. of Stockbridge.
Price: Moderate to Expen-
  sive.
Credit Cards: AE, MC, V.
Special Features: Restau-
  rant; No pets.

A brick Federal house, built in 1824, has been beautifully restored. In this historic property, the six guest rooms sit above a respected restaurant. Graceful and charming rooms feature antique furnishings. All have private bath and air-conditioning, and several have fireplaces. Owned and operated by a dynamic young couple who combine good taste and culinary talents.

*Colonial antiques highlight
the entry at the historic
Merrell Tavern Inn.*

Paul Rocheleau, courtesy Merrell Tavern Inn

MERRELL TAVERN INN
Owners: Faith & Charles
  Reynolds.

A s you walk through the massive door of this 1800s brick inn, you're transported back in

413-243-1794; 800-243-1794.
1565 Pleasant St., S. Lee,
MA 01260.
Rte. 102, just E. of Stock-
bridge.
Closed: Christmas Eve &
Christmas.
Price: Expensive.
Credit Cards: AE, MC, V.
Special Features: No smok-
ing; No pets; Inquire
about children.

time. For years it served as a stagecoach stop on the busy Boston–Albany Pike, until it outlived its usefulness. It lay idle and boarded up for over 100 years until purchased by the Reynoldses in late 1980. Now lovingly and carefully restored, the inn is listed on the National Register of Historic Places. The nine bedrooms, completely redecorated in 1992, are furnished with four-poster and canopy beds, and all have private baths, air-conditioning, and telephones; three have fireplaces. The Old Tavern Room features the original circular Colonial bar. A groomed lawn in back leads to the banks of the Housatonic River, where there is a screened gazebo. A full breakfast is served from a menu, and afternoon refreshments are also included.

OAK N' SPRUCE LODGE
Manager: Paul DiCroce.
413-243-3500; 800-424-3003.
P.O. Box 237, Meadow St.,
S. Lee, MA 01260.
Off Rte. 102, on Meadow
St., N. of village.
Price: Moderate to Expen-
sive (rooms only).
Credit Cards: AE, MC, V.
Handicap Access: Yes.
Special Features: Indoor
and outdoor Pools; Ten-
nis; Golf; Health Club;
No pets.

A full-service, but by no means fancy resort. For rent are 45 hotel rooms and 130 condominiums. Restaurant and bar in main building. New function and meeting facility. Beautiful natural scenery offsets the hodgepodge architecture and interiors. Very casual atmosphere. Breakfast is not included in the room rate but is available in the restaurant in the summer and fall, Tues.–Sun.

Monterey

MOUNTAIN TRAILS B&B
Managers: John & Maureen
Congdon.
413-528-2928.
P.O. Box 477, Monterey,
MA 01245.
At the jct. of Rtes. 23 & 57.
Price: Inexpensive to
Expensive.
Credit Cards: None.
Handicap Access: Yes.

A four-room B&B in the country, on ten acres of land. Two rooms have private bath, and two share. A full breakfast is served. Especially loved by hikers as the Appalachian Trail and Beartown State Forest are nearby, and it's also just one mile from Butternut Basin ski area. Children are welcome. A 20-minute drive to Tanglewood or Jacob's Pillow.

New Marlborough

THE OLD INN ON THE GREEN AND GEDNEY FARM
Innkeepers: Bradford Wagstaff & Leslie Miller.
413-229-3131.
Star Rte. 70, New Marlborough, MA 01230.
Rte. 57, in center of village.
Price: Moderate to Very Expensive.
Credit Cards: AE, MC, V.
Handicap Access: Yes.
Special Features: Restaurant; No pets.

A beautiful village rich in unaffected nostalgia is the setting for this 18th-century inn. Rooms in the inn have been lovingly restored and furnished in a simple, American country style; all share baths. Gedney Farm, a short walk from the inn, has 15 guest rooms, mostly two-level suites, carved out of a Normandy-style barn, which was built around 1900 as a showplace for Percheron stallions and Jersey cattle. All suites feature fireplaces in the living rooms, large bedrooms, and whirlpool tubs in the master baths. A recent addition to this special property is the restoration of a second barn — the horse barn — now serving as space for weddings, parties, meetings, an art gallery, concerts, and, in summer, the Gallery Cafe. The restaurant in the inn is one of the finest in the Berkshires.

RED BIRD INN
Managers: Don & Joyce Coffman.
413-229-2433.
Box 592, Gt. Barrington, MA 01230.
Adsit Crosby Rd., Rte. 57, New Marlborough.
From Gt. Barrington, Rte. 23 E. to Rte. 57.
Price: Moderate to Expensive.
Credit Cards: None.
Handicap Access: Limited.
Special Features: No smoking; No pets; Children over 12.

A former stagecoach stop, the 18th-century Red Bird Inn is located on ten acres on a quiet country road. The rooms are furnished with antiques, decorated with Ralph Lauren and Laura Ashley, and retain their original wide plank floors, fireplaces, and old ironwork. Some have private bath; some shared. A separate suite has one huge room with a queen-size bed, two twins, a sitting area, and private bath. The large screened porch is a popular feature with warm-weather guests. A full breakfast is served.

Otis

GROUSE HOUSE
Managers: The Goulet Family.
413-269-4446.
Rte. 23, Otis, MA 01253.
Near Rte. 8, on Rte. 23.
Price: Inexpensive.
Credit Cards: AE, MC, V.
Special Features: No Pets.

Next door to Otis Ridge Ski area, Grouse House offers five rooms, all with shared baths. Reduced rate on lift tickets for guests of the house. Guests can get breakfast at the ski lodge, as no breakfast is served at the inn. In summer, there are horseshoes and volleyball.

JOYOUS GARDE B&B

Owner: Joy Bogen.
413-269-6852.
Olde Quarry Rd./PO Box 132, Otis.
From Rte. 8 in the center of Otis village to Rte 23E; almost 1 mi. to L. onto Gibbs Rd., continue to fork in road; go L. and follow signs.
Price: Expensive to Very Expensive.
Credit Cards: AE, DC, MC, V.
Handicap Access: Yes, one room; ramp to breakfast room.
Special Features: No Smoking; No pets; Children over 11 welcome; call about younger ages.

In Arthurian legend, Joyous Garde was the name of Launcelot's castle retreat, and the Berkshires' own Joyous Garde — a hideaway down a country road — is just as magical. In two adjacent farmhouses and a cabaña, the common areas and bedrooms are a charming mix of elegant and casual, old-fashioned and up-to-date. Nine cozy bedrooms offer big beds dressed up with lush linens, striped and floral wallpaper and curtains, and whimsical accent pieces, many antique. Each bedroom has an updated private bath (one is just across the hallway). In the first house is also a serve-yourself breakfast alcove for early risers, a wicker-filled sunporch, and second-floor sitting areas, inside and out, across from an enormous stone chimney. Out back is a cabaña/sauna, Jacuzzi, and swimming pool. The second house, also a vintage farm building with arched stonework, includes a formal living room and dining room, where a full breakfast is served. Just beyond are a tennis court and trails for woodland hiking or cross-country skiing.

Owner Joy Bogen — once an opera and concert singer and the only student of Lotte Lenya — says she goes out of her way to provide extra services for her guests, such as making appointments for massage therapy or tennis instruction. Though the inn has no restaurant, Joy will make up picnics or light dinners and provides snacks for concert- or theater-goers returning in the evening for fireside socializing. She can also stage a full gourmet meal for special occasions. There's an antiques shop on the premises for guests, and many of the prints, paintings, and other pieces throughout the rooms are for sale, too. Joyous Garde was recently awarded three diamonds, the highest rating, from AAA.

STONEWOOD INN

Managers: Joan & Howard Basis.
413-269-4894.
Star Rte. 62, Box 42, Monterey, MA 01245.
E. of Gt. Barrington on Rte. 23 in W. Otis.
Price: Moderate.
Credit Cards: None.
Special Features: Hiking trails; No smoking; No pets; Children over 12.

A gracious, 1880s farmhouse, set on 15 pastoral acres, now owned by a decorator who has filled the rooms with antiques and country touches, in perfect harmony with the setting. There's a woodstove in the common room. Four large bedrooms share two baths. Only the mattresses — three king-size and one queen — are not antique, but are newly custom-made. There's an additional large suite, with private bath, suitable for four people. Full country breakfast may include baked apples, blueberry pancakes, or thick French toast — served on the screened porch in summer.

Sandisfield

DAFFER'S MOUNTAIN INN
Managers: Jean & Bill Daffer.
413-258-4453.
Box 37, Rte. 57, Sandisfield MA 01255.
Price: Inexpensive.
Credit Cards: MC, V.

Mostly a restaurant (closed Mondays), but with seven rooms upstairs that share several baths. Congenially run by hosts who cater effectively to their guests' needs. In fall, the large sign reads "Hunters Welcome." Very informal. Friendly groups return year after year. A full breakfast is included.

NEW BOSTON INN
Innkeeper: Paula McCarthy Tatko.
413-258-4477.
Rte. 8 & 57, 166D, Sandisfield, MA 01255.
Jct. Rtes. 8 & 57, Sandisfield. In the village of New Boston.
Price: Moderate.
Credit Cards: AE, MC, V.
Handicap Access: Yes.
Special Features: Pub.

Built in 1737, this remarkable old stagecoach inn, listed on the National Register of Historic Places, underwent a painstaking renovation in 1984, and the owners continue to make improvements. The eight guest rooms are, true to the period, snug. Low ceilings, wide-board floors, and multipaned windows hark back to the 18th century and, in most cases, are original. All rooms feature private baths and are decorated with early pine furniture and stenciling. All closets are cedar lined.

Our favorite space at the inn is the second-floor ballroom. After wandering through the cozy bedrooms, you enter the spacious ballroom, now called The Gathering Room, complete with an antique billiards table and a barrel-vaulted ceiling. The sense of openness, grace, and the continued presence of the past is romantic, especially the matching fireplaces at either end.

Another historic delight is the taproom, now open as a pub, that adjoins the low-ceilinged dining room. The 22-inch-wide oak boards on the wall are called "king's wood" because they were illegally retained by the colonists after the deputies of the king of England went about marking trees for the royal sawmills. In this room, as throughout the inn, the wood molding, plaster walls, slanted floors, venerable windows and doorways (there is hardly a right angle in the place) provide a powerful charm and sense of history. What's more, the New Boston Inn has a resident ghost. She is real enough to have been reported in *Yankee* magazine: an Irish maiden, dressed in bridal black (that's what they wore back then), who was shot by a scorned suitor in an upstairs room.

Sandisfield may be one of the more remote towns in Berkshire, but the New Boston Inn's return to life will make the ride out there more than worthwhile. Although the inn's restaurant is no longer open, the space is available for functions. A recent change is the landscaping of the back yard, which offers perennial gardens and a nice sense of privacy.

Sheffield

CENTURYHURST ANTIQUES & BED & BREAKFAST
Managers: Ronald & Judith Timm.
413-229-8131.
Box 486, Sheffield, MA 01257.
Main St., Rte. 7.
Price: Inexpensive to Moderate.
Credit Cards: AE, MC, V.
Special Features: Pool; No smoking; No pets; Children over 11.

This grand old home, nestled among towering trees, is listed on the National Register of Historic Places. The inn features four guest rooms that share two baths, and visitors are served an all-you-can-eat continental breakfast. A new post-and-beam barn behind the house serves as an antiques shop, specializing in antique American clocks, early 19th century furniture, and Wedgwood.

THE DEPOT
Owners: Dennis & Joan Sawyer.
413-229-8894.
Rte. 7A, Box 575, Sheffield, MA 01257.
From Rte. 7, follow Rte. 7A toward Ashley Falls.
Price: Inexpensive to Moderate.
Credit Cards: AE, MC, V.
Handicap Access: Yes.
Special Features: No pets.

The owners' home once served as the Sheffield train station, but was moved to this location in 1970. The guest rooms are located in a separate guest house. The five rooms all have private baths, refrigerators, air-conditioning, and color TVs. No breakfast is served, but a large kitchen, known as the Baggage Room, is available for the guests' use.

IVANHOE COUNTRY HOUSE
Managers: Carole & Dick Maghery.
413-229-2143.
254 S. Undermountain Rd. (Rte. 41), Sheffield, MA 01257.
On Rte. 41, 4 mi. S. of Rte. 23; 10 mi. N. of Lakeville, CT.
Price: Moderate.
Credit Cards: None.
Special Features: Pool; Children over 14 July–Aug. wkends.

Set along one of the most scenic roads of South Berkshire, the Ivanhoe provides comfortable rooms, all with private bath, at reasonable prices. Continental breakfast served at your door. Take a dip in the pool before dinner, play the piano if you wish, enjoy the fire in the chestnut-paneled public room, and select one of the many fine local restaurants for your evening meal. At the base of Race Mountain, traversed by the Appalachian Trail, 20 wooded acres hug this 1780-vintage country house. Golden retrievers are raised on the property, and guests are welcome to bring their own dogs (no cats!), for an additional $10.

ORCHARD SHADE
Owners: Debbie & Henry
   Thornton.
413-229-8463.
Box 669, Sheffield, MA
   01257.
On Maple Ave., off Main St.
   (Rte. 7) N. of Christ
   Church.
Price: Moderate to Expen-
   sive.
Credit Cards: AE, D, MC,
   V.
Special Features: Pool;
   No smoking; No pets;
   Children welcome.

This venerable 1840 house has operated as a bed and breakfast since 1888. Furnished with antiques, the public rooms have two spacious fireplaces to ward off the chill on cooler evenings. The large screened-in porch is perfect for relaxing after a busy day of Sheffield antiquing.

RACE BROOK LODGE
   B&B
Innkeeper: Eve Van Syckle.
413-229-2916.
864 S. Undermountain
   Rd./Rte. 41, Sheffield.
Two miles S. of Berkshire
   School.
Price: Moderate.
Open: Year-round.
Credit Cards: AE, MC, V.
Handicap Access: Ground-
   level entry to many
   rooms.
Special Features: Smoking
   restricted; Pets
   (well-behaved accepted);
   Children welcome.

This hideaway set in classic New England countryside offers rest and rustication to all. A large rambling barn, dating from the 1830s and recently renovated, embraces rooms and suites in what were once haylofts and workshops, with exposed original beams, stenciling, nooks and alcoves, and windows and stairs in unexpected places. The variety of bedroom, bathroom, and entrance arrangements can work for couples, family groups, or friends traveling together. The easygoing furnishings include chairs and sofas no one minds if you put your feet on — in fact, the whole place has been specifically designated a "chintz-free zone" to maximize informality. More rooms and suites, available seasonally, are in nearby cottages. (There are 14 rooms in the winter, 20 in the summer and fall.) In the lofty common rooms at the heart of the barn is the well-stocked, always-open, help-yourself kitchen, along with tables, a TV corner, and a horseshoe bar (check out the wine list). Out back, paths and terraces overlook Race Brook, and state forest trails lead to a waterfall, ravine, and the Appalachian Trail.

   With her unique brand of sophisticated gregariousness, innkeeper Eve Van Syckle ensures that her guests feel at home and looked after, yet free to follow their own agenda. A popular feature here is the dynamic Jazz Sunday (the third Sunday of every month). Plans are also afoot for workshops on antiquing and collecting, with trips to auctions.

RAMBLEWOOD INN
Owners: Martin & June Ederer.
413-229-3363.

The Ederers purchased A Unique Bed & Breakfast Inn in 1992 and have expanded the busi-

Box 729, Sheffield, MA
01257.
Rte. 41, 5 mi. S. of Gt.
Barrington.
Price: Moderate to Expen-
sive.
Credit Cards: MC, V.
Handicap Access: Limited.

ness to offer six guest rooms (four with private bath) and a ground-floor suite with full kitchen, bedroom, living room, and bath. Up a short hill off scenic Rte. 41, this Alpine structure at the edge of the woods has an attractive rustic look, with all the comforts of home, including central air-condition-ing. June is an English teacher and has named each room for a character in *Canterbury Tales*. The Miller's Room on the first floor has its own deck and, not surprising, the Wife of Bath's Room on the second floor is the largest in the house. Also new to the inn is a piece of lake-front property across the road, where guests may swim, canoe, and fish.

A full gourmet breakfast is served. The Berkshire School, site of the Berk-shire Choral Institute (see the "Music" section in Chapter Four, *Culture*), is a mile down the road.

STAGECOACH HILL INN
Manager: Danielle Pedretti.
413-229-8585.
Rte. 41, Sheffield, MA
01257.
On Rte. 41, several mi. N. of
Lakeville, CT.
Closed: Nov.–Apr.
Price: Inexpensive to
Moderate.
Credit Cards: AE, DC, MC,
V.
Handicap Access: Limited.
Special Features: Pool;
Children welcome in
cottage.

A time machine. Nostalgia for bygone eras (especially Colonial times as evident in the decidedly English pub and restaurant), plus charm and comfort greet the fortunate visitor to this ideally situated hostelry. Choice of rooms in the main house or cottage, all with private bath. There is access to the Appalachian Trail from the property.

STAVELEIGH HOUSE
Owners: D. Marosy & M.
Whitman.
413-229-2129.
Box 608, Sheffield, MA
01257.
Just S. of village, on Rte. 7.
Price: Moderate.
Credit Cards: None.
Special Features: No smok-
ing; No pets; Children
over 11.

This vintage 1821 house is set in the heart of Sheffield. Your hostesses believe in old-fash-ioned hospitality and have succeeded in creating a warm and comfortable interior, with hooked rugs and patchwork quilts in the five guest rooms (one with private bath; the rest share two baths). A full breakfast, with imaginative specialties, is featured. The grounds feature perennial beds, an herb gar-den, and a place to sit under the trees. There are two resident cats.

Stockbridge

**ARBOR ROSE BED &
  BREAKFAST**
Owner: Christina Alsop.
413-298-4744.
Box 114, Stockbridge, MA
  01262.
8 Yale Hill Rd., off E. Main
  St. (Rte. 102).
Price: Inexpensive to
  Expensive.
Credit Cards: AE, MC, V.
Special Features: No smok-
  ing; No pets; Children
  welcome.

The first thing you hear on turning into the driveway at Arbor Rose is the soothing sound of
rushing water. The house sits on a hill overlooking
an early 1800s mill and millpond — perfect for ice
skating in winter (and Arbor Rose has a box of
skates handy). The large white house has four guest
rooms, two with private bath. The charming decor is
highlighted by colorful paintings by the owner's
mother, Suzette Alsop, a noted local artist. There
are family pets — dog, cat, and horse.

BERKSHIRE THISTLE
Owners: Gene & Diane
  Elling.
413-298-3188.
Box 1227, Stockbridge, MA
  01262.
Rte. 7, N. of village.
Price: Moderate to Expen-
  sive.
Credit Cards: None.
Special Features: Pool; No
  smoking; No pets;
  Inquire about children.

The new owners of this bed and breakfast have
had years of training in the business, filling in
for Gene's parents at the Ellings' B&B in Great Barrington. Their location, midway between Lenox
and Stockbridge, is unbeatable, and though the
house is a recently built Colonial, it is comfortable
and beautifully sited, with a wraparound deck to
take advantage of the views. All four rooms have
private baths and air-conditioning. Easy access to
theater, Tanglewood, and great hiking trails.
Swimming pool and picturesque pasture with
grazing horses.

**THE INN AT
  STOCKBRIDGE**
Innkeepers: Nancy &
  Michael Rosenthal.
Owners: Lee & Don Weitz.
413-298-3337.
Box 618, Stockbridge, MA
  01262.
On Rte. 7, about 1 mi. N. of
  village.
Price: Expensive to Very
  Expensive.
Credit Cards: AE, MC, V.
Handicap Access: Limited.
Special Features: Pool; No
  smoking; No pets;
  Children over 12.

A marvelous, secluded inn run by friendly, professional people. The large, white-columned
house is decorated with impeccable taste, featuring
priceless antiques and many thoughtful touches.
All seven rooms have private baths and are air-
conditioned. Wine and cheese are served in the living room (warmed by a fire in chilly weather) and
breakfast in the formal dining room is incredible.
The breakfast pastries are all homemade, with
croissant French toast and cinnamon buns possible
offerings. Special private dinners can be arranged
on request.

THE RED LION INN

General Manager: C. Brooks Bradbury.
413-298-5545.
Main St., Stockbridge, MA 01262.
Village center, Rtes. 7 & 102.
Price: Expensive to Very Expensive.
Credit Cards: AE, D, DC, MC, V.
Handicap Access: Yes.
Special Features: Pool; Exercise Room; Massage Therapist.

In Colonial America, three years before the States became United, the Red Lion Inn first opened its doors to travelers on the stagecoach route linking Albany, Hartford, and Boston.

Today, over two centuries later, the Red Lion continues to welcome visitors and locals, and still with consummate Colonial charm. The present inn, rebuilt after a fire in 1895, is a veritable icon of the Berkshires, representing graceful country lodging at its best.

Antique furniture and a fine collection of china teapots adorn the lobby. Each private room is decorated with unique period appointments, carefully coordinated by the inn's owner, Jane Fitzpatrick, also owner of Country Curtains. Recent improvements have concentrated on creating larger rooms and increasing the number of suites, consistent with guest requests.

The atmosphere is faithful to the rhythms of a simpler, slower time while providing all contemporary comforts. Sipping a cool drink on a hot summer's day on the famous porch of the Red Lion, or meeting your companion in front of the cheery fireplace in the lobby in winter, you can't help but feel you're at the very heart of the Berkshires. The Red Lion roars with a quiet Rockwell charm.

Throughout the inn, the loving attention to detail is evident in every aspect of its operation. It's easy to feel at home here because all the inn's top quality services are offered by a vibrant, eager-to-please staff. During your stay in summer, don't be surprised if you find your porch or courtyard company to be an actor or actress of note, who spends evenings nearby on the boards of the Berkshire Theatre Festival and nights at the inn.

The Red Lion Inn is not, however, a particularly tranquil place. The main building is full of activity and people, and the street right outside (Rtes. 7 & 102) is sometimes noisy with traffic. There's a conviviality and gaiety about the lobby that some folks love and others don't. If you're in the latter category, take heart: there are several sweet Red Lion cottages that form a complex around the inn: the Stafford House, the O'Brien House, the more remote Buck House, and the Stevens House, just up the street.

Reservations should be made in advance at this popular inn, especially in the summer. The rooms have many fine complements: an excellent formal dining room; the Lion's Den, a pub featuring nightly entertainment; a courtyard for summer meals under the trees, surrounded by bushels of impatiens; the Pink Kitty, an outstanding gift shop; and a Country Curtains retail store.

THE ROEDER HOUSE
Innkeepers: Vernon &
   Diane Reuss.
413-298-4015.
Box 525, Stockbridge MA
   01262.
Rte. 183, just S. of Glendale
   village center.
Price: Expensive to Very
   Expensive.
Credit Cards: AE, MC, V.
Special Features: Pool;
   No smoking; No pets;
   Children over 9 in low
   seasons.

A delightful hideaway, in a small village far from the crowds, but close to summer attractions and just 3/4 mile from the new Norman Rockwell Museum. Awaiting lucky house guests are large, exquisitely furnished air-conditioned rooms, all with private bath and filled with priceless antiques and four-poster queen-size beds. The owners also run an antiques shop, and the entire house reflects their impeccable taste. A full breakfast is served on tables set with china, silver, and crystal on the charming screened-in porch, weather permitting.

The Taggart House B&B.

Ogden Gigli, courtesy the Taggart House

TAGGART HOUSE B&B
Owners: Hinckley & Susan
   Waitt.
413-298-4303.
18 Main St., Stockbridge.
Price: Very Expensive.
Credit Cards: AE, D, DC,
   MC, V.

A stunning array of art and antiques in the richly detailed architectural setting of a 19th-century mansion, with a fireplace around just about every corner, a billiards room, a paneled library, a concert-sized music room, and a secluded three acres of gardens and fields — this must be a description of a romantic country manor house in a Victorian

Special Features: No smoking; No pets; Inquire about children.

novel. Actually, the Taggart House is right on Main Street in Stockbridge, where resident owners Hinckley and Susan Waitt have transformed fiction into reality. Their personal collection of antique furnishings and artwork, with dramatic choices of color and texture, artfully blend elegance and whimsy, opulence and coziness.

Throughout the downstairs living rooms and the upstairs bedrooms are a variety of fabulous faux effects painted on walls and ceilings, including bois and tortoiseshell finishes. In the butler's pantry, trompe-l'oeil painting merges a real garden scene with an illusory one. The abundance of imaginative details also includes fabrics and wallpaper with William Morris designs, a canoe suspended from a frescoed ceiling over the billiards table, curtains drawn back with antlers, a collection of Native American artifacts in the library, and a pillowed nook halfway up the stairs. The cavernous music room has hosted chamber concerts from Bach to Gershwin — and an 18-foot Christmas tree. The four bedrooms feature rich and restful color themes, fireplaces, and luxurious antique beds; each room's private bath is equally sumptuous, with antique furnishings, heated towel racks, and even bath salts. Morning brings gourmet breakfasts, and there are some serve-yourself options, too. Afternoon tea can be provided, as well as early evening hors d'oeuvres.

WOODSIDE BED & BREAKFAST
Owner: Paula Schutzman
413-298-4977.
Box 1096; Stockbridge, MA 01262.
Rte. 102, W. of town.
Price: Inexpensive to Moderate.
Credit Cards: None.
Handicap Access: Yes.
Special Features: No smoking.

Here's an alternative to cozy and quaint — a country contemporary, comfortable and informal, just outside the village of Stockbridge. Two of the three guest rooms have private baths. A full breakfast is served on weekends; continental during the week. Ask about bringing pets — the answer may well be "yes." And it's "yes" to children.

Note: See also **Kripalu Center** under "A Yoga Retreat" in Chapter 6.

Tyringham

THE GOLDEN GOOSE
Innkeepers/Owners: Lilja & Joe Rizzo
413-243-3008.
Box 336, Tyringham, MA 01264.

The town itself is worth the trip. Beautiful, surprising and secretive, Tyringham is a gift. The Golden Goose is a white Colonial hideaway, with six cozy rooms, four with private bath, and one studio apartment in a setting of absolute peace and

On main st. of village,
across from town hall.
Price: Moderate to Expen-
sive.
Credit Cards: AE, D, MC,
V.
Special Features: No pets.

quiet. The deck and picnic tables watch over the
Appalachian Trail, so it's a perfect stopping place
for Trail hikers. Afternoon wine and cheese, and
hot cider in season, are served in the antique-furnished, fireplaced common rooms. Breakfast is a
hearty continental.

West Stockbridge

**CARD LAKE COUNTRY
INN**
Innkeepers: Ed & Lisa
Robbins.
413-232-0272.
4 Stockbridge Rd., W.
Stockbridge, MA 01266.
Main St., center of village.
Closed: March.
Price: Inexpensive to
Expensive.
Credit Cards: AE, MC, V.
Special Features: No pets.

Under new ownership since 1992, the inn offers
eight guest rooms featuring brass and iron
beds. Four rooms have private bath and four are
shared. Village shops across street are artsy-craftsy.
You may want to ask for a room at the back of the
inn, to avoid traffic noise. Restaurant and tavern on
the premises.

MARBLE INN
Owners: Yvonne & Joe
Kopper.
413-232-7092.
Main St., W. Stockbridge,
MA 01266.
Rte. 102, S. of town center.
Price: Moderate to Expen-
sive.
Credit Cards: MC, V.

The house that is Marble Inn was built in 1835
during the expansion of marble quarries and
limestone works in the area. In a cozy country
atmosphere guests will find four rooms, all with
private bath, furnished with antiques and fluffy
terry robes. A full breakfast is served from a menu,
with as many as seven entrée choices every day.
The inn's homemade jams are for sale to take home.

**INN AT SHAKER MILL
TAVERN**
Owner: Jonathan Rick.
413-232-8565; 800-322-8565.
Box 521, W. Stockbridge,
MA 01266.
On Rte. 102 in village.
Price: Expensive to Very
Expensive (2-bdrm. suite).
Credit Cards: AE, MC, V.
Handicap Access: Limited.
Special Features: Room
service for all meals;
Children and pets
welcome.

This may just be the best buy in the Berkshires.
Enormous, modern deluxe rooms (one with a
patio) with two queen-size beds come complete
with small kitchens. The suite has two full bedrooms, two full baths, large, fully equipped
kitchen, living room, two TVs, laundry, and just
about anything else you might want. All accommodations are in a converted barn located behind the
popular restaurant.

KASINDORF'S
Managers: Shirley &
  Meyer Kasindorf.
413-232-4603.
Box 526, W. Stockbridge,
  MA 01266.
Price: Moderate.
Credit Cards: None.
Special Features: No
  smoking; No pets;
  Children over 13.

A lovely, contemporary home set on five park-like acres. There are three rooms, one with private bath. Full breakfast and complimentary afternoon beverages.

The Colonial charm of the 18th-century Williamsville Inn.

**THE WILLIAMSVILLE
  INN**
Owners: Gail & Kathleen
  Ryan.
413-274-6118.
P.O. Box 138, W. Stock-
  bridge, MA 01266.
On Rte. 41, 5 mi. N. of Gt.
  Barrington.
Price: Expensive.
Credit Cards: AE, MC, V.
Special Features: Pool; Ten-
  nis; Inquire about pets;
  Children over 9.

The gracious, white Colonial home was built in 1797 and retains the charm of a bygone era. There are nine guest rooms in the main house, two with fireplaces. Two cottages and four more units, all with woodstoves, in the converted barn, bring the room total to 15. All rooms have private bath. Fine restaurant on main floor, pool, and clay tennis court give the inn added dimension. Summer guests will enjoy the sculpture garden, with changing exhibits. In winter there are Sunday evening storytelling programs. The inn is available for meetings and conferences.

LODGING CENTRAL COUNTY

Becket

CANTERBURY FARM
Managers: Linda & Dave
  Bacon.
413-623-8765.
Fred Snow Rd., Becket, MA
  01223.
On country road off Rte. 8,
  5 mi. N. of Rte. 20, E. of
  Lee.
Closed: Mid-Oct.–mid-
  June.
Price: Inexpensive to Mod-
  erate.
Credit Cards: None.
Special Features: Hiking
  trails; No smoking; No
  pets; Children welcome.

This 200-year-old farm is a B&B in summer and fall and an active cross-country ski center in the winter. Eleven miles of trails are available for hiking and mountain biking. The four guest rooms are furnished with antiques, braided rugs, and an overall sense of personal warmth. Ask for the room with the fireplace. Gourmet, family breakfasts.

LONG HOUSE B & B
Owners: Roy & Joan Sim-
  mons.
413-623-8360.
High St. Becket, MA 01223.
On Rte. 8, Becket.
Price: Inexpensive.
Credit Cards: MC, V.
Special Features: No smok-
  ing.

The Simmonses have been welcoming bed and breakfast guests since 1966. Their charming 1820 country home, listed on the National Register of Historic Places, has four cozy rooms, one with private bath. Convenient to Jacob's Pillow, hiking and nature trails. Full breakfast offered. In summer, a weekly plan can be arranged.

Dalton

THE DALTON HOUSE
Hosts: Gary & Bernice
  Turetsky.
413-684-3854.
955 Main St., Dalton, MA
  01226.
Price: Moderate to Expen-
  sive.
Credit Cards: AE, MC, V.
Special Features: Pool;
  No smoking; No pets;
  Children over 6.

The rooms in the Main House and Carriage House, 11 altogether, all have private baths. Set in a small New England village, the house has been partially furnished with antiques. Summer guests enjoy the pool, extensively landscaped lawn and flower gardens, and a picnic area.

Hancock

HANCOCK INN
Managers: Ellen & Chester
  Gorski.
413-738-5873.
Rte. 43, Hancock, MA
  01237.
On Rte. 43, via Rte. 22, N. of
  New Lebanon, NY.
Price: Moderate.
Credit Cards: AE, MC, V.
Special Features: No smok-
  ing; No pets; Children
  welcome.

Exceptionally cozy Victorian inn set in a quaint village that seems unaware of the 20th century's arrival. A tastefully furnished, family-run establishment, the inn has the charm of a delightful, forgotten keepsake discovered one day in your grandmother's attic. Six comfortable rooms, all with private baths and air-conditioning, above a respected and well-managed restaurant. A full breakfast is included.

**JIMINY PEAK, THE
  MOUNTAIN RESORT**
General Manager: Paul
  Maloney.
413-738-5500; 800-882-8859
  (outside Mass.)
Corey Rd., Hancock, MA
  01237.
Between Rtes. 7 & 10 mi. N.
  of Pittsfield.
Price: Expensive.
Credit Cards: AE, D, DC,
  MC, V.
Handicap Access: Yes.
Special Features: Pool; Ten-
  nis; Health Club; Trout
  Fishing; Alpine Slide;
  Downhill skiing; No pets.

This relatively new full-service resort truly has it all. Even in the 105-unit Country Inn, all units are suites featuring kitchens, living rooms with queen-size sofa beds, and a master bedroom with queen-size bed. There are also one- and two-bedroom condominiums for rent. Add to that several restaurants, tennis, swimming, health club, trout fishing, an Alpine Slide for summer, and — best of all — *great* downhill skiing, and you've got one of the Berkshire's most complete resorts. The Champions Cup Tennis Tournament takes place here in July. Conference facilities are available.

**KIRKMEAD BED &
  BREAKFAST**
Owners: Donald & Pat
  Bowman.
413-738-5420.
Box 169A, Stephentown,
  NY 12168.
From NY Rte. 22, in Stephen-
  town, take Rte. 43 E. to
  Hancock, MA. Inn just
  across NY/MA state line.
Closed: Thanksgiving &
  Christmas.
Price: Inexpensive.
Credit Cards: None.
Special Features: No smok-
  ing; No Pets; Children
  welcome.

Historic, 1767 stagecoach stop has seven comfortable rooms, with air-conditioning and private baths. Informal atmosphere on 30 acres, with meandering brook and nature trail. Breakfast around the large common table is ample and convivial, and the complimentary bedtime snacks are popular with guests of all ages. Children are welcome; the Bowmans have a crib, playpen, and high chair available. This bargain is hard to beat.

Hinsdale

MAPLEWOOD B & B
Innkeepers: Charlotte &
  Bob Baillargeon.
413-655-8167.
435 Maple St., Box 477,
  Hinsdale, MA 01235.
On Rte. 143.
Price: Inexpensive to Mod-
  erate.
Credit Cards: None.
Special Features: No smok-
  ing; No pets.

Country setting; country style. The house is set on six acres with a small pond and has four rooms, one with private bath. Full breakfast might feature fresh trout caught by Bob or corn pancakes with fresh, locally made maple syrup; special diets can be accommodated. Antiques in many rooms.

Lanesborough

TOWNRY FARM
Managers: Cliff & Barb
  Feakes.
413-443-9285.
The Greylock Rd., Lanes-
  borough, MA 01237.
Off Rte. 7, 0.75 mi. on way
  to Mt. Greylock.
Closed: Mid-March–mid-
  May; Mid-Nov.–mid-
  Dec.
Price: Inexpensive.
Credit Cards: None.
Special Features: No pets;
  Children over 6.

A former sheep farm, Townry Farm still feels like a working farm, with Belgian horses next door and 80 milking cows across the road. Three rooms in the 1750 Colonial house share baths. The reasonable price includes full breakfast, and Barb Feakes is an accomplished baker who is happy to instruct guests as she works and often has baked goods for sale to take home.

**THE TUCKERED
  TURKEY**
Managers: Dan & Marianne
  Sullivan.
413-442-0260.
Old Cheshire Rd., Lanes-
  borough, MA 01237.
From Rte. 7, turn E. on
  Summer St., then N. on
  Old Cheshire Rd.
Price: Moderate.
Credit Cards: None.
Special Features: No smok-
  ing; No pets.

A restored 19th-century Colonial farmhouse, set on close to four acres, with spacious views. Three antique-furnished rooms share baths. Guests are welcome to bring their children to play with the owner's younger two. Full breakfast served, along with a great sense of humor.

WHIPPLETREE BED & BREAKFAST

Owners: Chuck & Kristin Lynch.
413-442-7468; 413-443-9874.
10 Bailey Rd., Lanesborough, MA 01237.
On Rte. 7, 3.5 mi. N. of Berkshire Mall.
Price: Inexpensive to Moderate.
Credit Cards: None.
Special Features: Pool; No smoking; No pets.

Guests approaching Whippletree by day will see two flags flying from the front porch — the American flag is joined by that of Kristin Lynch's native Iceland. After dark, the landmark is the candles glowing in the downstairs windows, no matter what the season. This painstakingly renovated 1753 farmhouse at the base of Mt. Greylock has five rooms (one is a suite with kitchen, living room, bedroom, and separate entrance), and two with private baths. Throughout the spotless house there are quilts (Kristin is a prize-winning quilter), wall hangings, stenciling, and a number of antiques. Guests may use the family room or the more formal living room. Host Chuck Lynch serves a hearty continental breakfast. He tells prospective clients that Whippletree is dead center between Tanglewood and Williamstown, and five minutes away from downhill skiing.

Lenox

AMADEUS HOUSE

Owners/Innkeepers: Marty Gottron & John Felton.
413-637-4770; 800-205-4770.
15 Cliffwood St., Lenox, MA 01240.
Off Main St. in Lenox.
Price: Moderate to Expensive.
Credit Cards: None.
Special Features: No smoking; No pets; Children over 6.

Marty Gottron and John Felton purchased the house once occupied by the Cranberry Goose in April 1993, repainted inside and out, refurnished and decorated the rooms, and opened for business two months later. Each of the seven rooms (plus the third-floor apartment, available by the day, week, or month) is named for a composer. Two rooms share a bath; the rest have private baths. The Mozart Room on the first floor has a sitting area, a wood-burning stove, and its own front porch. All the rooms are comfortable and pretty, with a number of antiques and quilts. Guests are welcome to choose from a collection of several hundred compact discs in the common room, or take a book from the upstairs library shelves and spend the day on the wraparound porch. A full breakfast, complete with vegetarian hot entrée, is served, as well as complimentary afternoon tea with fresh-baked cookies, tea cakes, or scones. John is a writer and former journalist and Marty an editor, who met when both worked for *The Congressional Digest*. Their interests and hospitable ways make a stay at Amadeus House a comfortable and relaxing experience, steps away from the busy main street of Lenox.

THE APPLE TREE INN
Managers: Aurora & Greg
  Smith.
413-637-1477.
334 West St., Lenox, MA
  01240.
On Rte. 183, S. of Tangle-
  wood Main Gate.
Closed: Jan. 1–Apr. 22.
Price: Expensive to Very
  Expensive.
Credit Cards: AE, CB, D,
  DC, MC, V.
Special Features: Pool; Ten-
  nis; No pets; Children
  over 10.

Magically set, the Apple Tree Inn is indis-
putably the lodging that lies closest to the
front gates of Tanglewood. Aurora and Greg
Smith, innkeepers, have brought great warmth and
hospitality to this inviting if not elegant country
property. The guest rooms in the main house are
down-comforter dainty, some with antique brass
beds and fireplaces, two with shared baths. A separate unit with 21 additional rooms is less charming,
though the rooms are certainly convenient and
clean.

The Apple Tree would be worth a visit for the
views alone. There is no more magnificent
panorama in the Berkshires than the views from
the south rooms, from poolside, or from the
gazebo, which now serves as a restaurant. There is
also dining on the new deck. The downstairs parlor is thoughtfully appointed
and very comfortable; the bar has rich wood paneling, stained glass windows,
and a huge hearth. A crowning touch is the landscaping, boasting hundreds of
varieties of roses set among the apple trees — truly a visual feast throughout
late spring and summer.

BIRCHWOOD INN
Innkeepers: Joan, Dick, &
  Dan Toner.
413-637-2600; 800-524-1646.
Box 2020, 7 Hubbard St.,
  Lenox, MA 01240.
On corner of Main and
  Hubbard.
Price: Moderate to Very
  Expensive.
Credit Cards: AE, CB, D,
  DC, MC, V.
Special Features: Massage
  therapy; No smoking; No
  pets; Children over 11.

Elegant 1767 mansion high on the hill overlooking the charm of Lenox. The Toner family has
owned the inn since June 1991. They are gradually
renovating the rooms and recently have added
telephones, as well as new carpeting in the corri-
dors. There are ten rooms in the main house, eight
with private bath, and two suites in the carriage
house. A magnificent library extends along one side
of the house, with books, magazines, and games
galore. The wicker-furnished front porch is a popular spot in summer. A full gourmet breakfast, plus
wine and cheese in the afternoon, is included.

BLANTYRE
Manager: Roderick
  Anderson.
413-637-3556 (Winter: 413-
  298-3806).
16 Blantyre Rd., Lenox, MA
  01240.

There is, in Berkshire, no sanctuary so civilized
as Blantyre. Regally set amidst 85 conscien-
tiously groomed acres of lawns, trees, and hedges,
Blantyre offers its guests attentive and even inge-
nious service, great natural and architectural
beauty, palatial furnishings, and magnificent vistas.

Frank Packlick, courtesy Blantyre

Stately Blantyre.

Off Rte. 20, 3 mi. NW of Lee (and Mass. Pike).
Closed: Nov. 1–mid-May.
Price: Very Expensive.
Credit Cards: AE, DC, MC, V.
Handicap Access: Limited.
Special Features: Pool; Tennis; Croquet; Exercise Room; Sauna; Hot Tub; No pets; Children over 12.

Built by New York City businessman Robert Paterson in 1902, a replica of his wife's ancestral home in the Scottish village of Blantyre, east of Glasgow, Blantyre went through several hands in mid-century and fell into disrepair. In 1980 Jack and Jane Fitzpatrick bought the property and with their daughter, Ann, restored it to its present excellent condition: a baronial yet hospitable place — massive but comfortable, grand yet delicately appointed.

A member of the prestigious Relais et Châteaux, Blantyre was awarded the Relais et Châteaux Gold Medal in 1989, a very special award, bestowed on the hotel that receives the highest number of complimentary guest comments. The five original suite-size bedrooms, with four-poster beds, fireplaces, and magnificent bathrooms, are the true "jewels" in Blantyre's crown. There are three other rooms on the same floor, created in the "nanny's wing" on a different scale, smaller but just as elegant. Twelve more rooms are neatly tucked away in the original Carriage House. There are also two cottages on the grounds, both cozy, endearingly whimsical and brilliantly situated.

In addition to its superb accommodations, Blantyre has a magnificent gourmet dining room. The hotel maintains four Har-Tru tennis courts and two tournament-size bent-grass croquet courts. A delightful exercise room fashioned out of a former potting shed also provides a sauna and hot tub. Nearby is a lovely landscaped swimming pool. Tanglewood is a mere three miles to the west. Conferences and small meetings are welcome. (Please note that the grounds and buildings are *not* open to the public for casual viewing.)

BROOK FARM INN

Owners/Innkeepers: Joe &
Anne Miller.
413-637-3013; 800-285-
POET.
15 Hawthorne St., Lenox,
MA 01240.
Just off Old Stockbridge
Rd.
Price: Expensive.
Credit Cards: D, MC, V.
Special Features: Pool; No
smoking; No pets.

The Millers bought this inn in January 1992 and have upheld the special poetry feature started by the previous owners. A 1,400-volume library is supplemented by 75 poets on tape, and a reading takes place every Saturday at 4 p.m., accompanied by tea and scones. A buffet breakfast and afternoon tea are served daily to guests; on Sunday mornings musicians from the nearby Tanglewood Institute perform during breakfast. Twelve antique-furnished rooms, all with private bath, are offered in this large Victorian home, close to many Berkshire attractions. Several of the rooms have been renovated, with special attention lavished on the two large rooms at the front of the house, both with four-posters, sitting areas, and new bathrooms.

CANDLELIGHT INN

Managers: Rebecca & John
Hedgecock.
413-637-1555.
35 Walker St., Lenox, MA
01240.
On corner of Walker &
Church sts., near village
center.
Price: Moderate to Expensive.
Credit Cards: AE, MC, V.
Special Features: No pets;
Children over 9.

This comfortable, antique-furnished inn has eight large guest rooms, all with private bath, some retaining their original fixtures. Centrally located in the heart of Lenox, the inn features a charming restaurant on the main floor. Delightfully and professionally run by friendly hosts.

CLIFFWOOD INN

Owners/Managers: Scottie
& Joy Farrelly.
413-637-3330.
25 Cliffwood St., Lenox,
MA 01240.
Just off Main St., in village.
Price: Moderate to Very
Expensive.
Credit Cards: None.
Special Features: Pool;
No smoking; No pets;
Children over 12.

This very special inn, on a quiet, residential street, was built for an ambassador to France in the early 1890s. The elegant public rooms have tall ceilings, polished inlaid hardwood floors, and grand fireplaces. The seven guest rooms have private baths and air-conditioning; six even come with their own fireplaces. In summer, a continental breakfast is served on the spacious veranda overlooking the gardens and pool. On winter mornings, breakfast is served by a warming fire in the oval dining room with its ornate wood-carved fireplace mantel. Wine, hors d'oeuvres, and friendly conversation served early evening.

CORNELL INN
Owner: Jack D'Elia.
413-637-0562.
209 Main St., Lenox, MA
  01240.
On Rte. 7A, just N. of center
  of town.
Price: Expensive to Very
  Expensive.
Credit Cards: AE, DC, CB,
  D, MC, V.
Handicap Access: Yes.
Special Features: Spa
  (sauna, steam room,
  Jacuzzi); No pets.

The Cornell Inn just keeps getting better. It began life in 1888 as a large, well-built Victorian, and the owners keep making all the right improvements. Each of the ten bedrooms in the main house has its own bath and is furnished with brass or four-poster beds; several have wood-burning fireplaces. There are four additional rooms in the converted carriage house and ten in the adjacent McDonald House, which has recently been renovated. The McDonald House rooms have fireplaces and whirlpool tubs.

**CRANWELL RESORT
  AND GOLF CLUB**
General Manager: Joe
  Corso.
413-637-1364; 800-272-6935.
55 Lee Rd., Lenox, MA
  01240.
Rte. 20 S. of Lenox center,
  3.5 mi. from exit 2 Mass.
  Pike.
Price: Expensive to Very
  Expensive.
Credit Cards: AE, D, DC,
  MC, V.
Handicap Access: Yes.
Special Features: Pool;
  Tennis; Golf; No pets.

Cranwell is a 380-acre estate high on a hill with one of the finest views of the Berkshire Hills. The 1893 Tudor Mansion is surrounded by lawns, gardens, and a par-71 championship golf course. Guest rooms are in the Mansion (Cranwell Hall); Beecher's Cottage (the farmhouse built on the property in 1853 by Henry Ward Beecher); the Carriage House; and a group of one-bedroom cottages. The most luxurious bedrooms in the Mansion are spacious and individually decorated in the Victorian style, with private marble baths. In the various outbuildings, accommodations are slightly simpler and more contemporary, but some have the advantages of wet bar, refrigerator, and/or galley kitchens. Two dining rooms, a lounge, and numerous conference rooms complete the full-service offerings of this special property.

SUMMER HILL FARM
Owners: Sonya Chassell
  Wessel & Michael Wessel.
413-442-2057.
950 East St., Lenox, MA
  01240.
Off Rtes. 7 & 20 at Holmes
  Rd.; right on Chapman
  Rd.(becomes East St.) to
  red farmhouse on left.
Price: Moderate to Expensive.
Credit Cards: None.
Handicap Access: Yes.

Here is a piece of the old Berkshires, before the days of the grand "cottages" and the influx of New York society. The historic ca. 1750 farmhouse has six rooms, with a one-bedroom suite recently added in a cottage behind the house. All the rooms have private baths and color TVs and are furnished with Wessel family antiques. Michael is English, and Sonya lived in England for 36 years, which makes for an informal cosmopolitan atmosphere. Twenty acres of peaceful countryside at the foot of October Mountain, at the northern edge of Lenox, provide a peaceful stopping place away from the

Special Features: No pets;
Children under 1 and
over 4.

busy village. Wildflower walks, horseback riding, canoeing, and bicycling are just a few of the possible pastimes in the area. Horse Sense, a riding school for children run by the Wessels' daughter, shares the farm.

EASTOVER
Owners: Susan & Bob
McNinch & Ticki Winsor.
413-637-0625; 800-822-2386.
430 East St., Lenox, MA
01240.
From Rte. 7 in Lenox,
take Housatonic St. E.,
then L. onto East St.
for 1 mi.
Closed: 3 weeks in April.
Price: Moderate AP; wkly
rates also.
Credit Cards: AE, CB, D,
DC, MC, V.
Special Features: Indoor &
outdoor pools; Tennis;
Exercise Room; Sauna;
Driving range; Miniature
golf; Downhill skiing;
XC skiing; Toboggan run;
No pets; Inquire about
children.

Eastover makes no bones about it. Informality is the key! Though it is surely not everyone's cup of tea, it is a very picturesque, amiable place that is admirably free of pretension. As another of the celebrated Lenox "cottages," this grand Gilded Age house is obviously living out of character but seems to be thriving.

You need not leave the sprawling grounds of this former estate to enjoy tennis, swimming, biking, volleyball, sauna, exercise room, horseback riding, and all sorts of winter activities, including downhill and cross-country skiing and tobogganing on their own toboggan run.

Inspired by the remarkable spirit of the late founder, George Bisacca, the staff is up for anything as long as it's fun. To add to the festivities, there is dancing to live music during happy hour and again later in the evening. No liquor license here, so it's BYOB, but the band can play into the wee morning hours. This is not the place for the shy, the reclusive, or those who don't quite feel dressed without a jacket and tie or a skirt and heels. For the good sport, the incurably casual, or the curious, Eastover means relaxation, silliness, and whatever the weekend's theme may be.

Wander the grounds, but beware of the American buffalo, geese, burros, and other pets of the singular Bisacca. The founder's collection of Civil War artifacts and the museum in the "Heritage Room" will fascinate boys of any age and revolt most others. Corny, oddly quaint and yet decidedly trendy, Eastover caters to families, couples-only, and singles-only on different weeks and weekends. Call ahead to find out when you might go, depending on who you are. No matter what your status, Eastover has some fun planned for you.

THE GABLES INN
Manager: Frank Newton.
413-637-3416.
81 Walker St., Lenox, MA
01240.
In center of village.

Charming old home where Edith Wharton summered while her "cottage," the Mount, was being built. In the center of the village within walking distance of almost everything, including Tanglewood. There are 18 bedrooms, all with private

Price: Moderate to Very
Expensive.
Credit Cards: D, MC, V.
Special Features: Pool; Ten-
nis; No Pets; Children
over 16.

GARDEN GABLES INN
Owners: Mario & Lynn
Mekinda.
413-637-0193.
P.O. Box 52, 135 Main St.,
Lenox, MA 01240.
Price: Inexpensive to
Expensive.
Credit Cards: AE, D, MC,
V.
Special Features: Pool; No
pets; Children over 11.

GATEWAYS INN
Manager: Vito Perulli.
413-637-2532.
51 Walker St., Lenox, MA
01240.
Just off Main St., in center
of village.
Price: Expensive to Very
Expensive.
Credit Cards: AE, D, DC,
MC, V.
Special Features: Tennis;
No smoking; No pets;
Children over 12.

THE HILLTOP INN
Owner: Vito Perulli.
413-637-1746.
174 Main St., Lenox, MA
01240. In the center of
town.
Price: Very Expensive.
Credit Cards: AE, D, DC,
MC, V.
Handicap Access: Limited.
Special Features: No smoking; No pets; Children
over 11.

baths; nine with fireplaces. A handsome house.
Continental breakfast.

Since purchasing the property in 1987, the Mekinda family has brought new life to this inn. All 18 rooms have been upgraded to include private bath (three have whirlpools); eight rooms have fireplaces; some have private porches; and some have TV. The five acres of landscaped grounds include the largest outdoor pool in Berkshire County. Walking distance to Lenox shops and restaurants, and even to Tanglewood for the hardy. Breakfasts are extra special.

This Berkshire "cottage" was built in 1912 by Harley Procter of Procter and Gamble fame. Above an award-winning restaurant are spacious, elegant rooms, each with bath, three with fireplaces, a four-poster here, a canopy there, and peace and quiet everywhere. Arthur Fiedler stayed here when performing at Tanglewood, and the "Fiedler Suite" is especially lovely.

An upscale guest house opened in June 1993 by the owner of Gateways, with six elegant guest rooms and splendid public areas. The attractive Victorian, at the crest of Main St. across the street from Kennedy Park, has a wraparound porch and a handsome sitting/breakfast room overlooking the back lawn. The bedrooms are air-conditioned, and each has a private bath with period fixtures and decor, a fireplace (many with the original Victorian tiles), and cable TV. Duvets and cutwork linens add a romantic touch. The Norman Rockwell suite has a canopy bed, a sitting room with sofabed, and an especially splendid bathroom.

THE KEMBLE INN

Innkeepers/Owners:
Richard & Linda
Reardon.
413-637-4113; 800-353-4113.
2 Kemble St., Lenox, MA
01240.
Rte. 7A in Lenox.
Price: Expensive to Very
Expensive.
Credit Cards: AE, MC, V.
Handicap Access: Yes.
Special Features: No smok-
ing; No pets; Children
over 15.

The newest luxury bed and breakfast inn in Lenox is named for the actress Fanny Kemble, who once lived on the street named for her. It occupies yet another Berkshire "cottage" — this one the Georgian mansion built by Chester Arthur's secretary of state, Frederick T. Frelinghuysen, in 1881. Richard Reardon is a contractor and has supervised the complete renovation of the house, which included adding several bathrooms. Each of the 12 guest rooms has a private bath and air-conditioning, and the furnishings throughout the house are period reproductions. The Master Suite has a bedroom with fireplace and a bathroom with Jacuzzi and another fireplace. The most impressive features of the inn are the elegant and spacious common spaces on the ground floor — foyer, reception room, living room, dining room, and back porch — all with magnificent Adam-style paneling — and the views of the mountains to the back and historic Trinity Church to the front.

PINE ACRES BED & BREAKFAST

Manager: Karen Fulco.
413-637-2292.
137 New Lenox Rd., Lenox,
MA 01240.
Price: Moderate.
Credit Cards: None.
Special Features: No smok-
ing.

A bed and breakfast on a quiet back road, close to all the Berkshire highlights. Three rooms, shared bath, have a pleasant Colonial decor. In summer, a continental breakfast is served on the sun porch.

ROOKWOOD INN

Innkeepers: Tom & Betsy
Sherman.
413-637-9750.
11 Old Stockbridge Rd.,
Lenox, MA 01240.
Just off Main St. in center of
town.
Price: Expensive to Very
Expensive.
Credit Cards: AE.
Handicap Access: Limited.
Special Features: No smok-
ing; No pets.

A grand Victorian painted lady, on a quiet street, but only one block from town center. All 19 rooms have private bath and seven include fireplaces. The two-level turret room is a marvelous secluded aerie, and the three rooms in the new addition at the back of the house are particularly comfortable. The innkeepers have two small children, and guests are welcome to bring their own.

UNDERLEDGE INN

Managers: The Lanoue
Family.

Set high on a hill, off tree-lined Cliffwood St., this estate has 26-acre Kennedy Park at its back door. Perfect for hiking or cross-country skiing.

413-637-0236.
106 Cliffwood St., Lenox,
 MA 01240.
Just off Main St.
Closed: "Some winter
 months"
Price: Moderate to Expen-
 sive.
Credit Cards: MC, V.
Special Features: No smok-
 ing; No pets; Children
 over 9.

The mansion was built in 1900 as a summer home for two wealthy sisters. Rooms are large and several feature fireplaces. The gracious front porch and sunny terrace are perfect places to relax and watch the sunset before driving along the pretty back road to Tanglewood, no more than a mile away.

The Village Inn by moonlight.

Bruce MacDonald, courtesy the Village Inn

THE VILLAGE INN
Managers: Clifford Rudisill
 & Ray Wilson.
413-637-0020; 800-253-0917.
Box 1810, 16 Church St.,
 Lenox, MA 01240.
Off Walker St. in the center
 of town.
Price: Inexpensive to
 Expensive.
Credit Cards: AE, CB, D,
 DC, MC, V.
Handicap Access: Yes.
Special Features: No smok-
 ing; No pets; Children
 over 6.

Innkeepers Cliff Rudisill and Ray Wilson are cultivated, hospitable hosts whose personal warmth complements this old, highly respected hostelry. Their pride in restoration and furnishings is evident in their recently completed renovations. There are 32 guest rooms, all with private bath and telephone. Six rooms have fireplaces, and there is one suite with a kitchenette. All guest rooms are nonsmoking, as are the public rooms.

The inn was built in 1771 as a farmhouse; four years later, its original owner started to put up weary travelers arriving by horse-drawn coach. By 1815, he had sold his surrounding land, and it is surmised that he was by then exclusively an innkeeper.

Among the nice culinary touches offered today are the hearty breakfasts served on the sunny all-season porch and the English afternoon tea for which the Village Inn is justly famous (neither is included in the room rate). There is a full-scale restaurant, as well as a downstairs tavern featuring English ales. In summer, late night suppers are available after Friday and Saturday night Tanglewood concerts.

WALKER HOUSE
Innkeepers: Peggy &
  Richard Houdek.
413-637-1271.
64 Walker St., Lenox, MA
  01240.
Price: Moderate to Expensive.
Credit Cards: None.
Handicap Access: Limited.

Comfortable, well-furnished, 1804-vintage Federal house operated by two genuinely friendly people. The three acres of garden and woods behind the house are gorgeous. Eight rooms all have private baths and are named for famous composers. Sitting rooms offer an impressive collection of music and books, and a new feature is the 7-foot video screen in the Library Theatre, wonderful for opera, films, and sports events. Within walking distance of Tanglewood, Lenox shops, and restaurants.

Courtesy Lenox Library

WHEATLEIGH
Owners: Susan & Linfield
  Simon.
413-637-0610.
Box 824, Hawthorne Rd.,
  Lenox, MA 01240.
From Rte. 183 in Lenox, left
  on Hawthorne Rd. to
  Wheatleigh sign.
Price: Very Expensive.
Credit Cards: AE, MC, V.
Special Features: Pool;
  Tennis; No pets; Children
  over 11.

Wheatleigh is pure romance. An estate built for heiress Georgie Bruce Cook, wife of "Count" Carlos de Heredia, it encourages flights of imagination. The grounds and setting are absolutely captivating. From the broad terrace, the manicured lawns slope down to a grassy stairway and then to a fountain. Straight ahead is an awesome view of the Stockbridge Bowl with the Berkshire hills in the distance. The pool is hidden away in a knoll surrounded by trees, and the tennis court is off in another direction.

Owners Linfield and Susan Simon have preserved the expansive luxury of the interior space and decorative details in this turn-of-the-century mansion. The approach is by way of a winding driveway, then through an enclosed courtyard with a circular drive — reminiscent of a 16th-century private palazzo in the hills outside Florence. Once inside, the Great Hall is impressive with its magnificent Tiffany windows lining the grand staircase, newly added antique furnishings, and original brass chandelier. The dark-wooded Conservatory with its cooling breezes is perfect for summer dining.

The 17 guest rooms, completely redecorated in 1993, are baronial in size and nine still have their working fireplaces. The bathrooms are splendid, several with original fixtures. Wheatleigh contains an award-winning, prix-fixe restaurant, complemented by an award-winning wine list. The premises are available for business meetings, weddings, and parties.

The music room at Whistler's Inn.

Jonathan Sternfield

WHISTLER'S INN
Managers: Richard & Joan
  Mears.
413-637-0975.
5 Greenwood St., Lenox,
  MA 01240.
On corner of Rte. 7A &
  Greenwood St.
Price: Moderate to Very
  Expensive.
Credit Cards: AE, D, MC,
  V.
Special Features: No pets.

Charming, much-admired guest house created within an 1820s English Tudor summer estate. Cultivated, accommodating hosts (Richard is an author; Joan is an artist) will put you at ease. The inn is furnished with antiques, chandeliers, and Persian rugs, resulting in an Old-World Victorian atmosphere. The interior is full of pleasant surprises, including an extensive library. The 13 bedrooms, all with private bath, are quaint and cozy. From the stone-walled terrace it's possible to walk among seven acres of gardens and woodland. Full breakfast is provided.

<u>Note</u>: See also **Canyon Ranch** under "A Luxury Spa" in Chapter 6.

Peru

CHALET D'ALICIA
Managers: Alice & Richard
  Halvorsen.
413-655-8292.

Remote location in the wilds of the Berkshire hilltowns. Congenial home with three rooms, one with private bath. Full country breakfast. Ideal

East Windsor Rd., Peru,
MA 01235.
Off Rte. 8, 3 mi. on Rte. 143,
then L. on E. Windsor
Rd., 3 mi.
Price: Inexpensive.
Credit Cards: None.

for nature buffs, cross-country skiers, hunters, or simply for those seeking solitude. Friendly dogs and cats. Hot tub for total relaxation.

Pittsfield

**BERKSHIRE HILTON
INN**
General Manager: Tom
Guido.
413-499-2000.
Berkshire Common, West
St., Pittsfield, MA 01201.
Off Park Square.
Price: Moderate to Very
Expensive.
Credit Cards: AE, D, DC,
MC, V.
Handicap Access: Yes.
Special Features: Indoor
pool; Sauna; Jacuzzi.

Following a major renovation in 1989, this Hilton is far above the average. VIP rooms have a decidedly New England flair with prints on the walls, English-style furniture, and chintz. Even the corridor carpeting is classy. A publike casual restaurant, the Park Square Grille, with photos of Pittsfield's old Park Square for decoration, complements the more formal Rockwell's. For business people, there is extensive meeting space, from a grand ballroom to small meeting rooms. The Top of the Hilton has recently reopened, with a cocktail lounge and function rooms.

WHITE HORSE INN
Innkeepers: Ron & Paula
Virgilio.
413-442-2512.
378 South St., Pittsfield, MA
01201.
Rtes. 7 & 20, S. of town center.
Price: Moderate to Expen-
sive.
Credit Cards: AE, MC, V.
Special Features: No smoking; No pets; Children
over 11.

An attractive 1907 Colonial Revival set back from the busy main street, south of the center of Pittsfield. All rooms have private bath and have been totally redecorated by the new owners with pretty linens and wallpapers. Several rooms have fireplaces. There is a kitchenette for guests on the second floor, as well as a small sitting room. An extensive continental breakfast is served in the dining room, where guests have individual tables, or on the new deck in summer. Perennial gardens and a picnic table complete the picture.

Richmond

**A BED & BREAKFAST IN
THE BERKSHIRES**
Manager: Doane Perry.
413-698-2817.

Formerly Seychelles, the name has changed but the ownership has not. Personal attention continues to be lavished on this special home, just 3 1/2 miles from both Tanglewood and Hancock

Dublin Rd., Richmond, MA 01254.
Rte. 20 to Rte. 41S, then S. on Dublin Rd.
Price: Inexpensive to Expensive.
Credit Cards: AE, MC, V.
Handicap Access: Limited.
Special Features: No smoking; Well-behaved children & pets welcome.

Shaker Village. Its serene setting on 3 1/2 acres includes magnificent perennial gardens, a wildflower meadow, an orchard complete with hammock and returning bluebirds, and in winter cross-country skiing out the back door. The three guest rooms have private baths, hand-made quilts, antiques, down pillows and comforters, and fresh flowers. In summer, the full country breakfast is served on the spacious porch; there is also complimentary afternoon tea or sherry.

BERKSHIRE HILLS COUNTRY INN
Manager: Ann Meyer.
413-698-3379.
Dean Hill Rd., Richmond, MA 01254.
Off Rte. 41.
Closed: Nov.–May.
Price: Inexpensive.
Credit Cards: None.
Special Features: No smoking; No pets; Children over 17.

Great view of the Berkshires from this 147-acre hilltop property. The three rooms are comfortable; all share baths. Continental breakfast served. Children are not accepted.

ECHEZEAUX, A COUNTRY BED & BREAKFAST
Innkeepers: Ronald Barron & Ina Wilhelm.
413-698-2802 (winter 617-965-3957).
Cheever Rd., Richmond, MA 01254.
2.25 mi. N. on Swamp Rd. (from W. Stockbridge), then R. on Cheever to end.
Closed: Labor Day–last wkend. in June; 2 cottages available in fall.
Price: Moderate.
Credit Cards: None.
Special Features: Pool; No smoking; No pets.

Delightful country retreat, owned by a member of the Boston Symphony Orchestra and frequently rented to other BSO members, this house often fills the surrounding hills with music. The main house has four antique-furnished rooms, one with private bath. Full breakfast is served. Guests are just two miles from the front gate of Tanglewood.

MIDDLERISE BED & BREAKFAST
Managers: The White Family.

This renovated Cape-style house sits above the Richmond Valley and offers guests three cozy bedrooms, one with private bath. The rooms are

413-698-2687.
Box 17, Richmond, MA
    01254.
Off State Rd., Rte. 41.
Closed: Nov.–Jan.
Price: Moderate.
Credit Cards: None.
Special Features: No smok-
    ing; Inquire about pets &
    children.

quaintly furnished with antiques. Short drive to Tanglewood in one direction and Hancock Shaker Village in another.

PEIRSON PLACE
Owner: Margaret Kingman.
413-698-2750.
1238 State Rd. Richmond,
    MA 01254.
On Rte. 41, just N. of inter-
    section with Rte. 295.
Price: Moderate to Expen-
    sive.
Credit Cards: AE, MC, V.
Handicap Access: Yes.
Special Features: Pond with
    boats; Children over 12.

Dating to 1772, this four-story former tannery, where boots for the officers of the Northern Division of the Revolutionary War were made, sits on 200 acres near the secluded village of Richmond. Fifteen rooms are available in summer and fall, eight with private bath and several with fireplaces. The room count diminishes to five in winter and spring. A continental breakfast and afternoon tea are included, and in summer there is a popular breakfast buffet for an extra charge. Lunch and dinner for guests are sometimes available. There are a private pond with boats, cross-country ski trails, and a sauna. Many outbuildings add charm. A fascinating history goes with the former tannery; ask the owner, whose family built it.

Washington

BUCKSTEEP MANOR
Manager: Domenick Sacco.
413-623-5535.
Washington Mtn. Rd.,
    Washington, MA 01223.
Off Rte. 8 N. from Becket;
    ask at general store.
Price: Inexpensive to Mod-
    erate.
Credit Cards: MC, V.
Handicap Access: Yes.
Special Features: XC ski
    center; No Pets; Children
    welcome.

Deep in the Washington Mountain woods, a cross-country skier's paradise. Several rooms in the main house share baths and are comfortably furnished. Rooms in the lodge have private baths. In the summer a few cabins increase the number of accommodations, adding to the rustic feeling of the property. Hiking, biking, and birding opportunities abound. Great dancing and rock, country, bluegrass, and reggae concerts in the Barn and on the lawn in summer. Good vibes, funky buildings, and that mellow, laid-back feeling predominate.

Windsor

WINDFIELDS FARM
Owners: Carolyn & Arnold
  Westwood.
413-684-3786.
154 Windsor Bush Rd.,
  Cummington, MA 01026.
Off Rte. 9, outside W. Cum-
  mington, 1.7 mi. N. on
  Bush Rd. in Windsor.
Closed: Mar. & Apr.
Price: Inexpensive.
Credit Cards: None.
Special Features: No smok-
  ing; No pets; Children
  over 12.

Way out in the northern Berkshire hills, this country farmhouse offers a friendly welcome and two rooms with shared bath, furnished very comfortably with contemporary and antique furnishings. The property adjoins the Windsor State Forest, Windsor Jambs waterfall is within walking distance, and there are a swimming pond and miles of trails for hiking or skiing. Hearty breakfast.

LODGING NORTH COUNTY

Adams

Bascom Lodge, atop Mount Greylock.

Jonathan Sternfield

BASCOM LODGE
Managers: Appalachian
  Mtn. Club; Jean Cowhig.
413-443-0011 (9–5 daily).
P.O. Box 1800, Lanesbor-
  ough, MA 01237.

Let us now praise improbable places. Bascom Lodge, atop Mt. Greylock, is a marvel of dramatic beauty, adventure, and bargain-basement rates. Operated by the Appalachian Mountain Club and the Massachusetts Department of Environmen-

From Rte. 7 take North Main St. to Rockwell Rd., to the summit of Mt. Greylock.
Closed: Mid-Oct.–mid-May.
Price: Inexpensive.
Credit Cards: MC, V.
Handicap Access: Yes.
Special Features: Hiking trails; No smoking; No pets; Children welcome.

tal Management, the lodge at the 3,491-foot summit of the state's highest peak was built of stone and wood by the Civilian Conservation Corps during the Depression. Generations of hikers, birders, and clever travelers have celebrated the accommodations and have returned again and again.

The stone fireplace and hand-cut oak beams cultivate a sense of adventure, which the magnificent hills and trails confirm. This is lodging for the hearty, or at least the sporting. Though linen is supplied, you might want to bring a sleeping bag or extra blanket. The guest rooms are private or dormitory style; so, plan accordingly. Breakfast and dinner are served family style at a set time.

Workshops on topics ranging from birdwatching and backpacking to geology and photography are offered throughout the hiking season. We once even enjoyed a literary gathering up here, hearing selections from Thoreau's hiking notebooks read by a ruddy-faced AMC guide. While some rates at other more lavish places approach the upper end of the chart, the rates at Bascom don't even make it onto the bottom end!

North Adams

BLACKINTON MANOR
Hosts: Dan & Betsy Epstein.
413-663-5795; 212-787-6262.
1391 Massachusetts Ave., N. Adams, MA 01247.
One block off Rte. 2, minutes from Williamstown.
Price: Moderate to Expensive.
Credit Cards: None.
Special Features: Pool; Chamber Music; Hiking; No smoking; No pets; Children over 7.

This handsome Federal mansion offers the most elegant and romantic bed and breakfast experience in North Berkshire County. Reopened in 1993 after a complete renovation by new owners, the 1849 house is notable for its French–Italianate features — including intricate wrought-iron balconies, floor-to-ceiling pocket windows, and a spacious bay window. The bedrooms, most with private bath, have furnishings, fabrics, and wallpaper appropriate to the period. A full gourmet breakfast is served in the formal dining room or, in summer, on the screened porch or pool patio. The Epsteins are musicians — Dan is pianist for the Raphael Trio and Betsy is an opera singer and invested cantor — and house concerts and chamber music workshops are a regular part of life at Blackinton Manor. The Appalachian Trail is right out the back door, so hiking weekends are also a specialty.

HOLIDAY INN BERK-SHIRES

Centrally located in the heart of town and convenient to numerous area attractions, the com-

General Manager: Edward Bassi.
413-663-6500.
40 Main St., N. Adams, MA 01247.
Price: Moderate.
Credit Cards: AE, CB, D, DC, MC, V.
Handicap Access: Yes.
Special Features: Indoor pool; Sauna; Jacuzzi; No pets.

pletely renovated former North Adams Inn calls itself "the newest full-service hotel in the Berkshires." The 87 air-conditioned rooms, all with private bath, color TV, and telephones, are large and decorated in soft tones of purple and mauve. Plum Trees, a full-service restaurant, serves breakfast, lunch, and dinner. Conference and meeting facilities are available, and tours are welcome.

TWIN SISTERS INN
Manager: Gabriella Bond.
413-663-6933.
Box 311, 1111 S. State St., N. Adams, MA 01247.
Rte. 8, 2 mi. S. of North Adams city hall.
Price: Inexpensive.
Credit Cards: None.
Handicap Access: Limited.
Special Features: No pets; Children welcome.

Set on 10 acres, this former carriage house now serves guests as a bed and breakfast. Four rooms share two baths. The large living room has a fireplace, and there's a porch with a great view of the eastern Hoosac range, looking toward the Mohawk Trail. Continental breakfast served.

Williamstown

FIELD FARM GUEST HOUSE
Managers: Judy & David Loomis.
413-458-3135.
554 Sloan Rd., Williamstown, MA 01267.
From jct. Rtes. 43 & 7, 1 mi. on R.
Price: Moderate.
Credit Cards: None.
Handicap Access: Limited.
Special Features: Pool; Tennis; Hiking trails; No pets.

A Property of the Trustees of Reservations, Field Farm comprises 254 acres of land, excellent for hiking and cross-country skiing, and a house built in 1948 in the American Moderne style. Five guest rooms all have private bath, two have working fireplaces, and three have sun decks. A swimming pool and tennis courts are added attractions. Country living with views of Mt. Greylock and the Taconic Range, just minutes from the attractions of Williamstown.

GOLDBERRY'S
Hosts: Bev & Ray Scheer.
413-458-3935.
39 Cold Spring Road, Williamstown, MA 01267.

A bed and breakfast opened in 1991, in an ideal location within three blocks of the Williams College campus, the Williamstown Theatre Festival, and the Clark Art Institute. The 1830s house is comfortably furnished with antiques and appropri-

Rtes. 7 & 2, near Williams Inn.
Closed: 3 days at Christmas.
Price: Moderate.
Credit Cards: None.
Special Features: No smoking; No pets; Children over 3.

ate companion pieces, and guests are invited to use the living room, dining room, sun porch, and back porch overlooking the perennial gardens. Two of the three bedrooms have private baths. Bev Scheer's gourmet breakfast might include lemon ricotta or pumpkin pancakes and always lots of fresh fruit. This is a popular stopping place for Williams College alumnae and parents.

THE HOUSE ON MAIN STREET
Innkeepers: Phyllis, Bud, & Regina Riley.
413-458-3031.
1120 Main St.,
Williamstown, MA 01267.
Near jct. Rtes. 2 & 7, W. of Williams Inn.
Price: Moderate.
Credit Cards: D, MC, V.
Handicap Access: Limited.
Special Features: No smoking; No pets; Children welcome.

Once known as Victorian Tourist & Antique House, this bed and breakfast has been taking guests since the 1930s. The Rileys became innkeepers in 1991 and are proud of the comment of one satisfied guest: "You have achieved a great combination of Victorian charm and modern comfort."

Like many Berkshire houses, this one had its beginnings in the 18th century, with a major Victorian addition in the 1870s. The six guest rooms are light and spacious, with accents of antique furnishings, pretty country prints, and braided rugs. A healthful and hearty breakfast is served in the country kitchen, with a hot entrée every day. Guests may use the parlor and the wicker-laden screened porch. The congenial Rileys are well versed on the attractions of Williamstown, all within walking distance.

LE JARDIN
Manager: Walter Hayn.
413-458-8032.
777 Cold Spring Rd.,
Williamstown, MA 01267.
On Rte. 7 a few mi. S. of town.
Closed: Jan.–Mar.
Price: Moderate.
Credit Cards: AE, MC, V.
Special Features: No pets.

Just south of the heart of Williamstown, on a wooded hillside above Rte. 7, Le Jardin offers six cozy rooms, all with private bath, in a large country farmhouse. Well-known restaurant on the first floor.

THE ORCHARDS
Owner/General Manager: Sayed M. Saleh.
413-458-9611.
222 Adams Rd.
Williamstown, MA 01267. On Rte. 2, E. of town center.

This small luxury hotel, a member of Preferred Hotels & Resorts Worldwide, is reminiscent of an English country inn. Antique furnishings, complimentary afternoon tea, and spacious guest rooms featuring four-poster beds with down pillows are just a few of the amenities. Many rooms have wood-burning fireplaces and bay windows.

The interior courtyard at the Orchards.

Jonathan Sternfield

Price: Expensive to Very Expensive.
Credit Cards: AE, CB, DC, MC, V.
Handicap Access: Yes.
Special Features: Pool; Exercise Center with sauna, environmental chamber, and whirlpool; No pets.

The Orchards' award-winning restaurant features a menu that reflects New England's heritage and the chef's distinctive international talents. In summer al fresco patio dining is available overlooking the pond in the nicely landscaped inner courtyard. Chocolate chip cookies are a regular bedtime treat. Private conference and meeting rooms.

RIVER BEND FARM
Innkeepers: Jeff Miller & Bob Horan.
413-458-3121.
643 Simonds Rd., Williamstown, MA 01267.
Rte. 7, 0.75 mi. N. of jct. of Rtes. 7 & 2 in town center.
Price: Moderate.
Credit Cards: MC, V.
Closed: Christmas–April 1, except by advance reservation.
Special Features: No smoking; No pets.

A stay at River Bend Farm, an authentic 1770 Georgian house listed on the National Register of Historic Places and featured on PBS's "This Old House," comes as close to an 18th-century lodging experience as one can have. Built by Colonel Benjamin Simonds as a tavern, the house has numerous original features intact — wide pine floorboards, magnificent paneling, corner cupboards, and a central chimney containing five separate fireplaces, two ovens, and an attic smoking chamber. Furnishings, accessories, and fabrics used throughout the house are from the period or appropriate to it. Five guest rooms share two very large bathrooms (one was the buttery of the house and its walls are lined with crocks, paddles, and other implements). Breakfast (homemade breads, jams, and granola, an egg entrée, and River Bend's own honey) is served in the keeping room at the back of the house, and the former tap room is a guest parlor complete with the top ten *New York Times* best sellers. In summer, lawn furniture and a hammock are placed among the perennial and herb gardens, which feature a variety of 18th-century plants.

STEEP ACRES FARM
Owners: Mary & Marvin
  Gangemi.
413-458-3774.
520 White Oaks Rd.,
  Williamstown, MA
  01267.
From Rte. 7, E. on Sand
  Springs Rd., N. on White
  Oaks.
Price: Moderate.
Credit Cards: None.
Special Features: Pond for
  swimming, boating, and
  fishing; Hiking trails; No
  smoking; No pets.

Two miles from the center of Williamstown, Steep Acres offers a peaceful rural alternative to in-town lodging. The 1900 stone and shingle house sits on a hilltop on the Vermont state line, overlooking Mount Greylock. The Gangemis' 50 acres include a 1 1/2-acre pond for canoeing, trout fishing, and swimming (there are a diving board and raft), and trails for hiking and cross-country skiing. A patio off the sunporch — great for summer breakfasts or reading — seems to be perched at the top of the world. The house itself is far from rustic — an attractive decor combining late Victorian oak, wicker, and handsome fabrics. Four guest rooms share three baths. A full breakfast and afternoon refreshments are included.

WILLIAMS INN
Manager: Carl Faulkner.
413-458-9371.
Main St., Williamstown,
  MA 01267.
On the green off Rte. 7.
Price: Expensive.
Credit Cards: AE, D, DC,
  MC, V.
Handicap Access: Yes.
Special Features: Indoor
  pool; Sauna; Spa.

Though its architecture is not exactly in keeping with the classic Williamstown, the Williams Inn and its staff do please a great many North County travelers. Vast and modern, the facility offers an indoor pool, sauna, and spa, perfect for those cold or rainy days. On some nights there is live entertainment, such as jazz or folk music. And nearby are two of America's fine museums and the renowned Williamstown Theatre Festival. There is no charge for children under 14 in parents' room, and pets are welcome in ground-floor rooms.

**THE WILLIAMSTOWN
  BED AND BREAKFAST**
Owners: Kim Rozell &
  Lucinda Edmonds.
413-458-9202.
30 Cold Spring Rd.,
  Williamstown, MA
  01267.
Just off the circle where
  Rtes. 2 & 7 join.
Price: Moderate.

Open for business since 1989, the Williamstown Bed & Breakfast credits its success to a central, in-town location and a high proportion of returning guests. This spacious and airy Victorian has been completely renovated and tastefully furnished with a mixture of antiques and comfortable sofas and chairs. Each of the three guest rooms has its own bath and is individually decorated in period oak, maple, or mahogany furniture. Guests

Credit Cards: None.
Special Features: No smoking; No pets.

have exclusive use of the living room, dining room, and broad front porch. Lingering around the table after Kim Rozell's popular breakfasts, featuring homemade breads, muffins, and scones and always a hot entrée, is standard operating procedure at Williamstown B&B. Summer guests enjoy the perennial gardens and two hammocks for lazy afternoons.

LODGING OUTSIDE THE COUNTY

Salisbury, Connecticut

**UNDER MOUNTAIN
  INN**
Owners: Peter & Marged
  Higginson.
203-435-0242.
482 Under Mountain Rd.
  (Rte. 41), Salisbury, CT
  06068.
4 mi. N. on Rte. 41 from
  center of Salisbury.
Price: Expensive to Very
  Expensive (MAP).
Credit Cards: MC, V.
Special Features: No pets;
  Children over 6.

Have you been longing for a quiet day in the English countryside? Save the air fare and drive to the Under Mountain Inn, a 1730s Colonial set on three acres on a picturesque country road. Owner Peter Higginson is British — retired from the British Merchant Navy, in fact — and this veddy British man is a reflection of his heritage.

The menu in the dining rooms, warmed by a fire in winter, features such English staples as steak and kidney pie, bangers and mash, and shepherd's pie. On Fridays in summer, don't miss the fish and chips served with malt vinegar. The seven rooms in the inn are partially furnished with antiques, and all have private baths. Hartley and Gibson sherry in the rooms, afternoon tea, and Gilchrist & Soames soaps all add to the British atmosphere. A wealth of British books in the parlor invite a quiet afternoon far removed from the hectic city. Tally ho!

THE WHITE HART INN
Owners/Managers: Terry
  & Juliet Moore.
203-435-0030.
The Village Green, Box 385,
  Salisbury, CT 06068.
At intersection of Rtes. 41 &
  44, in center of town.
Price: Expensive to Very
  Expensive.
Credit Cards: AE, CB, DC,
  MC, V.

Those indomitable restaurateurs Terry and Juliet Moore (who also run the Old Mill in South Egremont) have restored this landmark inn to polished perfection. The oldest portions of the inn were built sometime prior to 1810, when records indicate the farmhouse was converted to a tavern. The public spaces display an air of country elegance and comfort, and 26 charming guest rooms all offer private baths, air-conditioning, phones, and cable TV. Breakfast, lunch, and a light dinner

Handicap Access: Yes.
Special Features: Pets in some rooms; Children welcome; Senior Citizen Discount.

are served in the Garden Room and in the historic tavern. Julie's New American Sea Grill is a popular destination for dinner and Sunday brunch. Whether planning a wedding reception, business meeting, romantic weekend, or escape from city pressures, the White Hart has it all.

Cummington, Massachusetts

SWIFT RIVER INN
General Manager: Robert F. Cowan.
413-634-5751; 800-532-8022.
151 South St., Cummington, MA 01026.
Off Rte. 9 between Pittsfield & Northampton.
Price: Expensive to Very Expensive.
Credit Cards: AE, D, MC, V.
Handicap Access: Yes.
Special Features: Pool; Jacuzzi; Tennis; Hiking; Fishing; Mountain biking; Cross-country ski center; Ice Skating; No smoking; No pets.

A full-service inn occupying a turn-of-the-century gentleman's dairy farm on 600 acres, Swift River Inn combines the best of country charm and modern comforts. Twenty-two air-conditioned guest rooms and suites have country quilts, authentic weathered beams or open lofts, private baths, color TVs and VCRs, and telephones. The room rate includes a continental breakfast. The Restaurant at Swift River Inn is open for breakfast, lunch, and dinner every day, and banquet and meeting facilities are available. The inn has a magnificent setting in the largely undiscovered Hill Town region of the Berkshires, and the recreational opportunities on the property are matchless, including 14 miles of trails for hiking, mountain biking, and Nordic skiing.

Averill Park, New York

THE GREGORY HOUSE
Owners/Innkeepers: Christopher & Melissa Miller.
518-674-3774; 800-497-2977.
Rte. 43, Averill Park, NY 12018.
Price: Moderate.
Credit Cards: AE, CB, D, MC, V.
Handicap Access: Limited.
Special Features: Pool; No smoking; No pets; Children over 9.

New owners have given the Gregory House a clean, more sophisticated country look and an award-winning restaurant presided over by Owner/Chef and Culinary Institute of America graduate Christopher Miller. Twelve guest rooms, all with air-conditioning and private baths, have stenciled walls and attractive country furnishings. A buffet continental breakfast is served to guests, and the cozy bar and the restaurant are open for dinner Tuesday–Sunday. Averill Park is convenient to Williamstown attractions and North County ski areas as well as to the Saratoga Performing Arts Center.

Berlin, New York

THE SEDGWICK INN
Innkeeper: Edie Evans.
518-658-2334.
Rte. 22, Box 250, Berlin, NY
12022.
Price: Moderate to Expensive.
Credit Cards: AE, CB, D,
DC, MC, V.
Special Features: Gift shop;
Smoking, Pets, and Children in annex only.

A 1791 house with restaurant and small motel unit (the annex) attached, set on 12 acres in the country. Privately owned and operated, this quaint, well-kept property offers comfortable rooms and proximity to Berkshire attractions. Rooms in the main house are preferred.

Hillsdale, New York

Jonathan Sternfield

**L'HOSTELLERIE BRES-
SANE**
Owners: Jean & Madeleine
Morel.
518-325-3412.
Box 387, Hillsdale, NY
12529.
At junction of Rtes. 22 & 23.
Closed: Mon. in summer;
Mon. & Tues. in winter;
every day March &
April.
Price: Moderate.
Credit Cards: None.
Special Features: No smoking; No pets; Children
over 12.

T his Federal-period brick house strikes a noble profile above a busy intersection in a small upstate New York village. Six delightful, large rooms, two with bath, are thoughtfully furnished by your French hosts. The owner/chef, hailing from the Bresse region of France, operates an extraordinary restaurant on the ground floor. Breakfast is available but not included in the room rate.

SWISS HUTTE COUNTRY INN
Managers: Gert & Cindy Alper.
518-325-3333; 413-528-6200.
Rte. 23, Hillsdale, NY.
2 mi. E. of Hillsdale on MA-NY border.
Price: Moderate to Expensive.
Credit Cards: MC, V.
Handicap Access: Yes.
Special Features: Pool; Tennis.

At the entrance to the popular South County ski area, Catamount, this property boasts several tennis courts, pool, lovely gardens, and, of course, an inviting downhill slope in its front yard. Comfortable, well-furnished rooms are split between the original wooden chalet and a newer building. An award-winning restaurant completes the picture. A modified American plan is available. Breakfast is not included with the basic room rate.

New Lebanon, New York

CHURCHILL HOUSE BED & BREAKFAST
Hosts: Michele & Michael Arthur.
518-766-5852.
Rte. 22 & Churchill Rd., P.O. Box 252, New Lebanon, NY 12125.
Rte. 22, 0.25 mi. S. of Rte. 20.
Price: Moderate.
Credit Cards: D.
Special Features: Hiking trails; No smoking; No pets; Children welcome.

Churchill House was built in 1797 for Rev. Silas Churchill and remained in the Churchill family until 1965. The Arthurs bought the property, which includes 18 acres of land, in 1991. Churchill House has five guest rooms, three with private bath, and two with an additional bed in the room. There is a charming room under the eaves, with trails of ivy stenciled by Michele. Each room has bathrobes, and the beds are mounded high with featherbeds. The living room and wraparound front porch with views of the Taconic Hills are for the guests' use. Afternoon refreshments and a full breakfast are served, with dietary restrictions accommodated (breakfast in bed or picnic breakfasts available with advance notice). Away from the madding crowds but handy to all Berkshire attractions.

Stephentown, New York

THE MILL HOUSE INN
Owners: Frank & Romana Tallet.
413-738-5348.
Box 1079, Hancock, MA 01237.
Rte 43, Stephentown, NY.
Price: Moderate to Expensive.
Credit Cards: AE, MC, V.

Old-World touches in a former sawmill enhance this cozy, well-regarded country inn. Furnished with antiques, the rooms are warm and whimsical. A living room with fireplace offers warm comfort. Seven rooms and five suites, several with fireplaces of their own, all have private baths, air-conditioning, and telephones. Set on three peaceful, rural acres with formal gardens, stone walls, garden paths, and a pool, it's the perfect

Handicap Access: Limited.
Closed: Mar. 15–May 15;
Sept. 1–Oct. 1.
Special Features: Pool; No
smoking; No pets.

romantic escape — a touch of country with a European flair. Afternoon tea and continental breakfast are served; a full breakfast is available à la carte.

MOTELS

South County

Barrington Court Motel (Managers: Peter & Linda Gorman; 413-528-2340; 400 Stockbridge Rd., Rte. 7, Gt. Barrington, MA 01230; on Rte. 7, N. of Gt. Barrington) Price: Moderate to Expensive. AE, MC, V. Limited handicap access. 21 motel units and 2 suites, refrig., coffee makers in every room. Suites have kitchenettes, Jacuzzi; pool. Two-night minimum in high season.

Berkshire Motor Inn (Managers: Fred & Rita Chittenden; 413-528-3150; 372 Main St., Gt. Barrington, MA 01230; On Rte. 7, just S. of Town Hall) Price: Moderate. AE, D, DC, MC, V. Indoor pool on premises.

Briarcliff Motel (Manager: Kelly Pyanson; 413-528-3000; 506 Stockbridge Rd., Gt. Barrington, MA 01230; on Rte 7, N. of town) Price: Moderate. AE, D, DC, MC, V. Handicap access. 16 units on spacious landscaped grounds, with view of Monument Mtn.

Days Motor Inn (formerly Lee Moter Inn; Owner: Balvant Patel; 413-243-0501; Rte. 102, Box 426, Lee, MA 01238; between Stockbridge and Lee) Price: Moderate to Expensive. AE, D, DC, MC, V. 24 units in convenient location to Tanglewood, Berkshire Theatre Festival, Jacob's Pillow, and other South County attractions.

Gaslight Motor Lodge (Owners: Barbara & John Cascio; 413-243-9701; Rte. 20, Greenwater Pond, Lee, MA 01238; 5 mi. E. of town) Price: Moderate. MC, V. 8 units on pond with own swimming, paddle boats, row boats, ice skating, cross-country skiing and hiking, as the Appalachian Trail crosses property. Refrig. in every room, complimentary coffee or tea in morning.

Lantern House Motel (Manager: Curtis Ruppert; 413-528-2350; Stockbridge Rd., Box 97, Gt. Barrington, MA 01230; on Rte. 7, 1 mi. N. of Gt. Barrington) Price: Moderate. (3-night weekend min. in summer). MC, V. Handicap access. Pool. Refrig. and color cable TV in rooms.

Laurel Hill Motel (Owners: Fred & Rita Chittenden; 413-243-0813; Box 285, Rte. 20, Lee, MA 01238; N. of Lee center) Price: Moderate. AE, D, CB, DC, MC, V. 20 unit motel with pool and view.

Monument Mountain Motel (Managers: Pat & Dick Roy; 413-528-3272; 249

Stockbridge Rd., Gt. Barrington, MA 01230; on Rte. 7, just N. of Gt. Barrington) Price: Moderate to Expensive. AE, CB, D, DC, MC, V. Far above an ordinary motel. Color cable TV, heated pool, lighted tennis courts, picnic tables, 20 acres that border the Housatonic River, spectacular flower gardens. No pets.

Pilgrim Motor Inn (Manager: Ben Patel; 413-243-1328; 165 Housatonic St., Lee, MA 01238; on Rte. 20, E. of Lee) Price: Expensive. AE, D, DC, MC, V. 34 units. Color cable TV in every room. Pool.

Pleasant Valley Motel (Owners/Managers: Vinnie & Suzie Patel; 413-232-8511; Rte. 102, W. Stockbridge, MA 01266; sandwiched between Exit 1, Mass. Pike & Rte. 102) Price: Expensive. AE, MC, V. Handicap access. Color cable TV in every room. Pool. Continental breakfast included summer weekends.

Sunset Motel (Owners/Managers: Ron & Puspa Patel; 413-243-0302; 114 Housatonic St., Lee, MA 01238; on Rte. 20, in town) Price: Inexpensive to Expensive. AE, CB, D, DC, MC, V. 22 units with AC, color cable TV, Pool. Convenient to Mass Pike, but may be noisy.

Super 8 Motel (Manager: Melanie Bourdon; 413-243-0143; 128 Housatonic St., Lee, MA 01238; just off Mass. Pike on Rte. 20) Price: Moderate. AE, D, DC, MC, V. Handicap access. Non-smoking rooms, free coffee & paper. VCRs for rent. This two-level motel, next to a Burger King and conveniently close to the Mass Pike, has 49 attractive rooms, decorated in cranberry and gray, all with private baths. Some come with king-size bed and others with two doubles. Color cable TV.

Central County

All Seasons Motor Inn - Berkshires (Manager: Gregory Abbott; 413-637-4244; 390 Pittsfield Rd., Rte. 7, Lenox, MA 01240) Price: Expensive. AE, D, DC, MC, V. Outdoor pool, tennis court. Restaurant & lounge. Color cable TV.

Berkshire North Cottages (Managers: James & Mary Dowling; 413-442-7469; 121 S. Main St., Lanesborough, MA 01237) Price: Inexpensive to Moderate. MC, V. 5 cottages, 3 with full kitchens, 2 with refrigerator only. Color cable TV. Closed Nov.–mid-May.

Heart of the Berkshires Motel (Owner: Sue Patel; 413-443-1255; 970 W. Housatonic St., Pittsfield, MA 01201; on Rte. 20, W. of town) Price: Expensive. Two-night minimum in summer. AE, D, MC, V. 16 units with color cable TV & AC in all rooms. Outdoor pool.

Huntsman Motel (Manager: Raman Patel; 413-442-8714; 1350 W. Housatonic St., Pittsfield, MA 01201; on Rte. 20, W. of town) Price: Moderate. AE, MC, V. 14 units plus a suite with kitchen. All units have color cable TV.

Inn at Village Square (Manager: Becky Pursell; 413-684-0860; 645 Main St., Dalton, MA 01226) Price: Moderate. AE, D, MC, V. Handicap access. A 16-unit motel, with a restaurant attached. Color cable TV.

Lamppost Motel (Manager: Arvind Patel; 413-443-2979; Rte. 7, Box 335, Lanesborough, MA 01237; on Rte. 7, N. of Pittsfield) Price: Moderate. AE, MC, V. 10 units, all with efficiency kitchens. Pool available. Color cable TV.

Lenox Motel (Owner: Ish Bhatia; 413-499-0324; Rtes. 7 & 20, Box 713, Lenox, MA 01240; N. of Lenox) Price: Expensive. AE, D, DC, MC, V. 17 units with AC, color cable TV, and coffee in rooms. Pool.

Mayflower Motor Inn (Manager: "Jay" Patel; 413-443-4468; Rtes. 7 & 20, Box 952, Pittsfield Lenox Rd., Lenox, MA 01240; N. of Lenox) Price: Expensive. AE, CB, D, DC, MC, V. Handicap access, color cable TV. Swimming pool, some views.

Mountain View Motel (Proprietor: Kishor Patel; 413-442-1009; 413-499 S. Main St., Lanesborough, MA 01237; Rte. 7, N. of Pittsfield) Price: Inexpensive to Moderate. AE, D, MC, V. Some handicap access. Color cable TV. Large rooms in motel. Cottages available year-round.

Pine Hill Cabins (Manager: Mary Diakiw; 413-447-7214; 269 Cheshire Rd., Pittsfield, MA 01201; on Rte. 8, N. of town) Price: Inexpensive. No credit cards. 5 cabins, no kitchens. Closed mid-Sept.–mid-June.

Pittsfield City Motel (Manager: Joe Hashim; 413-443-3000; 150 W. Housatonic St., Pittsfield, MA 01201; on Rte. 20, W. of town) Price: Inexpensive to Moderate. AE, D, MC, V. 38 units with AC, color cable TV in rooms. Pool.

Pittsfield Travelodge (Manager: Beatrice Crocker; 413-443-5661, 800-255-3050; 16 Cheshire Rd., Pittsfield, MA 01201; at junction of Rtes. 8 & 9) Near Berkshire Mall. Price: Moderate. AE, CB, D, DC, MC, V. Handicap access. Color cable TV.

Susse Chalet Motor Lodge (Manager: Frank Phelps; 413-637-3560; Pittsfield Rd., Lenox, MA 01240; on Rtes. 7 and 20, N. of town) Price: Expensive. AE, D, DC, MC, V. 70 units all with AC, color cable TV. Pool.

Tanglewood Motor Inn (Manager: Navin Shah; 413-442-4000; 626 Pittsfield Rd., Lenox, MA 01240; on Rtes. 7 & 20, N. of town) Price: Expensive. AE, D, MC, V. 22 units with AC, color cable TV. Pool.

Wagon Wheel Motel (Manager: Naresh Patel; 413-445-4532; Rtes. 7 & 20, Box 808, Lenox, MA 01240; 3 mi. N. of Lenox center) Price: Moderate to Expensive. AE, MC, V. Handicap access. Color cable TV. Some king-size waterbeds.

The Weathervane Motel (Manager: Raj Shah; 413-443-3230; 475 S. Main St., Lanesborough, MA 01237; on Rte. 7, S. of town) Price: Moderate. AE, CB, D, MC, V. 17 units. Color cable TV. Pool.

Yankee Motor Lodge (Owners: The Trombley family; 413-499-3700; Pittsfield Rd., Lenox, MA 01240; on Rtes. 7 & 20, near Pittsfield town line) Price: Expensive. AE, D, DC, MC, V. Handicap access, color cable TV. This stylish, 61-unit motel has a heated pool with rock waterfall in center, 12 rooms with fireplaces, some queen-size, four-poster beds, and manicured grounds. Three-night minimum.

North County

Berkshire Hills Motel (Managers: Jerry & Marguerite Vincz; 413-458-3950; Rte. 7, Williamstown, MA 01267; on Rtes. 7 & 2, 2 mi. S. of Williamstown) Price: Moderate. MC, V. Brick, 2-story motel, spacious, landscaped grounds, heated pool, homemade complimentary continental breakfast, charming rooms, and gracious, friendly innkeepers, keep guests returning year after year. Non-smoking rooms and king-size beds available. Color cable TV.

Best Western Springs Motor Inn (Managers: The Grosso Family; 413-458-5945; Rte. 7, New Ashford, MA 01237; halfway between Pittsfield and Williamstown on Rte. 7) Price: Moderate to Expensive. AE, CB, D, DC, MC, V. This is a well-run motel, conveniently located near several winter ski resorts. 40 standard motel rooms, complemented by two small chalets with fireplaces. Color cable TV; coffee-maker in every room. Pool, tennis court. The Grossos' award-winning restaurant across the street makes this motel especially attractive.

Carriage House Motel (Manager: Gerald Garneau; 413-458-5359; Rte. 7, New Ashford, MA 01237) Price: Inexpensive. AE, CB, D. DC, MC, V. Partial handicap access. Owned by Brodie Mtn., this gray & yellow motel with 14 units, sits high on hill, behind a respected restaurant. Guests have access to a pool, indoor tennis & racquetball, woods, brook, and trails.

Chimney Mirror Motel (Managers: Harm & Shirley Cyr; 413-458-5202; Rte. 2, Williamstown, MA 01267; just E. of town) Price: Moderate. AE, MC, V. 18 units. AAA-approved. Color cable TV; continental breakfast included in summer.

Dublin House Motel (413-443-4752; Rte. 7 at Brodie Mtn., New Ashford, MA 01267; near Lanesborough town line) Price: Moderate. AE, D, DC, MC, V. Owned by Brodie Mtn. Ski Resort, this 21-unit motel offers convenience over charm, but right at the base of the slopes. Two-channel TV.

Dug Out Motel (Managers: Mr. and Mrs. Gardner, and Melissa Pratt; 413-743-9737; 99 Howland Ave., Adams, MA 01220; on Rte. 8, going N. out of town) Price: Inexpensive. MC, V. Several units have handicap access. Color cable TV. Basic motel unit on road between Adams and N. Adams.

1896 Motel Brookside (Manager: Sue Morelle; 413-458-8125; Rte. 7, Williamstown, MA 01267) Price: Moderate. AE, D, DC, MC, V. As close to a country inn as a motel can get. The 16 attractive rooms have knotty pine, Waverly papers and fabrics, and vintage maple furniture. Scenic Hemlock Brook at the front door. Access to pool at 1896 Pondside. Remote color cable TV. Generous complimentary continental breakfast (as well as in-room coffee and tea).

1896 Motel Pondside (Manager: Sue Morelle; 413-458-8125; Rte. 7, Williamstown, MA 01267 - just north of 1896 Brookside) Price: Moderate. AE, D, DC, MC, V. Formerly the Elwal Pines Motel, purchased in 1993 by the owners of 1896 Motel and refurbished inside and out. Twelve rooms (each with 2 queen-size beds) and 1 efficiency suite have Cape Cod curtains and Waverly papers and fabrics in soft colors. Pool. Remote color cable TV. Complimentary Danish and coffee (as well as in-room coffee and tea).

Four Acres Motel (Managers: Marjorie & Keith Wallace; 413-458-8158; 213 Main St., Williamstown, MA 01267; on Rte. 2) Price: Moderate. AE, CB, D, DC, MC, V. Handicap access. Color cable TV. Common room with fireplace, garden area with shuffleboard, meeting rooms.

Green Valley Motel (Manager: Helen Derose; 413-458-3864; Rte. 7 N., 1214 Simonds Rd., Williamstown, MA 01267; on Rte. 7, N. of town) Price: Moderate. MC, V. 18 units. Color cable TV.

Jericho Valley Inn (Proprietor: Ed Hanify; 413-458-9511 or 800-JERICHO; Rte. 43, Box 239, Williamstown, MA 01267; 5 mi. S. of Williamstown, then 5 mi. W. on Rte. 43) Price: Moderate. AE, MC, V. Heated pool, on 350 mountain acres with spectacular views, fireplace lounge. Near Jiminy Peak and Brodie Mtn. Satellite color TV. Also has suites and cottages.

Kerry House Motel (413-443-4753; Rte. 7 at Brodie Mtn., New Ashford, MA 01267; near Lanesborough town line) Price: Moderate. AE, D, DC, MC, V. Owned by Brodie Mtn. Ski Resort, this new 9-unit motel is located on the slopes of Brodie Mtn. Some efficiency apartments are available. Two-channel TV.

Maple Terrace Motel (Managers: Ron Lagasse & Bill Francome; 413-458-9677; 555 Main St., Williamstown, MA 01267; on Rte 2, just E. of town green) Price: Moderate. AE, MC, V. Pool with mountain views. Spacious grounds well off the highway. Color cable TV.

New Ashford Motor Inn (Manager: Marguerite and Francis Gigliotti; 413-458-8041; Rte. 7, New Ashford, MA 01237; 1 mi. N. of Brodie Mtn.) Price: Moderate. AE, MC, V. Handicap access. Small motel made for the skier and traveler who does not insist on old-world charm. Four channels of TV.

Northside Inn & Motel (Managers: Linda & Fred Nagy; 413-458-8107; 45 N. St. Williamstown, MA 01267; on Rte. 7, N. of town) Price: Inexpensive. AE, DC, MC, V. Handicap access. 35 units with coffee shop for breakfast. Pool. Color cable TV.

The Willows Motel (Managers: Schlesinger Family; 413-458-5768; 480 Main St., Williamstown, MA 01267; on Rte. 2 E. of town) Price: Inexpensive. AE, D, MC, V. 16-room above-average motel. Heated pool. Color cable TV.

CHAPTER FOUR

What to See, What to Do
CULTURE

To glorify God's grandeur by gracefully combining Art and Nature — this was the goal of the Stockbridge Laurel Hill Society, as expressed in 1853. Thinking such as this represented an already well-developed Berkshire cultural awareness, with roots in Colonial times when the earliest local libraries, schools, churches, and newspapers were the centers of cultural activity. But it was in the mid-19th century that the tradition of a Berkshire cultural bounty, as we know it today, really took shape.

Jonathan Sternfield

Regarding Renoir, at the Clark Art Institute.

It is an artistic abundance all out of proportion to the county's size and population. In music, dance, theater, and other art forms, Berkshire has long had a cultural calendar of astonishing excellence and variety — especially for a mountainous area once thought of as remote. There are good reasons for this legacy.

In the mid-1800s, summers in the crowded eastern cities were not only unpleasant but frequently unhealthy. At the same time, particularly after the Civil War, improvements in transportation made the mountains much more accessible. And already in Berkshire, a few key families of taste, talent, and money were setting the tone of cultural sophistication that you will still find here today. If you have come to Berkshire to escape the city, you are part of a grand old tradition created by writers seeking quiet; painters seeking picturesque landscapes; actors, musicians, and dancers seeking summer audiences.

A local intelligentsia developed around Stockbridge and Lenox, helping to spark the Berkshire cultural bounty. No single family was more dynamic than the convivial and civic-minded Sedgwicks of Stockbridge, whose novelist daughter, Catherine, shares honors with poet William Cullen Bryant as Berkshire's, and America's, first popular writer. The Sedgwick house and family still grace Stockbridge today. The presence of Herman Melville and Nathaniel Hawthorne in the 1850s strengthened the literary tone, as did the charm of the even more popular Oliver Wendell Holmes, who summered in Pittsfield. Adding a dash of precocious 20th-century insight, Edith Wharton came and created an opulent European lifestyle and the novels to go with it. The list of famous artistic residents is lengthy and impressive. Our bibliography (in Chapter Eight, *Information*,) cites several engaging books that will tell you the whole fascinating story.

When the Berkshires became the "Inland Newport" during the late 19th-century Gilded Age, culture was imported here by the trainload. The whole phenomenon of culture rode into Berkshire on the power of big money: architectural indulgences, furnishings, musical instruments and people to play them, paintings, chefs with their foreign cuisines, and landscape gardeners: Whatever we think these days about the implicit politics of it all, we are the beneficiaries of so much inherited culture. Some of the historic estates here have become cultural centers, such as Tanglewood, for music, and the Mount, for theater. And yet, as if to remind us that beauty need not be ornate or expensive, the Shaker Village at Hancock is also a Berkshire cultural legacy of remarkable value and vitality. Don't miss it.

And finally, there is the philanthropy factor. The artistic institutions in Berkshire all have their patrons, large and small, typified by the Crane family and Crane Paper Co. of Dalton, which started the Berkshire Museum; by Francine and Sterling Clark, who created the Art Institute in Williamstown; and by the Tappan family, which gave Tanglewood to the Boston Symphony Orchestra. There are hosts of others. We owe them all our thanks.

Many of the famous artists drawn to the Berkshires have lived here seasonally, like Edith Wharton, or year-round, like Norman Rockwell. Thousands more have come just to perform or exhibit. But on every one Berkshire has left its mark. When asked what the Berkshires and Tanglewood mean to him, Seiji Ozawa, music director of the Boston Symphony Orchestra, replied: "Tanglewood has an absolutely special connotation for me. It was the first place I ever saw in America since I came to Tanglewood as a student in 1960 at the invitation of Charles Munch. For me and the orchestra, Tanglewood represents an opportunity to appreciate both the beauty of the Berkshires, and of the music we make here."

Art combined with Nature, up and down the county, from the fine woodwork in Colonist John Ashley's study at Ashley Falls to one of the few printed copies of the Declaration of Independence at Williams College's Chapin Library, from dioramas and Egyptian mummies at the Berkshire Museum in

Pittsfield to simply beautiful fresh flower arrangements at the Berkshire Botanical Garden in Stockbridge. In performance halls, museums, libraries, theaters, nightclubs, and historic homes, Berkshire is rich in art beyond measure.

The following descriptions will give you many ideas of where to go and what to do in Berkshire, but they will not tell you what's currently playing or showing.

For the larger seasonal schedules, such as Tanglewood, Jacob's Pillow, the museums, theaters, and other concert series, it's best to write for information. We provide many addresses for you. Tanglewood issues its summer schedule around March 15; other arts organizations soon follow. With such information in hand, you'll be better able to plan your own Berkshire festival. Telephoning is always a good idea for specifics, especially when you might travel a long way to see or hear a certain artist. Sold-out performances are not uncommon here. For information on cultural events as they happen, the *Berkshire Eagle* is the best bet. Especially comprehensive listings can be found in its magazine supplement, "Berkshires Week." For seasonal coverage, see the spiffy *Berkshire Magazine*, one of the best-looking, best-written regional magazines anywhere.

ARCHITECTURE

If roaming through New England in search of handsome buildings is your idea of fun, then you'll find Berkshire County an inexhaustible delight. True, you won't find the architecture of the Deep South or the Southwest here. But you will find in Berkshire virtually every other style that has ever been popular in North America, from Colonial times to the present. Few counties anywhere can claim this much architectural variety.

Berkshire is justly famous for the scores of mansions built during the opulent Gilded Age. Under "Historic Homes" in this chapter, in the chapters called *Restaurants* and *Lodging*, and elsewhere in this book, we describe several of the best surviving examples of these great "cottages," as they were called. But the saga of the sumptuous cottages isn't half the Berkshire building history.

Consider humbler examples: one-room schoolhouses, icons of America's simpler past. Still housing primary schools in some Berkshire towns, adapted to alternative uses in others, these white clapboard, bell-topped frame structures are often handsome and always charming. Some of the best are the ones in Alford, Washington and Lanesborough (a stone structure, c. 1800).

There are numerous Berkshire villages that seem like architectural set pieces, so artfully coordinated are their building styles and locations. They almost seem quaint by design. The villages of Alford, New Marlborough,

From the author's collection

The Stanford White designed Stockbridge Station, turn-of-the-century railway to the big city.

Stockbridge and Williamstown all have this look. There is a conspicuous absence of neon and plastic commercial clutter in these towns. Feelings of space and grace predominate. Yet also in each town, there is the clear sense that you are at the heart of a community where religion (churches), education (schoolhouses), government (town hall), domestic life (private homes), and the honor due the dead (cemeteries) all naturally fit together. People who live in cities or suburbs where all services are decentralized will find such Berkshire villages intriguing as well as architecturally beautiful. New Marlborough bears all of this out with its archetypal village green, surrounded in part by the Colonial-style *Old Inn on the Green* (1760), a fine Federal-style house (1824), and a Greek Revival-style *Congregational Church* (1839).

Then there are Berkshire farms. Almost any minor country road will lead you past splendid examples of gambrel-roofed barns or those New England rambling farmhouses that have spawned one extension after another. Often the oldest of these houses, or at least one of the farm's outbuildings, will be in the familiar saltbox (lean-to) shape. Some good rides for farm viewing include Routes 57 (New Marlborough); 41 (south from South Egremont or north from West Stockbridge); and 7 (north from Lanesborough). Dramatic Tudor-style barns from the Gilded Age are still in use at High Lawn Farm (on Lenox Rd., between Lee and Rte. 7, south of Lenox). But the most famous barn in Berkshire is the round stone barn at *Hancock Shaker Village*, described under "Museums" in this chapter.

<u>*South County*</u> towns have many impressive buildings, among them several interesting industrial sites. A standout is the *Rising Paper Mill* (c. 1875; Rte. 183 in Housatonic, north of Great Barrington), with its handsome mansard slate roof. A similar mansard slate roof style is pushed to artful extremes on

campus buildings at **Simon's Rock College of Bard** (Alford Rd., Great Barrington), resulting in structures that vaguely resemble Japanese pagodas.

On its **Congregational Church,** the village of Lee has the tallest wooden spire in the Berkshires. In South Lee (Rte. 102) is **Merrill Tavern,** a Federal-period building still functioning as an inn, exquisitely maintained by the Society for the Preservation of New England Antiquities.

Sheffield, architecturally lovely and filled with antique shops, appropriately prides itself on having preserved the **oldest covered bridge in Massachusetts** (1837; reached eastward off Rte. 7). Though this bridge is no longer open to motorists, you can walk through it, or even get married on it (arrangements can be made through the town clerk and justice of the peace). Otis, a Berkshire hilltown, is graced with **St. Paul's Church** (1829), a fine example of the Gothic Revival style.

Stockbridge, of course, will dazzle even the most jaded architecture buff. Architect Stanford White's turn-of-the-century work appears in impressive diversity here: a casino (now the **Berkshire Theatre Festival;** at Rte. 102 and Yale Hill Rd.); a mansion (**Naumkeag;** on Prospect Hill Rd.); a railroad station (now **Shogun,** a restaurant; on Rte. 7 south of the village); and a church (**St. Paul's Episcopal;** center of town). We describe the **Mission House,** a Colonial "Historic Home," later in this chapter. Two other Stockbridge churches well worth a look are the red brick **Congregational Church** (Main St., next to Town Hall); and the Chapel at the **Marion Fathers Seminary** (on Eden Hill, off Prospect Hill Rd.). Whereas the interior of the Congregational Church has a powerful beauty in its plainness, the Marion Fathers Chapel is beautiful for its finely crafted stone, woodwork, painting, and fabrics — much of it done by transplanted European artisans.

Three outlying sites in Stockbridge are worth a drive. The district originally called Curtisville, now known as Interlaken (Rte. 183, north of Rte. 102), boasts several strikingly pretty 18th- and 19th-century homes and a remarkable former tavern-inn, as well as **Citizens Hall** with its Victorian period Second Empire–style exterior details. Another building of note in rural Stockbridge is at Tanglewood's Lions' Gate (Hawthorne St., off Rte. 183) — where the replica of Nathaniel Hawthorne's **"Little Red House"** overlooks Stockbridge Bowl and the distant mountains. And just recently, the estate known as **Linwood** has opened to the public, as the site of the new **Norman Rockwell Museum.** The new museum is of some note, a Robert A. M. Stern–designed New England town hall upscale, but it is Charles E. Butler's unpolished marble cottage, **Linwood** (1859), that is the architectural highlight of this delightful Berkshire hilltop.

Finally, in South County, a ride out on the Tyringham Rd. (off Rte. 102, south of Lee) and then upland on Jerusalem Rd. will lead to **"Jerusalem,"** the remnants of a Shaker settlement dating from 1792. Five buildings remain, but none is open as a museum (as is Hancock Shaker Village, described under "Museums"). Jerusalem Rd. begins in tiny Tyringham Village. Along the

Tyringham Valley Rd. is the **Witch House,** a thatched-roof English cottage built by sculptor Henry Kitson in the late 1800s and known presently as *Tyringham Art Gallery;* see "Art Galleries," the next section in this chapter.

Central County abounds with notable architecture. In Dalton, a ride along Main St. (Rte. 9) provides views of the **Crane Paper Mills** (dating back to 1797) and several Crane family estates. In addition to other fine papers, Crane manufactures U.S. currency paper in these venerable mills. In 1816, Zenas Crane, company founder, built a dignified Federal-style house which still stands. There are also three 19th-century Richardsonian Romanesque churches on Main St. in Dalton proper.

In the hilltown of Hinsdale on Rte. 8 are some architectural surprises, vestiges of more prosperous, populous times when various mills were alive and well in the Berkshire highlands. The oldest (1798) Federal-style church in Berkshire is here. A Greek Revival town hall was built in 1848. The public library is in the high Gothic style, designed in 1868 by architect Leopold Eidlitz, who did St. George's Church in New York City and the New York State Capitol in Albany.

The only stone early Gothic Revival church in the county is *St. Luke's Chapel,* in Lanesborough (on Rte. 7). Like many other buildings cited in this book, St. Luke's is on the National Register of Historic Places.

Equal to any other village in Berkshire as an impressive architectural set piece is stately Lenox. This town has recently seen a commercial revival on its back streets that has spruced up the neighborhood, though some folks fear that it will soon be so trendy and chic as to lose its old New England charm. Recommended viewing in the historic center of the village includes the **Lenox Academy** (Federal style, 1803); the irresistibly photogenic **Church on the Hill** (1805); the **Lenox Library** (1815; see "Libraries" in this chapter). All three buildings are on Main St. (Rte. 7A). The **Curtis Hotel,** dominating the center of town, is now a wonderfully restored and converted apartment complex. From the Gilded Age to recent times, the Curtis was one of Berkshire's most fashionable addresses for travelers. Not far from Lenox village, on Rte. 20 heading toward Lee, is the **Cranwell** cottage with its architecturally daring, and very modern chapel, built in 1966, when Cranwell was the Jesuit-run Cranwell School. Often used for musical events, **Cranwell Chapel** produces an inspiring uplift for the eyes and mind, rising from its sunken altar to its broad "floating" ceiling. Tall, narrow, stained-glass windows encircle the sanctuary, enhancing the sense of spaciousness.

Pittsfield's architectural record is a distinguished though problematic one. Preservation and restoration nowadays receive good attention, as you'll see on a walk around Park Square. Several new buildings integrate quite well, we think, with the ornate elegance of the old Venetian Gothic Athenaeum, with the two churches, with the bank buildings, and with the courthouse — all dating from the 19th century.

The former *Berkshire Eagle* newspaper building (on Eagle St., off North St.) is a fine example of the Art Deco style, and it is set on a triangle, making it look like a miniature of Manhattan's Flatiron Building. Another important business structure in Pittsfield is the General Electric Plastics House, a handsome and interesting experimental and display house in the Plastics Division's new world headquarters complex. Address? "Plastics Ave.," of course (between Merrill Rd. and Dalton Ave.).

North County provides stark contrasts in architecture and much variety in the stories buildings tell about social history. The cities of Adams and North Adams are industrial and have seen better times. Urban renewal is proceeding, with a few of the abandoned textile mills converted to other uses, the idle *Sprague Electric plant*, awaiting a renaissance as a mammoth museum of contemporary art (visual and performing), or "Mass MoCA." Still, in otherwise rather grim cityscapes, there are sights worth a visit. In North Adams, the *Western Heritage Gateway State Park* celebrates a 19th-century architectural and engineering wonder, the *Hoosac Tunnel*. See "Museums" in this chapter. The spires of North Adams' many churches are a pretty sight when descending into the city from the west on Rte 2. In Adams, history lovers will want a look at the *Susan B. Anthony Birthplace* (1814; a private home near the corner of East Rd. and East St.); and the *Quaker Meeting House* (1782; near the end of Friends St.), another National Register of Historic Places building.

Williamstown, however, wins most of the architectural prizes in North County. Dozens of magnificent homes, an extraordinarily beautiful college, many quaint shops, and two masterfully designed art museums (the *Clark Art Institute* and the *Williams College Museum of Art*, both described under "Museums") — all await you there. *West Hall* (1790), at Williams College, is dignified and symbolizes the college's long history of loving attention to fine and sometimes dramatic buildings. A tour of the campus is well worth the time (413-597-3131 for information). The *Williamstown Memorial Library* (1815), which also houses the local history museum, is graced with elegant Palladian windows.

In Berkshire, a proud history still stands.

CINEMA

THE MAHAIWE

Reminding you of how movie palaces used to look, the Mahaiwe's ornate elegance survives. Now the spruced-up theater hosts special live concerts and occasional children's weekend movie matinees between conventional first-run movie offerings. Best of all, the Berkshire Film Society has wisely selected the

Jonathan Sternfield

Impresario Al Schwarz presides over the venerable Mahaiwe.

Mahaiwe as the site for its several interesting film festivals. More than the sum of its magnificent movies, the Mahaiwe is a local treasure.
The Mahaiwe: 413-528-0100; 14 Castle St., Great Barrington, MA 01230.

CLARK FILM SERIES

The Clark Art Institute shows films on artists and on art history as well as movies of a more general interest. A highlight of the fall '93 program was a showing of Alistair Cooke's masterful ten-part film, *America: A Personal History of the United States.* There is real variety in the Clark's film fare: call to get on their mailing list.
The Clark Film Series: 413-458-9545; South St., Williamstown, MA 01267.

IMAGES CINEMA

North County's most dynamic movie house is flying high. Threatened by skyrocketing rents, Images pulled itself together in the summer of '89, principally with the help of "Superman." The man of steel, also known as Williamstown resident and actor, Christopher Reeve, organized a fund-raising program that saved it. So Images lives on in refurbished modernity, for a fine future of feature films. Eclectic, exciting — the best from camp to classic. Mailing list available.
Images Cinema: 413-458-5612; 55 Spring St., Williamstown, MA 01267.

OTHER CINEMA

South County

Simon's Rock College of Bard (413-528-0771; Alford Rd., Great Barrington). Occasional classics and fun films, open to the public. Phone for information.

Central County

Berkshire Cinema 10 (413-499-2558; Berkshire Mall, Rt. 8 and Old State Road, Lanesborough) Dolby stereo, Kintek stereo, action, adventure, drama, comedy, popcorn.

Little Cinema (at Berkshire Museum, 413-443-7171; 39 South St., Pittsfield) Fine American and foreign films, nightly from late June through early September and again in the winter. This is *the* great little film festival in Berkshire, now featuring state-of-the-art projection and sound.

Pittsfield Cinema Center (413-443-9639; Rte. 20, West Housatonic St., Pittsfield) Unlimited free parking and a choice of eleven (that's 11), different commercial flicks nightly. A teenage hangout, but often showing first-run films as early as New York or Boston.

North County

North Adams Cinemas (413-663-5873; Rte. 8, Curran Highway) North County's multiplex, with six screens.

Williams College Museum of Art (413-597-2429; Williamstown) Often shows films in its auditorium, and these are free and open to the public.

Williams College (413-597-3131; Williamstown) Presents free American films in Bronfman Auditorium; and foreign films in Weston Language Center Lounge.

DANCE

**JACOB'S PILLOW
  DANCE FESTIVAL**
413-243-0745.
Box 287, Lee, MA 01238.
Off Rte. 20, in Becket, 8 mi.
  E. of Lee.
Season: Summer only:
  Tues.–Sun.
Tickets: $10–$35.
Gift shop.

America's first and oldest summer dance festival, Jacob's Pillow keeps step with the times, presenting the best in classical, modern, post-modern, jazz, and ethnic dance. Its schedule of offerings reads like a Who's Who of contemporary dance, featuring over the years Merce Cunningham, Dame Margot Fonteyn, Peter Martins, Alicia Markova, Twyla Tharp, Alexander Gudunov, Martha Graham, Paul Taylor, Alvin Ailey, and the Pilobolus troupe, among many others.

High on a hillside in Becket is the farm that famed dancer Ted Shawn bought after successfully touring with his wife, Ruth St. Denis, and the "Denishawn" troupe in the 1920s. Here Shawn worked to establish dance as a legitimate profession for men, founding a world-class dance performance center and a school for dance. The school continues to flourish along with the festival, honoring its founder's heartfelt philosophy that the best dancers in the world

Poet of time, space and silence, Merce Cunningham brings his virtuosity to the Ted Shawn stage, Jacob's Pillow.

Michael O'Neill, courtesy Jacob's Pillow

make the most inspirational dance instructors. In addition to performing here, some of the Pillow's visiting dance luminaries stay on to teach master classes in the compound's rustic studios.

Drive up to the Pillow early, if you can, and stroll among those studios where works are in progress, dancers are in development. Look through a window and watch choreography created before your very eyes. Walk down to the Pillow's natural outdoor theater, "Inside/Out," and watch avant-garde and experimental pieces in rehearsal and in performance. And after savoring that dance hors d'oeuvre, you might want to sup at the Pillow. Happily, here too there are several lovely options. You can dine at the Pillow Cafe, feasting under a brightly colored tent, or you can take your dinner over to the picnic area and possibly glimpse an occasional dancer who will be performing later in the Ted Shawn Theatre.

Recent performances at the Pillow have included the Paul Taylor Company, the witty Mark Morris Dance Group, the jazzy Hubbard Street Dance Company, and the hot young troupe, Philadanco, among others. The Pillow's Studio/Theatre, seating 160, adds a separate 12-week schedule of new and emerging, offbeat companies, complementing the Ted Shawn Theatre's exciting dance schedule.

ALBANY-BERKSHIRE BALLET
413-442-1307; 413-445-5382. 51 North St., Pittsfield, MA 01201 (Mail).
Concerts at various theaters.
Season: Intermittently year-round.

The *New York Times* dance critic Jennifer Dunning put it positively in her review: "Berkshire Ballet can be counted on for impressively clear classical technique and fresh performing." Said the influential *Dance Magazine*: "Berkshire Ballet displays solid training, a distinctly soft, lyrical style, and a wide choreographic range. In short, it is a company with integrity and taste."

Clemens Kalischer, courtesy Jacob's Pillow

Pilobolus, one of the many national troupes appearing at Jacob's Pillow.

Tickets: $12–$17; Discounts for seniors, children & groups.

Performing frequently at Berkshire Community College's Koussevitzky Theatre, at Great Barrington's Mahaiwe, and at the Palace Theater and the Egg in Albany, the Albany Berkshire Ballet also tours the Northeast. Lavish productions of *Cinderella* and *Giselle* have highlighted past seasons; one of our favorite Albany-Berkshire Ballet performances was the stunning *Arrow of Time*, by Laura Dean. Fall and winter concerts are capped with the traditional *Nutcracker* being staged at BCC and the Mahaiwe around Christmastime.

OLGA DUNN DANCE CO., INC.
413-528-9674.
7 Alford Rd., Gt. Barrington, MA 01230 (Mail).
321 Main St., 3rd Fl., Gt. Barrington, MA 01230.
Season: Year-round.
Tickets: $5–$25.

Since its founding in 1977, the Olga Dunn Dance Company has enjoyed such success that it spawned two offspring: the Junior Company and the Olga Dunn Dance Ensemble. Performing a free mix of exuberant, witty jazz and ballet, frequently with live musicians, the Company has also toured area schools, exposing children to the creativity of dance and the excitement of movement. Their annual performances at the Mahaiwe and at Great Barrington's Summerfest are highlights of the dance year. As Marge Champion, famed dancer and local Berkshire resident, put it: "The Olga

Dunn Dance Company has become the radiating center of our experience in appreciating and participating in the art of dance."

The artistry of Olga Dunn Dance.

Jonathan Sternfield

OTHER DANCE

With Jacob's Pillow bringing the world's best dancers to the Berkshires, it's not surprising that quality dance troupes would spring up here and there throughout the county.

In *South County*, Great Barrington leads the dance. Many of the most innovative performances take place at the *Simon's Rock "ARC,"* the school's barn-theater on Alford Rd. Simon's Rock (413-528-0771) has recently been offering two student-faculty dance programs during the school year, one in December, the other in May. These feature original music and choreography by members of the school's dance program. The *Barrington Ballet* (413-528-4963) gives classes and occasional performances, as does the Mill River-based *Anglo-American Ballet* (413-229-8776). Eurythmy performances are sometimes given by the *Rudolf Steiner School* (413-528-4015) on West Plain Rd. There is also a flourishing country and contra dance network in the Berkshires. Check the newspapers and bulletin boards for listings.

In *Central County*, keep an eye on the special events schedule at *Berkshire Public Theater* for dance happenings; the summertime festivals, including the Best of the Berkshires, brings various troupes to Pittsfield too.

In *North County*, the *Williams College Dance Department* sponsors an ongoing series with student and faculty choreography. Shen & Dancers, a Chinese company, have recently been the artists-in-residence; the Chuck Davis African Dance Collective has also been seen and heard in Williamstown, spreading the gospel of tribal movement.

GALLERIES

Since the arrival in Berkshire of nationally recognized turn-of-the-century sculptors Daniel Chester French (who sculpted the Lincoln statue for the Lincoln Memorial) and Sir Henry Hudson Kitson (who did *The Minute Man* at Lexington), the county has been home to an increasing number of talented visual artists.

Much of the art on display in local galleries reflects the uplifting reality of the Berkshire landscape. Many artists focus on the undulating hills and their ever-changing light. Of course local galleries also show other themes and styles as well, from traditional still-life sketches to intriguing abstract paintings. Some galleries show Berkshire artists exclusively; others bring in works from artists the world over. Galleries in the Berkshires are like delicate flowers and bloom best in warm weather. Unless you're rambling, it's wise to call ahead.

The biggest news in the Berkshire gallery world is the emergence of Housatonic as the modern art capital of the county. Led by the dynamic and trend-setting *Spazi Contempory Art* at Barbieri's Lumber Mill, this tiny, sleepy village now boasts close to two dozen galleries and artists' studios, making it a must stop on any Berkshire art tour.

Emerging also is West Stockbridge, with its jampacked outdoor, riverside sculpture garden and several new, intriguing galleries.

South County

SOUTH EGREMONT

Barbara Moran Fine and Decorative Arts (413-528-0749) Neat graphics, sculpture and objets d'art. Mostly contemporary, but also offers antique country-style furnishings and accent pieces.

Berkshire Women Artist's Collaborative (413-528-5628; Bott Hill Rd.) Refurbished gallery is showcase for the 75 members of the recently formed, local alliance.

Store Hill Gallery (413-528-1224; Rte. 23, between Kenver Ltd. and the Gaslight) The finest selection of oil, watercolor and acrylic paintings by Berkshire artists, including Sally Friedman, Warner Friedman, Joe Barber, Audrey Blafield, Ruth Green, and painter/gallery director Janet Rickus.

GREAT BARRINGTON

Galleria Arriba (413-528-4277; 40 Railroad St.) Contemporary Latin American art.

Geoffrey Young Gallery (413-528-6210; 292 Main St., 3rd Fl.) A small upstairs gallery, well worth your attention. Thematic and other imaginative shows guarantee an interesting angle. A stable of talented, perceptive artists produce the work; an insightful artist organizes the shows.

Lucien Aigner Studios (413-528-3610; 15 Dresser Ave.) Black and white photographs of Europe and the United States by the celebrated master photojournalist, Lucien Aigner. Please call for appointment. A permanent public exhibit of some of Aigner's pictures may be viewed at the Great Barrington Town Hall, on the 2nd floor, on weekdays.

Kaolin & Co. Pottery (413-528-1531; 80 Rt. 71) Wheel-thrown and handbuilt ceramics, some purely decorative, some both beautiful and functional. A distinctive pastel palette nicely complements alluring forms.

Mill River Studio (413-528-9433; 8 Railroad St.) Posters, hand-colored engravings, historic maps, and custom framing. A classy shop.

Momiji Gallery (413-528-4865; 16 Seekonk Rd.) Authentic, original Japanese woodblock prints, 18th through 20th centuries. By appointment only.

Sarah Fogerty's Frames on Wheels (413-528-0997; 84 Railroad St.) More than a mobile framer, Sarah Fogerty has her own land-based shop, filled with graphics and paintings, some by local artists. A light-filled studio for artful framing.

Tokonoma Gallery and Framing Studio (413-528-6966; Stockbridge Rd. in the Jenifer House Commons) Contemporary arts and crafts, much of it by area artists and artisans. Also hand-built furniture, pottery, jewelry, accessories, framed original Edward Curtis American Indian photographs, sculpture, and much more. Changing fine art shows, too.

HOUSATONIC

Front Street Gallery (413-274-6607) Co-op space is open on weekends and has the space to show large paintings.

Le Petit Musee (413-274-3838; 137 Front St.) Sherry Steiner's hole-in-the-wall gallery is so neat, and so tiny (7 by 11), that it's made it into *Ripley's Believe It Or Not*. Shows miniatures, smalls, and itty bitties, all of substantial quality. Step inside the gallery for an even better view.

The Housatonic Gallery (413-274-0236; 402 Park St, Rt. 183) The local Fine Arts and Crafts Guild shows its members' work here.

Spazi Contempory Art (413-274-3805) Leader of the Southern Berkshire pack in hip, contempory art, this lofty gallery space has been the scene of great shows, avant garde performance pieces, and outrageous openings.

LEE

Pierre Lapin Gallery (413-243-2221; Chambéry Inn, corner of Main and Elm) Contemporary American crafts.

SOUTH LEE

House of Earth Studio (413-243-1575; Rte. 102) Contemporary oil, acrylic, and watercolor landscapes in a rammed earth studio.

MONTEREY

Gallery in Monterey (413-528-6353; Rte. 23) An artist-operated gallery in one of the most talent-rich towns in South County.
Hayloft Art Gallery (413-528-1806; Rte. 23) Berkshire watercolors, including popular townscapes, by local artist Leonard Webber.

SHEFFIELD

Westenhook Gallery (413-229-8101; Rte. 7) Mixed media. Occasional show of wonderful miniature paintings, drawings, and etchings.

STOCKBRIDGE

Dolphin Studio (413-298-3735, West Main St.) Creations by the ffrench family, including ceramics, collages, jewelry, and Capreatures — furry, wooly capricious creatures by Crispina ffrench.
Holsten Galleries of Stockbridge (413-298-3044; Elm St., summer only) Outstanding contemporary objects of art: glass, ceramics, jewelry, paintings, and wall-hangings. One of the world's leading showrooms for sleek, sculptural glass.
Image Gallery (413-298-5500; Main St.) Modern arts (such as the intense and buoyant paintings of Stockbridge teacher, Leo Garel) and photography (usually by gallery-owner and master photographer, Clemens Kalisher).
Reuss Audubon Galleries (413-298-4074; Pine and Shamrock Sts.) This 19th-century house features a continuing, rotating exhibit of the "double elephant folio" bird prints from Audubon's Birds of America.

Ronrich Gallery (413-298-3556; Rte. 183, 2 mi. south of Tanglewood) Paintings and prints by American artists.

TYRINGHAM

Tyringham Art Galleries (413-243-3260; the Gingerbread House, Tyringham Rd.) Originally called "The Witch House," the studio of Sir Henry Hudson Kitson, this structure has a unique rolling thatched roof inspired by the hills; inside are contemporary paintings, sculpture, and graphics. Admission is $1.

WEST STOCKBRIDGE

Gigli Photography/Fine Arts (413-232-0232; Depot St.) Fine photographs and other art.
G/M Galleries (413-232-8519; Main St.) Exciting jewelry and unique art objects, as well as paintings and drawings.
Hotchkiss Mobiles (413-232-0200; 8 Center St., the old farmer's market, near the old train station) Original and colorful mobiles for moving art, both indoors and out. Museum quality at country prices.
Riversbend Gallery (413-274-6213; Rte. 41) 18th–20th-century American and European paintings.
Waterside Gallery (413-232-7187; 32 Main St.) Striking graphics, ceramics, jewelry, and sculpture. Some powerful pieces in many different media.

Central County

BECKET

Becket Arts Center of the Hilltowns (413-623-6635; Rte. 8) Local shows and programs.
The Gallery Up Yonder (413-623-8329; Yokum Pond Road) Mixed media.

LENOX

Artuoso Gallery (413-637-0668; 22 Church St.) Contemporary Judaic art.
Brushwood Studio (413-637-2836; Brushwood Farm, Rtes. 7 & 20) Paintings, furniture, and carved wooden horses make up one of the most intriguing collections in the county, gathered by artist-owner, Dudley Levenson.
Clark Whitney Gallery (413-637-2126; 25 Church St.) Contemporary art.

Concepts of Art (413-637-4845; 67 Church St.) Contemporary and traditional arts, including watercolor, and crafts, including glass, jewelry, pottery, and wood.

Ella Lerner Gallery (413-637-3315; 17 Franklin St.) 19th- and 20th-century paintings, drawings, graphics, and sculpture in one of the area's oldest galleries. Featuring the likes of Raphael Soyer, Salvador Dali, Pablo Picasso, and Leonard Baskin.

Hado Studio Gallery (413-637-1088; 70 Church St.; summer only) Contemporary paintings and sculpture.

The Hand of Man (413-637-0632; at the Curtis Shops, Walker St.) A wide range of appealing crafts, photographs, and paintings.

Hoadley Gallery (413-637-2814; 17 Church St.) Contemporary art crafts, with especially wonderful ceramics.

John Stritch Gallery (413-655-8804; 104 Main St.) Paintings, prints, and Tanglewood poster collection by popular Berkshire artist John Stritch. Artist's sculpture garden in Hinsdale is open by appointment (413-655-8804; Shady Villa, Hinsdale).

Sculptor John Stritch, at his Hinsdale Studio.

Warren Fowler

Stevens & Conron Gallery (413-637-0739; the Curtis Shops, 5 Walker St.) Watercolors and pastels, as well as traditional, contemporary crafts.

Stockwood Fine Art Gallery (413-637-4122; 81 Church St.) Stunning wood engravings by local master Michael McCurdy; also paintings and illustrations by Laurie Corimer, William Langley, and Joseph Sparaco, as well as etchings by Dale Bradley.

Towne Gallery (413-637-0053; 88 Main St.; downstairs below card shop) Regional paintings, graphics, sculptures, and crafts; framing; 19th-century Berkshire prints and maps.

Ute Stebich Gallery (413-637-3566; 104 Main St.) Outstanding international collection of extraordinarily beautiful art, from primitive African objects to sleek contemporary glass by Tom Patti. A must on any Lenox gallery hop.

PITTSFIELD

Berkshire Artisans (28 Renne Ave.; 1 block eastward off lower North St.) Exhibitions and workshops at the city's nonprofit municipal arts center.

Pasko Frame & Gift Center (413-442-2680; 243 North St.) Berkshire oil paintings by Walter Pasko, prints and etchings by Pat Buckley Moss, prints and other graphics.

Pittsfield Art League Cooperative Gallery (413-448-2691; 2 South St.) Recent shows included works by Lillian Bendross and John Frick, plus art by regular members.

Radius Art Gallery (413-445-7223; 137 North St.) Fine arts and crafts, often by local artists and craftspeople.

North County

ADAMS

The Alley (413-743-7707; 25 Park Street) Prints and sculpture.

Sylvia's Gallery (413-743-9250; Rte. 8) Paintings, graphics, and drawings by modern artists.

NORTH ADAMS

Up Country Artisans (413-663-5802; Heritage Park) A continuous, ever-changing show of some of the Berkshire's best artists and artisans.

WILLIAMSTOWN

Beaverpond Gallery (413-738-5895; Rte. 43) Berkshire watercolors, custom framing, art classes.

Elysian Fields (413-458-4707; 48 Spring St.) Berkshire landscapes, artful jewelry, and weavings.

HISTORIC HOMES

ARROWHEAD

413-442-1793.

780 Holmes Rd., Pittsfield, MA 01201.

Off Rte. 7, (about 1.5 mi.) near Pittsfield-Lenox line.

Season: Memorial Day Weekend–Labor Day, open daily; Sept.–Oct., closed Tues.–Thurs.; Winter by appointment.

Fee: $4.50; senior citizens $4.00; children 6–16, $3.00.

Gift shop.

In 1850, seeking to escape what he later called "the Babylonish brick-kiln of New York," Herman Melville gave in to his yearning "to feel the grass" and moved with his family to the Berkshires. By the time he came here, Melville had already published two tales of his South Sea adventures, *Typee* and *Omoo,* and he had earned a reputation as a man "who had lived among cannibals."

But Melville longed to be known as a great writer, and fresh from a new "close acquaintance" with the "divine" writings of Shakespeare, he took off on the grand literary whale hunt that was to be *Moby Dick.*

Melville's study at Arrowhead is undoubtedly the most interesting room in the house. Here he wrote looking northward at the Mount Greylock range with its rolling form reminiscent of a giant whale. The implements of the writer's trade and duplicates of many important books in his library are right here. Melville used to lock himself in, ordering the women of the house to leave meals on a tray outside the door.

Arrowhead is the home of the Berkshire County Historical Society, which offers excellent guided tours through the house. The other thoroughly "Melville" room is the kitchen, which is dominated by a grand stone hearth. The chimney above was immortalized in the charming Melville story, "I and My Chimney." Elsewhere, you'll see a collection of 19th-century period furnishings, fine arts, and textiles with Berkshire origins, several pieces of which belonged to Melville. The Ammi Phillips folk-art portraits are of particular interest.

Herman Melville, at about the age he wrote Moby Dick.

Nellie Fink

Outside, the piazza is impressive, as are the grounds; in fact, Arrowhead is a lovely picnic spot. The barn behind the house is the site of impressively varied cultural programs such as literary readings and historical talks. A film about Berkshire literary figures and artists is shown regularly. There is also an extensive herb garden and a vintage cutting garden on the grounds.

If you're hungry for still more of the literary Melville, you can visit "The Melville Room" at the Berkshire Athenaeum on Wendell Ave., also in Pittsfield. (See the Berkshire Athenaeum entry under "Libraries" in this chapter.)

THE MOUNT
Edith Wharton Restoration, Inc.
413-637-1899.
Box 974, Lenox, MA 01240.
On Plunkett St., Lenox, near southern jct. of Rtes. 7 & 7A.
Season: Summer: Tues.–Sun. 10–5; Fall: Fri.–Sun. 10–5.
Fee: $6.00; students 13–18, $4.50; senior citizens $5.50.
Book/Gift shop.

In February 1901, the writer and heiress Edith Wharton arrived at the Curtis Hotel in Lenox for a week in the country. She had summered in the area for the preceding two years, and now, having found the "watering place trivialities of Newport" all but intolerable, sought a new site on which to realize the design principles incorporated in her book, *The Decoration of Houses*.

The Georgian Revival house was modeled on Christopher Wren's Belton House in Lincolnshire, England. At first, Wharton retained an architect, her old associate, Ogden Codman. When his design fees grew exorbitant, she called upon Francis V. L. Hoppin to complete the job.

Edith supervised creation of the gardens, orchards, and buildings, while finishing her novel, *Disintegration*. The Mount was elegant throughout, boasting marble floors and fireplaces, and requiring 12 resident servants. Besides the 14 horses in their stables, the Whartons owned one of the earliest motorcars, a convenience that thrilled the visiting Henry James. In the fall of 1904, James and Wharton motored through Berkshire's autumnal splendor every day, enjoying social afternoons and evenings with visiting sophisticates.

Edith Wharton, at about the age when she began to develop both a writing career and grand residence in Lenox, at the Mount.

Nellie Fink

"The Mount was to give me country cares and joys," she wrote, "long happy rides, and drives through the wooded lanes of that loveliest region, the companionship of a few dear friends, and the freedom from trivial obligations which was necessary if I was to go on with my writing. The Mount was my first real home . . . and its blessed influence still lives in me."

Happily, its blessed influence lives on for all of us, as its physical and spiritual restoration continue. Since 1980, Shakespeare & Co. has been performing Shakespeare and plays based on Wharton's years at the Mount and has won national critical acclaim. When the National Trust for Historic Preservation bought the Mount to save it from commercial exploitation, Shakespeare & Co. stayed on; the house is run today by Edith Wharton Restoration, Inc. (EWR).

In the summer, besides house and garden tours of the Mount, EWR and Shakespeare & Co. continue to offer plays centering on Wharton's life and writings. Among the recent standout presentations was an adaptation of Wharton's *The Custom of the Country*, directed by Dennis Krausnick. Wharton's image has enjoyed a resurgence, with two powerful films of her novels (*Ethan Frome* and *The Age of Innocence*) released in recent years.

Edith Wharton Restoration is now being guided by former fundraiser and theatrical producer, Stephanie Copeland, who has strengthened the Mount as a locus for female energy, initiating the "Women on Women" lecture series with such dynamic speakers as Gloria Erlich (speaking on "The Sexual Education of Edith Wharton), Carole Klein, and Cynthia Griffin Wolff. With the grace of a Wharton afternoon gathering, tea is served after the lecture.

NAUMKEAG

413-298-3239.
Box 792, Stockbridge, MA 01262.
Prospect Hill Rd., Stockbridge.
Season: Memorial Day–Labor Day: House & Garden Hours, Tues.–Sun. 10–4:15; Open Mon. holidays; Labor Day–Columbus Day: House & Gardens open Sat., Sun. & Mon. holidays.
Fee: House & Garden $6; Gardens only $4; children 6–12, $1.50.
Gift Shop.

During the Gilded Age of the late 19th century, men and women of power played out their fantasies here, dotting the hillsides with dream houses. Some were outlandish, others were magnificent. In between was the very livable mansion of the lawyer Joseph Choate, the summer "cottage" the Choate family came to call "Naumkeag" (a native Indian name for "place of rest").

Here Joseph Choate found both a retreat from New York City life, as well as an enclave of great legal minds in Supreme Court justices Field, Brewer, and Brown, all Stockbridge residents!

Choate's was an illustrious career. He defended such notable clients as Stanford University, Bell Telephone, and Pullman Car; he dueled with the government on behalf of the New York Indians; and he fought against the graduated income tax, successfully postponing it for two decades.

In 1884, Choate persuaded David Dudley Field

The Choate mansion,
"Naumkeag."

Jonathan Sternfield

(his opponent in the Boss Tweed Affair) to sell him the property and he began construction. By the autumn of 1886, their 26-room shingled, gabled, and dormered Norman-style house was complete, with architectural design by Stanford White and imaginative gardens by the landscaping pioneer, Nathaniel Barret.

The house eventually came into the hands of Choate's daughter, Mabel, who maintained it while adding extensively to the gardens under the direction of landscape architect Fletcher Steele. The Fountain Steps, framed by birches; the Afternoon Garden, an outdoor room; further southward, the Chinese Pagoda and Linden Walk; uphill, the brick-walled Chinese Garden, where mosses and stone Buddhas gather with carved lions and dogs, all shaded by ginkgos; to the north, the topiary hedgework of the Evergreen Garden and the fragrance and color of the Rose Garden all reflect decades of inspired and distinctive garden design.

Now under the auspices of the Trustees of Reservations, Naumkeag is still intact, including its gardens, furnishings, and an extraordinary porcelain collection, much of it from the Far East. The tours are excellent. Some years at Christmas, Naumkeag is enlivened with decorations and toys from the Choate era.

Joseph Choate was generous, but also practical and witty. When the Stockbridge town fathers asked for a donation from him to build a fence around the cemetery, Choate denied them. "Nobody inside can get out," he said, "and no one on the outside wants to get in."

CHESTERWOOD
413-298-3579.
Box 827, Stockbridge, MA
01262.
Off Rte. 183, in Glendale.

When Concord, Massachusetts, native Daniel Chester French was commissioned by the town to create his first public monument, the 25-year-old French sculpted *The Minute Man*. Its life-

Season: May–Oct. daily 10–5.
Fee: Admission charged.
Gift shop.

like pose and exquisite sense of surface modeling won the artist national acclaim. He had produced his first American icon.

Years and scores of sculptures later, French sought a permanent country home to augment the New York City studio he maintained. In 1896, he and his wife, Mary, were shown the old Warner Farm and Boys School in the Glendale section of Stockbridge. After taking in the magnificent vista southward, toward Monument Mountain, French pronounced it "the best dry view" he had ever seen and promptly arranged to buy the property. Thereafter, he and Mary spent half of each year in New York City, half in Glendale at Chesterwood. "[Glendale] is heaven," he said. "New York is — well, New York."

French not only sculpted great public monuments, he created a grand residence, studio, and garden complex, which are an enduring and eloquent tableau of his artistry. It was here he created his masterpiece, the *Abraham Lincoln* that sits in the Lincoln Memorial in Washington. "What I wanted to convey," said French, "was the mental and physical strength of the great President. . . ." Visit Chesterwood today and you'll feel French's ability to sculpt that strength. In his studio, filled with memorabilia, you are invited to handle sculpting tools. Centerpieces in the studio are his marble *Andromeda,* an arrestingly erotic work unknown to most Americans; and the fascinating "railway" he had laid to facilitate moving his works-in-progress out into the revealing daylight. There is still a palpable sense of the sculptor's presence.

French designed magnificent gardens, and these are maintained superlatively today after his fashion by the property's management, the National

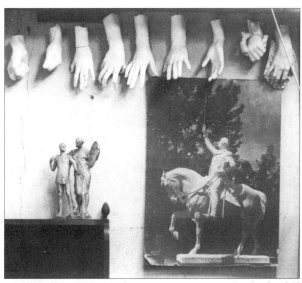

Hand studies in the Chesterwood studio of sculptor Daniel Chester French.

Jonathan Sternfield

Trust for Historic Preservation. Periodically, throughout the property, contemporary sculpture is exhibited. Come for a morning or afternoon at Chesterwood (the guided tour is definitely worthwhile) and enter the rarefied milieu of a gentleman sculptor. His artistry will inspire you.

Jonathan Sternfield

THE MISSION HOUSE
413-298-3239.
Box 792, Stockbridge, MA
    01262.
On the corner of Main &
    Sergeant Sts., in Stock-
    bridge.
Season: Summer:
    Tues.–Sun. 11–4; Open
    Mon. holidays.
Fee: $4; children 6–12,
    $1.50.

In 1735, an earnest minister from Yale came to the Berkshire wilderness to preach to the Mahican Indians. Establishing a settlement in the still-remote area, the sincere John Sergeant naturally drew the Indians to him, and thus began the town of Stockbridge. Sergeant learned the Indian language and preached two sermons in it every Sunday. In the springtime, he went out with the Indians to tap the sugar maples. His written account is the first in English to pass on this sugar production method. The minister frequently met with the Indians in the back of his simple log cabin, spending long hours listening to their problems. Under Sergeant's leadership, the Stockbridge Mission flourished.

To please his wife, Abigail, Reverend Sergeant built what is now called Mission House, high on Prospect Hill. The tall and ornate "Connecticut Doorway" that serves as the dwelling's front entry was carved in Westfield, Connecticut, and dragged by oxen 50 miles over rugged terrain to Stockbridge. It is not only a beautiful and noble doorway but also has special theological significance in that its panels represent the Ten Commandments, an open Bible, and St. Andrews' Cross. This front door and the front rooms were Abigail's domain; in the back, a separate entry and long corridor allowed the Indians access to the Reverend's study.

When John Sergeant died in 1749, the Stockbridge Mission was not long for this world either, and by 1785, the Indians had been displaced from Stockbridge, driven out for the most part by land speculators.

In 1927, Mission House was acquired by Mabel Choate, the art collector and philanthropist who was heir to Naumkeag (described above). She moved it to its present Main St. position, just a stone's throw from the site of John Sergeant's first log cabin. Boston landscape architect Fletcher Steele, who had designed the gardens at Naumkeag, planted an orderly, symmetrical 18th-century herb, flower, and fruit garden beside the restored, relocated Mission House. There are today apple and quince trees; herbs such as lamb's ear, rue, and southern wood; bright flowers; a grape arbor; and a "salet garden" filled with garden greens.

The Trustees of Reservations maintain Mission House now. Tours of the house take you back to the 18th century's furnishings and kitchen implements and the feeling of humble domesticity around the dominant central hearth.

COLONEL ASHLEY HOUSE

413-229-8600.
Box 128, Ashley Falls, MA 01222.
On Cooper Hill Rd., Ashley Falls, off Route 7A.
Season: Memorial Day–end of June, Labor Day–Columbus Day: Wed.–Sun.; rest of summer daily 1–5, exc. Mon. & Tues.
Fee: $3.50, children 6–12, $1.

In his military role as colonel and as a political radical, John Ashley was destined to become as prominent a citizen as the Revolution would produce in Berkshire. But he began his Berkshire life decades earlier, as a surveyor, trudging through the woods and swamps of Sheffield. With rod and chain, he and his cohorts mapped the wilderness.

Ashley loved what he saw, and by 1735 he had built a handsome home on the west bank of the Housatonic River, now the oldest house in Berkshire County. Framed of well-seasoned oak with chestnut rafters, it was the finest house in Sheffield. Woodworkers from across the colony came to carve paneling and to fashion the gracefully curved staircase. Ashley's study, with its broad fireplace and sunburst cupboard, is a room whose craftsmanship inspires confidence. It was here that Ashley met with a group of his neighbors in early 1773 to draft "The Sheffield Declaration," stating to the world that all people were "equal, free and independent." In Ashley's study, they asserted their independence from Britain, some three years before Thomas Jefferson and associates did so in Philadelphia.

Thanks to an excellent restoration and relocation (a quarter-mile from its original site) by the Trustees of Reservations, the Ashley House lives on. An herb garden flourishes outside while Colonial furnishings, a pottery collection, and the original wood paneling survive inside. If you're antique hunting in the Sheffield–Ashley Falls area, Colonel Ashley House will complement your visit.

The Sheffield Declaration, 1773

Resolved that Mankind in a State of Nature are equal, free and independent of each other, and have a right to the undisturbed Enjoyment of their lives, their Liberty and Property.

Resolved that it is a well known and undoubted priviledge of the British Constitution that every Subject hath not only a Right to the free and uncontrolled injoyment and Improvement of his estate or property. . . .

Resolved that the late acts of the parlement of Great Britan expres porpos of Rating and regulating the colecting a Revenue in the Colonies; are unconstitutional as thereby the Just earning of our labours and Industry without Any Regard to our own consent are by mere power ravished from us.

THE BIDWELL HOUSE
413-528-6888.
Art School Rd., Monterey, MA 01245.
Off Tyringham Road, 1 mi.
Season: Memorial Day–Columbus Day, Tues.–Sun., holidays, 11–4.
Fee: $4; Seniors, $3; children, $2.

Newest old house on the historic home circuit, Bidwell is actually one of Berkshire's oldest, dating from 1750. Surrounded by 200 acres of pristine Monterey woodland, the house looks much as it might have back in the 18th century. Drive down Art School Road, then keep driving, back into the woods, the deep woods where the past still lingers. There you'll find the unassuming Bidwell house, simple yet homey.

An active slate of lectures (such as "Fernside, the Shaker Village of Tyringham"), workshops (among them, cider pressing); and hikes (recently featuring the Historical Royal Hemlock Road) get this newest historical home off to a very promising start.

THE WILLIAM CULLEN BRYANT HOME-STEAD
634-2244.
Off Rte. 9 on Rte. 112 South Cummington, MA 01026.
Season: Summer: Fri., Sat., Sun. & Holidays 1–5; Labor Day–Columbus Day: Sat., Sun. & Holidays 1–5.
Fee: $4; children 6–12, $2; under 6, free.

On a farm of 465 acres, in a small gambrel-roofed cabin of rough-hewn lumber, two miles from the frontier village of Cummington, William Cullen Bryant was born in 1794. He went to Williams College but stayed only eight months, shortly thereafter taking up the law. From 1816 on, already a published poet, Cullen, as he was called, practiced law in Great Barrington.

On the record of about 30 well-respected poems written while in Barrington, on such local themes as Monument Mountain's Indian legend, the Green River, and native waterfowl, and with the influence of Catherine Sedgwick's brothers, Bryant became co-editor of the *New York Review* and *Athenaeum Magazine*, then editor at the *New York Evening Post* (one of America's oldest and most influential newspapers), and ultimately America's first popular and widely respected poet.

Bryant occasionally returned to his Cummington homestead, using the house as a country retreat. He also added to the house considerably, and today it stands gracious, its 23 rooms still filled with furnishings such as Bryant's Empire maple canopied four-poster. Well managed by the Trustees of Reservations, the house is a bit overloaded with Bryant memorabilia. Read the poems first, or the tour's fine points will elude you.

THE MERWIN HOUSE
413-298-4703.
14 W. Main St., Stockbridge, MA 01262.
In the center of Stockbridge.
Season: June 1–Oct. 15; Tues., Thurs., Sat., Sun., Noon–5.
Fee: $4; senior citizens $3.50; children over 12, $2.50.

"Tranquility" is the former home of Mrs. Vipont Merwin, and is a bit of 19th-century Berkshire refinement stopped in time. This charming brick mansion, built about 1825, is filled with period antiques (mostly Victorian); both furnishings and collectibles reflect global travel and domestic dignity. Merwin House is maintained as a property of the Society for the Preservation of New England Antiquities. For Stockbridge strollers, evening views through the multipaned front windows give an inviting glimpse of an elegant world gone by.

SEARLES CASTLE

Mark Hopkins was a founder and treasurer of the Central Pacific Railroad, and when he died, his widow, Mary, consoled herself with the creation of a grand castle in Great Barrington. The 40-room, Stanford White–designed castle was constructed between 1882 and 1887 of locally cut blue dolomite stone. Upon its completion, Mary Hopkins married her interior decorator, Edward Searles, a man 20 years her junior. Searles had spared no expense on the castle's interior, and many of the major rooms feature massive carved wood or marble fireplaces, each one unique. More than 100 of the world's best artisans and craftsmen were brought on site to work with oak carvings, marble statues, atriums, columns, and pillars.

When all the bills came in, they totalled $2.5 million, but Mary had the cash, and Edward, and the castle with its Greek Revival temple, indoor pool, golf course, and tennis court. First known as Barrington House, the castle has been a girl's school, an insurance company, and now serves as the home of the John Dewey Academy, a residential therapeutic high school. In 1982, Searles Castle was added to the National Register of Historic Places. Usually closed to the public, the building and grounds are visible to pedestrians walking along Main Street. Several times a year — for an Antiquarian Book Fair, for the Stockbridge Chamber Concerts, and at other special events — Searles Castle is open to the public, and well worth a visit.

Touring the Berkshire Mansions

For those who yearn to step back into Berkshire's Gilded Age, visits to Naumkeag, the Mount, and Tanglewood, described in this chapter, will make an excellent start. Elsewhere in this book, in the chapters on *Lodging* or *Restaurants,* other Gilded Age mansions are noted for their original beauty or their contemporary adaptations. But there is much more to know and to see — if you're willing to keep an eye out for certain opportunities. From time to time, local historical societies and garden clubs arrange visits to some of the best mansions, normally off limits because they are private homes. **Edith Wharton Restoration** at the Mount offers summer step-on guides who will lead your group of 20 or more on your own bus to some of the great houses. **Berkshire Walking Tours** (413-443-5017; Box 383, Pittsfield) also runs a similar service.

You can also guide your own tour of the Gilded Age "cottages." Many are visible from the road and are well worth a look. Their owners' privacy should be respected, of course. The stories of Berkshire's Gilded Age are endlessly entertaining, and Carole Owens' book *The Berkshire Cottages* tells them in lively detail. The business magnates, robber barons, philanthropists, architects and designers, artists in residence, and squadrons of domestic servants are all alive in Owens' pages. If you liked public television's *Upstairs, Downstairs,* then *The Berkshire Cottages* is your kind of book. Maps to guide your way are included. At most bookstores.

LIBRARIES

BERKSHIRE ATHENAEUM
413-499-9480.
One Wendell Ave. Pittsfield, MA 01201.
Season: Year-round, exc. summer, Mon.–Thurs., 9–9; Fri., Sat., 9–5. Late June–Labor Day, Mon., Wed., Fri., 9–5; Tues., Thurs., 9–9; Sat., 10–1.
Closed holidays.
Fee: Free.

The old Berkshire Athenaeum is a 19th-century specimen of the Venetian Gothic style, constructed next to the courthouse on Pittsfield's handsome Park Square. Built of Berkshire deep blue dolomite (a limestone) from Great Barrington, along with red sandstone from Longmeadow, Massachusetts, and red granite from Missouri, this Athenaeum was once Berkshire's central library and now serves Pittsfield's municipal courts.

The new Athenaeum is a three-level brick and glass facility featuring a tall and airy reading room with natural clerestory lighting and an outdoor reading terrace for adults and one for children.

There is an outstanding dance collection, a Local Authors Room, and a Local History Room (where some of the research for this book was done). The crown jewel of the Athenaeum is its Herman Melville Room, a veritable treasure trove of Melville memorabilia, from carved scrimshaw depicting the terror of the Great White Whale to first editions of the author's works. Look for *Moby Dick* in Japanese! Here also you'll find autograph letters from Melville, photos of his Pittsfield Farm, Arrowhead (see entry under "Historic Homes," in this chapter), and the desk on which he wrote his last haunting work, *Billy Budd.*

CHAPIN LIBRARY OF RARE BOOKS
413-597-2462.
Box 426, Williamstown, MA 01267.
On the 2nd fl. of Stetson Hall, on Williams College campus.
Season: Year-round: 10–12, 1–5, exc. weekends & holidays. Open July 4. Call for summer hours.

One of the best-rounded collections of rare books and manuscripts in the world is right here in Berkshire. Alfred Clark Chapin, Williams class of 1869, went on to become mayor of Brooklyn and to collect a magnificent library of first editions and manuscripts, specializing in historic literary and artistic masterworks. Since his presentation to Williams in 1923, other alumni have given their collections, and as a result, the Chapin is strong in all the significant fields.

Among the literary holdings are Shakespeare in First Folio, and first editions of Pope, Swift, Fielding, Defoe, Richardson, Sterne, Johnson, Scott, Byron, Burns, Browning, Keats, Shelley, Thackeray, and Dickens. There is also a fine T. S. Eliot collection. Representing American literature are first editions by such writers as Crane, Melville, and Whitman.

Scientific endeavor is represented by Tycho Brahe's *Astronomia* (1602), Harvey's *Anatomical Exercitations* (1653), Darwin's *Origin of Species* (1859), and a double elephant folio of Audobon's *Birds of America.*

Most powerful of all, perhaps, is the Chapin's collection of documents from the American Revolution. The valuables include a copy of the Articles of Confederation of 1777; copies of two versions of the Bill of Rights; a copy of the Committee of Style draft of the Constitution, with handwritten objections by one of its members; and General Greene's handwritten order for boats to cross the Delaware; and a copy of the Declaration of Independence that had belonged to one of its signers. This last was purchased at auction in 1983, with a bid of $412,500; the college and alumni both stunned the academic and art-auction world and endowed the Chapin and the Berkshires with yet another cornerstone of American history.

SAWYER LIBRARY
413-597-2501.
Williams College, Williamstown, MA 01267.
In the center of Williams College campus.
Season: Year-round; closed weekends when Williams is not in session.

Berkshire County's most comprehensive library, the Sawyer is an unmatched research resource. Here you'll find a wide array of the latest periodicals, shelves of newly released books, and a library staff as helpful as they come. The Sawyer is a very pleasant place in which to work, and unlike many college libraries, here most eyes are on the books.

LENOX LIBRARY
413-637-0197.
18 Main St., Lenox, MA
01240.
Season: Year-round; summer: Mon.–Sat. 10–5; rest of year, Tues.–Sat. 10–5; Thurs., open until 8.

Built in 1815 as the Berkshire County Courthouse, when Lenox was still the "shire town," this classic Greek Revival building became the Lenox Library Association in 1873. It is listed on the National Register of Historic Places, and if you're lucky enough to sit and read there some afternoon, you'll understand why. See especially the main reading room with its lofty illuminated ceiling and its amazing array of periodicals. This is Old World reading at its best. A solid collection of about 75,000 volumes plus a music room are available to the public. There is a closed collection of historical memorabilia too, including the infamous sleigh in Edith Wharton's novella, *Ethan Frome*. A lovely outdoor reading park makes warm-weather bookwork much fun.

Love and Death in Wharton's **Ethan Frome**

Though written after she completed her Berkshire life, Wharton's *Ethan Frome* is set in a Berkshire town, which she calls Starkfield. In the climactic scene, soulmates Ethan and Mattie decide to take a suicidal sled ride rather than having to live apart, separated by Ethan's snarling wife, Zeena. The snowy downhill race toward obliteration was based on an actual sledding accident in turn-of-the-century Lenox.

She waited while he seated himself with crossed legs in front of the sled; then she crouched quickly down at his back and clasped her arms about him. Her breath in his neck set him shuddering again, and he almost sprang from his seat. But in a flash he remembered the alternative. She was right: this was better than parting. He leaned back and drew her mouth to his. . . .

Just as they started, he heard the sorrel's whinney again, and the familiar wistful call, and all the confused images it brought with it went with him down the first reach of the road. Half-way down there was a sudden drop, then a rise, and after that another long delirious descent. As they took wing for this, it seemed to him that they were flying indeed, flying far up into the cloudy night, with Starkfield immeasurably below them, falling away like a speck in space. . . . Then the big elm shot up ahead, lying in wait for them at the bend in the road, and he said between his teeth: "We can fetch it; I know we can fetch it —"

As they flew toward the tree, Mattie pressed her arms tighter, and her blood seemed to be in his veins. Once or twice, the sled swerved a little under them. He slanted his body to keep it headed for the elm, repeating to himself again and again: "I know we can fetch it"; and little phrases she had spoken ran through his head and danced before him on the air. The big tree loomed bigger and closer, and as they bore down on it he thought: "It's waiting for us: it seems to know." But suddenly his wife's face, with twisted monstrous lineament, thrust itself between him and his goal, and he made an instinctive movement to brush it aside. The sled swerved in response, but he righted it again, kept it straight, and drove down on the black projecting mass. There was a last instant when the air shot past him like millions of fiery wires; and then the elm. . . .

Reading in the daylight-filled atrium, at the Simon's Rock Library, Great Barrington.

**SIMON'S ROCK
    LIBRARY**
413-528-0771, ext. 273.
Alford Rd., Gt. Barrington,
    MA 01230.
Season: Year-round, hours
    vary.

The Simon's Rock Library is certainly one of the best in South County, and the staff is always attentive to one's research needs. The college it serves may be small, but don't be deceived: this library's holdings are exceedingly well chosen. It is open to all visitors and to Berkshire County residents for borrowing. This is a library of half a dozen rooms, on two floors, in three interconnected pagoda-style buildings — all in a sylvan setting. Here, you can see art books you have only dreamt about; here you can answer that lingering question about the divisions of a nanosecond. With their big skylights, the reading rooms are highly recommended for naturally lit wet-weather browsing. And fascinating art exhibits almost always grace the library's skylit gallery.

**STOCKBRIDGE
    LIBRARY**
413-298-5501.
Box 119, Stockbridge, MA
    01262.
Main St., Stockbridge.
Season: Year-round, exc.
    Sun.

Parts of the Stockbridge Library date to 1864, and the reading room is one the most felicitous anywhere. Tall, stately, and obviously from another era, this book-lined salon sets the mood for study so strongly that it will woo you to sit awhile and peruse. The children's collection is also first-rate.

MUSEUMS

Sharing the aesthetic, at Pittsfield's Berkshire Museum.

George Dimock, courtesy the Berkshire Museum

THE BERKSHIRE MUSEUM
413-443-7171.
39 South St., Pittsfield, MA 01201.
Season: Year-round: Tues.–Sat. 10–5, Sun. 1–5; open daily July–Aug: 10–5. Member disc. available.
Gift shop.

Cultural hub for the whole county, Berkshire Museum offers strong collections of art and regional and natural history, as well as offering an exciting calendar of lectures, films, concerts, classes, and field trips.

Founded in 1903 by Dalton paper maker and philanthropist, Zenas Crane, the museum now also shows the Hahn Collection of Early American Silver; the Gallatin Collection of Abstract Art; the Spalding Collection of Chinese Art; the Proctor Shell Collection; and the Cohn Collection of Minerals.

The collections are far-ranging and impressive. There is 19th-century glass made in the towns of Berkshire and Cheshire, and there are pre-Christian glass bottles from Egypt. There are exhibits of shells and aquatic life, fossils, mushrooms, reptiles and amphibians, and "Uncle Beasley," the ten-foot-long model dinosaur who starred in the children's TV movie, *The Enormous Egg.* The Bird Room has a special section on Berkshire birds; the owl exhibit especially captivating. The Berkshire Animal Room presents native mammal specimens. A collection of beautiful dioramas by Louis Paul Jonas, Sr. shows the animals of the world in one-tenth scale. These wonderful miniatures, teeming with animal life and frequently heightened by dramatic weather, give even the most traveled viewer a colorful glimpse into other ecosystems.

Also on the first floor is the Museum Theater, a 300-seat facility that is site for lectures, plays, concerts, and the Little Cinema's admirable program of feature films. The theater is visually enlivened by two Alexander Calder mobiles, and now boasts state-of-the-art sound and projection.

Upstairs, American portraiture is represented by works of Copley, Stuart, and Peale, and the Hudson River School appears in works by Coles, Inness, and others. There is a gallery of abstract art, and also two European galleries devoted to the work of such English portrait painters as West and Reynolds, and European works by masters from the 15th to the 18th century. An ancient civilizations gallery includes "Pa-hat," the ever-popular Egyptian mummy, who lies resplendent amidst a first-rate collection of ancient reliefs and artifacts.

In the museum's center is the lofty and skylit Ellen Crane Memorial Room, a beautiful space that is now the museum's sculpture gallery, devoted to American and European pieces from the 19th and 20th centuries.

Downstairs, the museum has more than 20 exhibits of living fish, local reptiles, amphibians, and exotic habitats, such as coral reefs.

The museum has a year-round calendar of programs, events, lectures, and trips that could be a full-time education. "Art for Lunch" is one of the series aimed at enriching local lives. Bus trips are run with destinations like New York's Museum of Modern Art and the Frick. Berkshire Museum also presents an unusual concert series, "Close Encounters With Music," a series of concerts combined with talks.

"Head of a Young Man" (1503), by Albrecht Durer, one of the Clark's many outstanding drawings.

Albrecht Durer, courtesy
Clark Art Institute

STERLING AND FRANCINE CLARK ART INSTITUTE
413-458-9545.
225 South St.,
Williamstown, MA
01267.

Sterling Clark acquired his first Renoir in 1916. By the time he was finished, he owned 36. He bought what he liked, not what was popular, and was sometimes able to purchase a masterpiece for a song. Such was the case with the renowned *Nymphs and Satyr*, a larger-than-life scene of idyllic

Season: Year-round: 10–5, exc. Mon.; open Memorial Day, Labor Day & Columbus Day.
Fee: Free admission.
Gift shop.

eroticism by Bourguereau, which you will see in one of the first galleries.

Across the hall from the Bourguereau are galleries filled with 19th-century American classics — by Winslow Homer, John Singer Sargent, and Frederick Remington. Sterling Clark loved horses, so it's not surprising he loved his Remington showing the cavalry galloping forward, right out of the canvas.

The original Clark building — the white Vermont marble neoclassic structure whose interior is finished in Italian marble, plaster, and natural-finish oak — is elegant as a setting for art, and also efficient. Upon its opening it was called by the editor of *Art News*, ". . . very likely the best organized and most highly functional museum structure yet erected anywhere." Almost every gallery has some form of natural light, and the building is completely climate controlled. In addition, many galleries offer not only splendid art on the walls but peaceful views of the Berkshire hills as well.

Among the treasures here you'll find a small but impressive collection of Old Masters. But for many visitors, the centerpiece of the museum's collection is its gathering of French Impressionists; these were Sterling Clark's greatest artistic love, nurtured by his French wife, Francine. Among the standouts here, besides Renoir, are works by Monet and Degas, the latter in both his racehorse and ballet dancer series.

The Clark is no mere painting gallery, however. As you walk among its colorful masterworks and their accompanying drawings and prints, you'll also see some of the collection's antique furniture and silver, masterpieces of craftsmanship. The Clark is also an important art education center, with a broad spectrum of lectures open to the public, serving as classroom to a Williams College graduate program in art history as well.

Besides its extensive art lecture series, the Clark presents chamber music and film programs, described in the "Cinema" and "Music" sections of this chapter. In its spare time, the Clark hosts mimes, puppeteers, one-person shows, poets, and storytellers.

Even a short visit to the Clark is worth the trip, but linger if you can, and return often.

NORMAN ROCKWELL MUSEUM
413-298-4100.
Route 183, Stockbridge, MA 01262.
Season: Year-round: Daily 10–5; Winter, Mon.–Fri., 11–4; Sat.–Sun., 10–5.
Closed major holidays.

However one regards Norman Rockwell, the display of his life's work at the new Norman Rockwell Museum has deep resonances for every human being. A tour of this new, grand monument to his talents and insight is a must for every Berkshire resident and visitor.

Set on a gracious knoll overlooking the Housatonic River in the Glendale section of Stockbridge,

"Stockbridge Mainstreet at Christmas."

Fee: Adults $8; Children 6–18, $2; under 5, free. Gift shop.

the $4.4-million building designed by Robert A. M. Stern has a New England town hall look to it, with slate gables, clapboard siding, and fieldstone terraces. Inside are spacious, well-lit galleries showing off more than 150 Rockwells at any given time. Rockwell fan or not, there is much to see here, much delight in the windows into Norman Rockwell's world.

By the time he was twelve, Rockwell knew he wanted to be a painter. Ten years later, he had reached the height of his profession, selling a cover painting to the *Saturday Evening Post* and beginning a relationship that was to last for 47 years. His *Post* covers are just one highlight of the museum, which has the largest collection of Rockwell originals in the world (over 500).

A centerpiece of the entire museum is the skylit gallery where Rockwell's Four Freedoms are on permanent display. Rockwell created them during the Second World War, as depictions of what we were fighting to uphold: *Freedom of Speech; Freedom from Fear; Freedom of Worship; Freedom from Want.* These four archetypal American images constitute something of a shrine to patriotism.

In 1953, Rockwell moved with his family from Arlington, Vermont, to Stockbridge, where he continued his creation of classic Americana. Ten years later, his relationship with the *Saturday Evening Post* ended, and he signed on with *Look.* His palette and his cast of characters broadened. Where once he depicted white boys running from a prohibited swimming hole, now it was federal marshals leading a young black girl to school in Little Rock. From lovers and gos-

sips, he moved on to Peace Corps volunteers and astronauts on the moon.

The museum changes its exhibits periodically. Exhibits in 1994 include a collaborative exhibition with the Delware Museum of Art, featuring the works of Rockwell and Howard Pyle, one of Rockwell's most revered heroes; also "A Centennial Celebration," a retrospective celebrating Rockwell's centenary and highlighted by seldom-seen works from private collections.

If you have the time, by all means take one of the museum's tours. All sorts of colorful information will be passed along (such as pointers about the portraits of Grandma Moses and Rockwell's family contained within one painting). Helpful hints are given about how to appreciate Rockwell's attention to detail: "Notice the ring finger on the old woman's hand; it's been indented by many years of wear. . . ."

Next, you may want to stop in the attractive gift shop, selling Rockwell images on all manner of goods, from post cards and posters to coffee mugs and puzzles. There are Rockwell books as well.

Outside, just over the knoll past the Linwood mansion, stands Rockwell's studio, with a bucolic view of the Housatonic. The studio is a 19th-century carriage house, moved from the village to its present site in 1986, and now opened to the public for the first time. Inside Rockwell's studio, you get a real feel for the light in which he loved to paint, for the curious assemblage of artifacts he liked to surround himself with, and for the modest space he felt was his "best studio yet."

The Rockwell Museum offers a variety of community-oriented programs beyond its public exhibitions. Among our favorites is a sketch class taught by a succession of visiting artists. Special reference is made to Rockwell's work, as students are guided along in the development of the fine line.

Traditional sheepshearing in the shadow of Hancock's round stone barn.

Jonathan Sternfield

HANCOCK SHAKER VILLAGE
413-443-0188.
Box 898, Pittsfield, MA 01202.
Jct. Rtes. 20 & 41, 5 mi. W. of Pittsfield.
Season: April 1–Nov. 30; daily 9:30–5.
Fee: $10; children 6–17, $5; families $25.
Gift shops.

Founded in England in 1747, the Shakers originally called themselves the United Society of Believers in Christ's Second Appearing, but they soon became known as the Shaking Quakers for the tremblings they exhibited during religious dancing. In 1770, one of their members, Ann Lee, had a powerful vision, and as new leader of the sect, brought a small band to America. Here around 1776, Ann Lee founded the first American Shaker community, at Niskayuna, near Albany.

They practiced a religion that was also their way of life. All property and labor was shared. The community consciously kept itself insular from the outside world. The sexes were treated equally, but kept separate, for celibacy was a basic Shaker tenet. Sins were confessed publicly, but because the Shakers were pacifists, punishment was never physical. Since the sect did not reproduce its own, converts or New Believers were important, and Mother Ann made frequent missionary journeys through Connecticut and Massachusetts, seeking souls.

A community was established in 1790 at Hancock, just west of Pittsfield. There, the community, called the City of Peace, grew and prospered, its residents seeking to achieve heavenly perfection on earth through a highly structured, cloistered life. Design of clothing, furniture, implements, and buildings was strictly functional, with beauty being almost synonymous with simplicity. "Tis a gift to be simple," goes an old Shaker hymn; and such simplicity was a primary aim of both inner and outer life. "Beauty rests on utility," said their credo.

Of great beauty, then, is Hancock's symbol, the stunning Round Stone Barn. As splendid as the structure is to the eye, how much more splendid to the legs and arms of the single farmhand for whom the round barn was designed. With such an efficient architecture, one farmhand at the center could easily and quickly feed an entire herd of cattle.

When the sect was at its peak, in the mid-19th century, Hancock was one of 18 Shaker communities from Maine to Kentucky and had a population of about 300 members. The agricultural base of the village was augmented by cottage industries, fabricating such items as tin dustpans, flat brooms, and bird's-eye maple chairs. But because of the strict codes of celibacy, Shaker population at Hancock declined steadily until 1960, when the last of the Hancock Shakers moved away.

Since then, the village has been a living museum to accommodate visitors who want taste of the simple Shaker ways. The City of Peace now acts as a center of recreated Shaker activities, including workshops, candlelit dinners, and evening tours. An important event on the second weekend in July is the Americana artists and crafts show.

Visitors can tour the splendid Round Stone Barn and 19 other original Shaker buildings. And while you amble around the lovely old compound, you'll be able to see Shaker furniture, tools, and machines, some of them attended by craftspeople working in the Shaker way. Visit with the chair maker, the blacksmith, basket makers, or textile workers who spin or weave. In Hancock's workshops, you can learn to work like a Shaker, creating Shaker chair seats, oval boxes, natural cosmetics or herb wreaths. Take in the gardens, both herbal and vegetable, and from any of the village farm workers, you can get a sense of the power of Shaker simplicity.

WILLIAMS COLLEGE MUSEUM OF ART
413-597-2429.
Main St. (Rte. 2), Williamstown, MA 01267.
Across from Gothic chapel: set back from street.
Season: Year-round: Tues.–Sat., 10–5, Sun. 1–5.
Closed: Thanksgiving, Christmas & New Year's.
Fee: Free.
Gift Shop

The Williams College Museum of Art is a 19th-century structure that is strikingly new. Behind the original 1846 building, with its neoclassical octagonal rotunda, is an addition designed by Charles Moore, which opened in 1983, with further additions completed in 1986. Combining wit and sophistication, Moore created a versatile, multi-leveled exhibition space. His design for the building's rear facade is a continuation of his lighthearted approach, featuring what Williams students fondly call their "ironic columns."

Inside, the museum's permanent collection contains some 11,000 objects. To complement the Clark Art Museum's collection of 19th-century European art, WCMA emphasizes American art, 20th-century art, and the art of Asia and other non-Western civilizations. Thanks to a gift by the widow of American impressionist Charles Prendergast, the museum houses the finest collection in America of works by both Charles and his talented brother, Maurice, and is now the leading center in the world for study of the Prendergasts' work.

Frequent loan exhibitions focus on a wide range of subjects. Our advice: when in Williamstown, stop off at both the Clark Art Institute and the college museum.

Money paper, one of Crane Paper's most successful products.

Courtesy U.S. Treasury

CRANE PAPER MUSEUM
413-684-2600.
30 South St., Dalton, MA 01226.
Off Rte. 9, behind Crane office, Dalton.
Season: June to Mid-Oct., Mon.–Fri., 2–5.
Fee: Free.

One of Berkshire's most important creations is money. Not the finished product, mind you, but the rag paper on which every U.S. bill is printed. The Crane Paper Company makes it, and from Berkshire County to the nation and then the world, these treasured notes circulate.

While the mills themselves are no longer open to the public, the Crane Paper Museum, established in 1929, is open and tells a fascinating industrial tale. This magical, one-room brick museum — ivy covered and set in a garden — is really a restored paper mill building. The exhibits inside are mostly scale models, historical photographs, and paper samples. Crane produces only rag paper (nothing from wood pulp), and the exhibits show how the rags are soaked, softened, beaten to a pulp, and dried into paper stock. A 20-minute video on papermaking explains the process of watermarking, surface finishing (hard or soft), and anti-counterfeiting techniques. Also on display are historic documents, White House invitations, and U.S. and foreign currency, all printed on paper manufactured by Crane. At the end of your visit, you'll likely be offered an envelope of free Crane paper samples, including some of their luxurious stationery. It's that old rags to riches story come true again.

**STOCKBRIDGE
LIBRARY HISTORI-
CAL ROOM**
413-298-5501.
Main St., Stockbridge, MA
01262.
Season: Year-round, exc.
Sun.
Fee: Free.

Called W-nahk-ta-kook ("Great Meadow") by the Mahican Indians who settled there, the town of Stockbridge was incorporated by the English in 1739. A Colonial charter not only made the town official, but made it Indian property as well, and thereafter it was known as "Indian Town." The history of this great meadow and its town is displayed and explained in the Stockbridge Historical Room, a small museum in the basement of the Stockbridge Library. Here you'll see Indian artifacts, photos from the mid-1800s onwards, memorabilia from many famous residents and visitors to the village, and other intriguing historical bits that illuminate Stockbridge present.

**WESTERN GATEWAY
HERITAGE STATE
PARK**
413-663-6312.
9 Furnace St. Bypass, N.
  Adams, MA 01247.
In N. Adams freightyard
  district.
Season: Year-round, 10–5.
Fee: Donations accepted.
Gift shop & Restaurant.

Berkshire has always been somewhat isolated, nestled between long glacial ridges and separated from the rest of Massachusetts. In 1854, engineers and construction workers assaulted this situation, drilling and blasting a 4.3-mile-long tunnel through the northeastern ridge. This Hoosac Tunnel was the first major tunneling work in the U.S., and many new methods were devised over the 20-year construction — but at a cost of over $20 million and more than 200 lives. The building of the tunnel and related railroad development made North Adams the largest city in Berkshire in 1900. "We hold the Western Gateway," says the North Adams seal, and at the turn of the century, more than half of Boston's freight came through the tunnel.

Western Gateway Heritage State Park now celebrates the former Boston and Maine Freight House and the Hoosac Tunnel, both of which are on the National Register of Historic Places. Inside, you can see films, slide shows, written and visual histories of the railway and tunnel through the Hoosac barrier. Outside, there are shops, the restored freightyard, a restaurant (reviewed in Chapter Five, *Restaurants & Food Purveyors*), and the church-spired charm of North Adams.

**BERKSHIRE SCENIC
RAILWAY MUSEUM**
413-637-2210.
Box 2195, Lenox, MA 01240.
Willow Creek Rd. at the
  end of Housatonic St.
Season: June–Oct., week-
  ends & holidays, 10–4.
Museum & Gift Shop: Free.

Penned in by red tape and inter-railway line disputes, Berkshire Scenic has cut its cross-county route to a short back-and-forth in front of Wood's Pond. While it's technically true that you get to take a ride in their shined-up 1920s-vintage Erie Lackawanna passenger coaches, the ride at present is so brief as to be something of a tease. Things will change, we're reasonably sure, and one day soon you'll once again be able to tour southern Berkshire by rail, so keep your eyes on this one.

For now, you can take the "Short Shuttle," check out the toy trains in the old train station, or just admire backwoods Lenox.

OTHER MUSEUMS IN THE BERKSHIRES

Besides fine art and rare books, the many museums in Williamstown can take you in still other directions. The *Williamstown House of Local History* (413-458-5369; Main St.) will take you back in time through a collection of books, antiques and artifacts depicting Williamstown the way it was. You can go out at the *Hopkins Forest Museum* (413-597-2346; *Hopkins Memorial Forest,* the Rosenberg Center, and Buxton Garden; Northwest Hill Rd.), to such seasonal events as sheepshearing and maple sugaring, while the museum itself exhibits old photographs, farm machinery, and tools. And you can go up to the stars at the 19th-century flintstone *Hopkins Observatory* (413-597-2188; Main St.) via the projected shows at the *Milham Planetarium* (Fridays during the school year), or back, out and up to the real pulsars and quasars through the telescopes of America's second oldest collegiate observatory, in touch with the stars since 1836.

MUSIC

A moving bass passage through Tanglewood's park-like setting.

Courtesy the Boston Symphony Orchestra

TANGLEWOOD
413-637-1666 or 413-637-5165.
Boston Symphony Orchestra, Tanglewood, Lenox, MA 01240.

The rhapsody in green continues. Framed by towering pines, carpeted with lush lawns, endowed with spectacular mountain views, and animated by the Boston Symphony Orchestra and its students, Tanglewood remains *the* summer

Mail: 301 Massachusetts Ave., Boston, MA 02115. Mail (July & Aug.): Tanglewood, Lenox MA 01240. On West St., Rte. 183, in Lenox.
Season: Summer only.
Tickets: $10–$14 lawn, $13.50–$67 shed, $20–$30 concert hall.
Gift shop; cafeteria.

music festival in New England, an incomparable facility for all the world's musicians and music lovers. Whether you picnic on the lawn or sit closer to the BSO in the Shed, hearing music at Tanglewood is a rare experience. Sit inside and witness up close the artistry of Music Director Seiji Ozawa; or sit back on the vast expanse of lawn, sip your wine, watch the stars and satellites in the clear sky overhead, and just listen to these masters make music.

Critics assert that Tanglewood is too crowded, too expensive, too predictable, and too lax in its standards for music making or music listening, but this is belied by the powerful, positive feeling among musicians, students, and concertgoers alike. The sheer fun of seeing and hearing great music made in the great outdoors far outweighs any criticisms. We join in that good feeling and heartily recommend Tanglewood as a quintessential Berkshire entertainment.

Tanglewood began as the Berkshire Music Festival in the summer of 1934. Members of the New York Philharmonic were bused from Manhattan to the mountains and lodged in the area's hotels for the concert series. It was a sound success and repeated the following summer, but the New York orchestra withdrew. Serge Koussevitzky, the Russian-born conductor of the Boston Symphony Orchestra, was wooed and then won. The BSO signed on for a series of three concerts on a single August weekend in 1936.

The popularity of this series was immense, with nearly 15,000 people attending. And in the fall of that year, the Tappan family gave the BSO a permanent summer home in the Berkshires, their Tanglewood estate on the Stockbridge-Lenox border. For the first two summers, concerts were held in a large canvas tent, but during one 1937 program, a torrential thunderstorm not only drowned out Wagner's *The Ride of the Valkyries* but also leaked through, dampening instruments, musicians, and audience alike. During intermission, an impromptu fund-raising drive for the creation of a permanent structure, a "music pavilion," raised pledges totaling $30,000.

By the following summer, through the combined architectural efforts of the distinguished architect, Eliel Saarinen, and Stockbridge engineer, Joseph Franz, the Shed was a reality. Sensing the opportunity and the ideal setting, in 1940 Koussevitzky and the BSO added the Berkshire Music Center for advanced musicians, the only such school run by a major symphony orchestra.

For the school's opening ceremony, Randall Thompson composed his haunting *Alleluia* for unaccompanied chorus, a work that left such a lasting impression that it has been performed as the school's traditional opening music each summer since.

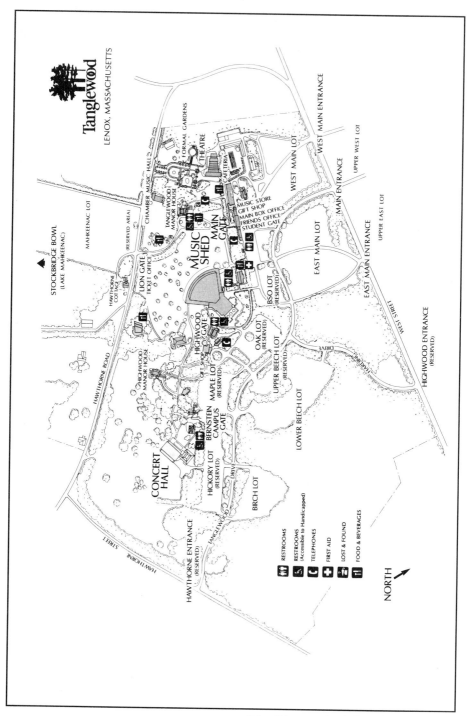

Barbara Peterson, courtesy the Boston Symphony Orchestra

The passion and artistry of Midori, a Tanglewood highlight.

Walter Scott, courtesy the Boston Symphony Orchestra.

Each summer, the Tanglewood Music Center Orchestra is recreated from that year's crop of students; for their weekly concerts, this impressive group is usually led by conducting fellows, but sometimes by the likes of Seiji Ozawa or Simon Rattle. So significant is this Tanglewood education that upwards of 20 percent of the members of America's major orchestras count themselves among Tanglewood Music Center alumni. Leonard Bernstein was a graduate, as are Seiji Ozawa and Zubin Mehta.

The Music Festival itself has evolved into a performance center of major proportions. With an annual attendance now of some 300,000 visitors (1993 set the record at 336,862), it has become a musical mecca. Pianists Emanuel Ax, Garrick Ohlsson, Peter Serkin, and Alicia de Larrocha; violinists Midori and Itzhak Perlman; and cellist Yo-Yo Ma return regularly. In addition to the regular Boston Symphony Orchestra concerts, Tanglewood presents weekly chamber music concerts in the concert hall, Prelude Concerts (Friday nights) and Open Rehearsals (Saturday mornings); the annual Festival of Contemporary Music; a Jazz Festival; and almost daily concerts by gifted young musicians at the Music Center. The Boston Pops comes to play as well. If you're staying in the Berkshires for a month or more and want to take in Tanglewood music frequently, join the "Friends of Tanglewood" and enjoy free entry to student concerts and other privileges.

A favorite of each season is "Tanglewood on Parade," an amazingly varied musical day lasting some ten hours and climaxing with booming cannon shots and fireworks. But whatever the scale of the offerings, and whoever you might get to see and hear, an evening at Tanglewood marks a high point in any summer.

The biggest news here is the addition of the new $9.7 million Seiji Ozawa Hall, opened in the summer of '94. Accommodating 1,180 inside, and an addi-

Where to Sit at Tanglewood

If you plan to picnic at Tanglewood before a performance in the Shed, it's best to arrive an hour or so in advance of concert time. Besides allowing time to eat before listening, arriving early affords a greater choice of spaces on the lawn, an important factor if you're to hear the music clearly. Although Tanglewood's amplification system is excellent and facilitates good listening from almost any lawn position, in our experience, places about 25 yards beyond the Shed-mounted speakers provide the very best lawn listening.

Inside the Shed, the last series of back rows are good only for saying you were there, allowing only the most distant orchestra views and suffering greatly from much-diminished sound. At the optimum speaker sites on the lawn, the sound is far superior.

If you're not picnicking and can afford to indulge (up to $60 tops), buy your way forward into the good seats where the sound is rich, sometimes robust and sometimes delicate, and where you can really see classical music in the making.

Seiji Ozawa Hall has its own lawn with seating for several hundred.

Regardless of where you sit, allow time for a walk in Tanglewood's beautifully groomed boxwood gardens. As the sun sets, on a clear day, you can see the hills in three states.

Festivals-Within-the-Festival at Tanglewood

Not content merely to satisfy the classical music lover, Tanglewood offers mini-festivals and series featuring contemporary, jazz, and popular music.

Recent offerings in the Contemporary Music Festival have been an appropriately eclectic mix, including a performance by the California E.A.R. Unit, an eight-player ensemble from Los Angeles. If you find the free spirit in you is being kept too staid by the classicist in you, leave time this summer for a dose of Tanglewood's Contemporary Music.

Artistry of an even jazzier sort is showcased during Tanglewood's annual Jazz Festival, and songs of a slightly different sort are featured during Tanglewood's Popular Artist Series, which is sometimes announced after the Tanglewood summer schedule is published; keep an eye on local papers during the months of May and June.

tional 700 on nearby lawns, the new hall has openable sides, giving it flexibility and versatility as well as excellent acoustics. The hall is located on the Highwood section of Tanglewood, now designated as the Leonard Bernstein campus.

SOUTH MOUNTAIN CONCERTS
413-442-2106.
Box 23, Pittsfield, MA
01202.

It's certainly appropriate that South Mountain's concert hall in Pittsfield is called the Temple. Built in 1918, this colonial-style Temple of Music was the gift of Mrs. Elizabeth Sprague Coolidge,

*On stage at South
Mountain.*

Clemens Kalischer

On Rtes. 7 & 20, about 1 mi.
S. of Pittsfield Center.
Season: Mid-Aug.–early
Oct.
Tickets: Prices vary each
concert $18–$20.

created to house the concerts of the Berkshire
String Quartet. The acoustically splendid 500-seat
auditorium, listed on the National Register of Historic Places, is set gracefully on its wooded South
Mountain slope.

Past standout performers at the Temple have
included Leonard Bernstein, Alexander Schneider,
Leontyne Price, and Rudolf Serkin. Currently, a typical season features concerts by leading American string quartets such as the Guarneri, the Juilliard,
and the Emerson, as well as other types of ensembles. A popular highlight of
every season is the concert by the Beaux Arts Trio.

South Mountain Concerts frequently sell out — be sure to call ahead. Unlike
Tanglewood, where watching the stars or basking in the sunshine may substi-
tute for close listening to the music, South Mountain's more limited season and
number of concerts are designed for the serious music lover only.

ASTON MAGNA
413-528-3595.
Box 28, Gt. Barrington, MA
01230.
In St. James Church, just S.
of the town hall.
Season: July and Aug.
Tickets: $15 single, $50 for
all 5 concerts.

There's a great deal of historic preservation
going on in the Berkshires, and none more
artistic than the renaissance of Baroque, Classical,
and early Romantic chamber music by Aston
Magna. Offering unique cross-disciplinary educational programs for professional musicians and a
short run of superb summer concerts, Aston
Magna has specialized in 17th-, 18th-, and early
19th-century music, always played on period
instruments or reproductions. Hear Bach, Handel,
Haydn, Mozart, Schubert, and their contempo-

Playing theorbo, Catherine Liddell — another Aston Magna revelation.

Wes Thomas, courtesy Aston Magna

raries as you might never have before, with festival director and virtuoso violinist Daniel Stepner, leading a distinguished roster of singers and instrumentalists.

Performances interpret the music as much as possible as the composer intended, hence the faithfulness to original instruments. Participants study the temperament and cultural milieu of the age and then make music that is buoyed with the period's sensibility as well.

Andrew Porter, writing in the *New Yorker,* has given this festival several reviews, noting that the string players are "probably as good as any in the world. The winds are in tune. The old self-consciousness has been replaced by confidence, by character and, beyond that, by something one might almost describe as a philosophy intelligently and joyfully embraced. For there is more to Aston Magna than authentic instruments, stylistic insights, and technical ability."

BERKSHIRE CHORAL FESTIVAL
413-229-8526.
Mail: 245 N. Undermountain Rd., Sheffield, MA 01257.
Concert Shed, Berkshire School, Rte. 41, Sheffield.
Season: July and August.
Tickets: $15–$18.

It started out as an experiment in mixing amateur, semi-pro, and professional singers into a makeshift chorus whose work together culminated in a single concert. Success there has led the Berkshire Choral Festival some 12 years later to evolve into a summer-long, professional quality chorus that can be counted on for some stirring moments.

Each summer now brings a five-concert Berkshire celebration featuring 200 voices, the Springfield Symphony, powerful soloists and conductors, all at one of the loveliest preparatory schools in New England, the Berkshire School (Rte. 41, Sheffield; 413-229-8511). *Berkshire Eagle* critic Elsbet Wayne found the closing performance of their '93 Berkshire season "refreshingly boisterous," praising the chorus for its "beautiful diction." This is still something of a pick-up chorus, now being remade annually with a corps of 200 experienced amateurs and some professionals.

BERKSHIRE OPERA COMPANY
413-243-1343
Cranwell Opera House, Rte. 20, Lenox.
Season: July and August.
Tickets: $30–$38

After nearly a decade, first under founder-director Rex Hearn and now conductor Joel Revzen, the Berkshire Opera seems stronger than ever. Performing once again in Cranwell's chapel, where they got their start, this talented group has won praise from both audiences and serious critics alike for their English-language renditions of chamber opera.

There are discoveries to be made here, and among them recently was Stockbridge resident Maureen O. Flynn, whom Hearn initially heard singing at the First Congregational Church in Lee and who has since gone from the Berkshire Opera to the Metropolitan and a brilliant international career.

Recent offerings have included Carlisle Floyd's *Susannah*, and Mozart's *Don Giovanni*. "Mozart was well served," wrote the *New York Times* critic of the latter production. "The Berkshire Opera Company fills a needed role in the rich summer life of the region, offering artfully prepared chamber operas."

NATIONAL MUSIC CENTER
413-637-4718
40 Kemble St., Lenox.
Season: Year-round concerts and workshops.
Prices and schedules to be announced.

Already overflowing with musical culture, Berkshire's cup nearly runneth over as we become the locale for the National Music Center. The brainchild of aging rocker Joey Dee (whose big hits were "The Peppermint Twist" and "Shout"), and spearheaded by the godfather of rock 'n' roll, the ageless Dick Clark, the National Music Center is the "campus" of the nonprofit National Music Foundation. Located on the outskirts of Lenox village, the Center has a twofold mission: "1. To educate the public about American music, in order to preserve our nation's musical heritage. 2. To provide for the retirement of professionals from the fields of music, radio and recording, with provision made for those who can't retire on their own."

Educational facilities will include an interactive museum, performance centers, a library and archive, a radio broadcast facility, and a recording studio. The center will offer workshops in every American music style, giving Berkshire a music balance unparalleled in modern country life.

The National Music Center's introductory offering, "An Evening with Dick Clark and Special Guests" in late September 1993 began with Karen Park, soprano, followed by tenor Ricardo Tamura, then went to such diverse performers as the jazz guitar specialist Larry Coryell and rocker Joey Dee and his wife, Lois Lee. The finish was downwright inspirational, with Arlo Guthrie —

backed up by son Abe's band, Xavier — leading the crowd in singing patriarch Woody Guthrie's "This Land is Your Land."

Watch for the center's growing and continuing calendar of concerts, workshops, and lectures.

NORFOLK CHAMBER MUSIC FESTIVAL
203-542-3000; 203-432-1966 off season.
During season: Norfolk, CT 06058; off season: 96 Wall St., New Haven, CT 06520.
Rtes. 44 & 272, in Norfolk.
Season: Mid-June–Mid-Aug.
Tickets: $8–$24. Subscription for 5 concerts $32–$90.

From mid-June to mid-August at Norfolk, visiting virtuosos perform regularly, among them the Tokyo String Quartet and the Vermeer Quartet. Orchestral and choral works are also featured. Concurrent with this series of concerts, Yale's Summer School of Music runs a program of classes for its students and regularly schedules recitals by young professional musicians — recitals that are open to the public free of charge (currently on Thursday evenings and Saturday mornings).

The setting is superb. Arrive early and you can picnic on the grounds of the elegant 75-acre estate on which the music center has grown. Norfolk's Music Shed is enclosed and beautifully crafted of acoustically resonant hardwoods. Some balcony seats along the sides may pose a viewing problem, but the sound is good everywhere, and the ticket prices are somewhat lower than at Berkshire County's more widely known music events.

For fall '93, Norfolk initiated a special series of Indian Summer concerts in October, effectively stretching their season over another month. In the southern foothills of the Berkshires, Norfolk is a quiet alternative to Tanglewood, offering chamber music at its finest.

MUSIC MOUNTAIN
203-824-7126.
Falls Village, CT 06031.
On Music Mountain Rd., off Rte. 7 opposite Housatonic Valley High School.
Season: Mid-June to Labor Day.
Tickets: $15.

Founded in 1930 by Chicago Symphony concertmaster Jacques Gordon, Music Mountain is the oldest continuing chamber music festival in America. In the acoustically excellent, 325-seat Gordon Hall, set on a woody hilltop, concerts are given by the resident summer group, the Manhattan String Quartet, and by visiting guest artists.

OTHER MUSIC

Astonishingly, there is much, much more music in the Berkshires: choral music, lyric theatre, opera, jazz, "world" music, other chamber concerts, and folk music series.

In **South County**, the **Berkshire Bach Society** (413-229-2224) has turned an auspicious opening into a fine regular series, both highly acclaimed and popular. Dedicated to the rediscovery of the largely unknown cantatas of Bach, the society offers lectures at the Albert Schweitzer Center in Great Barrington and performances at various area churches, September through May. New in South County — perhaps to help fill the void left by the unfortunate demise of L'Orchestra — is **Berkshire Friends of Music** (413-243-9744; 518-794-8151; P.O. Box 2397, Lenox, MA 01240), who fashioned an inaugural '93-'94 season of three concerts with various orchestras. First up was an all-Haydn program with the St. Cecilia Chamber Orchestra of Albany, then some Beethoven and others from our own Berkshire Symphony, of Williamstown, and some Haydn and Stravinsky from the Atlantic Sinfonietta of New York City. **Berkshire Chamber Music Society** (413-269-7190; Box 586, Otis, MA 01253) has a half-dozen fine seasons behind it, most recently offering six programs, including one by the 22-member Kiev Chamber Orchestra. Their season runs from late October through late May. **Simon's Rock College of Bard** (413-528-0771; Alford Rd., Great Barrington) is one of the liveliest promoters of professional music in South County, with various events during the academic year. Most recently, under the aegis of **South Berkshire Concerts**, they hosted the Da Vinci String Quartet. The **Curtisville Consortium** (413-698-2618) takes its name from the hamlet of Interlaken in Stockbridge, which was originally settled as Curtisville. The Consortium is a group of Boston Symphony musicians and guest artists who present a five-week-long series of concerts each summer at the Congregational Church in Interlaken. **Stockbridge Chamber Concerts** (413-449-8252), another well-received series, once again played their summer season at Searles Castle, Great Barrington.

In **Central County**, chamber music can also be enjoyed at the **Commonwealth Chamber Music Series** (413-637-3646) at the Town Hall Theatre in Lenox, and the **Armstrong Chamber Concerts**, at the same venue. And more chamber music is the feature of the **Richmond Performance Series** at the Richmond Congregational Church, Rte. 41. Each of these chamber music series features professional symphony orchestra veterans, making intimate music in special settings. **Berkshire Community College** (413-499-4660; West St., Pittsfield) offers a wide range of concerts, and the **Berkshire Museum**'s "Close Encounters with Music" series alternates between the Pittsfield home base and Great Barrington's St. James' Church, offering beautiful music and intriguing commentary by conductor/cellist Yehudi Hannani and guests. The **Berkshire Lyric Theatre**, under the direction of Robert Blafield, continues to play at a variety of county venues, including the Berkshire Museum and the Lenox Town Hall.

In **North County**, **Williams College** (413-597-3131) alone offers enough music to keep anyone humming, and their season kicks into high gear right after Tanglewood finishes. Among recent offerings have been performances by the *Williams Choral Society* at Chapin Hall (413-597-3146). Most of Williams' many musical offerings are under the auspices of the Williams Department of Music (413-597-2736; Bernhard Music Center). The *Thompson Concert Series* at Williams has recently offered Benefit Street, an original-instrument group playing 17th- and 18th-century music. The *Williams' Group for 20th Century Music* has lately produced concerts of note, starting the fall '93 season with a performance by the Florida State Brass Quintet. *Williamstown Chamber Concerts* (413-458-8273; P.O. Box 287, Williamstown, MA 01267) continues its winning ways, most recently presenting a song recital by baritone Kevin McMillan at the Clark Art Institute. ". . . McMillan delighted the audience with extraordinary brilliance and smoothness and a dynamic range that seemed endless," wrote *Eagle* critic Elsbet Wayne.

Also playing frequently in the Williamstown area is the *Berkshire Symphony*, that eighty-member North County orchestra led by conductor Ronald L. Feldman. Besides the already-mentioned Williamstown Chamber Concerts, the Clark Art Institute features other major musical performances as well; see the Clark's entry under "Museums" in this chapter.

Over in North Adams, *North Adams State College* (413-664-4511) sponsors a variety of musical events, among them, the *Smith House Concert Series*, which recently featured a recital by pianist Laura Kargul playing works by Beethoven, Chopin, Wagner, and Liszt.

Just *Outside the County*, in the Berkshire hilltown of Charlemont (Rte. 2, Franklin County), the *Mohawk Trail Concerts* (413-625-9511; 75 Bridge St., Shelburne Falls, MA 01370) presented a season of informal classical concerts at the Federated Church. In nearby Columbia County, NY, *Tannery Pond Concerts* (518-794-7887; Box 446, New Lebanon, NY 12125) most recently hosted that very popular Canadian ensemble, the St. Lawrence String Quartet. In adjacent Spencertown, NY, the *Spencertown Academy*'s concerts (518-392-3693; Box 80, Spencertown, NY 12165) are among the Berkshire region's neatest. Said the *Berkshire Eagle* of Spencertown, "Acoustically the hall is a little gem, and each featured artist, cognizant of these attractive surroundings, radiates a feeling of `I am happy to be performing here.'"

NIGHTLIFE

When the sun sets on Berkshire, what was quiet becomes quieter — except at the dozens of clubs across the county. From videotheques to cabarets, from hard rock to softly sung madrigals, nightlife in the Berkshires will satisfy most and truly please many. Here are the clubs, together with a few bands and individuals who've performed recently. Check the local papers for current listings.

Members of the Berkshire-based Big Waaagh Scratch Band get down with their instruments, including washboard.

Jonathan Sternfield

Starting in <u>**South County**</u>, in Ashley Falls, *The Lantern* (413-229-0088; Clayton Rd.), describes itself as "the best little bar in the Berkshires — where there are no strangers, just friends you haven't met yet." The Lantern hosts groups like the Blue Rhythm Band and Bandanna, and on the side, runs the occasional pool tournament. In Sheffield, the *Sheffield Pub* (413-229-8880; Rte. 7), often hosts karaoke nights, where you can sing your soul out, or just throw back a cold one. In Egremont, the *Egremont Country Club* (413-528-4222; Rte. 23), has a fairly irregular schedule of good live bands up in the clubhouse, where you, too, are invited to shake your stuff. In Great Barrington, the *Steak Out* is the newest scene, featuring dancing "to the hottest tunes spun by the best DJ's," six nights a week. At *Dos Amigos* (413-528-0084; 250 Stockbridge Rd., Rt. 7), the Vikki True Band is a regular, the singing is soulful, the scene lively. Just down the road, at *Spencer's* (413-528-3828; Jnct. of Rtes. 7 and 183), owner David Thorne and his jazz trio play dance music on Friday and Saturday nights (and then do a jazz brunch on Sunday mornings!). Way out in New Boston, at the *Silverbrook Cafe* (413-258-4597), "The Best Little Honky Tonk West of the Clam River," a whole lotta shakin' goes on, with bands like Stormy Weather. Nearby, in Housatonic, at the *Macano Inn* (413-274-6636; Rte. 183), a steady diet of driving rock keeps the blues away, with regular live bands such as the Equalites and Shockra. Over in Stockbridge, the *Lion's Den* under the Red Lion Inn (413-298-5545), presents almost nightly live entertainment of high quality, such as folksinger David Grover. On a hot night, the subterranean Lion's Den is thick with music, cigarette smoke, laughter, banter, and dish clatter, each apparently competing for center stage. Around the corner, at *Michael's* (413-298-3530; Elm St.) occasional live bands, like Ruby, liven the otherwise staid Stockbridge soundscape. *Oak n' Spruce* (413-243-3500; South Lee), frequently features live bands in their Bear Tree on Saturday nights, and almost always has karaoke or dancing to DJ-spun music. And over in East Lee, the *Belden Tavern* (413-243-4660; Rte. 20) regularly features Arnie Hays and the Belden Band, playing big band and swing.

In <u>*Central County*</u>, the *Candlelight Inn* (413-637-1555; 53 Walker Street), has recently featured Ed Linderman singing his "Songs for a Summer Night." Just down the block, the *Roseborough Grill* (413-637-2700; 83 Church St.), offers the town's most regular and intriguing cabaret, with players like Mike Schiffer and Minna Bromberg, as well as Michael Haynes playing dinner music and a late show by the Sweet Tarts. *Lenox 218* restaurant (413-637-4218; 218 Main St., Lenox) often features Piano Joe tickling the ivories on Friday and Saturday evenings. *Cranwell* (413-637-1364; Rt. 20), sometimes offers dinner music on weekend evenings, with the likes of Mike Schiffer.

For lovers of folk and down-home country music, *Bonny Rigg Inn* (413-623-8784; in Becket on Jacobs Ladder Rd.) frequently can stir something up, as can Pittsfield's *Itam Lodge* (413-443-7134; Waubeek Rd.). *Jack's Place* (413-442-0253; Rte. 7, Lanesborough), gets to percolatin' now and again, offering live country music Thursday through Sunday. But the hottest club for down-home music is the *Home Club* (413-655-2206; up on Rte. 8, Hinsdale) where solid touring acts are booked, where you can see Gloria Curtis and the Country Classics, Easy Livin', and even Box Car Willie.

In Pittsfield itself, the mood is mostly upbeat. *Jay's* (413-442-0767; 1220 North St.) is one of the hotter clubs, booking bands like Leon Savage, offering frequent comedy, karaoke and a massive infusion of videos. Also fun is the *Misty Moonlight Diner* (413-442-0028; 505 East St.), which offers karaoke on Friday nights. Mellowest of the clubs is probably *La Cocina* (413-499-4027; Wahconah St.). Though the fine musicians, such as Michael Haynes, provide dynamic listening, the crowd can occasionally eclipse the performers. Wednesday is usually open-mike night.

Up the mountain, in the town of Washington, lie two of the county's most spacious rock clubs, *Woody's Roadhouse* (413-623-8302), and *Bucksteep Manor* (413-623-5535; off Washington Mountain Rd.). Woody's is vast, the rock music driving (like Leon Savage), the crowds youngish. Action is nightly in summer, weekend nights only in winter. Bucksteep has cut back considerably on their rock fare, heading toward a softer, more country beat, with bands like Dooley Austin and Shake 'n' Bake. They also hosted a Squeeze Box Convention, something we'll want to hear next time around. In summer, occasional outdoor concerts on their lawns mark a high note in the Berkshire rock calendar. Out in Dalton, the *Hard Hat Bar and Grill* (413-684-9787; 26 Daly Ave.) books some wicked acts, recently offering Leon Savage.

In <u>*North County*</u>, the *Blarney Room* at Brodie Mountain (413-443-4752; Rte. 7, New Ashford) and *Kelly's Irish Pub* both present occasional live music. *The Springs* (413-458-3465; Rte. 7, New Ashford) offers a pianist at the grand piano, on Saturdays. Up Williamstown way, the *Williams Inn* (413-458-9371; Main St., Williamstown) is still hosting the popular Walt Lehman and his band, playing jazz. And during the summer, the finest late evening entertainment in the county might be found at various Williamstown restaurants in the form of the *Williamstown Theatre Festival Cabaret* (413-597-3400), a combination of theater apprentices, students and current WTF stars; call for current information.

Just *Outside the County*, over in Northampton, the *Iron Horse Music Hall* (413-586-8686; 20 Center St.) presents the region's best and most regular folk and jazz, offering concerts with such greats as Aztec Two Step and Acoustic Junction. Nearby, *Pearl Street* (413-584-7771; 10 Pearl St.) presents the hot stuff, such as Johnny Winter, with the accent on dancing.

Folk Festivals in Hilltown Farms

Just over the border, where the Berkshire Hills still run tall and majestic, a couple of major folk festivals have been drawing thousands of fans from all over America. For over 20 years now, the Rothvoss Farm in Hillsdale, NY, has been hosting the *Winterhawk Bluegrass & Folk Festival.* This is a big, three-day-long music fest in the country, held mid-July, and that old tribal feeling is quickly established. Recent standout artists have included Alison Kraus and Union Station, Jimmy Martin, and Riders in the Sky.

Just a week later, at another Hillsdale farm, the Long Hill Farm, the *Falcon Ridge Folk Festival* is coming on to its sixth season. This is another three-day music fest, with music almost nonstop, around-the-clock, day and night for every minute the gathering is on. Falcon Ridge covers its folk end of the deal quite well, with groups like the Fast Folk Musical Revue, but the festival goes way beyond in its musical offerings, most recently mixing in pop, blues, gospel, rock, funk, metal, jazz, reggae, New Age, and hip-hop. In between, musicians and ordinary folk were making up new forms of music, then improvising. Most recently, highlights of the planned fare included the glistening pop harmonies of the Story; stirring pop gospel from the Salt and Pepper Gospel Choir; and gut-wrenching blues from the soul of Rick Ilowite.

THEATER

WILLIAMSTOWN THEATRE FESTIVAL
413-597-3400.
Box 517, Williamstown, MA 01267.
1000 Main St.
Season: Summer only.
Tickets: $11–$28.

"Miracles every summer since 1955," the *Boston Globe* once wrote, and the miracles continue. On Berkshire summer nights, nowhere are the stars brighter than on stage at the Williamstown Theatre Festival. Here in a typical show you'll find the likes of Broadway and Hollywood luminaries Elaine May, Marsha Mason, Dick Cavett, Blythe Danner,

Michael York is challenged by Linda Purl, in Williamstown Theatre Festival's production of Ingmar Bergman's adaptation of Henrick Ibsen's A Doll's House.

Richard Feldman, courtesy the Williamstown Theatre Festival

Edward Herrmann, Richard Thomas, and Christopher Reeve — all performing live in the region's most sophisticated summer theater.

People Magazine once put it this way: "The showbiz capital of the U.S. may, for once, be on neither coast. The Williamstown Theatre Festival could boast the most powerful concentration of acting talent any place this summer."

Each summer, in addition to full-scale productions with first-rate sets and costumes on the Main Stage, WTF offers other more intimate theater experiences. There are the four productions of works-in-progress mounted at the Other Stage, which most recently included the U.S. premiere of Joanna Glass's *If We Are Women*, starring the silky smooth Blythe Danner. Regular festival activities also include special events at the Clark, late-night musical cabarets, occasionally providing surprise cameo appearances by Main Stage celebrities like Dick Cavett, inveterate songster and raconteur. There are Staged Readings; Museum Pieces, at the Williams College Museum of Art; Act I Performance Projects by the WTF young actor training ensemble, at work in Goodrich Hall on the Williams Campus; and a new Children's Theatre program presenting two original plays for pre-teens and their families. Most recently, the last two were adaptations of Kipling's "The Elephant's Child," and that all-time classic, "The Beginning of Armadillos."

And for the naturalist in you, WTF offers the Free Theatre, outdoors in the glades behind Mt. Greylock High School, Rte. 7 South. Here's a rare opportunity for a free theatrical picnic party, for you, your family and friends. You supply the lunch, WTF will supply the pastoral setting and complimentary, first-rate theater.

It's no mistake, then, that *Newsweek* ranked WTF as "the best of all American summer theaters," with "the cream of America's acting crop."

**SHAKESPEARE & COM-
PANY AT THE MOUNT**
413-637-3353 box office;
    413-637-1197 off season.
The Mount, Plunkett St.
    Lenox, MA 01240.
On Plunket St. in Lenox,
    near southern jct. of Rtes.
    7 & 7A.
Season: Summer only.
Tickets: $15–$25.

Shakespeare is alive and well in the Berkshires, alive, that is, on stage in Lenox, at Edith Wharton's palatial estate, the Mount (described in this chapter under "Historic Houses"). Shakespeare & Company has made splendid use of the Mount's rolling lawn, performing most of their plays outdoors on a stage built in a glade, against the lovely stone wall of a rose garden. Seating is either on your own blanket or on the company's low-slung aluminum chairs.

Under the powerful artistic guidance of English actor-director Tina Packer, her husband, actor-director Dennis Krausnick, and her associate, Scottish vocal maestro Kristen Linklater, Shakespeare & Company has brought new light, feeling, and clarity to Shakespeare's plays, making the works much more accessible to many people.

A bit of the zany, al fresco action in The Tempest, *as staged by Shakespeare & Company, at the Mount.*

Courtesy Shakespeare & Co

Part of the dramatic impact derives from the actors' ability to treat the audience as their alter ego, always privy to secrets of the drama. The plays are staged all around the seating area; intimacy with the action is inevitable, with stage and lighting design creating magical effects.

The company's inspired clowning is magical, too. Says Tina Packer, "The function of the clowns is of the utmost importance in Shakespeare's plays. The influence of *commedia dell'arte* on Elizabethan theater, with its knockabout and improvised humor, cannot be overemphasized. Because of the inordinate amount of 'seriousness' that has been attached to the 'Bard,' much of the sheer joy and fun of Shakespeare has been lost for modern audiences." Not so at the Mount, where you're in for a good time.

Wrote the *New York Times* critic Ben Brantley of the company's performance of *A Midsummer Night's Dream*: "The overall result is vulgar, overscaled and loud. And it works. . . . There are few productions of Shakespearean comedy in which the meaning of every joke (whether intended by Shakespeare or not) reads so clearly, and the audience was responsive to each one."

Having established a singularly rich tradition at the Mount, Shakespeare & Company has significantly enriched *that*, developing three new theaters — the 200-seat, outdoor Oxford Court; the 75-seat indoor Wharton theater, inside the Mount; and the 108-seat, indoor Stables Theatre. A recent summer saw five Shakespearean productions, four Wharton-oriented plays, and four or five modern plays. In addition, a Fall Foliage Festival presented dramatic adaptations of Wharton's *The Custom of the Country*, and "Kerfol: A Ghost Story," and a dramatic adaptation of Hawthorne's *Scarlet Letter*.

The company has toured, for performances and workshops, to Denver, Toronto, and other cities, and under the aegis of Joe Papp's New York Shakespeare Festival, they have also taken productions from the Mount to Brooklyn's Prospect Park.

In our opinion, Shakespeare & Company is a "must see" for locals and visitors alike.

BERKSHIRE THEATRE FESTIVAL
413-298-5576; 413-298-5536 off season.
Box 797, Stockbridge, MA 01262.
East Main St., Rte. 102, Stockbridge.
Season: Summer only.

In 1887, architect Stanford White completed his design for the Stockbridge Casino Company, created for the "establishment and maintenance of a place for a reading room, library and social meeting." Forty years later, when the structure had fallen into disuse, Mabel Choate, daughter of Ambassador Joseph H. Choate of Stockbridge, gave the building to the Three Arts Society, which

The BTF world premiere of Mark St. Germain's witty Camping with Henry and Tom *featured (L to R) Ralph Waite (as President Warren G. Harding), John Cunningham (as Henry Ford) and Robert Prosky (as Thomas Alva Edison).*

Charles Erickson, courtesy Berkshire Theatre Festival

Tickets: Main Stage, $15–$30; Unicorn Theatre, $12, Children's Theatre, $3.50. Gift shop.

in turn moved the Casino to its present site at the foot of Yale Hill and rented it to Alexander Kirkland and F. Cowles Strickland, who opened the Berkshire Playhouse in 1928.

Since that time, the Berkshire Playhouse, later renamed Berkshire Theatre Festival, has fostered the development and presentation of American drama. Major works by nearly every American playwright of note have been performed here, including plays by Lillian Hellman, Tennessee Williams, Eugene O'Neill and Thornton Wilder. The playhouse produced Wilder's *Our Town* and *The Skin of Our Teeth*, with Wilder himself playing featured roles.

In the summer of 1930, a budding actress named Katherine Hepburn came to Stockbridge to further her training at the Berkshire Playhouse. She first appeared in Barrie's *The Admirable Crichton*, and then was given the lead in a play called *A Romantic Young Lady*.

Other players arrived in Stockbridge already closer to stardom. Ethel Barrymore, James Cagney, Tallulah Bankhead, Ruth Gordon, Gene Hackman, Anne Bancroft, Dustin Hoffman, Al Pacino, Frank Langella, and Joanne Woodward are among the many prominent actors and actresses who have played the Berkshire Theatre Festival. And true to the policy that led to Katherine Hepburn's debut at BTF, and to Montgomery Clift's at age 13, the festival continues to encourage promising newcomers.

The last two decades have been a period of growth and refocusing for BTF. In the spring of 1976, the building was entered on the National Register of Historic Places. Since then, gradual refurbishment has continued, with a new paint job, and most noticeably, all new seats, making the theater truly comfortable at last.

Summer of '93 saw a changing of the guard at BTF, Emmy Award–winning artistic director Richard Dunlap stepping down and Julianne Boyd stepping in. Boyd opened with her own *Sweet & Hot*, the songs of Harold Arlen. Next up was a world premiere of Mark St. Germain's witty *Camping with Henry and Tom*. The season finished with the very powerful Hugh Whitemore drama, *Breaking the Code,* and the sly Noel Coward comedy, *Blithe Spirit*.

The Theatre Festival has expanded its educational and rehearsal facilities, principally upon the gift of the Lavan Center (formerly Beaupre Art School), a few miles north of the playhouse. Interns and apprentices live at the center and rehearse there, while pursuing a program of classes in acting, voice, movement, and design.

BTF also features shows at its 100-seat Unicorn Theatre, a showcase for younger artists. These are becoming increasingly substantial, most recently being highlighted by the painterly *Mississippi Nude*, by John Reaves, one artist's life in living color. A Summer Readings Festival also sees staged readings of important new plays and musicals, again at the Unicorn. And for the local community, BTF has several outreach programs, offering discount tickets to the elderly and dramatic production of prize-winning plays written by local grade schoolers.

Altogether, BTF seems more robust than ever, more completely fulfilling its self-prescribed mission. Year after year, we return to Stanford White's Stockbridge Casino with deeper love, admiration, and thanks for the Berkshire Theatre Festival.

Members of the Ensemble of Remscheid, Germany, perform in John Byfne's The Slab Boys, *another Berkshire Public Theatre international treat.*

Susanne Mies, courtesy the Berkshire Public Theatre.

BERKSHIRE PUBLIC THEATRE
413-445-4634 & 413-445-4631.
Box 860, Pittsfield, MA 01202.
30 Union St., in the center of town.
Season: Year-round.
Tickets: $10–$18, students & senior citizens $2 off.
Gift shop.

Iris and Frank Bessel and friends continue their dynamic doings in downtown Pittsfield. A theatrical powerhouse of local dramatic talent, the Berkshire Public Theatre has continued to strive toward its goal of being the county's only year-round, regional repertory theatre, and Frank Bessel is central to this endeavor. Under his leadership, BPT has always attracted talent. In the grand old Union Square Vaudeville Theatre, opened in 1912 and more recently purchased for the BPT by the city, Bessel's group has a work-play space, which they are intent upon restoring, expanding, and sharing as funds allow.

Such local artists as the Berkshire Lyric Theatre, Mixed Company, the Robbins-Zust Family Marionettes, the Olga Dunn Dance Company, and the Albany Berkshire Ballet have all used the BPT stage to good effect.

Theatrically, Bessel's company has evolved tremendously over the years. Among the most penetrating of its recent offerings — appropriately in its new Saturday Late Night Adult Theatre series — was Maria Irene Fornes' *Mud*, a relentless, Becket-bleak vision where life has no winners. Whatever one thinks of individual shows at the Berkshire Public Theatre, it's hard not to applaud the general enterprise. For bringing powerful year-round theater to the Berkshires, Frank Bessel and friends deserve a heartfelt Bravo!

The dynamic Hannibal Peterson performs his original music-theatre piece, Diary of an African American, *produced by the innovative Music-Theatre Group.*

Clemens Kalischer, courtesy the Music-Theatre Group

MUSIC THEATRE GROUP/LENOX ARTS CENTER
413-298-5504; 212-924-3108 off season.
During season: Box 1396 Stockbridge, MA 01262.
Off season: 29 Bethune St., New York, NY 10014.
Season: Jun.–Jul.
Tickets: $15–$20.

For their innovative and penetrating explorations of music-theatre, the Music Theatre Group/Lenox Arts Center has won 20 Obie awards in New York, and they bring to the Berkshires a world-class adventure for all lovers of music and drama. Under the leadership of producing director Lyn Austin, the group has tackled difficult, esoteric works and created ones that are close to sublime.

"The Music-Theatre Group blazes trails. . . ." raved the *Boston Globe*, and in the summer of '94 they are presenting a number of shows, including Ann Sinclair's *Gospel*, sung principally by Ann herself, and *Kartunes*, by poet Cornelius Eady. Productions are now staged at the venerable St. Paul's Church in Stockbridge and the Lenox Club in Lenox. Theater here is minimally staged; the emphasis is more on script and musical development as many of these works prepare for a New York run.

Said the *New York Times*: "The Music-Theatre Group/Lenox Arts Center has produced one of the most innovative and original bodies of work in American theatre."

OTHER THEATER

There are more than a dozen other theater companies in and about Berkshire.

In *South County*, the biggest little theater in the world is *Mixed Company* (413-528-2320; at the Granary, 37 Rosseter St., Great Barrington), where fall-off-your-seat comedy alternates with moving drama. Under the direction of Joan Ackermann and Gillian Seidl, Mixed Company has built a solid following, and there is often competition for the theater's few dozen seats. Ackermann's award-winning *Zara Spook and Other Lures* premiered here, as did her droll *Bed and Breakfast*, in which she played an addled Mrs. Digby. The company occasionally features revivals, like *Greater Tuna*, a laugh-till-you-cry look at the foibles of the Greater Tuna, Texas, radio listening area. More fun than a barrel of monkeys. And with considerably greater charm, too. Recent Mixed Company standouts have included John Goodber's *Happy Jack*, starring Bruce Mac-Donald and Gillian Seidl, and Joan Ackermann's award-winning *Stanton's Garage*.

The *Central County* theater scene has never been livelier. The *Berkshire Community College Players* regularly appear at the Robert Boland Theater at BCC (413-499-0886; West St., Pittsfield). *The Town Players* (413-443-9279) also occasionally perform at either BCC or the Berkshire Museum, and in a recent season, they presented *Barefoot In the Park*.

North County is especially theatrical. Besides the Williamstown Theater Festival, Williamstown has other theater companies, loosely grouped in a consortium called *Summer Stages*. These include the *Calliope Theatre Company*, the Starlight Stage Youth Theatre, and Thespis. Calliope Theatre Company (413-458-5024) was founded by four local female playwrights, and continues to offer innovative drama, usually on tour. The *Starlight Stage Youth Company* (413-458-4273), features young area residents who perform at the First Congregational Church. *Thespis* (413-458-8266) is a local non-Equity company that also performs at the Clark.

After such a busy summer season of theater, the fall-winter slack is picked up by *Williamstheatre*, the Williams College theater group (413-597-2342; Adams Memorial Theatre), producing impressive revivals of plays by the likes of Brecht and Becket; and by the drama department at *North Adams State College* (413-664-4511), whose fare recently ran from Ibsen to Rodgers and Hammerstein. Finally, the *Williamstown Community Theatre* (413-458-5833) performs two or three productions a year, an annual cabaret, one-act plays and an occasional radio play.

Outside the County, in neighboring Chatham, New York, just west of Central Berkshire, the *Mac-Haydn Theatre* (518-392-9292; Rte. 203), has been offering 15-week-long summer seasons of robust Broadway musicals since 1969.

Productions are staged in the round, and their high energy casts are guaranteed to deliver a supercharge of musical theater. Less than truly sophisticated and a bit out of the way, but usually a whole lot of fun. In New Lebanon, NY, at the *Theater Barn* (518-794-8989; Rte. 20), producers Joan and Abe Phelps zero in on musical comedy, with an occasional murderous dose of Agatha Christie thrown in. *Proctor's* in Schenectady (518-382-1083), and the *Egg* in Albany (518-473-1061), both provide stages for national acts, shows and dramas. Up in Bennington, Vermont, the *Oldcastle Theater Company* (802-447-0564; at Southern Vermont College) can always be counted on for some fun, such as *Nunsense: The Second Coming*. Back in Massachusetts, *StageWest* in Springfield (413-781-2340) provides top quality theatrical experiences, and the tiny *Miniature Theatre of Chester* (413-354-6565; in the Town Hall), has hosted some large-as-life drama, such as the telling instants dramatized in Emmy Award-winning, West Stockbridge playwright Lee Kalcheim's *Moving*.

SEASONAL EVENTS

There are a number of special Berkshire events tuned to the weather, and somehow the Berkshire year wouldn't unfold properly without them. In this context, we long for the return of the full-fledged Great Barrington Fair, an event which provides every camp and nostalgia lover a chance to step out of time and become bit player in the carny drama of yesteryear. Till the horses come home to Barrington, here are a few others of the best seasonal events, all still clearly worth your attention.

Berkshire Crafts Fair is a mid-August event, held at Monument Mountain Regional High School (413-528-3346; Rte. 7, between Stockbridge and Great Barrington). Top local and regional craftspeople offer their extraordinary creations, from handmade paper to handblown glass, from handwoven clothing to exotic woodenware.

The Best of the Berkshires Festival is Pittsfield's newest celebration of county-wide talents, in many fields, from music to dance, from food to drink. Held in mid-August, the festival brought a jolt of life to North Street, luring thousands to the traffic-free party. The Berkshire Public Theatre Children's Ensemble performed, as did acclaimed magician Timothy Wenk. This party looks like a comer.

Big Apple Circus declares: forget the three rings; less is more! With one ring under a colorful big top, this international troupe has been making an annual summer landing of late at the Jenifer House grounds in Great Barrington, wowing everyone who takes in the show. Each year, a totally new show is created around a specific theme — in recent seasons celebrating Coney Island and an adventure around the world. With acts from dozens of nations globally, this circus also brings the world right to you, high-lighting performers of enormous strength, dexterity, and balance. So remarkable are some of these showpeople, you come away not only enter-tained, but awed as well. And the band plays on: live music from the Big Apple Band, orchestrating from atop the curtained entry to the one ring. One ring? But what a ring! Modeled on the opulent spectacles of the Belle Epoque, when circus arts were on a par with opera and ballet, the Big Apple has a quaint elegance entirely absent in a larger circus. Great fun; highly recommended.

A Christmas Carol by Charles Dickens has been read for many a Christmas now; and for some years, there's been a live reading at the Stockbridge Library. Usually a week or two before Christmas, this little-publicized event is worth watching for. The Berkshire Theatre Festival often has a hand in the casting of indigenous Scrooges and Tiny Tims. Outstanding dramatizations of the story are staged annually by the Berkshire Public Theater, in Pittsfield. And God Bless You, one and all.

Fireworks over Stockbridge Bowl are spectacular because of echoes from the hills. The biggest bangs and most colorful starbursts come from Tangle-wood, on the Fourth of July, and following the 1812 Overture at the end of "Tanglewood on Parade," a highlight of the BSO Berkshire season.

Greylock Rambles are hikes and climbs to and around the lofty top of Mount Greylock in North County. Sponsored by the Appalachian Mountain Club and the Williams College Outing Club, the walks are often narrated by well-informed guides. Best time to go? Fall foliage, of course. In early October, the town of Adams sponsors an annual Mt. Greylock Ramble Weekend, with concerts, hayrides, and apple pie downtown, then a hike up the big hill.

Halloween Walk Through Ice Glen is a Stockbridge tradition, though inher-ent dangers give the event an uncertain future. By torchlight, residents explore the rocky hidden valley in dramatic procession. A towering inferno of a bonfire usually follows, but nearly took the nearby gas station with it one Halloween.

Harvest Festival at the Berkshire Botanical Garden, Stockbridge (described under "Nature Preserves" in the *Recreation* chapter) is an early-October event packed with seasonal goodies such as cider and doughnuts, apples and pumpkins, haywagon and fire engine rides, plants and seeds, and mayhem of all sorts appealing to children and grownups of every persua-sion. The event has recently been expanded to two days, with a live perfor-mance tent featuring the likes of the Bluestars. Besides a great plant sale and flea market, a book sale and second-hand clothes mart, the festival has also attracted a greater number of craftspeople, selling an increasingly refined collection of handcrafts. A true highlight of the Berkshire calendar.

The Great Josh Billings RunAground is likely Berkshire's greatest one-day party, an athletic extravaganza that involves thousands of participants

Bicycle-powered cider mill, a highlight of the Harvest Festival, at Berkshire Botanical Garden, Stockbridge.

Jonathan Sternfield

and many more admiring, supportive spectators. This late September biking-canoeing-running triathlon takes its name from Lanesborough's Henry Wheeler Shaw, an inveterate 19th-century prankster, who fashioned something of a career for himself as a humorist, under the penname of Josh Billings. "If a fellow gets to going down hill, it seems as if everything were greased for the occasion," wrote Billings (more or less); and every fall at the RunAground the bike racers, shooting down that last hill on Rte. 183 to Stockbridge Bowl, prove how right old Josh was.

As you bike your butt off from Great Barrington, or paddle your back out around Stockbridge Bowl, or run yourself ragged climbing up to Tanglewood, or as you do all three as some Iron Men and Iron Women do, or as you watch a friend in the race, remember the words of Josh Billings: "Be sure you are right, then go ahead; but in case of doubt, go ahead anyway." After the race, there's a huge party at Tanglewood with food, drink, dancing, and Berkshire camaraderie.

The **Monument Mountain Author Climb** is a literary event commemorating the August day in 1851 when Melville, Hawthorne, Holmes, and friends scaled the Great Barrington peak. They imbibed a good deal of champagne, weathered a thunderstorm, read William Cullen Bryant's poem about the Indian maiden who threw herself in sorrow from the top, and began a lasting friendship. Watch the *Berkshire Eagle* in late July for an announcement.

Naumkeag at Christmas is extra-special, because that's when the Choates' Christmas decorations are taken out and the house is made to look ever so festive. Look in on a quiet turn-of-the-century Christmas; it might make yours a bit merrier. The historic home in Stockbridge (described under "Historic Homes" in this chapter) offers this opportunity to the public on an irregular basis.

Octoberzest is a new fall foliage festival of music and ballet, presented at Simon's Rock by the Barrington Performing Arts. Mixing and matching poets with musicians, dancers with actors into various ensemble pieces really does add a zesty melange to the southern Berkshire fall. We hope their sprout develops legs, showing up fall after fall.

Summerfest in Great Barrington has become a highlight on South County's early summer schedule. Held on a Saturday evening in mid-June, the last edition was the most successful ever, raising thousands of dollars for Hospice of South Berkshire, and raising the spirits of thousands who attended. With the entire downtown closed off to motor traffic, locals and visitors have a grand old time — listening to music, watching dance or magic, or grazing on various snack foods. Dozens of performers, from the Olga Dunn Dancers to the Bluestars contribute their time and talent, making this a community celebration of unqualified good cheer.

The Tea Ceremony at Great Barrington Pottery is a moving meditation, a highly stylized form of social communion for both the Tea Mistress and those she serves. Enter the *Chashitsu* (Japanese Ceremonial Teahouse and Formal Garden) at Richard Bennett's Great Barrington Pottery (described in the *Shopping* chapter) and you'll be taken back in time to 14th-century Japan. Leading with the concept of *wabi* — quiet simplicity — both the building and the slow-moving ceremony gently harmonize you. Bow, as you must, to enter the ceremonial washing area, and follow the Tea Guide's instruction in the proper ritual cleansing. Then follow her, bowing, through the low door into the teahouse itself, a structure four-and-a-half *tatami* mats in size. In the *tokonoma*, or ceremonial alcove, observe the calligraphy, and below it, note the grace, elegance, and appropriateness of the flower arrangement, a bouquet the Tea Mistress has made especially to meet the mood of this day. Then observe the silent power of the Tea

Jonathan Sternfield

Mistress, for whom serving tea is "The Way." The Tea Ceremony at Great Barrington Pottery offers the most gracious service in the Berkshires. Advance reservations are required (call 413-274-6259), as seating is limited.

The Tub Parade is one of Berkshire's oldest annual events, dating back to the Gilded Age, and for the last four years, the late September parade has been revived without a hitch. Actually, there were plenty of hitches, but they were supposed to be there, hitching show ponies to the ornate, flower-decked carts they pulled. Under the auspices of the Lenox Village Association and the Colonial Carriage and Driving Society, the Tub Parade gives a glimpse back into the fancy-free world of turn-of-the-century Berkshire, where dogs rode with ruffled collars right next to their masters. Brief but brilliant, the Tub Parade is a new high note in the Berkshire fall calendar.

VIDEO RENTALS

With one exception, the following video rental outlets stock the standard Hollywood movies and a smattering of foreign art titles. *Either/Or Bookstore* on North Street, Pittsfield, offers the county's most eclectic and artful selection of films. If you're tired of the same old Tinseltown fare, head for Pittsfield's Either/Or.

South County

Alice in Videoland (413-528-4451; 301 Stockbridge Rd. [Rte 7], Great Barrington).
Crandall's Video (413-269-7200; Rte. 23, Otis).
Impoco's (413-528-9162; 54 State Rd. [Rte. 7], Great Barrington).
Movie Connection (413-528-3585; 986 S. Main St., Great Barrington).
Patrick's Video (413-528-5575; 740 Main St., Gt. Barrington).
Shanahan's Elm St. Market (413-298-3634; Elm St., Stockbridge).
Video File (413-243-0468; 60 Main St., Lee).
Video Shed (413-243-0743; 152 West Park St., Lee).
West Stockbridge Video (413-232-7851; Main St., West Stockbridge).

Central County

Action Video (413-499-4208; 44 S. Main St. [Rte. 7], Lanesborough).
Blockbuster (413-443-3323; 455 Dalton Ave., Pittsfield).
East Street Video (413-443-2000; 10 Lyman, Pittsfield).

Either/Or Bookstore (413-499-1705; 122 North St., Pittsfield).
Master Darkroom and Video (413-443-9763; 758 Tyler St., Pittsfield. 413-499-7989; 89 West Housatonic St., Pittsfield).
Nejaime's Video Oasis (413-442-6660; 598 Pittsfield Rd., Lenox).
Nichols Pharmacy (413-443-2568; 274 Wahconah, Pittsfield).
Patrick's Video (413-442-6666; 200 West St., Pittsfield).
Plaza Video (413-443-0943; 444 West Housatonic St., Pittsfield).
Pontoosuc Video (413-445-7525; S. Main St., Lanesborough).
Variety Video (413-637-2046; Housatonic St., Lenox).
Video Studio 12 (413-447-7595; 180 Elm St., Pittsfield).

North County

Adams Video (413-663-5440; 85 Main St., North Adams).
Video Studio (413-743-7007; Myrtle, Adams).
Video Studio of North Adams (413-664-7880; North Adams Plaza, N. Adams).

CHAPTER FIVE
Pleasing the Palate
RESTAURANTS & FOOD PURVEYORS

As "The Inland New-port" of the Gilded Age, the Berkshires had its complement of haute cuisine dining rooms and gourmet purveyors. Today, some of the county's best restaurants are found in the "cottages" of that era, at Orleton, now called the Gateways, and at Blantyre and Wheatleigh. But there is great dining in more humble Berkshire settings, too, in pre-Revolutionary farmhouses, old mills and inns.

Jonathan Sternfield

Considering the choices, at Jodi's.

When we first migrated to the Berkshires in the early 1970s, the cuisine was largely American, with a dash of the continental. But now the area has become abundant in many other cuisines and is studded with Japanese (Kintaro, Shuji's, and Shogun), Chinese (four Pandas, a Chopsticks, and a Great Wall), and even a few Vietnamese (Truc Orient Express and Dragon) restaurants. Can Korean, Burmese, and Thai be far away?

And now, Berkshire has spawned a dining club with accompanying magazine — *Eat Out in the Berkshires* — and an annual food fest, "A Taste of the Berkshires," an early fall extravaganza that truly celebrates the bounty of the our region. A dozen of the county's top farm and agricultural producers together with scores of the region's best restaurants provide sumptuous outdoor grazing. (Another food festival, "A Taste of Chesterwood," has graced the estate at Glendale in recent years, but it may not be repeated annually.)

Four new books of Berkshire recipes have also been recently issued. The Williamstown Theatre Festival's *As You Like It* is a prize-winning compilation of the favorite recipes of the festival's stars, directors, writers, and associates, offering the likes of Paul Newman's Italian baked scrod. For the Berkshire County Historical Society's *Berkshire Victuals,* editor Janet Cook researched all county cooks, both dead and alive, and came up with scores of delicious local recipes. Two other Berkshire-based books, *The Red Lion Inn Cookbook* by Suzi Forbes Chase and *Best Recipes of Berkshire Chefs* by Miriam Jacobs, celebrate respectively the cuisine of the county's best-known inn and the culinary specialties of a range of fine contemporary county chefs.

The number of restaurants in the county is vast — upwards of 200. There are dozens of specialty food suppliers, too, engaging alternatives to supermarkets. We have concentrated on the establishments we found most interesting and most successful. In the spirit of candid reporting, we have risked critical judgments and hope you'll agree that the risk is worth taking. *De gustibus non disputandum.*

A dining experience has many dimensions. The food, of course, is primary, but we have also based our judgments on other obvious factors: the range of the menu, the decor and ambiance of the restaurant, the quality of service, and value for price.

We found it equally easy in Berkshire to spend $5 or $25 for a meal, and in several instances we preferred the bargain food — and the service and ambiance that came with it. Remember: we designate each restaurant with a price code, signifying the approximate cost of a meal, including appetizer, entrée, and dessert, but not cocktails, wine, tax, or tip. Restaurants with a prix-fixe menu are noted accordingly.

Reviews are organized first by section of the county, then alphabetically by town, then by restaurant name. Food purveyors are grouped alphabetically by type, then by name of establishment. Every entry appears in the general index, too.

Bon appétit!

Dining Price Codes

Inexpensive	Up to $10
Moderate	$10 to $20
Expensive	$20 to $35
Very Expensive	Over $35

Credit Cards

AE - American Express
CB - Carte Blanche
DC - Diner's Club
MC - MasterCard
V - Visa

Meals (Note: meals offered may vary seasonally.)

B - Breakfast;
L - Lunch
SB - Sunday Brunch
D - Dinner

RESTAURANTS SOUTH COUNTY

North Egremont

ELM COURT INN
413-528-0325.
Rte. 71, N. Egremont.
Closed: Mon. & Tues. in
  winter.
Price: Expensive.
Cuisine: Continental.
Serving: D.
Credit Cards: AE, MC, V.
Reservations: Recom-
  mended.
Special Features: Fireplaces.

The Elm Court hosts, Glee and Urs Bieri, continue its excellent Swiss tradition, bringing polish and imagination to the dining experience. Glee handles the pleasantly decorated dining room, insuring her guests' good time. Urs is Swiss and a former executive chef at the United Nations. At the Elm Court, he's able to concentrate his substantial culinary talents on far fewer meals, and the results are extraordinary.

Among starters, both the lobster bisque and French onion soup are superior, the onion soup featuring a first-class Gruyère lid, the bisque delicate yet distinct.

The Elm Court's wine list offers a nice range of French, Swiss, German, Italian, and California bottles, at surprisingly affordable prices. Many good wines are priced around $15, with some of the best up around $100. Service is superior — and our waitress could confidently tell us just what was in the fillet of sole's sauce — a light hollandaise with diced tomatoes and herbs. Fillet goulash Forestière is another clear winner, the goulash made with the tenderest filet mignon.

Although the menu at Elm Court appears to be strictly for carnivores, a request from a vegetarian friend of ours brought out a vegetable plate that was both beautiful and delicious, with grilled golden bell pepper, zucchini, string beans, and shiitake mushrooms, along with pasta in tomato basil sauce.

Awesome desserts are standard fare here. The whipped cream served on most of these is about the finest we've tasted — stiff, rich, and only slightly sweetened. The pear tart is at once hearty and delicate with a thick, cakey crust. A recently sampled berries and cream in a cookie bowl was a true devastator: the berries ripe and sweet, the cream rich and mellow, the cookie bowl simply divine. The dessert menu also offers eight cognacs, two Armagnacs, two ports, and four cordials. Call the Elm Court for a reservation on weekend and holiday nights.

South Egremont

BERKSHIRE PLACE
413-528-5620.
Main St., S. Egremont.

Berkshire Place has set up shop in a woody, Colonial space, providing a small cafe, delectable take-outs, and an outstanding catering ser-

Price: Inexpensive.
Cuisine: International.
Serving: B, L.
Credit Cards: MC, V.
Special Features: Catering;
  Take-out service.

vice. The food is imaginative and well prepared, of the finest ingredients. As a lunch or snack spot, Berkshire Place offers the gourmet alternative, for those who care enough to eat the very best.

For lunch, soups, salads, pâtés, hors d'oeuvres, entrées, and pastas are offered; or you can choose one of the sandwich specials of the day. You're in a win-win situation here; you can't make a poor choice. Our introduction was a superb Bombay chicken salad sandwich on a baguette, beautifully garnished with both fresh fruit and vegetables amd remarkable for its tender, flavorful chicken, its curry spicing, and chunky texture.

Had we succumbed to a delicacy in one of the display cases, we might have tried the likes of crabmeat stuffed mushrooms, Technicolor coleslaw, Texas crab cakes, or Maine lobster lasagna. Whatever we ate, or imagined eating, we loved. The whiskey cake we actually had for dessert was as moist and boozy as it gets.

THE EGREMONT INN
413-528-2111.
Old Sheffield Rd., S. Egre-
  mont.
On side street off Rte. 23 in
  center of village.
Closed: Mon. & Tues.
Price: Moderate to expen-
  sive.
Cuisine: American.
Serving: SB, D.
Credit Cards: DC, MC, V.

In its latest incarnation, under the stewardship of innkeepers Jo-Ann Charde and Harvey Miller, the Egremont Inn has gotten a fresh paint job, a dash of elegance, and personable new hosts. Dining here has an old-fashioned, village-pub atmosphere matched by few other Berkshire restaurants.

Dinner could happen in the friendly tavern room, or in one of the four dining rooms adjoining. If it's a cool night, you'll almost certainly find yourself beside one of the inn's many crackling hearths. On your table will be fine linens, china, crystal, candlelight, and a seasonal bouquet.

In warm weather, the inn serves a delightful Sunday brunch out on its curved porch. Stick to the more familiar fare, the omelets, pancakes, and the like; our poached eggs on artichoke hearts in a phyllo basket with crabmeat and tomato-tarragon beurre fondue turned out to be less than the sum of its many parts. Altogether, though, the brunches we've enjoyed out on the inn's old porch have given us the sure and powerful feeling that all's right with the world.

We recently enjoyed a memorable dinner in the beautifully refurbished main dining room. New chef Jim Rondinelli created a native corn and lobster chowder with saffron and tarragon that was superb, thick with corn and lobster, a symphony of flavors.

Sautéed duck breast with green salad, poached pear, and green peppercorn sauce was magnificent in presentation, the duck breast sliced and artfully fanned out around the erect poached pear with individual raspberries adding accent at the plate's perimeter.

Desserts kept up the standard set by earlier courses, with a blueberry short-cake delivering the coup de grâce.

THE GASLIGHT CAFE
413-528-0870.
Rte. 23, S. Egremont.
Price: Inexpensive.
Cuisine: American.
Serving: B, L, SB; D (Fri. & Sat).
Credit Cards: None

The Gaslight is still the quaintest old-time country cafe in Berkshire. Penny candy is holding steady at a penny, though Fireballs have risen to a nickel and a Sugar Daddy'll set you back sixty cents. For kids, any news like this is good news, and for kids, the Gaslight is awesome. On our last visit, we saw whole families out of turn-of-the-21st-century Norman Rockwell pictures, kids licking ice-cream cones while their parents, in baseball caps, licked *their* ice-cream cones. At one table, Mike, the new owner, was offering an incentive to two young girls: finish your hamburgers and you'll get a free Tootsie Roll!

Not every meal comes with a free Tootsie Roll, but the food is always fun — well-prepared sandwiches, burgers, omelets, and pancakes. The quaint dining room has been enlarged, and the garden patio is open in season for Gaslight dining al fresco. No wonder that when *Yankee Magazine* toured the Berkshires, they found the Gaslight to be one of the most authentic New England eateries in the region.

Completing a fine meal, at John Andrew's.

Jonathan Sternfield

JOHN ANDREW'S
413-528-3469.
Rte. 23, S. Egremont.
W. of village 2.5 mi.
Price: Expensive.
Closed: Sun. dinner; Wed. in winter.
Cuisine: American.
Serving: D, SB.
Credit Cards: MC, V.

With a menu that changes every six to eight weeks and a flattering new interior decor, John Andrew's is bringing a degree of vitality, imagination, and finesse to dining that is a rare find anywhere. The restaurant's interior has been enhanced under the direction of designer Lindy Smith. Painted in a rough rouge, with many other colors hinted in the background and lighted by

Reservations: Recommended.
Special Features: Terrace dining; Fireplace.

dramatic wall sconces, the main dining room has some of the most flattering light in the county.

The food is just as pleasing. Chef Danny Smith continues to turn out a splendid array of consistently excellent, inventive, and beautifully presented meals.

As we considered the choices recently, three kinds of bread were served to us: rice, semolina, and sourdough. Intriguing appetizers included white cornmeal pizza with hickory smoked salmon, and mascarpone and panfried oysters over peppery greens, anchovy mustard vinaigrette.

Among the standout entrées we sampled, three-herb fettuccine with porcini, spinach, and pine nuts was unusually delicate; and "Duck Served Two Ways" was simply as flavorful as this bird gets. The duck leg was served confit style, the breast sautéed in a very hot pan with the sauce being a smooth wild thyme blossom honey.

If you're man or woman enough to move into the next course, chef Smith will continue to dazzle you with such desserts as warm strawberry compote with basil ice cream or ricotta cheesecake with strawberry coulis. The latter dessert, with its artistic swirls of strawberry coulis winding from the luscious-looking cheesecake, was as good-looking as it was satisfying. Among the homemade ice creams, the hazelnut is not to be missed.

MOM'S

413-528-2414.
Rte. 23, S. Egremont.
Price: Inexpensive.
Cuisine: American & Italian.
Serving: B, D, L.
Credit Cards: None.

Disregard novelist Nelson Algren's admonition: "Never eat in a place called 'Mom's.'" This one features a brookside dining room, serving breakfast and lunch all day long, and Mom's has one of the few open kitchens in the county, with chefs scurrying about and the pots and pans hanging from a wheel above. Omelets such as the feta and tomato are excellent; sandwiches are meaty and flavorful, with special accolades for the monstrous fresh turkey sandwich. There are also daily specials, good pizza, and a fine array of burgers. The Veggie Melt, with its generous layerings of avocado, sprouts, and cheese, makes a substantial vegetarian meal for any diner.

Mom's service is pleasant and efficient, even in times of great demand, and the brookside deck behind the restaurant, perched thirty feet above the Karner's Brook, is one of Berkshire's most tranquil and picturesque dining spots.

In the evening, Mom's turns a bit more formal, with delicious pasta dishes and meaty entrées.

THE OLD MILL

413-528-1421.
Rte. 23, S. Egremont.
Closed: Mon. in winter.

In the beautifully restored 1797 gristmill at the center of South Egremont, Britisher Terry Moore and his wife, Julie, run one of southern Berkshire's most popular dining spots.

Jonathan Sternfield

Elegant simplicity at the Old Mill.

Price: Moderate to expensive.
Cuisine: American.
Serving: D.
Credit Cards: AE, CB, DC, MC, V.
Reservations: Recommended for parties of 5 or more.
Special Features: Private dining room; Fireplaces.

Its 18th-century proportions, simple exposed beam construction, and artistic decor offer elegance without pretension. The comfortable bar accommodates those awaiting dining room tables, as well as the many who prefer the bar's more intimate seating and simpler menu. The main dining room was once the mill's blacksmith shop, and the anvil's massive stone foundation still sits surrounded by centuries-old wide-board flooring.

Happily, staff and cuisine match the splendid ambiance; service is friendly, attentive, and intelligent, while the menu gets more enticing every year.

A breadbasket with rolls, French bread slices, and sesame studded bread sticks is offered, along with herbed chèvre. Watch out: this chèvre is addictive, and if you're not careful, could cut into the main event. Under chef Jeff Niedeck's direction, a recent menu featured such delectable combinations as pan-seared almond-crusted trout with tomato-chive beurre blanc, medallions of venison with chanterelles and game sauce, and roast duck with prunes in port sauce and wild rice pancakes.

The lighter bar-menu meals are accompanied by a mountain of tasty shoestring fries — presenting both a challenge to finish and a struggle to resist.

Desserts are quite special; the profiteroles au chocolat are surely the best for many miles around. Another totally deadly dessert is the red-white-and-blue strawberry and blueberry Napoleon. Substituting puff pastry dough for mille feuille and dense whipped cream for the pastry cream, it is spectacular.

WINDFLOWER INN
413-528-2720.
Rte. 23, Gt. Barrington.

When you call for reservations at Windflower (as you must), they'll tell you right out they

Price: Expensive, prix fixe.
Cuisine: Eclectic.
Serving: D.
Credit Cards: None.
Reservations: Required.
Special Features: Non-
   smoking area; Out-
   door dining; Fireplace.

accept no credit cards and there's no smoking in the dining room. So, if you're carrying sufficient cash to cover the prix-fixe tab and like smoke-free dining, quite a good meal awaits you.

The atmosphere is country casual, and the young staff is both friendly and jocular. The menu is blackboard-style, changing daily to accommodate inn guests and the availability of certain meats and fish. (Windflower's roast duckling, in particular, is memorable.)

After your meal, adjourn to the living room by the fire to chat or play with the owners' three springer spaniels. The inn's guest book there is filled with the micro-stories and thanks of scores of pleased guests. Perhaps you'll inscribe your own.

Great Barrington

THE BACK PORCH
413-528-8282.
424 Stockbridge Rd., Gt.
   Barrington.
Closed: Mon.–Wed.(din-
   ner); please check for
   winter hrs.
Price: Inexpensive to Mod-
   erate.
Cuisine: International.
Serving: L, D.
Credit cards: AE, MC, V.
Special Features: Vegetar-
   ian dishes.

After selling his last restaurant (Mom's) a few years back, Cos Poulos is now back, doing what he does best: serving satisfying food in a warm and homey environment. There is indeed a back porch — though to those who come directly to the restaurant instead of through the Jenifer House Commons, it is the front porch. Front or back, it does make a pleasant dining spot.

Inside, the ambiance is oldish, woody, and eclectically decorated, a bit of a hodgepodge, but somehow in this space it works. The menu works, too. Luncheon choices we enjoyed included a juicy, flavorful steak sandwich and a satisfying shrimp salad plate. Fine dinners included chicken Liberator (charbroiled breast of chicken on linguine) and shrimp and scallop pesto. For dessert, an apple crisp was made with not-too-sweet Granny Smiths, giving it extra dimension.

BOILER ROOM CAFE
413-528-4280.
405 Stockbridge Rd., Gt.
   Barrington.
Closed: Mon., Tues.; first 2
   wks. in Apr.
Price: Expensive.
Cuisine: European,
   American.

Michelle Miller's extraordinary Boiler Room Cafe has moved to Great Barrington and is now more spacious (three individually decorated dining rooms and a terrace). The menu is even more robust and adventurous, changing seasonally.

The aesthetic is unchanged: country rustic.

Among recent summer offerings, Michelle's corn

The very talented Michelle Miller, at her Boiler Room Cafe.

Jonathan Sternfield

Serving: D.
Credit Cards: MC, V.
Special Features: Fireplace;
  Upstairs lounge.

fritters with maple cream made an awesome opener, just about the best fritters (they were actually closer to corn balls) we've ever tasted.

Popular recent entrées included a roast Puerto Rican chicken with black bean chili and pickled onions and grilled corn bread. Grilled swordfish charmoula with couscous and pear chutney was delicious, the fish seeming to melt in your mouth, the chutney a piquant accompaniment. A variety of modestly priced vegetarian plates, including a grilled pizza, make the Boiler Room a very comfortable destination for vegetarian dining.

As might be expected in a restaurant run by the founder of a fine bakery (Suchèle, in Lenox), desserts at Michelle Miller's Boiler Room are rich and good. Recent winners included a tart-sweet lemon Napoleon and a nutty polenta-walnut pound cake with raspberries, blueberries, and crème fraîche.

BRONZE DOG CAFE
413-528-5678.
Railroad Station, Gt.
  Barrington.
Closed: Wed.; Mon.–Wed.
  in winter.
Price: Moderate.
Cuisine: Wide variety of
  contemporary & regional
  sources.
Serving: L, D, SB.
Credit Cards: MC, V, D.
Special Features: Vegetarian dishes; Outside dining; Beautiful bar.

Heather Austin (Berkshire Coffee Roasting Company and Kintaro) and her friends have converted Great Barrington's interesting old railroad station into the appealing Bronze Dog Cafe.

Our first taste of Bronze Dog cuisine came at a Sunday brunch featuring strawberry-walnut cream cheese stuffed French toast. Simply delicious, and complemented by excellent Berkshire Coffee Roasting Company coffee.

Shortly after it opened, the Bronze Dog wisely struck a deal with another Bronz, the well-known Miss Ruby. Ruth Bronz is a talented and adventuresome chef who ran two successful versions of her Miss Ruby's Cafe (first in West Stockbridge and next in the Chelsea section of NYC) and authored her own cookbook. And though Ruth cooks only Thursday through Sunday nights, the menu is principally hers.

Grace and space, at the felicitous Bronze Dog Cafe.

Jonathan Sternfield

Among the appetizers, Ruth's corn batter cakes with black beans and grape-fruit salsa (and sour cream) is a true sensation. And the chicken, mushroom, and broccoli torte is a meal in itself.

Bronze Dog entrées are ever-changing and imaginative. When we visited, grilled polenta with assorted wild mushrooms and spicy greens was a vegetarian feast, a true counterpoint of intriguing tastes. Seared salmon with papaya-grapefruit salsa, grain medley, and steamed greens was every bit as good as it sounds.

Among the desserts, seasonal fruit poached in a huge pumpkin was something special. And Ruth Bronz's tart tatin is terrific, we're telling!

A Taste of the Berkshires

Settling into a September Saturday on Berkshire's crowded social calendar, "A Taste of the Berkshires" gives new meaning to the concept of grazing. If you love the nibbler's lifestyle, sampling a bit of this and a bit of that, then this festival is the ideal spot for you, with its tents poised just behind the Great Barrington bandstand. Unforgettable treats in our last outing included grilled shiitake mushrooms from Delftree and Maryland crab cake from Thornewood Inn, among many others.

Other facets of the food fest include a Berkshire's Best Pie contest, sheepshearing, and music, so the whole family can enjoy. One recommendation for this extravaganza: an empty stomach; don't leave home without it.

CASTLE STREET CAFE
413-528-5244.
10 Castle St., Gt. Barrington.
Closed: Tues.

Chef-owner Michael Ballon continues to preside over one of the liveliest and most consistently satisfying eating establishments in Berkshire. The decor is straightforward upscale bistro with exposed brick walls, white linen tablecloths, fresh

Chef/restaurateur Michael Ballon at the bar of his lively and delicious Castle Street Cafe.

Jonathan Sternfield

Price: Inexpensive to Moderate.
Cuisine: American, French, Italian.
Serving: D.
Credit Cards: D, MC, V.
Special Features: Cruvinet wine bar.

flowers and a handsome, inviting bar at the back of the dining room — a great spot for a cool drink late on a summer's night or a hot toddy after the movies at the nearby Mahaiwe. Table service is top-notch — attentive, well informed, and prompt. And unlike many other sophisticated restaurants which turn away the dessert and coffee crowd, Castle Street treats everyone with the same warmth and welcome.

Chef Ballon's excellence derives in part from his reliance on the best local suppliers for everything fresh — from goat cheese to French bread to produce. The menu tips its hat to these Berkshire provisioners by listing them prominently.

The eclectic menu combines French, Italian, and American influences. On our many visits we have enjoyed entrées such as perfect fettucine Alfredo with appropriately thick cream sauce, redolent with parmesan; the three-cheese eggplant roulade, which left the vegetable al dente and mixed the cheese with a pungent tomato sauce inside; and shellfish pasta that combined wonderfully fresh shrimp, scallops, and mussels in a garlic, basil sauce with al dente penne. Vegetarians and carnivores alike have a good range of choices.

Castle Street offers a modest array of uniformly excellent desserts. *Newsday* declared the chocolate mousse to be "the world's best," but two of our personal favorites are Castle Street's apple crisp and their bread pudding.

For its superior food, reasonable prices, and extraordinarily convivial atmosphere, Castle Street rates as one of Berkshire's very best.

THE DELI
413-528-1482.
345 Main St., Gt. Barrington.
Price: Inexpensive.
Cuisine: American.
Serving: B, L, D.

Where else could you have lunch with ex-Gov. Dukakis, Perry Como, Tex Ritter, Gilda Radner, Dr. Johnny Fever, Jacques Cousteau, Zonker Harris, Mrs. Emma Peel, Bebe Rebozo, Groucho, Zeppo, and Carlos Castenada? Only at the Deli, where the delicious sandwiches named after these luminaries actually appear on the menu. The sandwiches are huge (for a lighter lunch, try a "half," which is actually a less stuffed whole). Soups are delicious, too. Owner and chief sandwich artist Frank Tortoriello and his fun-loving staff create an air of summer camp all year long, serving up almost any sandwich you can imagine and many you never would. Try a Winter Sheik: cream cheese, walnuts, and honey on a bagel. Or perhaps you'd prefer a sandwich named after that famous actor, Avocado Montalban, a delicious layering of tuna, avocado, sprouts, tomatoes, and melted cheese. In or out of office, "Dukakis" here will always be "ex-Gov." — cold turkey, hot pastrami, and onions.

Breakfast starts here at 5:30 a.m., with omelets like the Cisco Kid, Eve Arden, Ken Kesey (Muenster and onions), and Miss Piggy rolling off Frank's pan till 10.

DOS AMIGOS
413-528-0084.
250 Stockbridge Rd. (Rte.7),
  Gt. Barrington.
Price: Inexpensive.
Cuisine: Mexican.
Serving: L, D.
Credit Cards: MC, V.
Reservations: Preferred for
  groups of six or more.
Special Features: Vegetar-
  ian dishes; Children's
  menu/highchairs; Enter-
  tainment.

Dos Amigos offers a pleasant, informal setting — bright colors and souvenirs from the border towns of Mexico. The distinguishing characteristic of its food is the abundance of fresh ingredients. The Special Taco is a meal in itself. The beef, particularly recommended, is given a long slow roast and is served shredded, not ground. Enchiladas and especially the enchilada sauce are both made very well here, too. A word about spiciness: they will make it hot, but to get it really hot, you must in graphic terms convey to the chef just how much importance you attach to self-immolation. On this score, it's a pity that whole jalapeños are not served as a garnish.

To complement — or to extinguish — your meal, various Mexican beers, wines, and bar drinks are available. A tasty large margarita is served in a glass the size of a birdbath, and specialty coffees are available as postprandials.

A small, enclosed outdoor patio in front of the restaurant offers fresh-air dining on warm days, though the nearby traffic on Rte. 7 sometimes is distracting.

Dos Amigos is one of Berkshire's most convivial eateries. It brings in musicians like David Grover for the kids on weekend afternoons, and Vikki True and other jazz artists at night. Altogether, Dos Amigos is like a friend in the Berkshires.

GREAT WALL CHINESE RESTAURANT
413-528-4838.
87 State Rd., Gt. Barrington.
Closed: Thanksgiving Day.
Price: Inexpensive.
Cuisine: Chinese.
Serving: L, D.
Credit Cards: None.

So what if they made the place out of the old Motor Vehicles Department? Now, instead of questions about past vehicular infractions or squinty eyesight, you can get healthy heapings of Char Har Kew (deep-fried shrimp with Chinese vegetables), or Sam Get Dai (roast pork, chicken, fresh shrimp, sautéed with mushrooms, bamboo shoots, and snow pea pods).

You can eat at the Great Wall — though the ambiance hasn't improved much since its days as the Bureau of Motor Vehicles — but their take-out is much more popular. Wherever you choose to eat, Great Wall provides great combination platters, Cantonese- and Szechuan-style dishes, and a vast array of appetizers, soups, and other entrées, all prepared without MSG. Call ahead, and ten minutes later your food will be waiting at the Great Wall.

Hickory Bill, himself, at Berkshire's best barbeque.

Jonathan Sternfield

HICKORY BILL'S BAR-B-QUE
413-528-1444.
405 Stockbridge Rd.,Gt. Barrington.
Closed: Mon.
Price: Inexpensive.
Cuisine: American.
Serving: L, D.
Credit Cards: AE, MC, V.

Hickory Bill's barbecue is just the best north of the Mason-Dixon, and we have many friends who regularly make pilgrimages to his smoker. Using a method developed in Texas in the 1920s by a Mr. Jack Tillman — a Texan known as the "Barbecue King" — Hickory Bill seasons the meat, places it in the pit (hot with hickory coals), then bastes it and carefully controls its lengthy cooking. All meats are smoked and cooked at least six hours; many are left in the pit overnight. The result is fantastic — smoky, juicy, tender beef ribs, spare ribs, fancy brisket, and chicken. As side dishes, Bill serves dynamite collard greens (with bits of brisket), barbecue baked beans, and Mexican corn bread (laced with jalapeño pepper). Mrs. Evelyn's sweet potato pie for dessert makes a fitting finish, and you'll go out smiling, we promise.

Out behind Bill's, at the edge of a wide lawn and on the banks of the meandering Housatonic, are a few picnic tables. The waitresses will cheerily make the 100-foot dash out to your table here, and you'll be in hog heaven.

JODI'S COUNTRY COOKERY
413-528-6064.
327 Stockbridge Rd., Gt. Barrington.
Price: Inexpensive to Moderate.
Cuisine: Italian.
Serving: B, L, D, SB.
Credit Cards: AE, D, DC, MC, V.
Reservations: Recommended.

Consistently popular with travelers and locals alike, this "country cookery" in an old farmhouse right on Route 7 continues to turn out three squares a day for the multitudes. Though Jodi's immediate locale (amid a shopping center, a car dealership, and a McDonald's) may not suggest country charm, proprietors Steven and Jodi Amoruso and their partner, Carole Altman, succeed in establishing a rustic ambiance. Both dining rooms are pleasant, spacious, and truly conducive to enjoying country cookery. The porch that wraps around the front of the old farmhouse is very popular spot in warmer weather, where, despite noisy traffic nearby, you can dine in the great Berkshire outdoors.

Though a few of our selections have been decidedly underseasoned, most have found their mark. Maryland crab cake was quite good, indeed. A delicious turkey sandwich was made from white meat carved off a bird in the kitchen, so fresh that the meat was still warm and steaming. Shrimp and lobster gumbo over saffron rice was memorable, even though the lobster was actually two midget crayfish.

KINTARO
413-528-6007.
286 Main St., Gt. Barrington.
Closed: Tues.
Price: Moderate.
Cuisine: Japanese.
Serving: L, D.
Credit Cards: MC, V.
Reservations: Recommended for party of 5 or more.

Kinataro brings serious sushi and delicious Japanese meals to downtown Great Barrington. In a spare, elegant space, successful cafe entrepreneur Heather Austin and partner, Hideo Kikushi, have created an instantly popular Japanese dining room and sushi bar. They offer sushi and maki at affordable rates; a luncheon plate called the Bento Tray that we could easily look forward to on a daily basis; and beautifully portioned, prepared, and presented entrées.

Watch your sushi deftly prepared by a seasoned professional at the sushi bar, or sit at one of the dozen tables surrounding.

The art of sushi, at Kintaro.

Jonathan Sternfield

Kintaro's is the only restaurant in Berkshire offering a range of premium sakis from various regions of Japan. Besides their Ki-ippon house saki, served hot, in a *tokkuri*, Kintaro will serve you seven other premium sakis. Ask for advice about the sakis; they will be happy to help.

Esprit de corps, in the charm of La Tomate.

Jonathan Sternfield

LA TOMATE
413-528-3003.
12 Railroad St., Gt. Barrington.
Closed: Mon.
Price: Moderate.

Chef Jean Claude Vierne and his wife, Nikki, host one of Berkshire's most satisfying and best-valued restaurants, a "Bistro Provençal" in the best tradition.

Recent enticing starters included escargot salon de Provence (escargots sautéed with a mushroom,

Cuisine: French.
Serving: L, D.
Credit Cards: AE, MC, V.

tomato, demi-glacé sauce), and chèvre rôtie (roasted imported goat cheese, fresh thyme, and olive oil). Soupe de poisson (saffron sole chowder and aïoli sauce) is practically a meal in itself, and truly delicious. Salads, such as the épinard aux lardons, should not be missed — this one combining spinach, bacon, and goat cheese vinaigrette.

Pastas are a true value at La Tomate. The fusilli marée haute, combining clams, scallops, and shrimp, transported us to some romantic seashore. La Tomate's entrées are almost as magical, from their individually marinated carré d'agneau to the homard bouillabaisse, a lobster-studded shellfish classic.

A fine fruit tart is a wonderful way to end a French meal, and here, happily, La Tomate again delivers. In fact, La Tomate delivers over and over again, bringing us back time after time.

MARTIN'S
413-528-5455.
49 Railroad St., Gt. Barring-
ton.
Price: Inexpensive.
Cuisine: American.
Serving: B, L.
Credit Cards: None.

Martin continues to pack them in daily. In his cozy, bright dining room, his extremely cheery staff serves just the food his customers want.

Breakfast is served here all day long, and the omelets are outstanding. Choose from ones made with smoked salmon and cream cheese, Brie, spinach and cheddar, or make one up yourself. Want even more from your eggs? Consider Martin's steak and eggs, eggs Benedict, or corned beef hash with poached eggs. Or how about apple pancakes for a solid way to start your day?

For lunch, there are burgers in many styles, including the Berkshire cheeseburger (mushrooms, onions, tomatoes and peppers). Sandwiches, salads, and soups are also well represented, as are daily specials such as beef bourguignon.

Beverages available include Heineken, Rolling Rock, Perrier, juices, and herbal teas. Though we've rarely made it to dessert, there are many fine selections to choose from, and recently we sampled a rather special poppy seed cake and a whiskey chocolate cake.

Best of all, Martin's has attracted an extraordinarily convivial crowd, so you're likely either to meet someone you know, or someone you'd like to know. Martin's supplies crayons at every table, so kids of all ages can color their paper placemats just the way they want. A few of these masterworks — many of them testimonials to Martin's excellence — are pinned up in an informal gallery.

THE PAINTED LADY
413-528-1662.
785 Main St., Gt. Barrington.
Price: Moderate.

Painted Ladies" are San Francisco's colorful old Victorian houses, and chef Dan Harris and wife Julie run the Berkshire version. A nice mix of California, French, and Italian wines is offered, at mod-

Cuisine: Northern Italian, Continental.
Serving: D.
Credit Cards: MC, V.
Reservations: Recommended.
Special Features: Vegetarian dishes.

erate prices. Fine, fresh little loaves of Italian bread seduced us into feeling we were in the right place at the right time.

Among the recent Painted Lady entrées, we've enjoyed a seafood crêpe, filled with shrimp, scallops, and lobster Newburg. This was delicate yet substantial, and we savored every bite. The raspberry and blueberry shortcake on a proper biscuit, with dense, slightly sweetened cream, put us over the edge.

We've made plans for our return.

PANDA WEST
413-528-5330.
300 State Rd., Gt. Barrington.
Price: Inexpensive to Moderate.
Cuisine: Hunan, Szechuan, Mandarin, Cantonese.
Serving: L, D.
Credit Cards: All major cards.

Panda-monium reigns! Berkshire has been innundated with good Chinese food!

First there were no Chinese restaurants in Berkshire, then there were only ersatz Chinese. Now there are *three* excellent Pandas, all serving Peking, Hunan, Szechuan, Shanghai, and Cantonese specialties.

With its expansive, woody dining room, the Great Barrington Panda is our favorite, though the menus of all three are nearly identical. Service is excellent, and no MSG, thank you. Try the steamed vegetable dumplings, served in a woven bamboo steamer and with a special spicy dipping sauce. Superb! Among our favorite entrées: Tangerine Chicken and Prawn Amazing.

In warmer weather, Panda's wooden deck, with its tree and umbrella-shaded tables, makes a fine outdoor dining spot. Even though you're right near Route 23, traffic's rarely noisy, and the trees and air surrounding are always invigorating.

RUBY'S DINER
413-528-8226.
282 Main St., Gt. Barrington.
Price: Inexpensive.
Cuisine: American.
Serving: B, L, D (Fri.& Sat.).
Credit Cards: None.

Recently opened (1993), Ruby's shows promise for filling Great Barrington's need for a good, old-fashioned downtown diner. Service is very friendly and folksy, the ambiance is updated down-home '50s, and the food is simple and pretty good. The turkey sandwich — always a test — is made here from white meat carved from a real bird roasted in their own kitchen. Breakfasts are hearty, families are welcome. Feel like slipping into a Norman Rockwell tableau? Stop in at Ruby's.

SPENCER'S RESTAURANT AT THORNEWOOD INN
413-528-3828.

Terry and David Thorne's remarkable restaurant-inn now offers a choice of four distinctive dining rooms: the library, the atrium, the porches, or the music room. With the feel of a well-deco-

Stockbridge Rd., Gt. Barrington.
Closed: Mon. & Tues.
Price: Moderate to Expensive.
Cuisine: Country Continental.
Serving: D, SB.
Credit Cards: AE, D, MC, V.
Reservations: Preferred.
Special Features: Vegetarian dishes.

rated British B&B replete with tiny bar, the Thornewood is strong on charm. On Sundays at brunch and on some weekend nights, innkeeper David Thorne changes hats, to lead his David Thorne Trio, a jazz ensemble whose mellowness can complement your meal.

We recently tried out their deck, overlooking Taft Farms and the Monument Valley, where we delighted in every instant of the evening sunset and our evening meal. Among the appetizers, mushroom charlotte with port and currant sauce was our favorite — a creamy mushroom pâté baked in a bread crust and set in an ambrosial sauce. Also offered were palate-pleasing eggplant rounds, slightly breaded and layered with goat cheese and served with a tomato-basil salsa.

For entrées, a vegetable pie with a French-bread crust and layered with roasted garlic and lemon pesto made vegetarian eating regal once more. Salmon stuffed with scallop mousse caught us by surprise — the counterpoint of subtle fish flavors and textures working rather well.

"Fresh homemade desserts prepared on the premises," says a Thornewood flyer, and their desserts deliver satisfactions aplenty. A simple lemon pound cake was light, delicate and delicious. Death by Chocolate, Spencer's dessert of the season, was aptly named, delivering as it does a base layer of chocolate walnut torte topped by a tall wedge of double chocolate mousse.

The talk of the Berkshires, at 20 Railroad Street.

Jonathan Sternfield

20 RAILROAD STREET
413-528-9345.
20 Railroad St., Gt. Barrington.

Born in 1977, 20 Railroad Street is the restaurant that successfully launched the Railroad Street revival. In the tall brick dining room, always con-

Price: Inexpensive.
Cuisine: American.
Serving: SB, L, D.
Credit Cards: MC, V.
Special Features: Open late.
Handicap Access: Yes.

vivial, you'll share dining space with jovial families, couples young and old, as well as softball teams and ski patrol squadrons. You'll hear about divorces and deals, patients and quarterbacks. In story or in person, most of southern Berkshire has been in 20 Railroad.

But 20 Railroad didn't build its popularity on good vibes alone. From the outset, it has served good food. Since other restaurants have joined the Railroad Street renaissance, 20 Railroad has gotten even better, broadening its menu and always serving half-a-dozen dinner specials that extend the range further.

For lunch, dinner, or whenever, 20 Railroad's starters, salads, sandwiches, and burgers are legendary. Unusual starters include the Plowman's Snack, a combination of Brie, soprassata sausage, and French bread; and hot and spicy chicken wings marinated in soy, ginger, sherry, and garlic. Pocket sandwiches are outstanding, with the vegetarian side pocket — lettuce, fresh veggies, and blue cheese in a pita all "smothered under melted swiss cheese" — being among our favorites. The restaurant also nurtures a whole Reuben family (available in halves). If you thought the Reuben family was of pastrami stock, go visit 20 Railroad, where Reubens are also made with ham (Mama Reuben), turkey (Rebecca Reuben), and roast beef (Roland Reuben). More than a dozen different burgers and an equal number of sandwiches fill out Railroad Street's printed menu.

On the chalkboard, specials usually include soups, a variety of meaty entrées, and sometimes a vegetarian dish. Portions are more than ample; preparation is always careful. Despite the hundreds of meals a day this restaurant frequently turns out, quality remains unwavering. Service is efficient and always friendly.

Once touted by the *Boston Phoenix* as "The Best Bar in the Berkshires," 20 Railroad Sreet is not doing too badly in the restaurant department, either.

The 28-foot-long bar dominating 20 Railroad Sreet was built in New York City in 1883 and was moved to Great Barrington in 1919. Originally, the bar was named "Mahogany Ridge," deriving its name from an inside joke among some regulars. When asked by their waiting wives where they had been, their usual reply was, "Oh, we hunted the state forest in the morning and posted 'Mahogany Ridge' in the afternoon." During the 1920s, through the end of Prohibition, the bar served as one of the area's speakeasies. Maybe that's why the talk comes so easy at 20 Railroad.

WILDFLOWER BAKERY & CAFE
413-528-0780.
50 Stockbridge Rd., Gt. Barrington.
Closed: Mon.
Price: Inexpensive.
Cuisine: American.
Serving: B, L.
Credit Cards: None.

Taking the old Bullwinkels' shop and totally restoring the beautiful structure that housed it, Wildflower Cafe presents a soothing ambiance in which to enjoy Berkshire cafe life. Coffees and teas are served, as are baked goods, such as scones and cinnamon walnut rolls. Soup can be had in a bread bowl, essentially a large sourdough roll that's been hollowed out. Once you've finished the soup, you eat the bowl, saturated as it is with savory flavors.

The best feature of Wildflower's is their country porch, a wraparound affair outfitted with comfy canvas recliners. A cup of tea and a scone out here will convince you this is Berkshire life as it should be.

Housatonic

JACK'S GRILL
413-274-3476.
Main St., Housatonic.
On Main St., midway between Rtes. 41 & 183.
Under new management; call for information.

Until recently, this interesting old store housed Embree's Restaurant. Now owned by the Fitzpatricks of the Red Lion Inn fame, the restaurant (at press time) is slated to reopen under the management of Lori Lee Sykes. Decor will be unchanged (happily). Menu to be determined.

Lee

Joanne Wentholt, restaurateur, greeting friends and customers at her outstanding Cactus Cafe.

Jonathan Sternfield

CACTUS CAFE
413-243-4300
54 Main St., Lee

Lee has become a hotbed of intriguing dining possibilities, none more exciting or more plea-

Price: Inexpensive to Moderate.
Cuisine: Mexican
Serving: L, D
Credit Cards: All major cards.

surable than the new Cactus Cafe. Cactus Cafe Cantina y Tacqueria has an exciting, home-cooked approach to Mexican cuisine, and at the same time takes innovative approaches to old standards. As a result, it has become the standard: the best Mexican food in Berkshire.

In the quaint, tin-ceilinged, Mexican motif that surrounds you, the exellent house-made chips and salsa will disappear quickly, and a wave of Central American warmth will wash over you. Sopa de Lima — scallops, swordfish, and shrimp in a lime bouillon — is sensational, an oceanic meal in itself. Other soups like gazpacho de camerón (shrimp gazpacho), and frijoles negros con crema (black bean soup with sour cream) also delight.

Antejitos, the appetizer course, is just as much fun. Ceviche, a mix of marinated shrimp, marlin, and scallops tastes like some newly created fish, and a mighty delicious one. And where else but at the Cactus Cafe might you sample entrées such as grilled tuna with peach and mango salsa, or smoked mushroom quesadillas?

Viva Cactus Cafe! Viva Mexico!

CYGNET'S AT THE BLACK SWAN INN
413-243-2700, 800 876-SWAN.
Rte. 20 W., Lee.
At Laurel Lake, N. of Lee.
Price: Moderate.
Cuisine: Continental.
Serving: L, D; winter: D.
Credit Cards: AE, CB, DC, MC, V.
Special Features: Atrium restaurant overlooking Laurel Lake.

In their atrium dining room overlooking Laurel Lake, the Black Swan Inn provides a dining experience with unexpected pleasures. Besides the felicitous setting, the restaurant offers an impressive continental menu and a wine list to match, a broad range of bottles of French, American, German, Italian, Australian, and Hungarian wines from $15 to $225. Dessert wines and wines by the glass are also offered.

The menu is nicely complemented by such a list. Chef John Allen and his staff turn out fine food, from a juicy New York sirloin steak to authentic Hungarian gulyas with homemade spaetzle. A seafood chowder, which included healthy bits of lobster, was satisfying in every respect. Chargrilled Gulf shrimp accompanied by corn fritters and aïoli was sensational, as was a superb entrée of blackened tuna with honey Dijon mustard. Vegetables accompanying the entrées were uniformly fresh, cooked al dente.

Among the desserts, a *palacsinta* — a Hungarian dessert crêpe with apricots and walnuts — offered an artfully arranged, walnut-sprinkled crêpe resting neatly beside a small pool of vanilla crème sauce, which itself was punctuated with perfectly symmetrical striations of chocolate sauce.

Owner Joe Sorrentino works the crowd, at Joe's.

Jonathan Sternfield

JOE'S DINER
413-243-9756.
63 Center St., Lee.
At corner of Center & Main Sts.
Closed: Sun.
Price: Inexpensive.
Cuisine: American.
Serving: B, L, D.

Joe's Diner: where time has stood still and isn't waiting for anything, where things are just as they were and just as they will be. Still bustling with the vigor of the 1940s, Joe's is the kind of diner that still stocks packets of Red Man Chewing Tobacco right next to buckets of lifetime-guarantee combs, where artichokes are forty cents apiece and a real New York egg cream will set you back all of 65 cents.

But it's not the funkiness or even the old-time prices that keeps Joe's jammed most of the day and night. Joe Sorrentino serves good food. With the help of many other assorted Sorrentinos and friends, this ex-army cook will happily serve you "breakfast at dinner, or dinner at breakfast," any way you like it. Joe creates a special each day, and many regulars are attuned to his menu. "We'll go through a whole hip of beef every Monday, 120 pounds of corned beef every Thursday," says Joe. If you're serious about taking in one of Joe's specials (like a roast beef dinner with vegetable, potato, and bread for four bucks), you'd better arrive early. We came on corned beef night recently and watched the last of the 120 pounds disappear quickly, leaving disappointed latecomers.

At Joe's you'll dine with anyone and everybody.

MORGAN HOUSE INN
413-243-0181.
33 Main St., Lee.
Closed: Christmas Day.
Price: Moderate to Expensive
Cuisine: New England contemporary.

The Morgan House has just changed hands and is run now by Lenora and Stuart Bowen; their new menu incorporates some of the old restaurant's most popular items together with chef (Lenora) Bowen's personal favorites. We found the makeover in the kitchen truly astonishing, restor-

Serving: L, D.
Credit Cards: AE, D, DC, MC, V.
Reservations: Recommended.

ing the venerable Morgan House to one of Berkshire's better restaurants.

Lobster, scallop, sweet potato cakes, roasted red pepper sauce was just as good as it sounds, an oceanic medley of delightful flavors. Chicken breast and pistachio terrine with onion cassis jam was intense and satisfying, too.

Chicken in a popover — the Morgan House version of a classic white meat chicken pot pie — was truly terrific, the popover a moist and chewy alternative to the standard flaky crust, every single piece of the chicken as moist and flavorful as the last. Roast duckling is prepared here with cider rum sauce and spiced pecans; roast leg of lamb with fresh mint, tomato, and hazelnut chutney. At first glance, the menu seems like standard American fare, but a closer look and several tastes will convince you that the latest incarnation of the venerable Morgan House may be its best ever.

OH CALCUTTA!
413-243-2220
Rte. 20 W at Canal St., Lee.
Price: Inexpensive to Moderate.
Cuisine: Indian.
Serving: L, D.
Credit Cards: MC, V.

Aschararj Singh Jaggi, Oh Calcutta!'s chef/owner, has put together a string of Indian restaurants (this is his fourth) that satisfy the longings of many for tastes from the subcontinent. Purists and East Indian nationals may not be thrilled here, but for those of us only vaguely familiar with the cuisine, Oh Calcutta! does quite nicely, thank you. From recipes created for the "Kings and Nawabs of Mogul India," Oh Calcutta! offers an array of vegetarian and nonvegetarian dishes that have brought us back many times.

For lunch there is a buffet which includes at least one kind of curry; Keema Matar (ground beef, peas, corriander, and ginger); Chicken Tandoori, marinated in yogurt, herbs, and spices, and grilled; as well as a variety of vegetarian dishes (Channa Baji, the sultan's summer supper!) and specialty breads (Oh Calcutta! serves four different kinds of paratha!).

Soups include a tropical coconut, featuring shredded coconut, cream, nuts, and sweet spices; and Dahl Shorba, a hearty stew of lentils, split peas, and fresh vegetables. All dinners are served with basmati rice, dal, and chutney.

Lamb Biryani (lamb chunks steamed with Basmati, cashews and raisins and garnished with fresh herbs) was quite good, as was Shrimp Tandoori Masala, in which the crustaceans are first charbroiled, then sautéed. The restaurant has many specialties for vegetarians, and many which are mildly seasoned.

Although Calcutta's ambiance could be nouvelle pizzeria just as easily as people's curry, the food is fun enough that you hardly notice.

SULLIVAN STATION
413-243-2082.

We've always enjoyed the wood-paneled interior of this converted 19th-century railway

Railroad St., Lee.
Price: Inexpensive to Moderate.
Cuisine: New England.
Serving: SB, L, D.
Credit Cards: MC, V.
Reservations: Accepted.
Special Features: Converted 19th-century train station

station, tastefully decorated with railroad maps and memorabilia. Now the food is good, too, making the station a smart stop for soups, salads, burgers, sandwiches, and quiches, as well as fancier entrées. Juicy burgers are served with a generous salad and twice-fried home fries, resulting in a filling, very satisfying plate. Here's a no-bones-about-it kinda place that unabashedly offers "Rack of Lamb" right in there with "Hot Dog." There are daily specials, friendly waitresses, and a folksy bar near the entry. Altogether, Sullivan Station is right on time.

South Lee

Dinner by the flower-decked fireside, at the Federal House.

Jonathan Sternfield

FEDERAL HOUSE
413-243-1824.
Main St., Rte. 102, S. Lee.
1 1/2 mi. E. of Stockbridge.
Closed: Mon.
Price: Expensive.
Cuisine: Continental.
Credit Cards: AE, MC, V.
Reservations: Recommended.
Special Features: Fireplaces.

The Federal House is elegant and European, with white linens, heavy silver, and fresh flowers adorning every candlelit table. More than likely, a fire will be crackling in the hearth of the tall, stately dining room, welcoming you on a crisp evening.

For starters, recent offerings included fresh ravioli stuffed with Vermont goat cheese, tomato, and garlic sauce; and warm cornmeal blini, rosemary smoked trout, sour cream, and green onions.

A simple green salad is highlighted by an absolutely first-class vinaigrette. The wine list at the Federal House is excellent, strong in French vintages, with Bordeaux from $15 to $130 and Burgundies from about $25 to $75.

Recent entrées included medallions of pork sautéed with mulled cider apple sauce, and boneless roast Long Island duckling with maple pecan and bourbon sauce.

Chef Ken Almgren is a dessert master, justly known for his apple fritters: feathery fruity pancakes in a sauce of ice cream, stiff whipped cream, and kirsch. This is a symphonic creation, and at least one for the table ought to be ordered to cap a Federal House feast. His profiteroles are nearly as good and make an exceptionally satisfying conclusion.

Federal House continues its tradition of uncompromising excellence.

HOPLANDS
413-243-4414.
Rte. 102, S. Lee.
1 mi. E. of Stockbridge.
Closed: Tues.
Price: Inexpensive.
Cuisine: American.
Serving: SB, L, D.
Credit Cards: AE, MC, V.

Hoplands has changed owners, chefs, and menus, but much remains the same. In a handsome brick inn built around 1803, Hoplands embraces you with antique ambiance. On the western wall is an antique map showing Stockbridge and Lee the way they used to be, when the township of Hoplands lay between them.

Hoplands is still a lunch and dinner spot, featuring Hop Burgers, sandwiches, pastas, and fresh fish. We recently sampled broiled shrimp stuffed with crabmeat, finding them quite satisfying. Not haute cuisine, but there was nothing fishy about it, either. Dinner entrées of note include apricot chicken and veal Marsala.

Hoplands feels like it's just off the beaten path, safely outside the commercialism of Lee and Stockbridge. Next time you're tired of the towns, head out Hoplands way for food, grog, and peace of mind.

New Marlborough

THE HILLSIDE
413-528-3123.
Rte. 57, New Marlborough.
Closed: Mon.; Mon. & Tues.
in winter.
Price: Moderate.
Cuisine: Continental.
Credit Cards: MC, V.
Serving: D.
Reservations: Recommended.
Special Features: Outdoor
dining; Fireplace.

Not much has changed at the Hillside, and that's the way we like it. Simple Swiss elegance is in evidence everywhere, from the pale blue table linen to the fresh-cut flowers, from the rubbed honey-colored woodwork to the exceptionally flattering candlelight. Waitresses are first rate, and the atmosphere is one of casual conviviality.

Hillside's onion soup is among Berkshire's best. The melon and prosciutto are excellent, the melon sweet and perfectly ripe, the prosciutto gamy, even tangy. Salad features alfalfa sprouts — another surprise in a European-flavored restaurant — and slices of golden bell pepper. This newly popular pepper is far sweeter than its red or green cousins and lends real excitement to greens.

Entrées are strictly meat, fish, and fowl, with the accent on excellent ingredients and preparation. The menu features many fine veal dishes. Excellent duck flambé is gamy and not fatty, though the orange sauce that comes on the side is far too sweet.

The cheesecake dessert is light and not too sugary, its topping of fresh strawberries showing off their natural sweetness. Chocolate crêpe filled with chocolate ice cream and topped with chocolate sauce is a semisweet winner at every layer. Coffee is excellent; espresso arrives in a stately demitasse with its own espresso pot for a second cup, covered with its own blue linen espresso cozy.

SATURDAY, DECEMBER 18TH	SATURDAY, DECEMBER 25TH
Warm Artichoke Paté with Morels and Tomato Chutney	CHRISTMAS
Roasted Lamb Loin with Black Trumpet Mushroom Crust and Pinot Noir Sauce *or* Swordfish Medallions with Three Sauces and Potato-Leek Gratin	Seatings from 2:30 pm
	Sweet Corn and Lobster Bisque
	Roast Prime Rib of Beef au Jus with Hazelnut Oil-Potato Purée, Collard Greens and Port-Braised Shallots *or* Poached Halibut with Beluga Caviar, Sautéed Spinach and Pesto Risotto
Chocolate Cabernet Tart or Praline Cheesecake with Caramel Sauce	
	Christmas Cookies and Chocolate Chestnut Terrine

Courtesy the Old Inn on the Green

A pair of warming wintertime menus from the Old Inn on the Green.

OLD INN ON THE GREEN AND GEDNEY FARM
413-229-3131.
Rte. 57 (6 mi. E. of Rte. 23), New Marlborough.
Closed: Mon.–Wed., winter only.
Price: Weekday: Moderate to Expensive. Weekends: Very expensive, prix fixe.
Cuisine: French, American.
Serving: D.
Credit Cards: None.
Reservations: Required.

The quintessence of Colonial charm, the Old Inn feels authentic in every detail. Innkeepers Miller and Wagstaff have astute instincts for putting the emphasis right where it belongs. Their careful restoration of a former stagecoach stop includes preservation of the authentic materials and quirks of the old building. You will find nothing synthetic here.

All four dining rooms and the bar are candlelit — and no other light. There are fireside tables and several dining alcoves that vie for the prize of "most romantic dinner spots in the Berkshires." And for warmer weather, there is now a charming

Special Features: Intimate candlelit dining rooms; Fireplaces; Outdoor patio.

backyard extension of the bar (a patio and awning) for al fresco drinks. Best of all, you can dine here dressed in your finest finery or in sports clothes and feel equally welcome and comfortable.

The inn's latest chef, Chris Capstick, has quickly established himself as a worthy successor to David Lawson, who moved over to Blantyre. The Old Inn's fixed price menu (announced via mailing list, a season in advance) still consists of essentially one set meal each night. With a little advance notice, vegetarians and fish eaters can be accommodated when the entrée is meat.

Serving its "Terrace à La Carte" menu every night but Saturday, the Old Inn has found a less formal way to satisfy a greater number of diners without in any way sacrificing their culinary design. Partner Brad Wagstaff maintains a thoughtful, high-quality wine cellar, as well as directing several wine tastings a year. Serious diners will want to be on the Old Inn's mailing list.

Sheffield

STAGECOACH HILL INN
413-229-8585.
Rte. 41, Sheffield.
On Rte. 41, several mi. N. of Lakeville, CT.
Closed: Wed.; also Nov.–May.
Price: Moderate.
Cuisine: English, Italian.
Serving: D.
Credit Cards: AE, DC, MC, V.
Reservations: Recommended.
Special Features: Outdoor dining; Private dining room; Fireplace.

When your coachman's looking for a pub to wet his whistle and yours, the Stagecoach Hill is as a good as we've got. The 18th-century pub has Watney's on draft, Smith's Taddy Porter in bottles, and can serve up a lager and lime without question. Well-cushioned couches provide luxurious seating in one cozy nook, where in winter a fire crackles in a double-sided hearth.

Under the direction of John Pedretti and his English wife, Ann, Stagecoach Hill maintains its British flavor throughout, from the London street signs in the bar to the hunting prints and portraits of the Royal Family on the walls, from the slightly dowdy character of its dining room to its steak and kidney pie.

On Saturdays, Stagecoach Hill serves traditional English roast beef and Yorkshire pudding. During the rest of the week, entrées consist of steaks, chops, fish, and fowl. Grilled salmon is succulent, firm, and delicious. Steak and kidney pie tastes authentically British.

A coach stop since the early 1800s, Stagecoach Hill Inn continues to serve "Fine Victuals and Ardent Spirits." For English fare in the Berkshire Hills, tie up your horses here and have a pint, a chat, and a kidney pie.

Stockbridge

THE CAFE
413-298-4461.
Off Main St., (in the Mews),
  Stockbridge.
Closed: Tues. & Wed. during winter.
Price: Inexpensive.
Cuisine: American.
Serving: B, L.
Credit Cards: None.

The Cafe is a Stockbridge delight, with its enclosed porch, its skylit atrium, and its ample menu. Breakfast is still something of an event, with offerings such as eggs Florentine and "Not Just French Toast," a heavenly layering of cream cheese and orange marmalade between two slices of challah French toast. And lunch is even more so, with fare such as mesquite-grilled chicken breast sandwich, Cajun burgers, and Hawaiian chicken salad. There's Rolling Rock on tap, Heineken and Samuel Adams in the bottle, and wine by the glass, as well as soft drinks, teas, and coffees.

JILL'S
413-298-0224
Elm St., Stockbridge.
Price: Inexpensive.
Cuisine: American/Middle
  Eastern.
Serving: B, L.
Credit Cards: D, MC, V.

Simple and to the point, Jill's is an unpretentious luncheonette, delivering wholesome, fresh-made lunches and snacks at modest prices — sandwiches, soups, and Middle Eastern specialties. A Greek pita we recently enjoyed was chockablock full of fresh cut greens, olives, feta, and artichoke hearts. A wide range of herbal teas, sparkling waters, and sodas is offered to go with your meal. Ice creams and delicious desserts could top it all off.

MICHAEL'S
413-298-3530.
Elm St., Stockbridge.
Price: Moderate to Expensive.
Cuisine: American, Italian.
Serving: L, D.
Credit Cards: AE, CB, DC,
  MC, V.
Special Features: Late night
  menu.

Michael's has come a long way. With its expanded atrium in the back, boasting twin oversized TVs, Michael's is geared toward fun. Occasional live entertainment in the back supports that effort, adding a real spark to sleepy Stockbridge nightlife.

Up front, Michael's is much more sedate, a family restaurant frequented by locals and tourists alike. A far-reaching, moderately priced menu is at the heart of this restaurant's continued popularity. A house specialty is tortellini with shrimp and broccoli in a pesto sauce. But to our surprise, when we tried it, the very little taste we first perceived failed to be enhanced by considerable seasoning.

We have had pretty decent fare at Michael's, lunches that worked and late-night snacks that hit the spot. They've come a long way at Michael's — with miles to go before they sleep.

MIDGE'S
413-298-3040.
Elm St., Stockbridge.
Price: Inexpensive
Cuisine: American
Serving: L.
Credit Cards: None

Midge's offers relief from the pervasive Stockbridge preciousness. By serving good soups and sandwiches at reasonable prices, this lunch shop champions the ordinary in us all, providing sustenance to the people, not least in the form of good ice cream cones for strolling on warm days. If you're a people, you want to head down to Midge's.

Located until 1994 in an alley off Elm St., Midge's new quarters are next door in Shanahan's Market.

NAJI'S
413-298-5465
40 Main St., Stockbridge.
Closed: Mon. in winter.
Price: Inexpensive.
Cuisine: Lebanese/Greek.
Serving: L, D.
Credit Cards: AE, MC, V.
Special Features: Catering;
   Take-out service.

In the space that housed the original Alice's Restaurant, in the Romanesque trompe l'oeil decor that graced Bernard Mallon's last eatery, Naji's has opened its doors, serving pizza (here or to take away), Middle Eastern delicacies, and other gourmet foods. If their menu seems too tame, check over the deli cases, filled with bowls of shrimp with pasta, stuffed grape leaves, egg rolls, artichoke hearts, etc., etc. A falafel plate we recently tasted was just the falafel itself, on a plate, a specialty that suffered from the skimpiness of its ingredients and the icy cold pita in which it was wrapped. Cold curried shrimp with linguine was much better, a satisfying luncheon at a fair price. Desserts included a delicious blueberry crumble cake and authentic baklava.

Naji's is a friendly place, and regulars of all varieties stop by for their Middle Eastern provisions. Maybe you'll join them; we'll probably see you there.

THE RED LION INN
413-298-5545.
Main St., Stockbridge.
Price: Expensive.
Cuisine: Traditional American.
Serving: B, L, D.
Credit Cards: AE, DC, MC, V.
Reservations: Recommended.
Handicap Access: Yes.

At the Red Lion, choices abound. Where would you like to dine — in the cozy Widow Bingham Tavern, the inn's quaint formal dining rooms or, during summertime, out in the flower-decked garden? The main dining room requires jacket for gents, seating guests in a 19th-century, chandelier-lit space dotted with dozens of antique teapots, the collection of a former owner, Mrs. Plumb. Widow Bingham Tavern, by contrast, is dimly lit, rough-hewn, and intimate, with one especially cozy alcove you can reserve; and there is no dress code here. A similar policy applies to the rear porch and shaded garden, one of the most pleasant outdoor restaurant settings in Berkshire.

But before dinner, if time and weather allow, have a cocktail out on the legendary front porch at the Red Lion and drink in some old-world feeling. This

William Tague

The Red Lion Inn, Stockbridge

is the most seasoned porch in the Berkshires and has seen more rocking and more rockers than all others combined.

Rock vigorously; prepare for the feast to come. Carefully prepared by chef Steven Mongeon, the menu is traditional New England fare — solid, with steaks, fish, and poultry. A vegetarian plate is available, but not worth a detour. Appetizers are traditional, relying more on fine raw ingredients than inventiveness. Entrée portions are more than ample. Lamb chops are an inch-and-a-half thick. The meat is consistently succulent, cooked to order, and delicious. Duckling comes with a cranberry demi-glaze and nearly crowds its wild rice and green beans off the plate, so generous is the portion.

If you're person enough, proceed to the desserts, considering among others the bread pudding, Indian pudding, pecan ball covered with butterscotch sauce, or pecan pie. You'll never leave the Lion hungry.

The Red Lion also serves breakfast (an elegant bargain), lunch, various in-between-meals, snacks and, in summer, a most welcome, light late-night menu. We recently enjoyed an eggs Benedict made with Berkshire smoked salmon one afternoon in the Red Lion's garden, altogether one of the best brunch plates we'd ever eaten in Berkshire. The inn's lively, music-filled tavern downstairs, the Lion's Den, offers tasty sandwiches and desserts. When the inn is busy, breakfast may be restricted to lodgers; be sure to phone ahead. Watch for special holiday and Sunday dinner menus announced in the *Berkshire Eagle*. Whatever the day, service is exemplary throughout the Red Lion, a bright, attentive enthusiasm that never becomes intrusive.

SHOGUN
413-298-4490.
Rte. 7, Stockbridge.

Shogun is housed in the venerable Stockbridge Station, an 1893 English Gothic Revival building designed by Stanford White. The staff has

At Stockbridge Station, S. of village.
Closed: Mon., Tues. lunch in winter.
Price: Moderate to Expensive.
Cuisine: Japanese macrobiotic.
Serving: L, D.
Credit Cards: AE, D, MC, V.
Reservations: Recommended.
Special Features: Open late; Vegetarian dishes.

recently been upgraded with the addition of samurai chef Yo Hattori, with 20 years' sushi experience. The good news here is that the sushi is delicious and half-price(!) Tuesday to Friday. Entrées and desserts are also well-prepared, fine-tasting fare. The bad news is that the service here doesn't even begin to make it onto the charts. We've been walked out on during lunch, having to finish our meal self-service style; and we've seen parties literally standing and screaming for their much-delayed food.

Stockbridge Station deserves better and so do you.

West Stockbridge

CAFFE POMO D'ORO
413-232-4616.
6 Depot St., W. Stockbridge.
Closed: Tues. & Wed. in winter.
Price: Inexpensive to Expensive.
Cuisine: Tuscan Italian/Continental.
Serving: B, L, D (wkends in summer).
Credit Cards: None.
Reservations: Recommended.
Special Features: Vegetarian dishes.

In a corner of the restored and refurbished West Stockbridge train station, Scott Edward Cole has opened the new Caffe Pomo d'Oro, an Italian-flavored provision company. The space is lofty and skylit, the floor terra-cotta tile, the fixtures woody, the walls white, and exotic gourmet provisions everywhere.

Serving breakfast and lunch, and dinners on Friday and Saturday nights, the Caffe has become a favorite in West Stockbridge. Among the more enticing antipasti on a recent menu was Lattaio, locally produced buffalo mozzarella served with fresh tomatoes and basil. A torta pomodòro — red and yellow tomato tart filled with ricotta, mozzarella, pecorino Romano, and basil — was even better than it sounds. Satisfying luncheon sandwiches, served on a sliced baguette, included hickory smoked turkey breast, soprassata, buffalo mozzarella, and a Black Forest ham. A refrigerated display case up front holds dozens of other offerings.

Beverages run the gamut from Mad River Natural Sodas (like a super snappy Black Cherry Explosion) to Reed's Ginger Beer, with marvelous teas and coffees as well.

Dinner entrées change every weekend, recently including a huge half of Muscovy duck, roasted with red wine and thyme, wild rice, and a confit of sun-dried tomato; and roasted pork loin, wrapped in herbs and pancetta, served with rosemary potatoes Anna and steamed green beans.

For desserts, try the blackberry French bread pudding, or chef Cole's cinnamon roll with its chewy, buttery pastry dough and creamy cinnamon swirl — the best in the Berkshires. His raisin scone is as good as any you might ever taste in old England.

For a light continental breakfast, lunch, an elegant coffee break, gourmet provisions, or a weekend dinner out, Caffe Pomo d'Oro is our stop of choice in West Stockbridge.

LA BRUSCHETTA RISTORANTE
413-232-7141.
1 Harris St., W. Stock-
  bridge.
Closed: Wed.; Mon.–Wed.
  in winter.
Price: Expensive.
Cuisine: Italian.
Serving: D.
Credit Cards: AE, MC, V.
Reservations: Recom-
  mended.
Special Features: Overlook-
  ing a river.

Fresh from his stint as chef at Blantyre, chef Steven Taub has realized every chef's dream-come-true, opening his own successful restaurant. In the space formerly occupied by Truc Orient Express (they've moved entirely into their other building next door), La Bruschetta has brought first-class Italian dining to West Stockbridge. The wine list, too, is one of Berkshire's better lists and certainly its best priced.

An antipasto of fried eggplant slices layered with pesto of green olives, capers, and herbs was symphonic and simply satisfying simultaneously. Even more exciting was a lobster and scallop sausage served hot on a bed of diced ripe tomatoes, basil, tarragon, chive, shallot, extra virgin olive oil, and sherry vinegar.

Among the excellent pastas we've sampled are pappardelle (wide-cut pasta), cooked with wild and domestic mushrooms in cream; and farfalla (bow-tie pasta), with smoked sausages, roasted peppers, basil, Niçoise olives, and olive oil.

Entrées, entitled here "Primo," are primo indeed. Pan-roasted boneless trout stuffed with spinach and sorrel with a lemon, caper, brown butter, and herb sauce is superb, and at $9.95, the deal of deals. Equally excellent is their fresh breast of duckling with a sauce of sun-dried tomatoes, fresh basil, white wine, and demi-glacé.

Desserts are suitably decadent, with Chef Taub's awesome tiramisu, a creamy cappuccino mousse cake, leading the pack. While La Bruschetta is still developing its atmosphere, its food is immediately among the best in the region.

SHAKER MILL TAVERN
413-232-8565; 800-322-8565.
Rte. 102, W. Stockbridge.
Price: Moderate.
Cuisine: American & Ital-
  ian.
Credit Cards: AE, MC, V.
Reservations: Recom-
  mended on wkends.

Calling itself "A Classic American Tavern," Shaker Mill Tavern will chill, grill, bake, sizzle, or broil it to get it just the way you like it. What was a lively place has gotten livelier; and the good food has gotten even better. Besides a vast selection of sandwiches, burgers, tidbits, soups, salads, pasta, kebabs, and . . . pizzas(!), Shaker Mill has one of the most effervescent beer

Special Features: Outdoor dining; Private dining rooms; Fireplaces.

lists in the Berkshires, including: Samuel Smith's Pale Ale (England); Pinkus Original Weizen (West Germany); Aass Pilsner (Norway); and John Courage Draft (England).

In its expansive, woody dining rooms, Shaker Mill continues to please.

TRUC ORIENT EXPRESS
413-232-4204.
Harris St., W. Stockbridge.
One block off Main St. (Rte. 102), over Williams River.
Closed: Nov.–May.
Price: Moderate to Expensive.
Cuisine: Vietnamese.
Serving: L, D.
Credit Cards: AE, MC, V.
Reservations: Recommended.
Special Features: Vegetarian dishes; Outdoor dining.

Truc has moved to its annex barn, a space it sometimes occupied in busier times. As soon as you enter the building, you will see that owners Luy Nguyen and Trai Duong have dedicated themselves to quality and artistry. The decor is gracious and welcoming . . . and a welcome relief from pervasive New Englandiana. Here you can pretend you're somewhere in exotic Southeast Asia.

The one word of caution: abandon caution. In selecting items from this generally Vietnamese menu, it is best to experiment. Ask the waiter for his recommendations, or give the chef free rein, specifying only the principal ingredient you want and the amount you're willing to spend. In this manner, the only weakness of Truc's menu — its Americanized alternatives for the timid — may be confidently avoided.

Of the appetizers, the best we have tried is the Truc special shrimp roll, a triangular package of crabmeat, pork, vegetables, and shrimp, served with a garnish of ruby red lettuce and a spicy sweet-and-sour Vietnamese dipping sauce.

Two fine entrées at Truc are the sweet and sour fish and the Nahtrang pork barbecue. The fish is a deep-fried flounder in a light, crisp batter, dressed in a sauce that is neither too sweet nor too sour, neither syrupy nor thick. The absence of red dye is greatly appreciated and underscores the importance attached in this cuisine to ingredients that are fresh and to cooking techniques accentuating this freshness. The barbecued pork is ground, slightly spiced, and seared on a bamboo skewer over an open flame. This is a good hearty entrée with plenty of pork, enough to satisfy the lusty American appetite.

Although the dessert course does not play a major role in a Vietnamese meal, we have found both the crème caramel and lemon mousse pleasing if untraditional.

For an extraordinarily comfortable and gracious gourmet Vietnamese meal, Truc is the only game in town.

The warmth and cheer of a fireside dinner, at the Williamsville Inn.

Jonathan Sternfield

THE WILLIAMSVILLE INN
413-274-6118.
Rte. 41, W. Stockbridge.
About 10 mi. N. of Gt.
  Barrington, in hamlet
  of Williamsville.
Closed: Mon.–Wed. in
  winter.
Price: Expensive.
Cuisine: Country French.
Serving: D.
Credit Cards: AE, MC,
  V.
Reservations: Requested.
Handicap Access: Yes.
Special Features: Fireplace.

This 18th-century inn has always afforded true early American ambiance, with fine fare to match. Under the skilled guidance of chef Dennis Powell, Williamsville has lifted itself another notch. At a nicely appointed table, our meal began well with superior popovers delivered hot and steamy in a linen-covered breadbasket.

Among the appetizers, the chef recommended the catfish beignets — hot-sauce marinated, farm-raised catfish, dredged in a seasoned flour, sautéed to a golden puff, and served with a sauce of mayonnaise, sour cream, and Dijon mustard. Superb! Among the entrées, grilled boneless breast of duck was a standout, succulent with gamy juices, a marinade of seasoned oil, fresh rosemary and garlic, and an orange-fig sauce. Braised veal shanks Milanese style were just as good, the veal braised in a rich stock with onions, fennel, celeriac, and chopped tomatoes, and served with saffron risotto. The excellent desserts included a harvest apple pie, replete with cranberries and pear, winning all prizes.

With its crackling fires in winter and year-round country charm, Williamsville ranks among Berkshire's best restaurants. On Sundays, November through April, an evening of storytelling is offered, complete with a prix-fixe dinner. Through the summer, enjoy the fine offerings of the sculpture exhibit before dinner.

RESTAURANTS CENTRAL COUNTY

Lenox

APPLE TREE INN
413-637-1477.
224 West St., Lenox.
On Rte. 183, S. of Tangle-
  wood main gate.
Closed: Mon.–Wed. off
  season.
Price: Expensive.
Cuisine: Continental.
Serving: SB, L, D.
Credit Cards: AE, DC, MC,
  V.
Reservations: Recom-
  mended.
Handicap Access: Yes.

Up above Tanglewood, looking over Lake Makeenac (Stockbridge Bowl) and all of southern Berkshire, the Apple Tree Inn sits majestic. Its octagonal dining room delivers daytime vistas that are powerfully distracting from food, friends, or conversation. By night, hundreds of tiny "starlights" glow from the ceiling. Now Greg and Aurora Smith have added a delightful deck with awning, overlooking the lake, giving Apple Tree the best-dressed view in the Berkshires.

On a recent visit we enjoyed a five-onion soup combining Bermuda and Spanish onions with shallots, leeks, and scallions and served with seasoned croutons, a robust beginning to any meal. Artichoke hearts with chèvre were also a winner, the artichokes breaded and served with a vinaigrette.

Four imaginative pastas were offered, our favorite being penne with smoked scallops and shrimp, enhanced by the addition of shiitake mushrooms and scallops. Among the fine selection of meat and fish entrées, we were most delighted by the veal Normandy, the tenderest of veal served with apples and a cream brandy sauce. Grilled salmon steak was also superb, marinated as it was with shallots, garlic, basil, olive and raspberry vinegar, then charcoal-grilled and topped with lemon butter.

BLANTYRE
413-637-3556 (Winter: 413-
  298-3806).
Off Rte. 20, several mi. NW
  of Lee.
Closed: Nov. 1–May 31.
Price: Very expensive, prix
  fixe.
Cuisine: French.
Serving: D.
Credit Cards: AE, MC, V.
Reservations: Required.
Special Features: Fireplaces;
  Private dining room.
Handicap Access: Yes.

Blantyre is a true representation of Berkshire life as it was lived in the Gilded Age. Motoring up the castle's gently curving drive, you pass acres of closely cropped lawn. Once you are inside the expansive Tudor manor hall, the paintings, antiques, carpets, houseplants, and even the array of coffee-table magazines all will tell you this is the realm of the rich. Not a detail is missed here, from Tilo Kaufman's magnificent carved and painted rocking horse (whose soul brother rocks at the Red Lion), to a sterling potpourri bowl the size of a birdbath. Blantyre, the house, is baronial. Read the story of its builders and its style in Chapter Three, *Lodging*.

*Making dinner selections,
in the baronial splendor of
Blantyre.*

Jonathan Sternfield

Dinner here is decidedly theatrical. To begin, the tuxedo-attired maître d' offers drinks (serve-yourself style at the open rolling bar) for which you sign. On a couch that had room for an entire retinue, we enjoyed our cocktails and studied the menu and wine list, a dazzling array of dining and drinking choices.

Under the prix-fixe scheme, chef David Lawson (formerly of the Old Inn on the Green), presented a menu of many delights. Among the appetizers we sampled, pot-au-feu pheasant was as delicate as a game soup can be. And mousseline of fresh and smoked trout, with flageolet beans and lemon beurre blanc, was superb, seeming almost like an essence of trout.

A complimentary small lobster tail with pureed celery root came next, a powerful and delicious delivery from out of nowhere. Among the entrées, noisettes of venison, chive spaetzle, and sauce poivrade with cèpes was sensational, the deer tender and slightly gamy, the sauce supporting and augmenting its flavors perfectly. Magret duck breast, one of chef Lawson's signature dishes, was no less superb, served with potato-caramel flan and braised red cabbage with chestnuts.

From its spectacular wine cellar, Blantrye offers a tremendous range of the best vintages from France, Italy, Germany, and California. With our meal, we drank two splendid reds, Château Lynch Bages 1982, and a Jordan, vintage 1989. Though our first bottle of the Lynch Bages proved "off," the wine steward smoothly and quickly replaced it with a good bottle, never doubting our judgment on this hundred-dollar vintage.

Desserts were suitably divine, a pear cobbler with cinnamon ice cream and fresh berries taking us to the lower stratosphere of heaven. We settled in then with bananas Foster and a sorbet sampler, all fruity delicious.

Service through all courses was assured and knowledgeable, formally correct, but still somehow friendly. Forever bordering on perfection, Blantyre has somehow taken a giant step closer.

Jonathan Sternfield

Afternoon chat in the company of a cat, on the outdoor deck at Cafe Lucia.

CAFE LUCIA
413-637-2640.
90 Church St., Lenox.
Closed: Sun. & Mon. off season.
Price: Moderate to expensive.
Cuisine: Italian.
Serving: D.
Credit Cards: AE, CB, DC, MC, V.
Reservations: Recommended.
Special Features: Vegetarian dishes; Outdoor dining.

Moving into its maturity, Cafe Lucia improves with age, a tall order for a restaurant that was excellent right from the start. Choose either the dining room in the sleekly remodeled house that was once an art gallery, or in mild weather the shaded deck under a great green awning. On weekends especially, you may have to wait a few minutes for a table.

Lucia currently serves dinner only, a limited selection of excellently prepared specialties. Antipasti include carpaccio (thinly sliced raw beef) with a caper and mustard sauce; and locally smoked salmon with red onions, extra virgin olive oil, lemon, and capers. Five pasta dishes are offered, among them just about the best cannelloni we've ever eaten. This unusual version is stuffed with spinach, goat cheese, sun-dried tomatoes, and mascarpone, then baked in a light tomato basil cream sauce. Superb!

Outstanding entrées include chicken scarparello (chicken and homemade sausage roasted in white wine and balsamic vinegar, with onions, olives, capers, peppers, and mushrooms); and Lucia's signature dish — osso buco con risotto (a milk-fed veal shank sautéed, then braised in a veal sauce seasoned with diced carrots, onions, celery, and fresh herbs).

Desserts are rich, with a superior tiramisu leading the way.

THE CANDLELIGHT INN
413-637-1555.
53 Walker St.
Price: Expensive.
Cuisine: Continental.
Serving: SB, L, D.

The Dutch have a word for it: *gezelligheid* — hominess taken to its highest power of coziness — and without doubt the Candlelight Inn wins our "Golden Tulip" award for the most *gezellig* dining room in the Berkshires.

We found a recently sampled swordfish in

Credit Cards: AE, CB, DC, MC, V.
Reservations: Recommended.
Special Features: Fireplaces.

tomato basil beurre blanc quite good, though a bit less than the sum of its fine parts. Desserts restored the mood, especially the lemon mousse torte and an all-American apple crisp.

Though slightly uneven, the entire meal was served with such unpretentious grace and warmth that we finished feeling quite satisfied.

In warmer weather, the Candlelight offers dining al fresco in their lovely backyard garden. In this leaf-shaded glade lies the catbird seat of Lenox, and from your perch there, you can watch much of the town's activity — passersby on Church Street, and the pilgrims coming or going to Tanglewood.

CAROL'S
413-637-8948.
4 Franklin St., Lenox.
Closed: Wed. off season.
Price: Inexpensive.
Cuisine: American.
Serving: B, L.
Credit Cards: None.

Despite its cinder-block ambiance, Carol's continues to delight, offering some of the best breakfasts and lunches around. Carol's own, homemade, seven-grain whole-wheat bread is featured as a sandwich bread or breakfast toast (also available by the loaf for take-home). The home fries on breakfast plates are sensational. The pancakes are fun (buckwheat, blueberry, or chocolate chip!), and the omelets imaginative (Kitchen Sinker — onions, bacon, mushrooms, cheese, and sour cream on the side).

Lunches feature meaty sandwiches, such as the Gobble It Up — turkey breast, onion, and spicy mustard on their homemade sourdough, topped with melted cheese. A variety of salads and vegetable/cheese sandwiches make Carol's an appealing option for vegetarians and vegetable lovers.

CHURCH STREET CAFE
413-637-2745.
69 Church St., Lenox.
Price: Moderate.
Cuisine: American.
Serving: L, D.
Credit Cards: MC, V.
Reservations: Recommended.
Special Features: Outdoor dining.

We're wary of heaping any more praise on this excellent eatery. Already occasionally overwhelmed by its summertime popularity, Church Street continues to be our pick for the best all-round restaurant in the shire town. Clayton Hambrick and co-owner Linda Forman have expanded their restaurant three times. Church Street's patio is one of the prettiest in the county, and its interior dining rooms resemble art galleries — which they are.

Given their only moderately expensive prices, this restaurant is an uncommonly good bargain. Soups are imaginative and hearty, salads are fresh. The wine list is unpretentious, refreshingly brief, and intelligent. Service here is cordial and attentive; and even when Church Street is busy, which is often, meals generally unfold at the customer's preferred pace.

Things Southern, like gumbos or "New Orleans Shrimp," show Hambrick and his well-trained staff at their best.

All Church Street desserts are created in house; each has earned applause. Mocha torte, misnamed but divine, features Heath Bars blended into chocolate-and-mocha ice cream, then topped with hot fudge. Swedish cream is a slightly sour, creamy custard under a delicate strawberry sauce. Apple cake is moist, none too sweet, and accompanied by fresh-whipped High Lawn Farm cream.

CRANWELL
413-637-1364.
Rte. 20., Lenox.
Price: Expensive.
Cuisine: Continental.
Serving: D, SB.
Credit Cards: AE, MC, V.
Reservations: Recommended.

Cranwell was originally Wyndhurst, the "cottage" of John Sloane, a formal Tudor estate, with gardens by Frederick Law Olmsted. Now it's a resort and conference center, and a restaurant.

You'll likely be served in the Wyndhurst Room, a grand space with ornate, high ceilings, and tall, majestic windows. Tables are lace covered, candle-lit, and flower decorated, and altogether the effect is one of hushed dignity. Cranwell's latest menu is imaginative and well prepared, their chef and obviously large kitchen staff working well together. We sampled many, many dishes at their Christmas Buffet, a superior feast.

The buffet featured roast beef with Yorkshire pudding; stuffed loin of pork with apples, raisins, apricots, and lingonberry sauce; breast of chicken with shiitake mushroom sauce; mélange of seafood with sherry cream and lobster sauce; and fresh pasta, prepared individually, to order, with marinara, Alfredo, or tomato concasse and wild mushroom sauce. A vast array of salads, breads, and vegetables complemented the meal(s) nicely.

For dessert, we tried the warm plum pudding, the cheesecake, the chocolate and white chocolate mousse, the raspberry nut torte, and the pecan and apple pies. Solid and delicious.

CROSBY'S
413-637-3396.
62 Church St., Lenox.
Price: Inexpensive.
Cuisine: International.
Serving: L.
Credit Cards: MC, V.
Special Features: Catering; Take-out service.

Since Crosby's is one of Berkshire's best caterers, fine food has been issuing here for years, and it's once again available to diners, with lunch served Wednesday through Sunday. We had a wild mushroom and wild rice soup whose subtle flavors and textures satisfied many appetites at once. Comfortable from that first course, we then launched into a wonderful smoked turkey sandwich on a baguette that came across as perfect in every respect.

We felt catered to, and you will too, at Crosby's.

A tuxedoed waiter pours wine with panache, at the Gateways.

Jonathan Sternfield

THE GATEWAYS INN
413-637-2532.
71 Walker St., Lenox.
Closed: Sun. & Mon. off
  season.
Price: Expensive to Very
  Expensive, prix fixe.
Cuisine: Continental.
Serving: D.
Credit Cards: AE, DC, MC,
  V.
Reservations: Required.
Special Features: Vegetar-
  ian dishes; Dress require-
  ments; Outdoor dining;
  Private dining room;
  Fireplace.

Only eight restaurants in New England have been awarded a four-star rating by Mobil, and the Gateways continues to be top rated (translated by Mobil as "outstanding — worth a special trip"). Every dimension of dining is elegant at Gateways, from the splendid china and silver to the French-folded damask napkins, from the lively floral centerpieces to the woven silver breadbasket.

In the rather formal dining room of "Orleton," the 1912 mansion built by Harley Procter of Procter and Gamble soap fame, you'll be treated like the magnate himself. Appetizers include duck salad with raspberry vinaigrette, and lobster and sweetbread crêpes. Of the five soups offered, we found both the baked French onion and the lobster and clam bisque to be fine, indeed.

Among the entrées, pheasant in a sauce of white grapes, juniper berries, brandy, and cream is sensational, an enticing counterpoint of gamy, sweet, and creamy. Provincial rack of lamb, one of the restaurant's specialties, is superb. Roasted with garlic, toasted bread crumbs, and parsley, and served with its own natural juice, the lamb is exceptionally tender, juicy, and flavorful.

Desserts at Gateways are sumptuous. Chocolate hazelnut cake is unexpectedly light, undeniably delicious. The Viennese apple strudel is a divine, old-world pastry, with raisins and walnuts, topped with some Lenox-made Denham's vanilla ice cream.

For those sweet days of summer, spring, and fall, Gateways has opened its patio. Here, under a striped awning, you can enjoy both the Berkshires and some of Berkshire's best dining.

LENOX HOUSE
413-637-1341.
Pittsfield-Lenox Rd. (Rtes. 7 & 20), Lenox.
Just N. of village.
Price: Moderate to Expensive.
Cuisine: Continental.
Serving: L, D.
Credit Cards: AE, CB, DC, MC, V.
Reservations: Recommended.
Special Features: Children's menu; Private dining room; Fireplace.

As the competition for your dining dollar heats up, restaurants are forced to refine themselves. Lenox House had a long way to go, and, remarkably, their kitchens have made great strides. Everything about our most recent meal there suggested a new approach — from the fresh, still moist and hot popovers served soon after we ordered, to the affable and assured service of our European waiter.

One entrée we tasted stood out in particular, a New England seafood pie, featuring scallops, clams, lobsters, and potatoes topped by a puff pastry. Just great!

Lenox House has taken the challenge and moved up on the pack.

LENOX 218
413-637-4218.
218 Main St., on Rte. 7A., Lenox.
Price: Moderate.
Cuisine: New American, Continental.
Serving: L, D, SB.
Credit Cards: AE, DC, MC, V.
Handicap Access: Yes.

Chef Jimmy DeMayo has always served an appealing plate. Teaming up with chefs Hugh Pecon, Jr., and Christina Gonzalez, De Mayo continues to preside over one of the area's sleekest dining spots. Lenox 218 is noticeably interior-decorated, with shiny black tables (cloth-covered for dinner), comfy black and brass chairs, vaulted ceilings with fans and skylights, and lots of framed prints.

DeMayo ran the popular Candlelight Inn and Painted Lady restaurants before he founded Lenox 218, where his artistry continues. Soups are hearty and fresh. The chicken pot pie is meaty, its crust flaky. Fresh New England salmon cakes with tomato salsa sauce are sensational, offered in summertime with a sweet ear of corn. Recent dinner entrées have included roast Long Island duckling with raspberry Chambord sauce, and a brochette of Cajun swordfish with peppers and mushrooms. Presentation is excellent, with each very hot plate succeeding in every way.

PANDA HOUSE
413-499-0660.
664 Pittsfield-Lenox Rd.,
Lenox.
Price: Moderate.
Cuisine: Szechuan,
Mandarin, Hunan.
Serving: L, D.
Credit Cards: AE, MC, V.

Though not a chain, this Panda very much resembles the others in Berkshire, except that it's on the strip just south of Pittsfield. As with the other local Pandas, the food is delicious, chock-full of good ingredients that have been well prepared. Threatened with extinction elsewhere, Pandas are now thriving in Berkshire.

ROSEBOROUGH GRILL
413-637-2700.
83 Church St., Lenox.
Closed: Tues. & Wed. in
winter.
Price: Moderate to Expen-
sive.
Cuisine: American.
Serving: L, D, SB.
Credit Cards: AE, MC, V,
D.
Reservations: Recom-
mended.
Special Features: Old New
England home, variety of
dining nooks.

The Roseborough Grill picks up where Cheese-cake Charlie's left off, redecorating the expansive interior of this old Lenox house and giving the neighborhood yet another expensive eatery. Chefs David Pullaro and Laura Shack turn out a generally appealing array of lunches and dinners, but by us they haven't been infallible.

Out on their slender porch one evening, we savored the splendors of Roseborough's red pepper and basil penne with sautéed garlic shrimp. In a slightly spicy, light shrimp broth with slivers of red pepper, this culinary creation was simply superb.

But when we returned for lunch the very next day, our choice — smoked salmon on a Brooklyn bagel — was a disappointment. The cream cheese came in an unappetizing plastic cup, the lid freshly pulled back, the cream cheese sitting flat where it had been squeezed by machine. The fish tasted fine, but the bagel shoulda stayed in Brooklyn. In all fairness, this smoked salmon on a Brooklyn bagel tasted better than it looked.

We thought it imaginative of the Grill to offer their Roseborough Pie, a four-berry pie that included blackberries, blueberries, strawberries, and raspberries. The secret here would be to let the berries play off each other, but unfortunately we found that their flavors blended together, no single berry flavor being truly distinct.

Still, this place is good and will get better. And Roseborough offers one of the more active entertainment schedules, with live music inside.

**THE SWEET BASIL
GRILLE**
413-637-1270.
306 Pittsfield-Lenox Rd. at
Brushwood Farm, Lenox.
Closed: Mon. in winter;
February.
Price: Moderate.
Cuisine: Italian.
Serving: L, D.

Sweet Basil occupies an impressive structure, the original "Brushwood Farm." The front section of this attractive, rambling building is one of the oldest houses in Lenox, reaching back to the 1750s. There is a comfortable mix of Colonial and Victorian styles here. Sweet Basil now makes fullest use of the place, seating diners upstairs as well as on ground level. We recently dined in a low-ceilinged upstairs

Credit Cards: AE, MC, V, D.
Reservations: Recommended.
Special Features: European country atmosphere in a 1700s house; 5 separate dining rooms.

room, where we enjoyed the random-width flooring and Colonial proportions of the room, though we disliked the "easy-listening" music that was piped into a minispeaker near our table.

Chef-owned Sweet Basil is Rick Penna's essentially Italian grill. Two soups were offered on a recent night: pasta fagioli and cream of roasted garlic. Appealing appetizers include deep fried calimari and roasted garlic rounds. Shrimp alla Ricardo is sautéed shrimp with fresh tomatoes, basil, ripened Brie, garlic, onion, and freshly grated Parmesan cheese in a light cream sauce served over a monstrous bed of linguine.

All entrées are accompanied by pasta. Portions are very hearty, value is very evident. Specialty coffees are offered to close out your meal, as is homemade cannoli and spumoni. Looks like Sweet Basil is here to stay.

THE VILLAGE INN
413-637-0020.
16 Church St., Lenox.
Closed: Mon. & Tues. for dinner.
Price: Moderate.
Cuisine: Regional American/New England.
Serving: B, SB, D.
Credit Cards: AE, CB, DC, MC, V.
Reservations: Recommended.
Special Features: Traditional English tea served every afternoon.

For over 200 years, the Village Inn has glowed at night, and the glow continues. In the soft amber light that pervades this Colonial way station, you can see the luster of old-world attention. Not a detail is missed, and whether you dine in the dining room or out on the glass-enclosed porch, the ambiance will be as cozy as it gets.

As we go to press, the Inn will be serving dinner under a new chef, specializing in regional American cuisine at moderate prices, with emphasis on New England dishes. Breakfast is served every day till 10:30 a.m., till noon Sunday, and tea is served every afternoon (see sidebar below).

High Tea at The Village Inn

English tea is available every afternoon from 2:30 to 4:30, featuring an assortment of homemade scones with strawberry preserves and clotted cream, as well as a dessert tray. A choice of select teas accompanies this delightfully light repast.

A considerably more elaborate high tea is offered on one Sunday afternoon each month from January through May. On those occasions (be sure to phone — reservations are required), the event begins with live chamber music, then proceeds into the dining room for traditional English high tea — a light supper in three courses. The first course includes finger sandwiches as well as the customary scones with clotted cream and strawberry preserves. The second course is a hot savory such as creamed mushrooms on toast, Welsh rarebit, or asparagus wrapped in ham with cheese sauce, and the finale is a traditional English trifle. The accompanying teas are an unsually large assortment from the John Harney Tea Company of Connecticut.

The ornate elegance of Wheatleigh.

Jonathan Sternfield

WHEATLEIGH
413-637-0610.
West Hawthorne Rd.,
  Lenox.
Price: Very Expensive, prix
  fixe.
Cuisine: Contemporary
  French.
Serving: B, L, D.
Credit Cards: AE, CB, DC,
  MC, V.
Reservations: Required.
Special Features: Fireplaces;
  Private dining room.

There are many places in Berkshire where you can look back in history to the Gilded Age. Wheatleigh, a grand 19th-century Palladian villa built for New York heiress Georgie Bruce Cook and her husband "Count" Carlos de Heredia, is a "cottage" that is carrying on in the grand tradition.

Wheatleigh has had its share of fine chefs. Now Peter Platt from Chicago has settled into its kitchens and is turning out some of the finest fare in all the Berkshires.

The extraordinary wine list, studded with scores of the finest vintages available, earned the 1989 Wine Spectator Award of Excellence as one of the most outstanding restaurant wine lists in the world.

During the high season, Wheatleigh has opened its more modestly priced (but still expensive) Grill Room. Outstanding entrées on a recent menu included Thai-style free-range chicken with almonds, cashews, and jasmine rice; and a bouillabaisse of mussels and scallops with julienned vegetables. Though this is the lesser of Wheatleigh's dining rooms, you'd never know it.

In the main dining room, from the imaginative lists of hors d'oeuvres, recent standouts included ballotine of free-range pheasant with red cabbage, caraway, and applewood-smoked bacon with calvados sauce; and a warm salad of roasted California squab with sweet corn pancakes and a black truffle sauce. Entrées of great note included roasted loin of veal with fresh Oregon white truffle sauce, sweetbread, and wild mushroom raviolis; and an awesome roasted loin of wild Texas antelope with dauphinoise potato and a fresh red currant sauce.

For an extra ten dollars, you can gorge on the grand assortment of desserts. And if you're a real major-leaguer, you can go beyond the standard prix-fixe menu (priced at $65), and move up to the Menu Table d'Hôte ($80), which includes soup, appetizer, entrée, and a trio of desserts — or way up to the Menu Dégustation Classique (priced at $90), which provides an even greater sampling of chef Platt's culinary masterworks.

The Critics on Wheatleigh

Our adoration of Wheatleigh is apparently shared by others:

"Sets a table fit for a prince."
— Marion Burros, *New York Times.*
"One of the finest tables in the United States."
— *Elle Magazine.*

Hancock

THE HANCOCK INN
413-738-5873.
On Rte. 43, reachable via Rte. 22 N. of New Lebanon, NY.
Closed: Mon. & Tues.; Mon.–Thurs. off season.
Price: Expensive.
Cuisine: Continental.
Serving: D.
Credit Cards: AE, MC, V.
Reservations: Recommended for parties of 5 or more.

Built in the early 19th century as a private residence, the Hancock Inn continues to offer cozy warmth and intimate hospitality. The fare served by innkeepers Ellen and Chester Gorski is some of the region's best.

For appetizers, smoked salmon blini got a recent dinner off to a smashing start, the three little dill pancakes layered with delicious smoked salmon and topped with a dollop of red caviar-sprinkled sour cream. The salad that comes with every dinner at Hancock is among Berkshire's best; fresh tender greens, small slices of apple, and crumbled blue cheese are just three of its many excellent ingredients.

Among the latest entrées, one of our favorites was a special of Yukon pork, with sautéed tender pork medallions in Yukon Jack, and served with similarly prepared pear slices. Superb. We longed to try the duckling in port wine with figs, but alas, the early diners had beaten us to the bird.

Desserts, such as their homemade maple-walnut ice cream topped with homemade butterscotch bourbon sauce, capped a most memorable meal. Reserve early, as the Hancock can serve only a limited number of lucky diners.

Pittsfield

Jonathan Sternfield

Dinner in the lodge beneath a birch bark canoe, at Dakota.

DAKOTA
413-499-7900.
1035 South St., Pittsfield
Price: Moderate.
Cuisine: American.
Serving: D.
Credit Cards: AE, DC, MC, V.
Reservations: Recommended for parties of 5 or more.
Special Features: Fireplace.

With its pine walls, raised fieldstone fireplaces, mounted deer and moose heads, and overhanging birch-bark canoes, Dakota successfully communicates the feeling of a grand hunting lodge. In addition, the restaurant fills its odd spaces and some of its walls with truly authentic Native American artifacts, all of museum quality. The restaurant is vast, spacious and comfortable. Well managed and conceived, it is likely the county's single most popular restaurant.

With good reason. The restaurant usually operates with clockwork precision, serving an imaginative, well-prepared menu that features Texas mesquite broiling. You can choose from steak kebab and shrimp, salmon, swordfish, and chicken teriyaki, among others. A lobster pond up front offers lobster lovers their pick, with the day's price per pound clearly posted above.

All meals come with huge slabs of freshly baked whole-grain bread and privileges to a bountiful salad bar. The wine list offers two dozen popular varieties. Desserts are dandy and prices are moderate, making Tony Perry's Dakota a Berkshire roadside delight.

THE DRAGON
413-442-5594.
1231 W. Housatonic St., Pittsfield.
Price: Inexpensive.
Cuisine: Vietnamese.

Pittsfield's premier Vietnamese restaurant, Kim Van Huynh's Dragon has only gotten better with age. The restaurant interior is welcoming, and the food continues to be authentic and frequently outstanding.

Serving: D.
Reservations: Not accepted.
Special Features: Vegetarian specialties.

Kim's hot soup with crabmeat, vegetables, and button mushrooms is superb — a soup that's hot in two ways. His Vietnamese pancake is spectacular: a rice batter crêpe filled with shrimp, pork, mushrooms, bean sprouts, and onion, and served with nuoc mam' sauce. A vegetarian version of this pancake is also available. A spate of squid dishes is offered, from squid curry and squid sate' to squid with black bean sauce. In all, forty-eight entrées are currently on the menu, in sections for Chicken, Pork, the Chef's Suggestions, Rice Noodle Dishes, Beef, Seafood, and Vegetarian.

Table service, Elizabeth's style, at Elizabeth's Cafe and Pizzeria, Pittsfield.

Jonathan Sternfield

ELIZABETH'S CAFE PIZZERIA
413-448-8244.
1264 East St.
Across from "the G.E."
Price: Inexpensive.
Credit Cards: None.
Special Features: Specialty pizzas; No smoking

Right in the heart of Pittsfield's industrial downtown, Elizabeth's stand's like a tiny beacon to homeyness. Its arty interior is a tip that you might get a mix of the modern and traditional here, and indeed you do. Elizabeth's attracts such a loyal following that you'd better get there early if you want one of their few dozen seats.

Soups here are excellent; we still recall a fresh tuna in a tomato-base broth, with onions and risotto. The specials are announced to you by a playful, knowledgeable waitperson, as excited about the restaurant as its loyal fans. Polenta here is extraordinary, a far cry from the bland mush served at most restaurants.

The salads at Elizabeth's are clearly among the region's best, at any price. Our insalata mista was chunked with delicious feta cheese, studded with old-world olives, stripped with roasted pepper, crowned with slices of kiwi, and supported by a bed of the freshest, youngest, tenderest baby salad greens from the very heart of the lettuce.

As good as the soups, salads, sandwiches, and entrées are at Elizabeth's, it is their pizza for which they are justly renowned, especially their "white pie," called Rustica. "Imagine yourself a painter," the menu gamely beckons, "before you lies a canvas of silken dough. It beckons you in some primitive way. 'Come close,' it says. 'Caress me with oils, flavor me with herbs and cheeses, paint me with fresh vegetables. Use me, I am yours.'"

Over the counter trading, at the Highland.

Jonathan Sternfield

THE HIGHLAND
413-442-2457.
100 Fenn St., Pittsfield.
Closed: Mon.
Price: Inexpensive.
Serving: L, D.
Credit Cards: None.
Reservations: Not accepted.
Special Features: Nonsmoking area.

The Highland has been serving square meals to Pittsfielders since 1936.

"Spaghetti!" answered the owner when we asked him what kind of food his restaurant serves. "Spaghetti and anything from a hamburger to filet mignon." With lots of veal in between and homemade pudding and cream pies to finish.

Ted Williams and other legendary ballplayers hang out here (in oversized photographic form); and if you weren't looking closely, you could easily be in a bar near Fenway Park or Yankee Stadium, but in the '30s or '40s.

The Highland is homey: the food's pretty good, folks are friendly, prices are right. We recently enjoyed a Highland Yankee pot roast sandwich on rye, with lettuce and mayo, for $2. Infinitely more class, taste, and value than any Big Mac, a Highland meal has proved itself, satisfying Berkshire locals and tourists just passing through, pleasing just plain folks for over half a century.

PANDA INN
413-445-5580; 413-443-0819.
795 Dalton Ave., Pittsfield.
Price: Inexpensive to Moderate.

Newest Panda on the block, this Coltsville outpost is one of the best, with a huge glassed-in atrium that's daylight-filled every day, rain or shine.

Cuisine: Chinese.
Serving: L, D.
Cards: AE, MC, V.

Panda's all-you-can-eat "Most Valuable Buffet" is a Chinese-food lover's dream. Here are half-a-dozen of your favorite entrées, spread out before you with an open invitation to take whatever you want. There are also two soups, hot and sour and egg drop, spring rolls, and dozens of other offerings, from pork fried rice to Chinese dumplings.

Most Valuable Buffet is amazing, but Panda Inn does much else besides, and for your health's sake uses only vegetable oil and low-sodium ingredients during food preparation. Beyond their standard (but certainly excellent) Panda-style entrées, Panda Inn offers Neptune's Blessing, a Shanghai dish of shrimp, lobster, scallop, and crabmeat, sautéed with broccoli and snow peas in a traditional sauce.

TEO'S HOT DOGS
413-447-9592.
1410 East St., Pittsfield
Price: Inexpensive.
Serving: L, D.
Cuisine: American
Credit Cards: None.

Easy to miss but hard to forget, this doggery wins no prizes for ambiance. Instead, it concentrates on serving cold beer and a genuinely zesty miniature hot dog that you can have topped with "the works," a "chili-sauce/chopped-onions/mustard" combo that may lead to gastrointestinal meltdown unless you're blessed with an industrial-strength stomach. But relax: even strong men posing as restaurant reviewers often eat these little dogs with less than everything on 'em. We do recommend living dangerously, though: order two or three.

Mysteriously, the dogs taste best when ordered through the tiny, screened take-out window. On your way into or out of Pittsfield, this is a good bet for fast but original food.

TRUFFLES & SUCH
413-442-0151.
Allendale Shopping Center,
  (Rtes. 8 & 9), Pittsfield.
Closed: Sun.
Price: Moderate to Expen-
  sive.
Cuisine: American.
Serving: L, D.
Credit Cards: AE, CB, DC,
  MC, V.
Reservations: Recom-
  mended.

Truffles & Such is a first-class and creative dining room. The setting is modern, with sleek tables and chairs and a sophisticated buzz in the air. Owners Mike and Irene Maston have created one of the Berkshires' best restaurants.

A peasant soup with sausage and potato, sampled on a recent outing, was as hearty and earthy as it should be. A Caribbean crab cake, with ginger and green peppercorns, accompanied by spicy avocado remoulade and roast pepper sauces, made a pretty plate, but the hot stuff was too timid.

Entrées were similarly well conceived, e.g., chicken livers with sliced green apples, an exquisite combination prepared to perfection. The menu offers more than a dozen inventive entrées, half-a-dozen salads, and an equal number of appetizers.

For lunch, Truffles & Such is equally creative, featuring many of their best dinner salads, soups, and appetizers, as well as pastas, eggs dish, specialties, and unusual sandwiches like Sir Wasso's Chicken Sandwich, a broiled chicken breast in orange, soy, and sesame marinade on French bread. Daily specialties include fillet of sole aux noisettes, with almonds, walnuts, and hazelnuts.

For dessert you can choose from among such diverse items as kiwi tart, deep-dish sour-cream apple pie, fine Napoleons, chocolate hazelnut tortes, and chocolate . . . truffles and such.

RESTAURANTS NORTH COUNTY

Adams

BASCOM LODGE
At the summit of Mt. Greylock.
413-743-1591 (Winter: 603-466-2721).
On top of Mt. Greylock, off Rte. 7 to S. Main St., Lanesborough, then 7 mi. up on Rockwell Rd. to the top. Accessible from N. Adams also.
Closed: Late Oct.–mid-May.
Price: Inexpensive.
Cuisine: American.
Serving: B, L, D.
Credit Cards: MC, V.
Reservations: Required.
Special Features: 100-mi. view.
Handicap Access: Yes.

Whether you've climbed on foot, on bike, or in your car, this mountaintop restaurant is a welcome stopover. Breakfast and special dinners are the main events, served in the rustic stone and wood lodge. Berry-laden pancakes shine in the morning, the weekly barbecue buffets and New England dinners star at night. Whatever the hour, the views are breathtaking, the elevation heady. Reservations are required, and the restaurant is open seasonally, from mid-May till mid-October.

New Ashford

MILL ON THE FLOSS
413-458-9123.
Rte. 7., New Ashford.
Closed: Mon.
Price: Expensive.
Cuisine: French.
Serving: D.

The atmosphere at Maurice Champagne's Mill on the Floss is informal and warm, with massive rough-hewn beams overhead, candlelight, and firelight from the brick hearth in colder weather. The focus of the dining room is, however, its open kitchen, where, behind a Dutch tile counter and a gleaming array of hanging copper pots, chef Cham-

Mastering the art of French cuisine — Chef Maurice Champagne.

Jonathan Sternfield

Credit Cards: AE, CB, DC, MC, V.
Reservations: Recommended.

pagne in his tall white toque prepares meals before your very eyes.

Soups are superb, the split pea full-bodied yet delicate; the onion soup bold in broth with still-firm bread and perfectly browned Gruyère topping. Escargots in garlic butter are plump and flavorful, handsomely presented, and sprinkled with bread crumbs. Eggplant parmigiana, served here as an hors d'oeuvre, ought not be passed by.

Entrées are uniformly excellent. Chicken Maurice is a succulent, boneless chicken breast in a light brown sauce, topped with béarnaise. Shrimp and scallop Creole on a bed of rice is piquant and oceanic simultaneously — a satisfying, spicy dish. Crispy duckling à l'orange comes with its skin crisp yet chewy, its meat succulent and flavorful with very little fat.

Desserts range from a delicate crème caramel to a heavier though no less artful gâteau de la maison. Cold Grand Marnier soufflé with raspberry sauce is an airy confection sprinkled with slivers of almond and covered with fresh raspberry sauce.

THE SPRINGS
413-458-3465.
Rte. 7.
Closed: Christmas.
Price: Moderate.
Cuisine: Continental, American.
Serving: L, D.
Credit Cards: AE, CB, DC, MC, V.
Reservations: Recommended.
Handicap Access: Yes.

A large, popular restaurant, owned and operated by the Grosso family since the 1930s. The original building burned in the mid-1970s, and its replacement has a somewhat baronial interior. The eclectic menu includes complimentary relishes, cheese bread, baked stuffed clams, and, at dinner, a sherbet palate cleanser. The Springs has become an institution with local folk and return travelers.

North Adams

THE FREIGHTYARD PUB
413-663-6547.
Furnace St., N. Adams.
In Heritage State Park.
Price: Inexpensive.
Cuisine: American.
Serving: L, D.
Credit Cards: AE, MC, V.
Special Features: Fireplace.

One of the few pubs in all of Berkshire, the Freightyard is a two-story brick tavern in a historic district.

A kielbasa made locally in Lanesborough, presented with sauerkraut, is among the best we've tasted. Chicken teriyaki, a dish easy to spoil, comes off quite well. Burgers, soups, and sandwiches are the basic fare. A generous, well-stocked salad bar can fill any stomach space left.

JACK'S HOT DOGS
413-664-9006.
12 Eagle St., N. Adams.
Off Main St.
Closed: Sun.
Price: Inexpensive.
Serving: B, L.

Premier doggery in North County, Jack's continues a 70-year family tradition by serving outstanding dogs with all the trimmings. Jack's is supplier of the official dog for the North Adams State vs. Williams College hot dog eating contest. As one local put it, "You haven't really been to North Adams till you've been to Jack's."

Williamstown

CHOPSTICKS
413-458-5750.
412 Main St.,
    Williamstown.
Price: Inexpensive to Moderate.
Cuisine: Chinese.
Serving: L, D.
Credit Cards: AE, MC, V.

Major source of North County's hot and sour soup, Moo Shu Pork, King-Pao Chicken, and other essentials of life, Chopsticks has settled in. Their menu lists over a hundred standard Chinese dishes from various regions, with starred dishes prepared hot and spicy. For those with asbestos throats and a taste for chili oil, these dishes can be made even hotter on request. Ask for no MSG, and no MSG shall be forthcoming.

There are few surprises here, but the food is well prepared, the sauces special. The atmosphere is pleasant, the service accommodating, and there is a full bar with a small wine list. Purists have complained about the quality of the martinis at Chopsticks, and a bottle of Tsing Tao Chinese beer or even a glass of Chinese white wine may be a better choice of beverages. There is a large bar with a wonderful tropical fish tank.

COBBLE CAFE
413-458-5930.
27 Spring St., Williamstown.

We've followed the Cobble Cafe's progress with pleasure. After smoothing some rough

Closed: Easter, Thanksgiving, Christmas, New Year's Day.
Price: Inexpensive.
Cuisine: American.
Serving: B, L, D.
Credit Cards: None.

spots, Sandy Smith's restaurant has come into its own, delivering well-prepared, imaginative cuisine in low-key, collegial surroundings.

Highlights of our most recent outing here included a superior appetizer of sole cakes in red pepper sauce, a starter with soul. A Roquefort and pear salad proved an exciting bridge to the entrée, although it might have served better *after* the main course. All the entrées we recently sampled were quite fine, but one was truly sensational: a duck breast with cranberry salsa, served with rice, haricots verts, and a black-bean crêpe.

Desserts, such as apple crisp cake and Chocolate Decadence, a chocolate mousse cake, continued the magical spell. Cobble Cafe is a highlight of the Spring Street renaissance.

HOBSON'S CHOICE
413-458-9101.
159 Water St.,
Williamstown.
Price: Moderate.
Serving: L, D.
Credit Cards: MC, V.
Reservations: Recommended.

Locals know that Hobson's Choice is a good one in Williamstown for lunch, a quiet drink, dinner, or a late evening's snack. Dark wooden booths line the walls of the restaurant's two rooms, creating a sense of privacy — even intimacy. Hobson's is a comfortable place to linger.

With chef Dan Campbell playfully holding court from the open kitchen behind the salad bar, you're likely to get a custom-cooked meal, just the way you like it. "You look like the Cajun shrimp man," proffered the chef as we picked out our salad fixings. "How would you like it — extra spicy?"

"Regular spicy," was our reply, and we got it just that way, a delightful spread of seafood on wild rice.

Hobson's offers a wide variety of chicken (grilled, blackened, barbecued, teriyaki, and Santa Fe style), beef, fish, pasta, and vegetarian specialties, all flavorfully prepared. They make their own soups, and onion soup gratinée is especially good.

A comfortable, well-stocked bar includes a nice selection of imported beers and ales, plus a modest wine list. Hot mulled cider, espresso, and cappuccino provide warmth and cheer for the more abstemious.

LE JARDIN
413-458-8032.
777 Cold Spring Rd.
South of Williamstown.
Closed: Tues. off season.
Price: Moderate to Expensive.

High on a hill, lit like a fairy castle, Le Jardin appeals to the eye as you stroll up its path, past a tranquil pond. Inside, the mood is that of a country inn. Formerly chef at the Springs (New Ashford) and also at Blantyre (Lenox), chef Walter Hayn serves more of a continental menu than

Cuisine: French.
Serving: D.
Reservations: Recommended.
Special Features: Fireplace; Vegetarian dishes; 3 dining rooms.

strictly a French one, with a greater emphasis on steaks and chops than on subtlety of sauces.

A favorite among Williams grads, Le Jardin offers a pleasant evening without getting too fussy. Though the menu is in French, it is also in English, and the food generally holds up well in the translation from kitchen to dining room. We found the breads and salads less than distinguished, but the hearty, homestyle entrées, served with broccoli and cheese, roasted potato and sweet potato, precisely matched the conviviality of the dining room. And besides all their visual appeal, the sole, duck, and other entrées proved to be nicely done.

Among the enticing desserts, a particularly sinister one was chosen by a member of our party, our dear friend falling fatally for Death by Chocolate Gâteau.

News of the day, Orchards style.

Jonathan Sternfield

THE ORCHARDS
413-458-9611.
222 Adams Rd., Williamstown.
Price: Expensive.
Cuisine: American, French.
Serving: B, SB, L, D.
Credit Cards: AE, CB, DC, MC, V.
Reservations: Recommended.
Special Features: Private dining room.

The Orchards, having changed hands, continues to serve fine meals in a gracious setting. In its appointments and attention to tableware, the Orchards still gets high marks. The tables are set with real Irish linen and graceful stemware and accented with colorful fresh bouquets. The dining rooms' walls are covered in a green plush velvet. Sailing-ship models in glass cases separate several of the dining rooms, and the restaurant has about it the feel of a club for people of substantial resources.

Recent appetizers ranged from an extraordinary apple walnut tortellini with sliced duck breast and calvados allemande to a hearty New England clam chowder with huge slices of fresh clam. The grilled swordfish entrée is served with Anjou pear chutney and rosemary-lime beurre blanc, the roast rack of lamb being "wrapped in a macadamia nut crust."

For dessert, a pear tart with almond paste crust confirmed that the Orchards would draw us back again soon.

Hanging out with Bo Derek, Zonker Harris and Dr. Strangepork, among many others, at Pappa Charlie's.

Jonathan Sternfield

PAPPA CHARLIE'S DELI SANDWICH SHOP
413-458-5969.
28 Spring St.
Price: Inexpensive.
Cuisine: American.
Serving: B, L, D.
Special Features: Open late.

Pappa Charlie's reigns supreme as a people's place and local hangout, convenient to the Images Cinema just down the street. It still serves good sandwiches and such. If you think you're seeing double when eyeing "the Deli" in Great Barrington together with this one, well, maybe you are. Reports are unconfirmed, but apparently there was a great Deli Schism somewhere back in ancient history, with the southerly Deli forces seceding from the northerly ones. Whatever the case, many of the same crazily named, delicious sandwiches, and elaborately adorned, well-stuffed bagels, are available here as at Barrington's "Deli." Anyone for a bite of a "Bo Derek"? Or an "Avocado Smoothie" — bagel of your choice, spread of cream cheese, slices of avocado: all zapped in the steamer? Both offer great satisfaction. There is fine hot and cold cider here, too, even homemade root beer; also exotic fruit juice combos (our favorite is strawberry-banana-OJ). The cooler holds one of North County's better arrays of domestic and imported cheeses.

Robin at work, making Robin's one of Williamstown's truly outstanding restaurants.

Jonathan Sternfield

ROBIN'S
413-458-4489.
117 Latham, Williamstown.
Closed: Mon.–Thurs. in
   winter.
Price: Expensive
Cuisine: Eclectic Californ-
   ian/Mediterranean/New
   England.
Serving: B (on Sun.), L, D.
Credit Cards: AE, MC, V,
   D.
Reservations: Recom-
   mended in summer.
Special Features: Wrap-
   around deck under pine
   trees; Catering and take-
   out service.

At the foot of Spring Street, Robin's is a welcoming outpost for imaginatively prepared, thoroughly satisfying food. "A pleasure," said the *New
York Times*, and we heartily concur. The menu
changes daily, featuring organic local produce in
season and influences from both California and the
Mediterranean. And the expansive, tree-shaded
deck has established Robin's as the *primo* warm-
weather eatery in Williamstown.

Enticing openers from a recent menu featured a
delicious Berkshire pâté with Niçoise olives, Dijon
mustard, and grilled garlic bread. Entrées included
black lobster and shrimp ravioli in a pesto cream
sauce, and a mixed grill of wild boar and venison
sausages and duck leg confit with apple cider
sauce. Extraordinary!

SAVORIES
413-458-2175.
123 Water St. (Rte. 43),
   Williamstown.
Closed: Mon.
Price: Moderate to Expen-
   sive.
Cuisine: Contemporary
   American.

Savories took over the old River House and
hasn't looked back since. Whether you dine in
their tavern — sampling fare such as the "best
burger ever," according to a friend of ours who
ought to know — or in the open-hearth ambiance
of their more formal dining room, you're in for a
fine meal.

Handhewn beams and quaint quilts, part of the charm of Savories.

Jonathan Sternfield

Serving: D.
Credit Cards: AE, MC, V.
Reservations: Recom-
mended.
Special Features: Fireplace.
Handicap Access: Yes.

Recent dinners have opened with a complimentary plate of sesame crackers, thin-sliced Jarlsberg,
and equally thin-sliced Granny Smith apple. With a
choice of five dressings, the salads should have
kept things going, but seemed slightly unremark-
able. Entrées revived the party. Idaho rainbow
trout, sautéed with cornmeal crust and finished
with thyme and pecan brown butter, was almost as good as it sounds. Grilled
jerked chicken with spicy-sweet Caribbean glaze brought out the big band.
Other enticing entrées included a pork tenderloin that was accompanied by an
inspired apple-onion tart and a truly deadly sirloin steak Kansas City, grilled
with blue cheese and bacon. The service was well meaning, but overextended.

Desserts such as a lemon pound cake with berry compote or tiramisu offer a
fine finish to one of Williamstown's better meals.

RESTAURANTS OUTSIDE THE COUNTY

Hillsdale, New York

**L'HOSTELLERIE
   BRESSANE**
518-325-3412.
At junction of Rtes. 22 & 23,
   Hillsdale.
Closed: Mon.

Jean Morel, chef-propriétaire of L'Hostellerie
Bressane, is a member of the Académie Culinaire
de France and L'Association des Maîtres Cuisiniers
de France, and winner of the latter organization's
1985 Toque d'Argent (on display at the restaurant).

Price: Expensive to Very Expensive.
Cuisine: French.
Serving: D.
Credit Cards: AE, MC, V.
Reservations: Recommended.
Special features: Fireplace; Vegetarian dishes.

His honors are well earned, because for Jean Morel, cooking is not only an art, it is a calling, a national responsibility.

At L'Hostellerie Bressane, in the sleepy hamlet of Hillsdale, you are likely to be greeted by chef Morel's wife, the directress of the inn; and she will escort you through their cozy dining rooms, aglow with candlelight. The red-brick inn was built in 1783 by a former officer in the American Revolutionary Army, and the Morels have lovingly restored it. Table linens and silver are appropriately fine, with the Morels' collection of colorful antique presentation china giving the chef's creations a splendid background. Each entrée arrives on a plate of a different design.

The wine list at L'Hostellerie befits a great French restaurant, featuring an extraordinary choice of rare wines. For example, you could order a Château Margaux 1955 ($375); a Mouton Rothschild of the same vintage ($425); or a Lafite Rothschild 1953 ($450). Good if less great French wines are also available from around $20.

In keeping with his passion to pass on the secrets of great French cooking, master chef Jean Morel teaches cooking classes at his L'Hostellerie Bressane. Courses are usually four days, with a daily schedule that features a 10 a.m. to 2:30 p.m. cooking class, followed by lunch with questions and answers. On Fridays, the class returns to the kitchen at 6:30 pm to watch the staff prepare the restaurant dinners. Students may either commute from their own lodging, or stay with the Morels at L'Hostellerie.

Chef Morel's range is impressive. For hors d'oeuvres, consider his *gâteau de foie blond au coulis de tomate* — chicken liver soufflé with a touch of garlic, light and livery; or his cold mussels with mustard sauce — a showpiece with a red cabbage leaf acting as a visual center, the sauce a sassy complement to the plump, fresh shellfish.

Soups are superb. A *gratinée lyonnaise accompagnée des oeufs aux deux alcools* (onion soup with egg yolk, Madeira, and cognac) has a symphony of winey flavors supporting the onion. *Soupe de moules au safran* (mussel soup with saffron) has all the finesse needed to carry off a successful marriage of these two subdued flavors. *Crème de pois à l'oseille* (pea soup with sorrel) is a creamy sensation.

Entrées include aiguilletes of duck with raisins and Sauternes cream sauce — slices of duckling breast, an exciting combination of flavor and texture. The trout is exceptionally delicate, and poached salmon studded with red peppercorns is delicious and rich. Vegetables include fresh salsify, imported from Belgium, and sautéed cucumbers, as well as slightly undercooked *riz sauvage* (wild rice).

Dessert soufflés, which can be a climactic event, need to be ordered in advance with your meal. Chef Morel is so masterful at these, it is almost a sin not to partake. Each soufflé is accompanied with stiff, slightly sweetened whipped cream. For those who don't favor soufflés, chef Morel makes his own ice cream (in flavors like hazelnut), sorbets, tarts, and mousses.

SWISS HUTTE
518-325-3333.
Rte. 23, Hillsdale.
Price: Expensive.
Cuisine: French, Swiss.
Serving: D.
Credit Cards: MC, V.
Reservations: Recom-
 mended.
Special Features: View of ski
 slopes; Outdoor dining.

From its scenic locale at the base of Catamount ski resort, Swiss Hutte lets you watch skiers in winter, listen to the birds near the deck in summer, or just feel cozy in its woody dining room in spring or fall. Fresh bouquets of flowers adorn each linen-draped table, and brass candle lanterns add a soft glow.

We enjoyed an appetizer of tortellini Swiss Hutte. This Gruyère-filled pasta was covered with a creamy sauce, garnished with sprinkles of parsley and a tomato puree. The onion soup was hearty, with a stringy Gruyère lid that made it difficult to eat but well worth the effort. Though we would have liked a few more traditionally Swiss entrées to choose from, the Wienerschnitzel and steak au poivre convinced us that this standard continental menu was just fine, when prepared as well as this. The steak was as fine a peppery rendition as we've tasted, succulent, tender, with a robust sauce. Vegetables here are uniformly excellent, from sweet carrots to cabbage. Swiss rosti (potato pancake) is superb, the ample plate-sized pancake that comes with your entrée being sufficient for a meal in itself.

Save room for dessert! We sampled an incredible raspberry cream pie and a rich, airy apple puff pastry, both of which featured fresh, whipped cream.

New Lebanon, New York

SHUJI'S
518-794-8383.
At junction of Rtes. 20 & 22,
 New Lebanon.
Closed: Mon.; mid-
 Nov.–end of Mar.
Price: Moderate to Expen-
 sive.
Cuisine: Japanese.
Serving: D.
Credit Cards: AE, MC, V.
Reservations: Recom-
 mended.
Special Features: Tatami
 rooms: Vegetarian
 dishes.

The atmosphere at Shuji's combines the Victorian splendor of former Governor Tilden's mansion (he's the fellow who lost the U.S. presidency to Rutherford B. Hayes in 1876 by a single electoral vote) with the delicacy of Japanese domestic decor. In four of the mansion's upstairs rooms, you must remove your shoes to enjoy the cushioned realm of tatami. With authentic pillow chairs to recline upon, even diners unaccustomed to this type of sitting will be comfortable. Two of these tatami rooms are for private parties only. Downstairs there is Western-style seating.

Mishiko, chef Shuji's wife, will greet you with

Jonathan Sternfield

welcoming Japanese hospitality. The service, usually provided by young Americans, is well versed, attentive, and graceful.

Shuji's menu is authentic, comprehensive, and imaginative. You could start with some plum wine or hot saki, but you might also like a Samurai Lord (the Far Eastern sour made with Suntory whiskey) or a Black Belt (vodka, kahlua, and saki). Ashai and Kirin Japanese beers are also available.

For appetizers, Shuji offers sashimi (raw fish), sushi (raw fish with rice), tempura (batter-dipped, deep-fried vegetables and fish), and maki (raw tuna and rice wrapped in seaweed). Their chicken Kushikatsu — breaded fried chicken and onion on a stick — was a delicious way to open a Japanese feast.

Several elaborate dinners are offered regularly, among them "King of the Sea" and the "Japanese Gourmet Dinner." The "King" is a melange of lobster, crab, shrimp, scallops, clams, and vegetables, all lightly steamed in a seasoned broth. Shuji's Japanese vegetables are grown especially for the restaurant. The eight-course "Gourmet Dinner," delicious as it is, may be misnamed, being better suited to gourmands or possibly sumo wrestlers. When you have lost count and think you're home, Shuji hits you with course number eight, a huge, half-inch-thick porterhouse steak cooked teriyaki style. The *wasabi* (hot green horseradish) that accompanied the superior sushi caused at least one of us to experience intimations of immortality.

For lighter meals, Shuji's also features two delectable vegetarian dinners, one a tempura and the other a teriyaki. And from the ocean comes Shuji's seafood *misonabe*, a Japanese-style bouillabaisse with half a lobster, king crabmeat, shrimp, scallops, tofu, and vegetables, cooked with a soy-flavored sauce in an earthenware pot.

At dessert time, stick to Shuji's simpler fare, such as artfully served fresh fruit or sherbet.

To Shuji With Love

For more than 25 years now, Shuji's has delighted regional diners who've yearned for an elegant, Japanese culinary experience. The back of their latest menu bears witness to their popularity, with signed testimonials from the likes of Seiji Ozawa, Paul Newman, Richard Chamberlain, and Norman Mailer. Wrote Governor Mario Cuomo: "Shuji's. What a wonderful place to have a 37th wedding anniversary dinner!"

OTHER RECOMMENDATIONS

Besides the few outside-the-county restaurants we've reviewed here, several others stand out. Three of these are good bets if you're headed to or from the Berkshires on the south end. *Charleston* (517 Warren St., Hudson, NY; 518-828-4990) is John Manikowski and Carole Clarke's restaurant (they ran the superb Konkapot Restaurant in Mill River), specializing in international cuisine. The setting is simple but gracious, the food extraordinary. The newly renovated **White Hart Inn** (the Village Green, Salisbury, CT; 203-435-0030) is a tastefully revised 19th-century lodging that houses three distinct dining rooms, all quite appealing. The White Hart is under the capable guidance of Terry and Juliet Moore, who also own and operate the popular Old Mill restaurant in South Egremont (see pages 160–61).

FOOD PURVEYORS

From the freshest sweet corn from the farm stand, raced from purchase to pot, to the latest imported gourmet specialty, appearing by candlelight on a Tanglewood picnic blanket, food you can buy in the Berkshires ranges from pure and simple to sophisticated and innovative. The food and beverage purveyors listed below are sources for baked goods, coffee and ice cream, produce and other farm products, picnic provisions, and health and gourmet food. And a surprising array of unique food specialties is created and produced in the Berkshires; they're listed at the end of the chapter.

BAKERIES

European pastries, New York bagels, French baguettes, and grandma's pies: breads and baked goods from Berkshire bakeries offer the staff of life and all its variations. Many of these bakeries also provide dining areas.

Bagels, Too (413-499-0119; 166 North St., Pittsfield) Several great flavors of New York-style bagels are made on the premises, accessorized by cream cheese spreads, lox, soup, and specialty coffees. Take them away or eat them on the spot. Raved Today Show's Willard Scott: "Best bagels outside of NY!"

The Baker's Wife (413-528-4623; 312 Main St., Great Barrington) Breads are baked on a weekly schedule and include, among others, five-grain, honey-oat, Italian twist, korn rye, San Francisco sourdough, seedy oat, and wheat germ. Tasty muffins range from a honey-sweetened ginger-pumpkin to sour cherry-pecan, from cranberry-hazelnut to blue cornmeal-blueberry. There's a piano, too. Closed Tues.

Christina's Just Desserts and Country Cafe (413-274-6521; 218 Pleasant St., Housatonic) The bakery offers chocolate truffles, cakes, pastries, and breads; enjoy a light lunch in the cafe.

Clarksburg Bread (413-458-2251; 37 Spring St., Williamstown) Wholesome offerings baked fresh from scratch daily: bread, muffins, scones, cookies, biscuits, coffee cakes, pies, and other assorted pastries. Juices, cheese, and yogurt are also available, as are tea, coffee, and gift items. Closed Mon.

Daily Bread (413-528-9610; 17 Railroad St., Great Barrington; Main St., Stockbridge; Main St., Lenox) Give us our daily bread: real, crusty sourdough French baguettes fresh out of the oven, and almond crescent cookies, hazelnut torte, sticky buns, and other necessities of life. Closed Mon.

Heritage Country Store Bake Shop (413-664-4886; Western Gateway Heritage State Park, North Adams) Follow your nose to the bake shop here, for Grandma Jackie's Pies, and breads, pastries, cheesecake, and a selection of local food products. They bake to order, too, and take obvious pride in their creations.

Suchèle Bakers (413-637-0939; 31 Housatonic St., Lenox) Geraniums in the window, Victorian accouterments inside, and tarts and tortes, sticky buns, muffins, wholesome bread, pastries, cakes, fresh fruit pies, and more, baked daily. Closed Mon. off season.

Wildflower Bakery & Cafe (413-528-0780; Rte. 7, Great Barrington) Variations on a scone: cranberry-orange, peach-hazelnut, and blueberry, for starters. Sourdough bread, plain and fancy, shares space with several other tempting varieties, including some made without dairy products. These and pastries and other goodies are baked on the premises daily. The cafe also offers soups and sandwiches, coffees, fruit juices, and sodas, with seating inside and out. Closed Mon.

COFFEE SPECIALISTS

Berkshire Coffee Roasting Company (413-528-5505; 286 Main St., Great Barrington) A top choice for exceptional coffee in an unpretentiously funky setting, conducive to the related activities of conversation, relaxing, people-watching, reading, or admiring the latest art exhibit on the walls. The

Restaurateur Heather Austin, partner in Kintaro and Bronze Dog, steam heats a fragrant cofffee at her Berkshire Coffee Roasting Company.

Jonathan Sternfield

beans responsible for all this pleasure are imported green, then roasted here. Choose from a selection of coffee flavors, and cappuccino, espresso, hot chocolate, cookies, muffins, and biscotti (try the chocolate-covered variety). Bags of coffee beans are for sale, too. The popular coffee take-out set-up thoughtfully provides raised lids for preserving the foam on your cappuccino.

Cold Spring Coffee Roasters, Ltd. (413-458-5010; 47 Spring St., Williamstown) More than 60 varieties of specialty coffees are roasted on the premises here (and there are 25 varieties of loose teas). Order cappuccino, latte, or espresso, and treat yourself to ice cream and other goodies in a cafe atmosphere. There's an array of tea- and coffee-making gear, too.

The Flavored Bean Coffee Company (413-637-9814; Lenox House Country Shops, Lenox) Green Mountain all-natural roasted coffee, fat- and sugar-free goodies, bread mixes; tea and tea accessories, create or have them customize a gift presentation; other kitchen and dining accessories.

FARM, ORCHARD, AND PRODUCE MARKETS

Besides, I had my crops to get in, — corn and potatoes (I hope to show you some famous ones by and by), — and many other things to attend to, all accumulating upon this one particular season.

From Herman Melville to his Lenox neighbor Nathaniel Hawthorne,
in a letter written at Melville's Pittsfield farm, Arrowhead, in 1851.

Fresh tomatoes right off the vine, crisp and juicy apples, enormous heads of organically grown lettuce, perhaps the descendants of Melville's corn and potatoes — bounty from Berkshire fields and hills is available at area produce markets, farm and orchard outlets, seasonal farm stands, and farmers' markets, where area growers truck in their harvests to a central outdoor location one or two days a week. You'll also find sources of non-Berkshire produce throughout the county, for those occasions when only kiwi fruit or bok choy will do.

Fruit-picking opportunities and maple sugaring expeditions at area farms are also listed.

The Berkshire County Extension Service (413-448-8285; 44 Bank Row, Pittsfield) can provide up-to-date information on seasonal farm stands and farmers' markets

Bartlett's Orchards 413-698-2559; Swamp Rd., Richmond) "Buy 'em where they grow 'em." Apple varieties throughout the season include Empire, Macs, Delicious (red and gold), Cortland, Northern Spy, Macoun, Ida Red, Jonagold, and more. Each variety is labeled with a description of its distinct flavor and best use. Bartlett's own cider is all-natural and preservative-free. The shop also stocks an array of apple products and other country-gourmet condiments and preserves; the bakery offers doughnuts, turnovers, pies.

Burgner's Farm Products (413-445-4704; Dalton Division Rd., Pittsfield) A neighborhood gathering place for fresh produce, including Burgner's own, especially their corn in season; plus other fruits and vegetables from local farms and farther afield. Eggs plus chicken and turkey products are also a specialty (see Poultry Markets).

Caretaker Farm (413-458-4309; Hancock Rd., Williamstown) Great organic produce and fresh organic bread.

The Corn Crib (413-528-4947; Rte. 7, Sheffield) Their own farm produce, plus that of other local farmers — fresh fruit, veggies, plants, perennials. **Carol's Cookery** has homemade pastries, soup, and bread; **Dolls & Dwellings** offers dolls, supplies, doll houses, miniatures, dried flowers.

Guido's Fresh Market Place (413-442-9912; 1020 South St., Pittsfield) The best place to buy vegetables and fruit in the county, with local produce in season and a multi-cultural array of standards and exotics from all over the world year-round — baby carrots, cilantro, radicchio, endive, fresh herbs, oriental vegetables, tropical fruits, mushrooms. A true marketplace ambiance, '90s-style, with distinct Guido touches: the signs posted at the carefully arranged but overflowing produce bins are polite and informative, and you can get help carrying your bags out to your car if you want. Also at Guido's are Berger's Bakery and Deli, Hillsdale Meat Market, Mountain Seafood, and Pasta Prima (described in the appropriate categories below), and all sorts of cooking supplies, health foods, earth-conscious cosmetics, gourmet items, candles, baskets, Guido's T-shirts. . . . Tip: if you can schedule your Guido's trips to avoid high-season weekends, it's a good idea. Plans are afoot for a South County Guido's as well.

Farmers' Markets

Farmers' markets, where local growers set up temporarily to offer this week's freshest harvest, have been springing up throughout the county. Held during the all-too-short Berkshire growing season, the markets' days, times, and exact locations may vary; check a newspaper or the extension service (413-448-8285). In *Pittsfield*, the Allendale Shopping Center hosts a market on Wednesday & Saturday mornings, and downtown Pittsfield sets up an open-air market on Columbus Ave. on Friday. In *Great Barrington*, the Farmer's Market is on Saturdays between Memorial Day and Columbus Day from 8:30 a.m to 12:30 p.m. in the yard of the old train station, with vegetables plus local cheeses and hand-crafted products related to farming. In *Williamstown*, on Saturday mornings, July through September, local farmers are at the foot of Spring St.

Picking Your Own Fruit

A berry or apple picking expedition is a great way to enjoy the Berkshire countryside, and to provide the makings for a special dessert or pancake breakfast. Be sure to call ahead at the following farms and orchards for picking conditions.

Blueberries abound at Blueberry Hill Farm, which offers 320 acres for family picking from late July until frost (East St., 7 mi. up the Mount Washington ridge; call 413-528-1479 for a recorded message about the status of picking). Three acres of *strawberries* are at Crooked Row Farm (413-698-2608; Dublin Road, Richmond) from 8 a.m. to 12 noon, and 5 to 8 p.m. *Raspberries and apples* at Windy Hill Farm (413-298-3217; Rte. 7, Great Barrington) are waiting to be picked in season; there's also a garden shop and nursery. Open Apr.–Oct. Also check with Taft Farms, Great Barrington; the Corn Crib, Sheffield; Mountain View Farm, on Partridge Rd. in Pittsfield, and Jaeschke's in Adams, for various fruit-picking excursions in season.

The Price of Strawberries

Yesterday i picked one quart ov field strawberrys, kaught 27 trout, and gathered a whole parcell ov wintergreen leaves, a big daze work.

When i got home last night tired, no man kould have bought them ov me for 700 dollars, but i suppoze, after all, that it waz the tired that waz wuth the munny.

Thare is a grate deal of raw bliss, in gitting tired.

Wisdom from Josh Billings, 19th-century Lanesborough
humorist and professional misspeller.

Jaeschke's Brothers Farms (413-743-3896; West Rd., Adams) The farm store is in Pittsfield, 736 Crane Ave. (Allendale area; 413-443-7180). You can also pick — or pick up — apples and pears at the orchard after the pro pickers have been through.

Maple Sugar and Syrup

Maple sugaring and syrup-making is a Berkshire tradition. Watch the process or participate at the following places during the season (usually March), or just pick up some of the final product at any time of year.

Quimby's Sugar House (413-458-5402; Rte. 43, Hancock) holds open house during the last two Sundays in March, beginning at noon. And *Sunset Farm Maple Products* (413-243-3229; Tyringham Rd., Tyringham) has an open sugar house 7 days a week from 9 a.m. to dusk. *Turner Farms Maple Syrup* (413-528-5710; Phillips Rd., S. Egremont) The sugar shack operation is open to the public; groups of 15 or more should make appointment for a tour. Other sources of local maple products include *Baldwin's* in West Stockbridge (413-232-7785) for their own table syrup made from maple and cane sugar; *Gould Farm* (413-528-2633; Road Side Store, Rte. 23, Monterey); *Holiday Farm* (413-684-0444; Rte. 9, Windsor); *Lone Maple Sugar House* (413-258-4706; Rte. 57, Sandisfield); *Mill Brook Sugar House* (413-637-0474; 317 New Lenox Rd., Lenox); *Monterey Maple* (413-528-9385; Hupi Rd., Monterey); *Soda Springs Farm* (413-229-8865; Home Rd., Sheffield); and *Swann Farm* (413-298-3535; Cherry Hill Rd., Stockbridge).

Maple sugaring, Berkshire style.

Eleanor Kimberley

Taft Farms (413-528-1515; Rte. 183 & Division St., Great Barrington) Taft Farms' own delicious produce in season, including potatoes, tomatoes, peppers, broccoli, cucumbers, and their famous just-picked sweet corn. It's all grown according to the "integrated pest management" system, which minimizes or eliminates the use of pesticides. Taft also offers fruit and vegetables from other climes, such as radicchio, kiwi fruit, or pomegranates. Baked goods, jams and jellies, cider, and seafood from the fish market (Thursday through Saturday) will provision you healthfully, delectably, and completely. Flowers and plants from the greenhouse, too.

GOURMET & DELI MARKETS, & CATERERS

The small grocery markets and specialty food shops and caterers of the Berkshires will please the palates of just about everyone, from the classicist to the experimenter. These markets and food specialists combine the latest culinary styles with ethnic traditions and personal service, and also magnificently maintain the celebrated Berkshire custom of the gourmet picnic. There's an old-time country store or two thrown in here, too.

Berger's Specialty Foods (413-442-1898; 1020 South St., Pittsfield, at Guido's) Some assert that the best baguettes to be found in the Berkshires are here; others avoid the controversy by selecting from the abundant variety of cheeses, crackers, condiments, pasta and other salads, and gourmet items from far and wide. Berger's also caters and does gift baskets.

Berkshire Hills Market (413-458-3356; 60 Spring St., Williamstown) It's a new but old-fashioned market, with a little bit of the best of everything, including fresh meat and fish, and smoked meat and sausage made on the premises. Gourmet items, including coffee and tea of the day, are to-go and by the pound. There's more: fresh produce, deli items, overstuffed sandwiches, gift baskets, and boxed meals. Call in orders.

Berkshire Place Gourmet Foods (413-528-5620; Main St., South Egremont) Fine foods to eat-in or take-out, catering. (Reviewed in *Restaurants*, above.)

Caffe Pomo d'Oro (413-232-4616; 6 Depot St., West Stockbridge) Gourmet provisions and a cafe in a sunny room in West Stockbridge's small-scale downtown. Cheese and deli items, bread, imported gourmet foods, even their own gourmet vinegar. Catering. (Reviewed in Restaurants, above.)

Cheesecake Charlie's (413-637-3411; 72 Main St., Lenox) Toasted Almond, Creamsicle, Piña Colada, Peppermint Patty — these are only a few of the cheesecake flavors that you can get here. Available in different sizes, and they'll ship it too.

Chez Vous Catering (413-298-4278; Box 1162, Stockbridge) Elegant food, beautifully presented, including Oriental roast beef, Madeira chicken, lentil salad plates, and desserts.

Country Glazed Hams (413-637-2288; Brushwood Farm, Lenox) Honey-glazed hams, spiral-sliced, are the specialty here; plus smoked and deli meats, gourmet coffee, fresh baked goods, overstuffed sandwiches, and seemingly the world's record for the number of different gourmet mustards.

Crosby's (413-637-3396; 62 Church St., Lenox) A gourmet shop and caterer renowned for imaginative offerings of fine food; take-out and eat-in lunches. (Reviewed in *Restaurants*, above.)

Gorham & Norton (413-528-0900; 278 Main St., Great Barrington) This authentically old-fashioned market has up-to-the-minute good things: groceries, gourmet items, imported cheese, an excellent wine selection. Real people work here, too; recently when they didn't happen to have a certain item, they immediately suggested other sources and offered to call them to make sure.

Karner Brook Country Store and Deli (413-528-5125; Rte. 23, S. Egremont) Organic coffee, freshly brewed and whole beans; gourmet foods, breads, and made-to-order deli sandwiches.

The Marketplace (413-528-5554; Rte. 7, Great Barrington) What a great idea: take out a complete fine restaurant meal, lunch or dinner, with the latest gourmet spin. A variety of salads, hot and cold, fish, cold cuts, and more are also take-out ready. All explained and served up with enthusiasm and panache.

Merrimac Smoked Fish, Inc. (413-528-2004; 955 S. Main St., Great Barrington) Their own fine smoked salmon, the equal of any produced in the U.S., smoked and peppered bluefish, and other gourmet and homemade seafood items.

Mazzeo's Market (413-448-8323; 251 Fenn St., Pittsfield; and 413-298-0220; Main St., Stockbridge) The Pittsfield market is larger, with a larger meat and deli operation, but both places stock baked goods, groceries and produce, and a full range of deli and gourmet items, with an emphasis on Italian imports. Generous subs-to-order at the Stockbridge location are a lunch option.

Jane McWhorter

Monterey General Store (413-528-4437; Rte. 23) Not necessarily a gourmet shop, but an established oasis in southeastern Berkshire, this old-time general store stocks fresh vegetables, cold cuts, preserves, and locally made maple syrup. With a lunch room in the back and a front porch for people-watching, this spot is a perennial gathering place.

Old Egremont Store (413-528-4796; Rte. 71, N. Egremont) Another old-time general store, this has a deli with soups and sandwiches, pastries on weekends, and coffee, not to mention the post office.

Samel's Deli and Catering (413-442-5927; 115 Elm St., Pittsfield) Bread, chicken, wine, cheese, pepperoni, legendary pickles, and much more in the deli and gourmet line. They deliver in the Pittsfield area.

Savories (413-458-2175; 123 Water St., Williamstown) This restaurant has a country deli with take-out choices that include homemade potato salad, pies, and meat prepared for grilling. (Reviewed in *Restaurants*, above.)

The Store At Five Corners (413-458-3176, fax 413-458-0931; junction of Rtes. 7 & 43, South Williamstown) The country store for the '90s, with well-chosen wine and beer selections, juices and waters, imported and domes-

---

Picnic Provisions

A three-hour's business from turkey to ice cream.

From a letter of Evert A. Duyckinck, literary editor, describing the famous picnic on Monument Mountain in 1850 with Hawthorne, Melville, and Oliver Wendell Holmes.

The Berkshires are ideal picnic territory, whether the context for your al fresco dining is a hike, literary or otherwise, an all-day canoe trip, or the prelude to an outdoor performance at the Mount or Tanglewood. Your picnic may also start with turkey and end with ice cream, but the picnic specialists listed here also offer many other options. And, of course, you can provision your picnic yourself, at any of the markets and gourmet shops described above.

Cheesecake Charlie's makes a special New England Clambake Picnic for Two, which includes lobster, mussels, clams, shrimp, corn on the cob, melon, and bread. Cher's in the Glendale section of Stockbridge on Rte. 183 has boxed picnic meals featuring sandwiches; no advance notice needed. Picnics from *Crosby's* may be selected from a variety of menu choices, including vegetarian, with a day's notice. The raspberry chicken salad picnic is especially recommended. The Great Barrington *Marketplace* will customize a gourmet picnic, with 24 hours' notice. At *Mazzeo's Market* in Stockbridge, you can rent or buy a picnic basket, which in either case will be filled with a selection of gourmet cheese, fruit, desserts, fresh-baked bread, overstuffed sandwiches, barbecued chicken, other gourmet items, and beer or wine. *Nejaime's* in downtown Lenox and Stockbridge also does picnics. *The Red Lion Inn* offers pick-up picnics, too. *Robin's Restaurant* in Williamstown will pack up entrées and side dishes; no notice needed. *Samel's Deli* has boxed meals ideal for portable dining. *The Store at Five Corners* will pack a picnic from their deli. *Truffles & Such* will also create gourmet picnics-to-go.

tic cheeses, fresh-baked breads and treats, homemade fudge, picnic and gift baskets, gifts, fresh produce, deli items such as sandwiches and salads, fancy preserves, gourmet coffee and ice cream, and various international offerings. Enjoy breakfast and light fare here, too, in all this abundance. And they ship and cater. In a building that was a tavern in 1770; the Greek Revival façade was added in 1830.

Truffles & Such (413-442-0151; Allendale Shopping Center, Pittsfield) A restaurant (see review) with take-out and catering. The pasta or bean salads are highly recommended and the desserts are simultaneously heavenly and sinful — try a "potato," a cake and marzipan concoction dusted with cocoa and studded with almond "eyes."

Other area restaurants or markets with catering services include the the *Castle Street Cafe, Harry's Supermarket, Hickory Bill's, the Silver Screen,* and the *Sweet Basil Grille.*

Pasta Possibilities

Pasta Prima (413-499-7478; 1020 South St., Pittsfield, at Guido's) Fresh pasta made on the premises, even before your very eyes. Have it cut to order or purchase in sheets for cutting at home. Selection of other pastas of the dried variety, sauces, and Parmesan and Romano cheese for grating.

Wright Pasta Company (413-528-6930; Main St., Egremont) A host of creative flavors, currently including sage, tomato basil, black pepper, and lime cilantro. Flavors are all natural; the flour is 100% semolina

---

HEALTH/NATURAL FOOD STORES

Berkshire Co-op Market (413-528-9697; 37 Rosseter St., Great Barrington) Open to the public, but co-op members get a 7% discount. Ingredients for healthy eating and living, including organic produce, much of it grown locally; and baked goods, macrobiotic foods, bulk pasta, beans, grains, and herbal remedies. Food products here have no white sugar, additives, or preservatives.

Clearwater Natural Foods (413-637-2721; 11 Housatonic St., Lenox) Fresh bread, sandwiches, a wide range of groceries, including macrobiotic and allergy-free selections, organic produce, and nondairy and dairy ice cream. Look for monthly specials.

Locke, Stock and Barrel (413-528-0800; 265 Stockbridge Rd./Rte. 7, Great Barrington) Where health food meets gourmet food, artfully and abundantly arranged: a large selection of cheeses, and cold cuts, fish, honey, teas, yogurt, juices, fresh tofu, flours, grains, rices, and soy and tamari sauces. There's a wall-length case of frozen health foods, and vitamins, mineral supplements, and natural cosmetics.

Sprout House (413-528-5200; 284 Main St./PO Box 1100, Great Barrington) Steve Meyerowitz, the "Sproutman," has sprouting kits and books, indoor vegetable kits and organic seeds; via mail order and wholesale.

Sunflower Natural Foods (413-243-1775; 42 Park St., Lee) Organic and natural items include bread, coffee, fat-free snacks, and natural personal care items; products are available here that are wheat-free, gluten-free, sugar-free. Vitamins, books, even a health video club.

Wholesome Harold's (413-637-3411; 72 Main St., Lenox) Natural and organic whole foods, bulk items, and produce, in a space shared with Cheesecake Charlie's.

Wild Oats Co-op (413-458-8060; Rte. 2, Colonial Shopping Center, Williamstown) Organic and local produce, whole foods, gourmet and specialty items, vitamins, natural cosmetics, along with food and health books and magazines. Members get discounts but the public is welcome.

ICE CREAM

Berkshire-made ice cream, plus that of those two guys from Vermont, can be found in strategic locations throughout the county. Reliably delicious *Friendly* ice cream, in cones, containers, and sundaes, is also available at one of the many Friendly restaurants near you.

Ben & Jerry's Ice Cream (413-448-2250; 179 South St., Pittsfield) Vermont's famous ice cream, in cones, cakes, sundaes, and containers; frozen yogurt. Worth standing in line for.

Bev's Homemade Ice Cream (413-637-0371; 38 Housatonic St., Lenox) Bev's is made daily on the premises, and comes in traditional to exotic flavors. You can also get ice cream sodas and sundaes, malteds, and egg creams, plus coffee and baked treats.

The Ice Cream Scene (282 Main St., Great Barrington) Gourmet to soft-serve to frozen yogurt and other goodies.

MEAT, FISH, & POULTRY MARKETS

Burgner's Poultry Farm (413-445-4704; Dalton Division Rd., Pittsfield) Burgner's raises and sells turkeys and chickens; order them uncooked, roasted, or stuffed and roasted, in all sizes. Burgner's turkey pot pies are local favorites. The farm store also carries eggs, produce, and their homemade bakery items and fresh homemade potato salad and cole slaw (see Farm Markets).

Greilich's Meat Market (413-743-0012; 24 N. Summer St., Adams) A small and friendly family operation with German- and Polish-style sausage, kielbasa, bratwurst, and homemade bacon, in a no-frills, back-of-the-house shop with a view of Mount Greylock thrown in for free.

Hillsdale Meat Center (413-442-8135; 1020 South St., Pittsfield, at Guido's) Excellent cuts of meat tantalizingly displayed, with helpful service.

Mazzeo's Market (413-448-8323; 251 Fenn St., Pittsfield; and 413-298-0220; Main St., Stockbridge) The Pittsfield store offers full meat market service; ask for a special cut in advance.

Pizza

Pizza cravings will be easily satisfied anywhere throughout Berkshire County, but all pizzas are not created equal. Top choices include the following:

Manhattan Pizza Company (413-528-2550; 490 Main St., Great Barrington) Pizzas here are big, flat, oozing, and delicious. They reheat well, and are available by the slice. The *East Side Cafe* (413-447-9405; 378 Newell St., Pittsfield) is essentially a bar, and they make pizza only on Thurs.–Sun. evenings from 5:00 p.m. on; it's small, thin, crisp, and tasty. *Elizabeth's Cafe Pizzeria* on East St. in Pittsfield (reviewed in *Restaurants*, above) offers signature "white pies" with abundant toppings, and fresh, innovative ingredients. The unbeatable taste of a wood-fired brick-oven pizza is somewhere *Over The Rainbow* (413-445-6836; 109 First St., Pittsfield). Generous toppings and imaginative combinations include chicken pesto, spinach and broccoli, or the "primavera" — eggplant, black olives, broccoli, and more. Take-out or eat in and watch the flames in the oven.

W.T. Seafood (413-499-3474; 1020 South St., Pittsfield, at Guido's) A variety of fresh and frozen former denizens of the sea.

Otis Poultry Farm (413-269-4438; Rte. 8, Otis) "Custom Laid Eggs" says the sign, and you can get them and chickens, geese, ducks, and capons, too. Their excellent frozen chicken and turkey pies are a staple of well-stocked Berkshire refrigerators. Various homemade goodies join sheepskin gloves and slippers and so forth in the country store.

Pleasant St. Market (413-274-3344; Pleasant St./Rte. 183, Housatonic) Butcher service and excellent homemade Polish sausage.

Additional options for meat and fish include *South End Market* (413-442-6906; 519 South St., Pittsfield), *Harry's Supermarket* (413-442-9084; 290 Wahconah St., Pittsfield), *Swanson's Seafood & Deli* (413-743-9040; 87 Summer St., Adams), *Vic's Seafood* (413-528-9510; at Taft Farms, Great Barrington, Thurs.–Sat. only), *The Other Brother Darryl's* (413-269-4235, 800-6FLOPIN;

Rte. 8, Otis); they offer wholesale seafood to retail customers, and promise "still-floppin'" freshness).

WINE & LIQUOR

Keep in mind that Massachusetts law prohibits the sale of alcoholic beverages on Sunday; stock up beforehand.

The Buttery (413-298-5533; Elm St., Stockbridge)

Country Spirits (413-528-6644; 389 Stockbridge Rd., Great Barrington)

Domaney's (413-528-0024; 66 Main St., Great Barrington)

Gorham and Norton (413-528-0900; 278 Main St., Great Barrington)

Liquors Inc. (413-443-4466; 485 Dalton Ave., Pittsfield) The biggest and best for discount wine, beer and spirits.

Liquor Mart (413-663-3910; State Rd., Adams)

Nejaime's Wine & Liquor (413-448-2274; 598 Pittsfield-Lenox Rd.), **Nejaime's Stockbridge Wine Cellar** (413-298-3454; Elm St.), and **Lenox Wine Cellar and Cheese Shop** (413-637-2221; 33 Church St.) In addition to wines, beers, and spirits, they offer gourmet and deli items, and helpful, knowledgeable assistance.

Queensborough Spirits (413-232-8522; Main St., West Stockbridge)

South Egremont Spirit Shoppe (413-528-1490; Rte. 23)

Spirit Shop (413-458-3704; 280 Cole Ave., Williamstown)

Stockbridge Wine Cellar (413-298-3454; Elm St., Stockbridge)

Trotta's Discount Liquors (529-3490; Rte. 23 & S. Main St., Great Barrington)

Val's Pipe & Package Store (413-743-0962; 7 Columbia St., Adams)

Berkshire Food and Beverage Specialties

Nurtured by Berkshire soil, or created by Berkshire entrepreneurs, this select group of food and beverage specialties includes condiments and sauces; breads and other baked goods; sweets and sweeteners; and dairy products, spring water, and soft drinks. Some are world famous; all are locally treasured. There's no individual retail outlet for many of these products, but look for them at Guido's, Bartlett's, the Store at Five Corners, Berkshire Cupboard, and most other gourmet shops, farm and produce markets, and many supermarkets. In some cases, you can also contact the food entrepreneur for more information. Or consider giving — or receiving — a gift basket or box with a selection of these unique items, cleverly packaged by Gifts of the Berkshires (800-BERKCTG) through Berkshire Cottage, the Great Barrington kitchen and gourmet store (see Chapter Seven, *Shopping*).

Continued on next pages

Beverages

Berkshire Spring Water (413-229-2086, 800-244-3212; Norfolk Rd., Southfield) Bottled daily at the spring, it's sodium-, bacteria-, and additive-free. Have it delivered, or buy it in 1-gallon jugs in supermarkets. *Gilly's Hot Vanilla* (413-637-1515) was created by Lenox resident Joanne Deutch as a hot-chocolate alternative; just add hot water to the vanilla-flavored powder. And there's no caffeine. Buy it by the bag locally, or have a cup at many local eateries. *Squeeze Beverages* (413-743-1410; 190 Howland Ave., Adams) are soda drinks with fabulous flavors: sarsaparilla, cream, birch beer, gentian root, cranberry, and "half and half" — half grapefruit, half lemon-lime. Cola and root beer for traditionalists, too, and some sugar-free choices .

Bread & Baked Goods

Berkshire Mountain Bakery (413-274-3412; Housatonic) doesn't sell retail, but their traditional sourdough breads should be sought out at area natural food stores. The peasant bread and the raisin bread are particular favorites; try their crisp biscotti, too. *Cedars of Lebanon* (413-743-1791; 131 Columbia St., Adams) makes pita bread that's in area supermarkets and groceries and is pure, simple, and delicious. *Nejaime's Lavasch* (413-298-4246; 13 Park St., Stockbridge) is deliciously addictive: a Mideast specialty, lavasch is a crusty cracker-like bread. Nejaime's is made with a variety of flavorings, all good.

Condiments & Sauces

Bear Meadow Farm (413-663-9241) products from Florida include preserves, mustards, vinegars, chutneys, apple ketchup. *Buddy Boys' Boss Sauce* was created to jazz up dorm food, so the story goes. This spicy, tomato-based ketchup-alternate comes in cool and hip 12-oz. bottles, and was created by a young Lenox entrepreneur. It's a barbecue sauce and a condiment for chicken wings, fried rice, stir-fries, grilled meat. *Donna Marie's Sauce for Pork* was recently concocted by a Berkshire entrepreneur from brown sugar, tomato concentrate, vinegar, spices, and (the key secret ingredient) lime juice. Designed for pork chops, it also works for other meat, rice, and vegetables — try with a stir-fry. No preservatives or additives. *Hickory Bill's Barbecue Sauce* from his Great Barrington restaurant (see the review above) comes in a variety of moods, from mild to hot, including "medium," "mad," and "mean." Saucy mixtures from Williamstown include *Sloan Tavern Honeysuckle Mustard* (413-458-5503); homemade smoked *White Oaks Farm Apple Barbecue Sauce*; and *Pat Green's Supreme Gourmet Sauce*, a meat marinade, cocktail sauce enhancer, and chicken or turkey salad ingredient with a tomato foundation. And from Washington, don't miss *Rosh's Hot Wing Sauce*.

Dairy Products

Monterey Chèvre is made from the milk of goats at *Rawson Brook Farm* (413-528-2138; Box 426, New Marlboro Rd., Monterey) and from acid starter from France. It's sold deliciously plain, or flavored with chives and garlic, or with a particularly tasty combination of wild thyme and olive oil. It is sold younger than

*Afternoon milking time
for High Lawn's Jersey
Cows.*

Jonathan Sternfield

imported chèvre and has a milder, more delicate flavor. Milk (with the cream on top) and light or heavy cream from *High Lawn Farm* (413-242-0672) is available at many grocery stores or can still be delivered to your door. Admire the Jersey cows as you drive by the farm on Lenox Road in Lee.

Desserts, Sweets, and Sweeteners

Baldwin's Extracts (413-232-7785; Depot St., West Stockbridge) offers "since 1888, the best in vanilla." This manufacturer of flavoring extracts and maple table syrup uses only the best — the Bourbon Vanilla Bean from Madagascar — for their Pure Vanilla Extract. It's made in a copper percolator (the "still") and aged in 100-year-old oak barrels, which you can see in their small and fascinating retail outlet in a former carriage shop. Inhale essence of vanilla and admire the ranks of extract bottles — including lemon, orange, mint, and more — on the old-fashioned counter. Also available is *Baldwin's Table Syrup*, a blend of maple and cane sugar syrup from a recipe created in the 1920s.

Catherine's Chocolates (413-528-2510; Stockbridge Rd., Great Barrington) are made on the premises from a century-old family recipe. These smooth and flavorful concoctions include chocolate truffles, a variety of hand-dipped candies, and fudges and brittles and barks. The nonpareils are, in fact, unequaled. By the piece, the pound, or in a boxed gift assortment. *David Rawson's honey* from Richmond is pretty close to nectar for the gods, who get it in 1-lb. jars at Bartlett's. *Desserts by Jayne Church* of Pittsfield are not shy; get acquainted with Chocolate Decadence Cake, the Cannonball, or Industrial Strength Cheesecake. *Laura's Homemade Scottish Shortbread* (413-443-7330; 78 Jefferson Place, Pittsfield) comes in attractive boxes of rich, sweet, buttery squares.

And . . .

The *Delftree Corporation* (234 Union St. North Adams, 413-664-4907) grows shiitake mushrooms on hardwood logs in a 19th-century textile mill building in North Adams. They're shipped all over the place, but available here.

CHAPTER SIX

For the Fun of It

RECREATION

Berkshire is a sporting landscape, beckoning boaters, hikers, horseback riders, runners, skaters, skiers, swimmers, and nearly every other variety of sportsperson. Mountains and trails, lakes and rivers—all the county's topography seems perfect for sport. And there's no doubt about it: Berkshire mountain air is downright invigorating. The ski areas assure groomed winter sport with extensive snow-making, and in warmer weather, Berkshire's golf courses and tennis courts draw sportspeople from all quarters.

Jonathan Sternfield

Heading south: Canada geese and a flotilla of canoeists muscle their way downwind at Stockbridge Bowl during the annual Josh Billings RunAground, a high point in the Berkshire sporting calendar.

Berkshire also offers many unusual sports, from ballooning to croquet to soaring. There is a center for yoga and health arts, with a staff of 150 (Kripalu); a luxury spa with a multi-million-dollar state-of-the-art fitness center and over 50 classes a day to choose from (Canyon Ranch); and two YMCAs offering programs from camping and tennis to aerobics and sailing.

There's baseball both soft and hard, in leagues both amateur and professional, and there are nature centers that offer instruction, creative activities, and adventure for explorers of all ages. And for you cave men and women out there, Berkshire offers mysterious caves under the mountains, perfect for dark, dank spelunking fun.

SPORTING GOODS STORES

The following stores provide sporting goods for a range of activities. Additional listings are provided under individual sports, e.g., bicycling, skiing.

South County

Gaffer's Outdoors 413-229-0063; 216 Main St., Sheffield.

Gerry Cosby & Co. 413-229-6600; Undermountain Rd., Sheffield.

Gilley's Sporting Goods 413-528-9898; 20 Stockbridge Rd. (Rte. 7), Great Barrington.

Central County

Arcadian Shop 413-637-3010; 333 Pittsfield-Lenox Rd., Lenox.

Champ Sports 448-2123; Berkshire Mall, Lanesborough.

Dave's Sporting Goods 413-442-2960; 1164 North St., Pittsfield.

Dick Moon Sporting Goods 413-442-8281; 114 Fenn St., Pittsfield.

Klein's All Sports 413-443-3531; Berkshire Mall, Lanesborough.

Main Street Sports and Leisure 413-637-4407, 800-952-9197; 102 Main St., Lenox.

Pittsfield Sporting Goods 413-443-6078; 70 North St., Pittsfield.

North County

Berkshire Outfitters 413-743-5900; Route 8, Adams.

D & M's Outpost 413-663-3484; 40 Holden St., N. Adams.

Goff's Sports 413-458-3605; 15 Spring St., Williamstown.

The Mountain Goat 413-458-8445; 130 Water St., Williamstown.

Points North Fly Fishing Outfitters 413-743-4030; Rt. 8, on Adams/Cheshire line.

Sports Plus 413-743-4204; Park St., Adams.

BALLOONING

Take off to a world of splendid silence, where the sky doesn't seem the limit, where the wind guides you gently over the Berkshire hilltops. While there is no ballooning outpost in Berkshire County proper, there are two outfits nearby, and on some flights, you'll surely drift over these hills. Both *Balloon School of Massachusetts* (413-245-7013; Dingley Dell, Palmer), and *American Balloon Works* (518-766-5111; Kinderhook, NY) can arrange hot-air flights for you. Guaranteed to give you a new perspective on things!

BASEBALL

Professional baseball in the Berkshires began in the 19th century, but it wasn't till the Roaring Twenties that the hardball action was continuous. The Pittsfield Hillies played some admirable ball in the A-level Eastern League, even winning a couple of pennants, but then the Depression came, and baseball went. Through some of the 1940s, the Pittsfield Electrics played to large home crowds, finally being short-circuited by the advent of televised baseball. For 15 years after, the only pro ball in the Berkshires was on TV, featuring the Red Sox. Then, in 1965, a Red Sox farm club came and played at Pittsfield's Wahconah Stadium, and Berkshire baseball reawakened with a bang. The Pittsfield-Berkshire Red Sox played in the AA Class of the Eastern League. Starring George "Boomer" Scott and Reggie Smith (both of whom went on to shine with the Boston Red Sox), the club drew nearly 80,000 fans for the season. The Red Sox farm club moved from the Berkshires in 1976, and it wasn't till 1984 that professional pitches were being thrown again in the county.

Jonathan Sternfield

Grounding out, at the Pittsfield Met's Wahconah Park.

Now it's the **Pittsfield Mets** playing Wahconah, and once again there's an opportunity to watch budding big leaguers in the Berkshires. The fastballs are wicked, homers are truly belted, and the playing field is real dirt (and grass). As a bonus, magic moments, perhaps out of a Norman Rockwell painting, are thrown in for free, as in the evening game delays when the setting sun shines directly in the batter's eyes and the game is temporarily suspended due to sunshine.

The Pittsfield Mets 413-499-METS (6387); Wahconah Park, 105 Wahconah St., Pittsfield.

Softball is rapidly becoming the most popular participatory sport in America, with nearly one out of every ten adults now playing. And in the Berkshires, too, softball is played with a passion. Nowhere is the action thicker than at the Berkshire County Softball Complex, a three-field park that sees at least six games a night during the summer. The complex is a not-for-profit corporation headed by banker Jim Bridges and is home to the Berkshire County Slow Pitch Softball League, a 30-team men's league, sponsored by local businesses. Other action at the complex includes a Men's Fall Softball League, a 15-team Women's Slow-pitch League and the 12-team men's General Electric League. To facilitate matters, the complex has a two-story clubhouse with bar and restaurant.

Berkshire County Softball Complex 413-499-1491; 1789 East St., Pittsfield.

BICYCLING

Cycling to the finish, at the annual Josh Billings RunAground.

Jonathan Sternfield

How sweet is the cycling! From the views, the rolling terrain and the variety of roadways, Berkshire bicycling seems to be custom-made for man and machine. For racers, there's the **Josh Billings RunAground** in September, and in October, the **Berkshire Community College Marathon**, a 14-mile race. In North Adams, the **Greylock Cycling Club** sponsors an annual Greylock Hill Climb, a 9.2-mile, decidedly uphill race.

For those who are touring, the back roads are tranquil, the main roads not too scary, and the mountain climbs intriguing. Mountains with roads to their summits make for a fun and challenging day trip, and in the south, the 2,600-foot Mt. Everett is a delight, while in the north, it's the 3,500-foot Greylock that commands premier attention. Climbing is the hard part, elevating you to stunning views available only to people in high places. Descents are exhilarating, but can be dangerous, so be sure to check your brakes before such an outing.

A relatively new species to these hills — the mountain biker — seems to be thriving; 18-speed machines and their smiling power plants are rolling through the picturesque landscape, often leaving the blacktop behind and riding up into the mountains, on hiking trails. Not too steep, not too tortuous, the Berkshire hills beckon those who have enough brawn, coupled with the right machine. Mountain bikers frequently gather at the *Mountain Goat*, 130 Water St., Williamstown, at 5:30 on Tuesday and Wednesday evenings, taking to the hills en masse for some "undulating all-terraining." Mountain bikers should remember that the trails, listed under the "Hiking" section in this chapter, have been established primarily for hikers.

Similarly, cyclists out on the roadways should remember that even on the most remote thoroughfare, cars do come by, do have the right of way, do hurt should you cross paths. It all seems very obvious until you get out there, intoxicated by the pastoral symphony around you, blithely forgetting you're on the road. So: right-hand riding, single file. After dark, the state says you must have a headlight, a red rear reflector, as well as side and pedal reflectors. In traffic, turns require hand signals with the left hand: extended for left turn, raised for right turn, held low for stopping. Helmets are a recommended nuisance, helping, in a crisis, to keep your head together.

An extremely detailed county map is available by mail from the Berkshire County Commissioners (413-448-8424; Superior Court Building, 76 East St., Pittsfield 01201; $6.00, checks payable to "County of Berkshire").

North Adams resident Lewis Cuyler is an avid bike rider and a writer as well, and his *Bike Rides in the Berkshire Hills* is a fine guide to pedaling through these valleys and over the mountains (see the Bibliography in Chapter Eight, *Information*).

BICYCLE DEALERS

South County

The Bike Doctor 413-229-2909; 145 E. Main, Ashley Falls
Gaffer's Outdoors 413-229-0063; 216 Main St.
Harland B. Foster 413-528-2100; 15 Bridge St., Gt. Barrington.

Central County

Arcadian Shop 413-637-3010; Pittsfield-Lenox Rd. (Rte. 7), Lenox.
Main Street Sports & Leisure 413-637-4407; 102 Main St., Lenox
Mean Wheels 413-637-0644; 55 Housatonic St., Lenox.
Ordinary Cycles 413-442-7225; 251 North St., Pittsfield.
Plaine's Ski & Cycle Center 413-499-0391; 55 W. Housatonic St., Pittsfield.

North County

The Mountain Goat 413-458-8445; 130 Water St., Williamstown.
Spokes, Bicycles & Repairs 413-458-3456; 620 Main St., Williamstown.
The Sports Corner 413-664-8654; 61 Main St., N. Adams

BOATING

Berkshire has been called the "American Lake District," and thanks to great glacial activity in its formative stages, the area is indeed blessed with many beautiful bodies of water. Besides the dozens of lakes and "bowls," scores of smaller ponds dot the landscape. For the boating enthusiast, opportunities abound. Here then, are Berkshire's best boating lakes, from ponds suitable only for canoe and rowboat, to grand lakes, where you can go powerboating, water-skiing, and sailing.

South County

Benedict Pond Beartown State Forest; 413-528-0904; Blue Hill Rd., Monterey.
Sylvan pond suitable for canoe or rowboat only.
Camp Overflow 413-269-4036; 5 mi. from Rtes. 8 and 20, in Otis.
Goose Pond Tyringham Rd., Lee. Boat rentals.
Laurel Lake Rte. 20, Lee. Boat rentals.
Lake Garfield Kinne's Grove, Rte. 23, Monterey. Boat rentals.
Otis Reservoir 413-528-0904; Reservoir Rd., off Rte. 23, Otis. Small power-boats, sunfish, and sailboats for rent at the largest of Berkshire's lakes.
J&D Marina, 413-269-4839; and Miller Marine, 413-269-6358.
Prospect Lake 413-528-4158; Prospect Lake Rd., N. Egremont. Canoe, paddleboat, rowboat, and sailboard rental and instruction at a private-access family campground and lake.
Sandisfield State Forest 413-258-4774; West St., Sandisfield.
Stockbridge Bowl Rte. 183, Stockbridge. Free launching sites on one of the county's prettiest lakes, just below Tanglewood.

Central County

Greenwater Pond Pleasant Point, Becket. Boat rentals.
Onota Lake Onota Blvd., Pittsfield. Free launching area for motorboats. Good windsurfing. Onota Boat Livery (413-442-1724; 455 Pecks Rd.) rents small powerboats.
Pittsfield State Forest 413-442-8992; Cascade St., Pittsfield.

Pontoosuc Lake Rte. 7, Pittsfield. The only place in Berkshire where you can rent a ski boat. U Drive Boat Rentals (413-442-7020; 1651 North St.) also rents smaller powerboats, sailboats, and jet skis.

Preparing to dock, at Pittsfield's Pontoosuc.

Jonathan Sternfield

Richmond Pond Swamp Rd., Richmond. Boat rentals.

North County

Clarksburg State Forest 413-664-8345; Middle Rd., Clarksburg. Hoosac Lake Rte. 8, Cheshire. Boat rentals and launching site.

Privacy Campground 413-458-3125; Rte. 43, 5 mi. south of junction with Rte. 7, Hancock. Pond for canoeing and rowboating.

Savoy Mountain State Forest 413-663-8469; Off Rte. 2 in Florida, Rte. 116 in Savoy. North Pond and South Pond are two jewels in the hills, quite remote, rarely busy.

BOWLING

Strike after strike is being bowled in Berkshire, and if you're eager to get in on the action, there are eight locales throughout the county. In *South County*, head for *Cove Lanes* (413-528-1220; 109 Stockbridge Rd., Gt. Barrington) or *Lee Bowling Lanes* 413-243-0095; Rte. 102, Lee). *Central County* offers

Candle Lanes (413-447-9640; 255 North St., Pittsfield); *Dalton Community House* (413-684-0260; 400 Main St., Dalton); *Imperial Bowl* (413-443-4453; 555 Dalton Ave., Pittsfield); and *Ken's Bowl* (413-499-0733; 495 Dalton Ave., Pittsfield). In <u>North County</u>, bowling's best at *Mt. Greylock Bowl* (413-663-3761; Roberts Dr., N. Adams) and *Valley Park Inc.* (413-664-9715; Curren Hwy., N. Adams).

CAMPING

It's easy to get back to nature in the Berkshires. Nine of the county's state parks offer camping, with facilities ranging from showers and flush toilets to campsites that are little more than terraces hewn out of the mountainside. There are also more than a dozen private campgrounds in the area, and these usually offer more amenities, making a long summer stay quite comfortable. Wherever you camp, the rolling hills are a soothing sight for sore eyes.

> *The delights of camping? You will live outdoors, sleep on the fragrant spruce boughs under the transparent tent roof, lazily loaf in "hammock grove," and, by means of frequent walks compassing noble scenery, cultivate the most enormous of appetites.*
>
> The Book of Berkshire, 1889

Campsites in *state parks* are available on an unreserved basis, but please be aware that owing to budget restrictions at the state level, some state parks and forests may be closed. It is therefore a good idea to obtain complete information in advance from *Massachusetts Environmental Management Department*, Region Five Headquarters, Box 1433, Pittsfield, MA 01201; telephone 413-442-8928.

Fees are as follows at all state parks and forests: Season pass $15; *Camping*: wilderness, per night: free; unimproved toilets $4; flush toilets $5; flush toilets with showers $6; water utility fee $1; sewer utility fee $1; group camping $8; log cabins, one-room $8; three rooms $10; *Day use* per car $2 per day.

State campgrounds, noted below with an asterisk (*), are of two kinds: "Type-1" denotes facilities with showers and flush toilets; "Type-2" denotes those with outhouses.

South County

* **Beartown State Forest** (Manager: Thomas W. O'Brien; 413-528-0904; Blue Hill Rd., Monterey, MA 01245; Mailing Add: Box 97, Monterey, MA 01245; N. from Rte. 23 in Monterey) On Benedict Pond; 10,555 acres, 12 Type-2 campsites, bicycling, boating, fishing, hiking, hunting, horseback riding trails, picnicking, xc skiing, snowmobiling, swimming.

Camp Overflow (413-269-4036; Box 645, Otis, MA 01253; 5 mi. from Rte. 8) 100 sites, electric hookups, dumping station, camp store, fishing, swimming, boating, seasonal rates, right on Otis Reservoir.

Laurel Ridge Farm Camping Area (413-269-4804; Old Blandford Rd., E. Otis, MA 01029) Electric and water sites.

Maple Glade Campground (Managers: Thomas & Karen Shaffer; 413-243-1548; 165 Woodland Rd., Lee, MA 01238; across from October Mtn. State Forest) 70 sites; hook-ups available. $15 for tents, $17 with water. Small store, swimming pool.

* **Mount Washington State Forest and Bash Bish Falls State Park** (413-528-0330; East St., Mt. Washington, MA 01258; From S. Egremont, take Rte. 41 S., then next right onto Mt. Washington Rd. and follow signs) 3,289 acres, including spectacular Bash Bish Falls, boating, bicycling, canoeing, 15 Type-2 wilderness campsites, fishing, hiking, horseback riding trails, hunting, snowmobiling, xc skiing. Nearby Mt. Everett State Forest offers three-state views from its road to the summit.

* **October Mountain State Forest** (413-243-1778 or 413-243-9735; Woodland Rd., Lee, MA 01238) Follow signs from Rte. 20 in Lee. 16,021 acres, 50 Type-1 campsites, bicycling, fishing, hiking, Appalachian Trail, horseback riding, hunting, xc skiing, snowmobiling. Some campsites wheelchair accessible.

Prospect Lake Park (413-528-4158; Prospect Lake Rd., N. Egremont, MA 01252) 130 sites, tennis, swimming, boat rentals, basketball court, volleyball, snack bar, playground.

* **Sandisfield State Forest** (Manager: Thomas W. O'Brien; 413-528-0904; West St., Sandisfield, MA 01255; off Rte. 57 at Pine Woods Rd., then to West St.) 11,000 acres, part of York Lake recreation area, which includes Campbell Falls and West Lake. Rest of park offers wilderness hiking, bicycling, boating, fishing, hunting horseback riding trails, picnicking, xc skiing, snowmobiling, swimming.

* **Tolland State Forest** (Manager: Paul Adams; 413-269-7268; Rte. 8, Otis, MA 01253; 5 mi. from Rte. 8) 90 Type-1 campsites, on 8,000 acres, including lovely Otis Reservoir. Private, secluded campsites, some on the lake or overlooking lake. Bicycling, boating, fishing, hunting, hiking, horseback riding trails, picnicking, xc skiing, snowmobiling, swimming.

Central County

Bissellville Estate & Campground (Owners: Eugene & Lorraine Brunet; 413-655-8396; Washington Rd. [Rte. 8], Hinsdale, MA 01235) 13 campsites with sewer hookups; 18 with water & electricity; 13 with all three. Closed winter.

Bonnie Brae Cabins and Campsites (Manager: Richard Halkowicz; (413-442-3754, 108 Broadway St., Pittsfield, MA 01201; 3 mi. N. of downtown Pittsfield, off Rte. 7 at Pontoosuc Lake) Full hookups, free showers, trailer rentals, new pool, cabin rentals May 1–Oct. 31. Closed Nov.–Apr. 30.

Bonnie Rigg Campground (Managers: Paul and Kathryn Neske; (413-623-5366; P.O. Box 14, Chester, MA 01011-0014; corner of Rtes. 8 & 20 in Becket) 200 campsites, but by owner/membership only. Call for information. Adult lounge, playground, swimming pool, sauna, jacuzzi.

Bucksteep Manor (413-623-5535; Washington Mtn. Rd., Becket, MA 01223; 10 mi. E. of Pittsfield, across from October Mtn. State Forest) 15 sites, 9 cabins; showers, swimming pool, tennis, hiking, xc skiing, weekend restaurant.

Mount Greylock State Reservation (413-499-4262; Rockwell Rd., Lanesborough, MA 01237; from Rte. 7 in Lanesborough, take N. Main St. to Rockwell Rd.) 10,237 acres which includes the state's highest peak (see Chapter Three, *Lodging*, for historic Bascom Lodge). 100-mi. view from War Veterans Memorial Tower, 35 wilderness campsites, 45 mi. of trails including the Appalachian Trail, xc skiing, hunting, snowmobiling, picnicking.

* **Pittsfield State Forest** (413-442-8992; Cascade St., Pittsfield, MA 01201; From Rte 7 take West St. to Cascade St.) 9,695 acres with streams, waterfalls, wild-flowers, panoramic views, and famous Balance Rock. Two camping areas offer 31 Type-1 and Type-2 campsites, plus boating, canoeing, xc skiing, ski lodge, bicycling, fishing, hiking, picnicking, hunting, interpretive programs, snowmobiling, swimming, and wheelchair-accessible picnic areas and trails.

Ponterril (Manager: Kevin Fitzpatrick, Pittsfield YMCA; 413-499-0640; North St., Pittsfield, MA 01201; off E. Acres Rd. at Pontoosuc Lake N. of Pittsfield via Rte. 7) 12 campsites, swimming pool, tennis, sailing and sailing instructions.

Summit Hill Campground (Manager: Vicki Roberts, 413-623-5761; Summit Hill Rd., Washington, MA 01235) 110 campsites for tents and trailers, 83 sites with electricity and water, adult lounge, swimming pool and recreation hall. Closed in winter.

* **Windsor State Forest** (413-698-0948; in winter 413-442-8928; River Rd., Windsor, MA 01270; Off Rte. 9 just E. of Windsor town line; off Rte. 116 in Savoy) 1,626 acres with spectacular falls at Windsor Jambs. 24 Type-2 campsites, bicycling, fishing, hiking, hunting, picnicking, swimming, xc skiing, snowmobiling.

North County

Brodie Campgrounds (Managers: Brodie Mtn; 413-443-4754; Brodie Mtn. Ski Resort, New Ashford, MA 01237; off Rte. 7, just N. of Lanesborough town line) 120 campsites for tents and trailers, rented seasonally. Heated swimming pool, tennis, recreation hall.

Clarksburg State Park (413-664-8345, in winter 413-442-8928; Middle Rd., Clarksburg, MA 01247; From Rte. 8 N. take Middle Rd. in Clarksburg)

3,250 acres of unspoiled forestland with panoramic views; Mauserts Pond offers landscaped day-use area; 47 Type-2 campsites; boating, canoeing, xc skiing, fishing, hiking, hunting, snowmobiling, picnicking, bicycling, swimming.

Historic Valley Park Campground (Manager: Les Griffin; (413-664-9228; Box 751, N. Adams, MA 01247) 100 campsites with electric and water hookups, laundry, camp store, recreation hall, hiking trails on beautiful Windsor Lake, public and private beaches with lifeguards. $14 a day.

Privacy Campground (413-458-3125; Hancock Rd., Williamstown, MA 01267; on Rte. 43, 5 mi. S. of Rte. 7) 475 acres, 35 sites, waterfall, pond, 10 mi. of hiking trails, paddle boats, volleyball, badminton, horseshoes, tetherball, basketball, campfires, waterwheel, windmill, trolley car, playground, sauna. 4 small cabins.

* **Savoy Mountain State Forest** (413-663-8469; Central Shaft Rd., Florida, MA 01256) 11,000 acres, including Bog Pond and Tannery Falls; 45 Type-1 campsites in old apple orchard, 3 log cabins with grand stone chimneys, overlook South Pond and are available for year-round rental by writing RFD 2, N. Adams, MA 01247; picnicking, boating, bicycling, canoeing, xc skiing, fishing, hiking, interpretive programs, snowmobiling, swimming.

CAMPS

There's a colorful list of overnight, resident summer camps in the Berkshires — some specializing in sports, some tuned to the arts, some with other

Campers greeting the day.

Ralph Schulman, courtesy Camp Mohawk

enthusiasms. If you or your youngsters are interested in dance or the theater, hiking or canoeing, tennis or gymnastics, dressmaking or computers, Berkshire has a camp for you. Most camps take advantage of the beauty of their natural settings, and for many of them that includes lakes and mountains. Warm days and cool nights make for season-long aquatics and sound sleeping. Berkshire cultural life also enriches campers' time here, with Tanglewood and Jacob's Pillow being two of the more popular side trips.

The Indians were the first campers in the Berkshires, and many of its camps still bear Indian names. Following is a list of addresses and telephone numbers. "Full program" indicates availability of both arts and sports activities.

South County

Camp Half Moon Directors: Til, Edward & Gretchen Mann; 413-528-0940; 400 Main St., Gt. Barrington, MA 01230; Day & Resident Camp; Coed; Full program.

Camp High Rock Director: Chris Coker; 413-528-1227; Mt. Washington, MA 01258; Sessions for coed groups and adults; Full program.

Camp Kingsmont Director: Keith Zucker; 413-232-8518; RFD #2, W. Stockbridge, MA 01266; Coed; Nutrition and dietary education program, physical fitness.

Camp Lenox Directors: Monty and Richard Moss; 413-243-2223, summer, 413-269-6036, winter; Rte. 8, Lee, MA 01238; Coed; Sports.

Crane Lake Camp Directors: Barbara and Ed Ulanoff; 413-232-4257, summer, 212-362-1462, winter; State Line, W. Stockbridge, MA 01266; Coed; Full program.

Eisner Camp Institute Director: Dave Friedman 413-528-1652, summer, 212-249-0100, ext. 496, winter; Brookside Rd., Gt. Barrington, MA 01230; Coed children's and adult retreats; Full program and Jewish education.

Central County

Belvoir Terrace Directors: Nancy Goldberg and Edna Schwartz; 413-637-0555, summer, 212-580-3398, winter; Cliffwood St., Lenox, MA 01240; Girls; Fine and Performing Arts.

Camp Becket Director: Mark Smith; 413-623-8972; Becket, MA 01223; Boys; Full program; Operated by Two-State YMCA.

Camp Emerson Directors: Addie and Marvin Lein; 413-655-8123, summer, 914-779-9406, winter; Long View Ave., Hinsdale, MA 01235; Coed 7-15, Full program.

Camp Greylock Director: Bert Margolis; 413-623-8921, summer, 212-582-1042, winter; Rte. 8, Becket, MA 01233; Boys; Full program.

Camp Mah-Kee-Nac Directors: Danny and Nancy Metzger; 413-637-0781, summer, 201-429-8522, winter; Lenox, MA 01240; Boys; Sports.

Camp Romaca Director: Brenda Levine; 413-655-2715, summer, 800-779-2070, winter; Long View Ave., Hinsdale, MA 01235; Girls; Full program.

Camp Taconic Directors: Robert and Barbara Ezrol; 413-655-2717, summer, 914-762-2820, winter; Hinsdale, MA 01235; Coed; Full program.

Camp Watitoh Directors: Sandy, William & Suzanne Hoch; 413-623-8951, summer, 914-428-1894, winter; Center Lake, Becket, MA 01223; Coed; Full program.

Camp Winadu Directors: Arleen and Shelley Weiner; 413-447-8900, summer, 407-994-5500, winter; Churchill St., Pittsfield, MA 01201; Boys; Full program.

Chimney Corners Camp Director: Susan Frantz; 413-623-8991; Becket, MA 01223; Girls; Full program; Operated by Two-State YMCA.

CANOEING AND KAYAKING

William Tague

Berkshire whitewater has challenged generations of canoers.

Besides all of Berkshire's lovely lakes to canoe and kayak, the paddler has several rivers to choose from, with stretches varying from lazy flatwater to rushing rapids. The Housatonic River rises near Pittsfield and flows southward, between the Taconic Range and the Berkshire Plateau, heading for the

Atlantic Ocean, near Stratford, Connecticut. Four Berkshire trips down the Housatonic are recommended by the Appalachian Mountain Club: Dalton to Lenox (19 mi.); Lenox to Stockbridge (12 mi.); Stockbridge to Gt. Barrington (13 mi.); and Gt. Barrington to Falls Village, Connecticut (25 mi.). Send for *The AMC River Guide to Massachusetts, Connecticut and Rhode Island* ($9.95, from AMC 5 Joy St., Boston, MA 02108) or ask local booksellers.

In **South County**, the stretch on the Housatonic from Gt. Barrington to Bartholomew's Cobble in Ashley Falls is classic, lazy river paddling. Canoes can be purchased and rented in Sheffield at *Gaffer's Canoe Service* (413-229-0063; Rte. 7) or *South County Paddling* (413-229-2541: 10 Miller Ave.).

> Henry Parker Fellows, describing an 1881 canoe trip down the Housatonic through Great Barrington: "The Housatonic is a confirmed coquette, constantly flirting with one mountain range or another, and frequently with several at the same time."

For lovely lake paddling, canoes can be rented at *Prospect Lake* (413-528-4158; Prospect Lake Rd., N. Egremont) and *Lake Garfield* (413-528-5417; Rte. 23, Monterey).

In early April, the West Branch of the Farmington River swells, and the stretch south of Rte. 23, along Rte. 8 in Otis and Sandisfield, is the site of an annual Olympic kayak racing event. In early spring, this stretch is a Class Three rapids and makes for exciting white-water paddling and great viewing.

Up in **North County**, the Hoosic River flows northwards, and in those parts, **Berkshire Outfitters** (413-743-5900; Rte. 8, Adams) are the canoe and kayak specialists, renting craft and offering sound advice on the best in area boating.

A Canoe Guide to the Housatonic River: Berkshire County is a nifty little booklet published jointly by the Housatonic River Watershed Association and the Berkshire County Regional Planning Commission. In it, you'll find a couple of nice line drawings, a neat history of the river and its flora and fauna, as well as dozens of access points with river descriptions. Highly recommended for any Housatonic paddling; see local booksellers.

CROQUET

In the Berkshires, croquet has had a small but tenacious group of followers who have fought heated battles on the lawns at the Lenox Club and at J.

Gould's, next to Tanglewood. Several clubs were formed in the early 1980s and have constructed tournament-grade lawns in Lenox, Richmond, Sandisfield, Stockbridge, and Tyringham. This complex of courts now gives the Berkshires the largest number of croquet lawns in any area of the country.

How does someone who is intrigued by this wicket sport find a way to learn the game and actually play? Local clubs are privately run, so watch the newspapers for announcements of tournaments open to the public. And, there are two beautiful courts on the grounds of Blantyre, in Lenox, which offers its resident guests the use of imported equipment and lessons by a certified professional, during the season from July to September. See Chapter Three, *Lodging*, for more information on Blantyre.

FITNESS FACILITIES

Getting in shape was never so organized. Used to be, you did your work, you had your fun, it kept you in shape. Now, most jobs age us before our time, and Berkshire has joined the growing revolution to reverse that trend. Residential fitness facilities, where you check in and stay awhile, are listed later in this chapter, Canyon Ranch as a "Luxury Spa," Kripalu as a "Yoga Retreat." Here are some other exercise and recreation centers around the county.

Berkshire Health & Fitness Center (413-528-9977; 955 S. Main St., Gt. Barrington) Aerobics, Nautilus, free weights, Air-dyne bicycles, Concept II Rowing machines, nutrition consultation, trained staff, showers and dressing rooms.

Berkshire Nautilus (413-499-1217; 205 West St., Pittsfield) Nautilus, stationary bikes, rowing machines, treadmill, StairMaster, whirlpool, sauna, steam, and certified instruction.

Berkshire West (413-499-4600; Dan Fox Dr.; Pittsfield) Nautilus, stationary bikes, free weights, tennis, racquetball, aerobics, treadmills, nautilus, freeweights, saunas, steam room, hot tub, and certified instruction. Also has a nursery.

Eden Hill Recreation Center (413-298-5222; Congregation of the Marians, Prospect Hill, Stockbridge) Olympic-size heated indoor poor, gym, weight room with Universal machines, Ping-Pong, billiards, and men and women's sauna. Swimming and aerobic instruction available.

Fitness Express (413-528-5600; 740 Main St., Gt. Barrington) Aerobics, ballet, karate, myotherapy.

The Health Club (413-243-3500; Oak 'n' Spruce, Meadow St., S. Lee) Universal equipment, Nautilus, StairMaster, stationery bicycles, free weights, indoor pool, hot tub, saunas, tennis, basketball, aerobics classes.

Lenox Fitness Center (413-637-9893; Main St., Lenox) Nautilus, stationary bikes, rowing machines, StairMasters, aerobics, steam rooms, tanning booth, and certified instruction.

FOOTBALL

There are high school games and pick-up touch football games throughout the county, but only in Williamstown will you see spirited collegiate gridiron action, as presented by the Williams College Ephmen (named after their school founder, Ephraim Williams). This is football at its sweetest, where opposing players help each other up after bruising tackles, where the announcer's game call includes such literate descriptions as: ". . . Number 84, leveled by a plethora of Ephmen," or ". . . Number 17, overwhelmed by a veritable deluge of jumbos!"
Williams College Football, Weston Field, Williamstown: 413-597-2344.

GOLF

In 1895, Joseph Choate, Jr., son of the prominent Stockbridge lawyer, returned from a Canadian trip with three rudimentary golf clubs. Using tomato cans for holes, he made a course in his backyard at Naumkeag and gave birth to golf in the Berkshires. Three years later, having perfected his swing, Joseph Choate, Jr., won the National Championships with a record low score.

Golf has grown in the Berkshires, and there are now more than a dozen courses county-wide, with hardy sportsfolk teeing up from March through November. Every course and club runs tournaments, and a call or visit to the pro will give you exact dates. Long-distance driving options have expanded, too. First there were wood woods, then metal woods, and now, new for the nineties — developed from Pittsfield-GE engineered resins — Lexan woods, by Thermo Par. And if you just have to hit some in the dark of night, *Baker's Driving Range & Miniature Golf* (413-443-6102: Rte. 7, Lanesborough) keeps its driving range open from 10 a.m. till 10:30 p.m. Other possibilities in the miniature division are the *Par 4 Family Fun Center* (413-499-0051; Rte. 7, Lanesborough), *Jiminy Peak* (413-738-5500; Hancock), the *Diversions Restaurant and Fun Center* in N. Adams (413-662-2688; N. Adams Plaza), and in South County there's *Rainbow's End Miniature Golf* (413-528-1220; Rte. 7, Gt. Barrington) inside Cove Bowling Lanes.

GOLF CLUBS

Price Code — Greens Fees
Inexpensive   Under $15
Moderate $15 to $30
Expensive   Over $30

South County

Egremont Country Club Pro: Bob Dastoli; 413-528-4222; Rte. 23, S. Egremont; 18 holes; Par 71; 5,900 yards; Price: Moderate.

Greenock Country Club Pro: Tom McDarby; 413-243-3323; W. Park St., Lee; 9 holes; Par 70; 5,990 yards; Price: Moderate.

Stockbridge Golf Club Pro: Jim Walker; 413-298-3423; Main St., Stockbridge; 18 holes; Par 71; 6,294 yards; Price: Expensive; Must be introduced by a member.

Wyantenuck Country Club Pro: Dennis Perrone; 413-528-3229; Sheffield Rd., Gt. Barrington; 18 holes; Par 70; 6,137 yards; Price: Expensive.

Central County

Bas-Ridge Golf Course 413-655-2605; Plunkett Ave., Hinsdale; 9 holes; Par 70; 5,164 yards; Price: Inexpensive.

Berkshire Hills Country Club Pro: Jim Turbeville; 413-442-1451; Benedict Rd., Pittsfield; 18 holes; Par 72; 6,606 yards; Price: Moderate; Must be introduced by a member.

Country Club of Pittsfield Pro: Brad Benson; 413-447-8504; 639 South St., Pittsfield; 18 holes; Par 71; 6,100 yards; Must be introduced by a member.

Cranwell Golf Course Pro Bran Meekins; 413-637-1216 or 413-637-0441; 55 Lee Rd. (Rte. 20), Lenox; 18 holes; Par 70; 6,387 yards; Price: Moderate.

General Electric Athletic Association Pro: Ed Rossi; 413-443-5746; 303 Crane Ave., Pittsfield; 9 holes; Par 72; 6,205 yards; Price: Inexpensive.

Pontoosuc Lake Country Club 413-445-4217; Ridge Ave., Pittsfield; 18 holes; Par 70; 6,305 yards; Price: Inexpensive.

Skyline Country Club Pro: Jim Mitus; 413-445-5584; 405 S. Main St., Lanesborough; 9 holes; Par 72; 6,643 yards; Price: Inexpensive.

Wahconah Country Club Pro: Paul Daniels; 413-684-1333; Orchard Rd., Dalton; 18 holes; Par 71; 6,541 yards; Price: Expensive.

North County

Forest Park Country Club 413-743-3311; Country Club Ave., Adams; 9 holes; Par 68; 5,100 yards; Price: Inexpensive.

North Adams Country Club 413-664-9011; River Rd., Clarksburg; 9 holes; Par 72; 6,070 yards; Price: Inexpensive.

Taconic Golf Club Pro: Rick Pohle; 413-458-3997; Meacham St., Williamstown; 18 holes; Par 71; 6,614 yards; Price: Expensive.

Waubeeka Springs Golf Links Pro: Tom Toski; 413-458-8355; New Ashford Rd. (Rte. 7), Williamstown; 18 holes; Par 72; 6,296 yards; Price: Moderate.

HIKING

If you would be happy in Berkshire, you must carry mountains in your brain.

Oliver Wendell Holmes

Massachusetts may be the sixth smallest state in the union, but its forest and park system is the sixth largest. And of the state's quarter-million protected acres, nearly 100,000 are in Berkshire County. With trails along lake and riverside, up hills and steep mountains, the Berkshires offer all types of terrain for anything from an afternoon's jaunt to a full-fledged pack trip. There are 21 state parks in the county, all of which have interesting trails, and the seven Berkshire Nature Centers each have scenic paths. In addition, the Appalachian Trail runs straight up the center of Berkshire County, entering near Bartholomew's Cobble in Ashley Falls and exiting near Clarksburg.

Thou who woulds't see the lovely and the wild
Mingled in harmony on Nature's face,
Ascend our rocky mountains.

From William Cullen Bryant's poem, "Monument Mountain"

Monument Mountain makes an exciting climb in any weather, over giant glacial boulders or up well-marked trails. Most of the cross-country ski trails noted later in this chapter are also excellent hiking trails. Although a compass and maps are advisable for any deep-woods hiking, it's comforting to note that in Berkshire County, no matter how wild your surroundings, you are never more than five miles from the nearest paved road. Nevertheless, for hikes of any length, and especially for those taken alone, always notify a friend of your plan and your estimated hour of return.

STATE PARKS IN THE BERKSHIRES

South County

Beartown and East Mtn. State Forest 413-528-0904; Blue Hill Rd., Monterey; 10,500 acres.
East Mtn. State Reservation 413-528-2000; Rte. 7, Gt. Barrington.
Mt. Everett State Reservation, Mt. Washington State Forest, Bash Bish Falls 413-528-0330; East St., Mt. Washington; 3,289 acres.
October Mtn. State Forest 413-243-1778, 413-243-9735; Woodland Rd., Lee; 15,710 acres.
Otis State Forest 413-528-0904; Rte. 23, Otis.
Sandisfield and Cookson State Forest 413-258-4774; West St., Sandisfield (New Marlboro); 4,378 acres.
Tolland State Forest 413-269-6002, 413-269-7268; Rte. 8, Otis; 8,000 acres.

Central County

Mt. Greylock State Reservation 413-499-4263, 413-499-4262; Rockwell Rd., Lanesborough; 10,327 acres.
Pittsfield State Forest 413-442-8992; Cascade St., Pittsfield; 9,695 acres.
Windsor State Forest 413-684-0948; River Rd., Windsor; 1,626 acres.

North County

Clarksburg State Park 413-664-8345; Middle Rd., Clarksburg; 346 acres.
Savoy Mtn. State Forest 413-663-8469; Rte 2, Florida and Rte. 116, Savoy; 10,500 acres.

History of the Trustees of Reservations

In 1890, long before the present national interest in the environment, a young landscape architect returned from study in Europe with a deepening concern for the need to preserve the natural beauty and historic sites of his community.

Early that year, Charles Eliot (1859-1897), just 31 years old and son of Charles W. Eliot, then president of Harvard University, proposed the establishment of an organization "empowered to hold small and well distributed parcels of land . . . just as the Public Library holds books and the Art Museum pictures for the use and enjoyment of the public."

The Trustees of Reservations was incorporated by the Massachusetts General Court a year later, 1891, the first independent organization in the United States established for the purpose of preserving land.

The Trustees of Reservations; 572 Essex St., Beverly, MA 01915.

For more detailed information on the county's 21 state parks, write: *Massachusetts Department of Environmental Management* (617-727-9800; 100 Cambridge St., Boston, MA 02202) or its Region V office (413-442-8928; Box 1433, Pittsfield, MA 01202).

Excellent hiking opportunities await you at the following properties of the Trustees of Reservations:

Bartholomew's Cobble 413-229-8600; Weatogue Rd., (Rte. 7A), Ashley Falls (Sheffield).
Monument Mtn. Stockbridge Rd. (Rte. 7), Gt. Barrington.
Notchview Reservation 413-684-0148; Rte. 9, Windsor.
Tyringham Cobble 413-298-3239; Jerusalem Rd., Tyringham.

Berkshire County Land Trust

The Berkshire County Land Trust and Conservation Fund is an offshoot of Berkshire Natural Resources Council, a private, not-for-profit environmental advocacy group, established in 1967. Led by director-lobbyist George Wislocki, this group believes that the wealth of Berkshire lies in its quality of life, in its natural environment and cultural heritage. Of the 600,000 acres in Berkshire, some 120,000 are parkland. The council works with state and local agencies to ensure that those lands are properly protected from abuse.

There are about 200 land trusts in America, many of them in New England. By all counts, Berkshire's is one of the more successful. In Pittsfield, the Trust was responsible for increasing the Pittsfield State Forest by 1,800 acres. Along the Housatonic, south of Pittsfield, the Resources Council is coordinating the creation of a 12-mile-long river park, reaching to Woods Pond in Lenox. The Land Trust facilitated the preservation of Gould Meadows, that gorgeous 95-acre pasture reaching from Tanglewood to Stockbridge Bowl. The Stockbridge-Yokun Ridge Reserve is another land corridor the Trust is assembling to remain forever wild, an eight-mile-long, 6,300-acre spread of Berkshire park.

The Land Trust helps keep Berkshire beautiful.

Berkshire County Land Trust and Berkshire Natural Resources Council, Inc.
Director: George Wislocki; 413-499-0596; 10 Bank Row, Pittsfield, MA 01201.

There are several hiking clubs in the Berkshires, and among them, the *Appalachian Trail Club* and the *Williams Outing Club* (413-597-2317) are the most active. Each runs organized hikes through the county. The map at the end of the book shows the entire length of the Appalachian Trail in Berkshire County.

A young and knowledgeable outfit, *Berkshire Hiking Holidays*, offers to guide you along the Appalachian and Taconic Range trails in half- or whole-day hikes, while arranging your tickets to a later Tanglewood concert, perhaps, and your sumptuous dinner and comfortable lodging to follow. Trail snacks and lunches are included, of course, as are stopovers at scenic vistas and cascading waterfalls. From a long, vigorous hike up a mountain to a slow meander through a birch-shaded path, Berkshire Hiking will help you find your way back to nature. Packages vary from a weekend to 10 days in length; and this is no camp-out type hiking, with your nightly stay arranged in comfortable, even luxurious accommodations. If you like meeting nature while maintaining your comfort quotient, Berkshire Hiking may be just the guide group you're after. ***Berkshire Hiking Holidays*** (413-637-4442; P.O. Box 2231, Lenox, MA 01240).

Two excellent books on Berkshire hiking are available: *Hikes & Walks in the Berkshire Hills* by Lauren Stevens; and for North County, *The Williams College Outing Club Trail Guide*, first published in 1927 and now in its seventh edition. Stevens' book covers not only a wide variety of challenging hikes for the energetic and ambitious, but also a large number of easy strolls for those with less time or gumption; and there's a section on walks for the blind and physically handicapped. There is also the extremely detailed *Appalachian Mountain Club Trail Guide*. See the Bibliography for further details on all these books.

Various literati have climbed Berkshire mountains and recorded their impressions. In his *Notebooks*, H. D. Thoreau wrote perhaps the most rhapsodic passage of all, about awakening after a night alone on top of Mt. Greylock.

As the light increased I discovered around me an ocean of mist, which by chance reached up exactly to the base of the tower, and shut out every vestige of the earth, while I was left floating on this fragment of the wreck of a world. . . . As the light in the east steadily increased, it revealed to me more clearly the new world into which I had risen in the night, the new terra-firma perchance of my future life. There was not a crevice left through which the trivial places we name Massachusetts, or Vermont, or New York could be seen, while I still inhaled the clear atmosphere of a July morning, — if it were July there. All around beneath me was spread for a hundred miles on every side, as far as the eye could reach, an undulating country of clouds, answering in the varied swell of its surface to the terrestrial world it veiled. It was such a country as we might see in dreams, with all the delights of paradise.

HORSEBACK RIDING

There's a slew of riding academies and stables in and around Berkshire County. A quick look in the Yellow Pages opens the barn door to information on horse breeders, dealers, trainers, shoers, and saddle shops. The following is a list of riding possibilities.

Aspinwall Riding School 413-637-0245; 279 Pittsfield Rd. (Rte. 7), Lenox; English lessons, indoor and outdoor rings; year-round.

Bonnie Lea Farm 413-458-3149; 511 North St. (Rte. 7), Williamstown; private and group lessons; English, dressage; indoor and outdoor rings, guided trail rides; year-round.

Bradford Manor Farm 413-232-4496; 6 W. Center Rd., W. Stockbridge; English, Western, jumping, trail rides, hay rides, outdoor ring; year-round.

Eastover 413-637-0625; 40 East St., Lenox; trail rides for guests only at Eastover resort; year-round.

Overmeade School of Horsemanship 413-499-2850; 822 East St., Lenox; English private and group lessons; year-round.

RCR Stables 413-637-0613; 430 East St., Lenox; guided trail rides.

Stepping Stone Stable 413-684-3200; 619 East St., Dalton; summer riding program, year-round lessons.

Undermountain Farm 413-637-3365; Undermountain Rd., Lenox; English lessons, trail rides; spring through fall.

HUNTING AND FISHING

Fly fishing the Green River.

Jonathan Sternfield

The first settlers found Berkshire teeming with fish and game; and though the wildlife is presently less plentiful, there are still so many deer they must frequently be avoided on the roadways, still enough wild turkey, bear, pheasant, quail, rabbit, raccoon, fox, coyote, and gray squirrel to satisfy nearly every hunter's aim. In Berkshire's waters, large and small mouth bass, northern pike, white and yellow perch, horned pout, and trout of all varieties still swim in abundance. Numerous brooks, rivers, ponds and lakes are stocked with trout each year.

Essential equipment for any hunting or fishing is a pamphlet containing abstracts of the *Massachusetts Fish and Wildlife Laws*, available free at local sporting goods shops; from the **Division of Fisheries and Wildlife** (617-727-3151; 100 Cambridge St., Boston 02202); or from the **Western Wildlife District Manager**, Tom Keefe (413-447-9789; Hubbard Ave., Pittsfield, 01201). This pamphlet carefully outlines the rules and regulations of Massachusetts fishing and hunting, and without it, you may well violate the law or risk injury. Also essential is a license, and this can be obtained through either city or town clerks, through the Division of Fisheries and Wildlife at the Boston address above, or through many local sporting goods stores (see the list at the beginning of this chapter).

Such a license permits hunting, fishing or trapping, but in no way permits trespassing on private property, whether posted or not. Permission to hunt or fish on private property must be obtained from the landowner. State lands impose no such restriction, and the game population there is generally higher. A chat with the local sporting goods proprietor or with fellow hunters at early morning coffee will often yield secrets about the most reliable hunting areas.

For stores carrying fishing gear, see the list of sporting-goods shops at the beginning of this chapter.

A LIST OF TROUT-STOCKED BERKSHIRE WATERS

South County

Alford Seekonk Brook, Green River.

Egremont Green River, Hubbard Brook.

Great Barrington Green River, West Brook, Thomas & Palmer Brook, Williams River, Lake Mansfield.

Lee Beartown Brook (west branch), Hop Brook, Goose Pond, Greenwater Brook, Laurel Lake, Washington Mountain Brook.

Monterey Lake Buel, Lake Garfield, Rawson Brook, Konkapot River.

New Marlborough Konkapot River, Umpachene Brook, York Pond.

Otis Farmington River, Otis Reservoir, Dimock Brook, Little Benton Pond, Big Benton Pond.

Sandisfield Buck River, Clam River, Farmington River.

Sheffield Hubbard Brook, Konkapot River.

Stockbridge Marsh Brook, Stockbridge Bowl.

Tyringham Hop Brook, Goose Pond Brook, Goose Pond.

FISH, EXCLUSIVE OF TROUT, IN BERSKHIRE WATERS

TOWN	WATER	NP	LMB	SMB	CP	WP	YP	BB
South County								
Egremont	Prospect lake				✔		✔	✔
Lee	Goose Pond		✔	✔	✔		✔	✔
Lee	Laurel Lake		✔		✔	✔	✔	✔
Monterey	Benedict Pond		✔				✔	✔
New Marlborough	Thousand Acre Swamp			✔	✔		✔	✔
Otis	Benton Pond			✔	✔	✔	✔	✔
Otis	East Otis Reservoir		✔	✔	✔	✔	✔	✔
Stockbridge	Stockbridge Bowl		✔	✔	✔		✔	✔
Central County								
Becket	Center Pond		✔	✔	✔	✔	✔	✔
Becket	Yokum Pond		✔				✔	✔
Hinsdale	Ashmere Lake		✔	✔			✔	
Pittsfield	Onota Lake	✔	✔		✔		✔	✔
Pittsfield	Pontoosic Pond		✔		✔		✔	✔
Pittsfield	Richmond Pond		✔	✔	✔		✔	✔
Windsor	Windsor Pond		✔		✔		✔	✔
North County								
Cheshire	Cheshire Reservoir	✔	✔		✔		✔	✔
Clarksburg	Mauserts Pond					✔		✔

Symbols

NP— Northern Pike
LMB— Largemouth Bass
SMB— Smallmouth Bass
CP— Chain Pickerel
WP— White Perch
YP— Yellow Perch
BB— Brown Bullhealds
(Horn Pout)

West Stockbridge Williams River, Cone Brook, Flat Brook.

Central County

Becket Shaker Mill Brook, Greenwater Pond, Yokum Brook, Westfield River (west branch), Walker Brook, Shaw Pond.

Dalton Sackett Brook, Housatonic River (east branch), Wahconah Falls Brook.

Hancock Kinderhook Creek, Berry Pond.

Hinsdale Bennet Brook, Housatonic River (east branch), Plunket Reservoir.

Lanesborough Town Brook, Sachem Brook, Lake Pontoosuc.

Lenox Sawmill Brook, Marsh Brook, Yokum Brook, Laurel Lake.

Peru Trout Brook.

Pittsfield Daniel Brook, Housatonic River (southwest branch), Lulu Cascade Brook, Sackett Brook, Smith Brook, Onota Lake, Lake Pontoosuc, Jacoby Brook.

Richmond Cone Brook, Furnace Brook, Richmond Pond, Mt. Lebanon Brook.

Washington Depot Brook.

Windsor Westfield River (east branch), Windsor Jambs Brook, Windsor Pond, Windsor Brook, Westfield Brook.

North County

Adams Anthony Brook, Hoosic River (south branch), Tophet Brook, Southwick Brook.

Cheshire Hoosac Lake, Hoosic River (south branch), Dry Brook, Kitchen Brook, South Brook, Thunder Brook, Penniman Brook.

Clarksburg Hoosic River (north branch), Hudson Brook.

Florida Deerfield River, North Pond.

North Adams Notch Brook, Windsor Lake.

Savoy Chickley River, Cold River, Westfield River (east branch), Center Brook.

Williamstown Broad Brook, Hemlock Brook, Green River (west branch), Green River, Roaring Brook.

NATURE PRESERVES

In addition to its vast forests, Berkshire is blessed with several nature preserves, each of which shows off the county's flora and fauna. Half a dozen of them provide miles of rich trail life, while Bartholomew's Cobble features geologically ancient stone outcroppings.

South County

Bartholomew's Cobble 413-229-8600; Weatogue Rd. (Rte. 7A), Ashley Falls (Sheffield). Bartholomew's Cobble, a National Natural Landmark is a 277-acre sanctuary with outcroppings of marble and quartzite, about 500 million years old. The terrain supports wildflowers, trees and ferns in great variety and number. It's a fine place to view the Housatonic River and its surrounding valley. On the site is the Bailey Museum of Natural History (Closed: Mon., Tues.). Group tours on request; picnic privileges available. Season: Apr. 15–Oct. 15; Fee.

Berkshire Botanical Garden 413-298-3926; Junction of Rtes. 102 & 183, Stockbridge. Formerly known as the Berkshire Garden Center, this has been the foremost botanical complex in the county for more than 50 years. Spread over 15 acres of gently rolling land, the magnificent plantings include primroses, conifers, day lilies, perennials, and shrubs. There's a terraced herb garden, a rose garden, raised-bed vegetable gardens, and exotic flowers in abundance. And the Botanical Garden has greenhouses (one of them is a well-designed passive solar model) growing seedlings, cuttings and plants of all sorts. It has a Visitor Center, where you may join the club or ask a few questions; and it has a Garden Gift Shop and an Herb Products Shop, both of which offer garden items, some of them practical, some merely beautiful or sweet smelling.

   The Botanical Garden runs a full schedule of activities, May through October, ranging from flower shows and herb symposiums to lectures on flower arranging and on English Country gardens. They also have a fine reference library, filled with books, magazines, and the latest seed catalogs. This library is open to the public, and its staff is available for your gardening questions.

   The Botanical Garden calendar culminates with the Harvest Festival in early October. Besides cider and apples, donuts and cakes of all kinds, and an ever-expanding luncheon menu, the day's fare includes rides on a 1923 fire truck, mazes, face-painting and balloons for the kids, and a book and clothing tag sale where it's still possible to buy a good-as-new Brooks Brothers suit for a few dollars.

Ice Glen Ice Glen Rd., Stockbridge. Cross the footbridge over the Housatonic River, follow the trail southward and walk a primeval path of glacial boulders. The trail is tricky and not recommended for the weak-kneed. Traditionally, the townsfolk of Stockbridge walked this path, bearing torches, on Halloween night.

Central County

Canoe Meadows Wildlife Sanctuary 413-637-0320; Holmes Rd., Pittsfield; 262-acre preserve of forest, ponds, streams, the Housatonic River banks and flood plain; owned and managed by the Massachusetts Audubon Society; Fee.

Dorothy Francis Rice Sanctuary South Rd. (off Rte. 143), Peru; 300-acre preserve of woodland trails, owned and managed by the New England Forestry Foundation; Free.

Notchview Reservation 413-684-0148; Rte. 9, Windsor; 3,000 acres of forest, crossed by miles of trails; owned and managed by the Trustees of Reservations; Fee.

Pittsfield State Forest 413-442-8992; Cascade St., Pittsfield. 10,000 acres of forest, fields, ponds, streams; trails for walks, hikes, x-c skiing, horseback riding; Free

Pleasant Valley Wildlife Sanctuary 413-637-0320; 472 West Mountain Rd. (off Rte. 7, opposite the Quality Inn), Lenox; 700 acres of forest, field, ponds (beaver dams), and streams with miles of trails; educational programs; owned and managed by the Massachusetts Audubon Society; Fee.

North County

Duvall Nature Trail Rte. 116 (at Hoosac Valley High School), Adams; two miles of nature trails overlooking the Greylock Range; Free.

Hopkins Memorial Forest 413-597-2346; Bulkley St. (off Rte. 7), Williamstown; 2,500 woodland acres on the slopes of the Taconic Range with miles of hiking trails; Free.

POLO

Polo is no longer available right here in Berkshire County, as of this writing, but those yearning to hear the thwack of mallet on ball, the thunder of hooves on turf, can go outside the county to the *Millbrook Polo Club* (518-398-7145; PO Box 297, Pine Plains, NY 12567). There is an eight-goal league with seven teams; match games are on Wednesday and Friday at 6, Sunday at 1. For those interested in taking up the sport, the club offers a clinic, usually on Saturday morning. Call in advance to confirm the exact schedules of games and clinic.

RACQUET SPORTS

RACQUETBALL

There's a lively racquetball scene in Berkshire, with courts in Lenox, Pittsfield, New Ashford, and North Adams. The *North Adams YMCA* (413-663-6529; 22 Brickyard Court), has two nice courts. At the *Brodie Mtn. Racquet Club* (413-458-4677; Rte. 7) in New Ashford, there are five courts, open from 8:30 a.m. to 10 p.m. *Pittsfield YMCA* (413-499-7650; 292 North St.) has four; and *Berkshire West* (formerly the Racquet Club at Bousquet; 413-499-4600; Dan Fox Dr., Pittsfield) has four. Both Pittsfield facilities offer top-flight teaching programs.

SQUASH

Squash in Berkshire? Yes, but it's mostly the garden variety. As for the sporting type, the situation is decidedly less bountiful. Many squash courts do exist, but, alas, most are open only to people associated with the private schools maintaining them. For travelers and locals alike, there is only one squash facility in Berkshire offering public access: the *Pittsfield YMCA* (413-499-7650; 292 North St.). Luckily the Y's court is new, well built, and lively.

TENNIS

In the Berkshires' Gilded Age, at the close of the 19th century, tennis was played on lawns, close-cropped and lined with lime. Wheatleigh was an especially favored site, and the lawn tennis parties there featured men in long, white linen trousers and ladies in ankle-length tennis dresses. Most of the grass courts are front lawns now, and though a few Berkshire connoisseurs still play on turf, tennis — here as elsewhere — is now played principally on clay, composites and hard courts.

Several tournaments are annual events and can be counted on to test the best skills or provide exciting viewing. Starting in late summer, tournaments are run by the *YMCA's Ponterril facility* (413-499-0687 or 413-499-0640 Rte. 7, Pontoosuc Lake, Pittsfield).

Southern Berkshire has traditionally been lacking in public tennis courts, the Simon's Rock courts having to partially meet the needs. But now *Monument Mountain High School* and the Berkshire Hills Tennis Association have created seven new hard courts at the school, for both scholastic and community play. The courts are open to the public, with priority given to the school's tennis teams' needs.

Veteran Grand Slam champion Rod Laver belting a backhand at Jiminy's Champion's Cup Tournament.

Jonathan Sternfield

Also new in Berkshire tennis is what we hope will become an annual event at *Jiminy Peak*, the Champions Cup. Featuring tennis legends such as Rod Laver, Cliff Drysdale, and Bob Lutz, the Champions Cup afforded locals an up-close and personal view of tennis greats who'd won more than 30 Grand Slam titles between them. Rod Laver, in particular, is fun to watch — the sporty, trim master in his early fifties, still belting the ball, still one of the boys, sipping a brew after the match.

Tennis great Pam Shriver has also been making regular sojourns in Berkshire, training and teaching at Canyon Ranch. Winner of 21 singles and 90 doubles titles, Shriver lends her professional wisdom, her world-class athleticism, and her personable style to two annual 4-day clinics, usually assisted by her touring friend, Elise Burgin. There are on-court group clinics, video assessment of your play, tennis talks, analysis of a pro match, and exhibition play with the Canyon Ranch teaching pros.

TENNIS FACILITIES

South County

Egremont Country Club; 413-528-4222; Rte. 23, S. Egremont; 4 hard-surface courts; Fee.

Monument Mtn. Regional High School Rte. 7, Gt. Barrington; 7 hard courts, used by school students on weekdays from 3 p.m.

Monument Mtn. Motel 413-528-3272; Rte. 7, Gt. Barrington (opposite Friendly's); 1 lighted all-weather court; Fee. Call for reservation.

Greenock Country Club 413-243-3323; W. Park St., Lee; 2 clay courts; Fee.

Oak n' Spruce Resort 413-243-3500; Off Rte. 102, S. Lee; 2 clay courts; Fee.

Prospect Lake Park 413-528-4158; Prospect Lake Rd., N. Egremont; 2 courts; Fee.

Simon's Rock College of Bard 413-528-0771; Alford Rd., Gt. Barrington; 4 hard courts plus backboard; Summer memberships available.

Stockbridge Golf Club Pro: James Walker; 413-298-3838; Main St., Stockbridge (behind Town Hall); 3 clay, 2 hard-surface courts; non-members may arrange for lessons only.

Stockbridge Public Courts Pine St., 2 hard courts; The Plain School, Main St. (Rte. 7); 2 hard courts; For town residents and registered hotel guests.

Central County

Berkshire West (formerly the Racquet Club at Bousquet) Pro: Dave Bell; 449-4600; Dan Fox Dr., Pittsfield; 7 outdoor courts and 5 indoor hard courts; Memberships available.

Cranwell Resort 413-637-0441; Rte. 20, Lenox; 2 Har-Tru courts; Fee.

Jiminy Peak 413-738-5500; Hancock; 7 outdoor courts; instruction, tournaments. Fee.

Pittsfield Public Courts free to the public when school is not in session; all are asphalt courts.

    Herberg Middle School Pomeroy Ave.; 4 courts.

    Lakewood Park Newell St.; 2 courts.

    Pittsfield High School East St.; 4 courts.

    Taconic High School Valentine Rd.; 4 courts.

Ponterril/YMCA Pro: Sherry Scheer; 413-447-7405 or 413-499-0640; Rte. 7, Pontoosuc Lake, Pittsfield; 6 outdoor clay courts; Members only, but when courts are free, nonmembers may use them for a fee, and summer memberships are available.

North County

Brodie Mountain Tennis & Racquetball Club Pro: Mark Upright; 413-458-4677; Rte. 7, New Ashford; 5 indoor courts; Memberships available.

North Adams Public Courts free to the public; all courts are asphalt.

    Greylock Recreation Field Protection Ave. (off Rte. 2), 2 courts.

    Noel Field (in back of Child Care of the Berkshires); State St. (Rte. 8A); 2 courts.

Williams College 413-597-3131; Main St. (Rte. 2), Williamstown; 12 clay and hard-surface courts; Summer memberships available: apply to Buildings and Grounds Department.

RUNNING

If you're a runner, you've run into the right neck of the woods in the Berkshires. With terrain and roadways of all types, clean mountain air, and

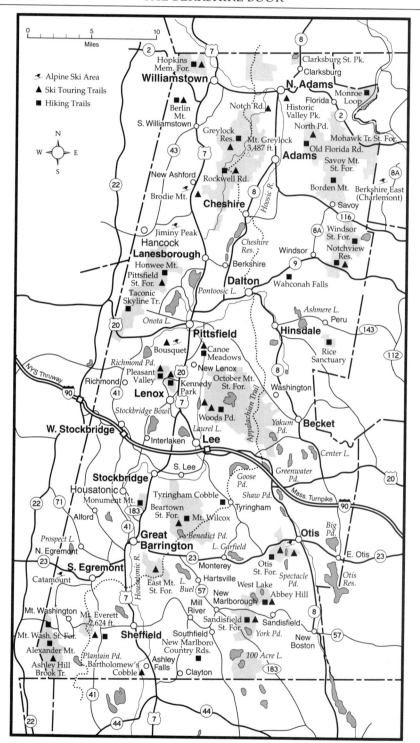

Berkshire Recreation Sites

Runners at Mount Hope Farm, Williamstown.

William Tague

inspiring vistas at every turn, Berkshire draws out the relaxed runner in you, that meditative runner who can run forever. Most back roads and byways have little traffic, and for all the jogs we've taken, each new jaunt refreshed the impression of running through one giant park. For the rugged cross-country runner, some of the trails outlined in the "Hiking" section are suitable, though it must be remembered that these trails are basically for hikers. If you're a racer, or yearn to be, many towns and organizations across the county run road races; exact dates and entry information for these can be obtained from local Chambers of Commerce.

SKATING

For ice skaters, there are many smooth and slippery possibilities in the Berkshires, most of them framed by the hills. There are three rinks open to the public: one at the *Pittsfield Boys Club* (413-448-8258; 16 Melville St.); another at *Chapman Rink* (413-597-2433) in Williamstown (*Williams College*); and the third in North Adams at the *Vietnam Veterans Memorial Skating Rink* (413-664-9474; S. Church St.). All the rinks offer low-priced children's programs.

Outdoor skating on flooded fields is a Berkshire tradition, and during the colder months, you can do that both day and night on the Common in Pittsfield, at the Dalton Community House, and on the Stockbridge Town Field. Lake and pond skating is exquisite in Berkshire, and many of the "Swimming" sites noted later in this chapter are partially cleared after the snow flies. Occasionally, all the elements work together to produce natural rinks of glass ice or "black ice."

For those who prefer their skating on wheels, many of the county's smoother back roads make for ideal blacktop cruising. And there is one roller rink in Berkshire: *Roller Magic* (413-458-3659; Rte. 2, Colonial Shopping Center, Williamstown). Rollerblading, or in-line roller skating, has taken off of late, and bladers can now be seen skating the hills three seasons a year. Some prefer using poles, some blade without. The best introductory package is offered by the versatile folks over at Lenox's *Main St. Sports & Leisure* (413-637-4407; 102 Main St.), where for about $10, you can rent rollerblade skates, wrist guards, and knee pads, and view an instructional video.

SKIING — DOWNHILL

Berkshire downhill ski areas go back to the 1930s, and there's some evidence that three significant advances in modern skiing had their origins in the Berkshires: the surface ski lift, snowmaking, and the ski bar. More recently, with Brodie Mountain's "Master Blaster" snowguns and Jiminy Peak's "Snow-Coat," a vinyl blanket to protect the snowy slopes in rain, Berkshire ski areas have continued to be innovative, always questing for better, more consistent conditions over a longer season.

But it's not the technology that makes Berkshire skiing so appealing, so increasingly popular. The Berkshire hills are challenging yet picturesque, without being imposing. From the summits of the area's ski mountains, the vistas are splendid — mountains on the horizon (like the Catskills, seen from atop Butternut) and skinny bands of civilization below. With seven major ski areas in the region to choose from, skiers in the Berkshires can pick their mountain for a week or tour the hills and ski a different area on different days. Each ski mountain has its own character, each caters to a slightly different skier yet always welcomes all. Jiminy Peak and Berkshire East have the highest proportion of trails suited to advanced skiers only; but Butternut, Catamount, and even Bousquet have dicey runs, demanding enough for many experts. Every Berkshire ski area offers instruction, and some make a specialty of ski training for youngsters, such as Bousquet with its ski school or Otis Ridge with its ski camp.

BERKSHIRE SKI INFORMATION

From *Outside* Massachusetts: 800-237-5747.

Berkshire Ski Conditions: 413-499-7669. New England Ski Council reports are broadcast twice daily from radio station **WBEC-AM** and **FM, 1420** and **105.5,** respectively, on the dial, Pittsfield.

WHERE TO BUY AND RENT SKI EQUIPMENT

Besides the ski areas themselves, all of which have fully stocked ski shops, renting and selling equipment, the following specialty shops sell skis and related paraphernalia.

Arcadian Shop 413-637-3010; 333 Pittsfield-Lenox Rd., Lenox.
Goff's Sports 413-458-3605; 15 Spring St., Williamstown.
Main St. Sports 413-637-4407; 102 Main St., Lenox.
Kenver Ltd. 413-528-2330; Rte. 23, S. Egremont.
The Mountain Goat 413-458-8445; 130 Water St., Williamstown.
Pittsfield Sporting Goods 413-443-6078; 70 North St., Pittsfield.
Plaine's Ski & Cycle Center 413-499-0294; 55 W. Housatonic St., Pittsfield.
The Sports Corner 413-664-8654; 61 Main St., Adams.

South County

BUTTERNUT BASIN
413-528-2000.
Rte. 23, Gt. Barrington, MA 01230.
2 mi. E. of town, toward Monterey.
Trails: 22 Downhill (20% Beginner, 60% Intermediate, 20% Expert). XC trails (7 km.).
Lifts: 6 Chairlifts (1 quad; 1 triple, 4 doubles); 1 Poma; 1 rope tow.
Vertical drop: 1,000 ft.
Snowmaking: 100% of area.
Tickets: 1994 $36 Adults, $28 Junior, $28 Senior, $10 Children.
Open: Wkdays 9–4; Wkends 8:15–4.
Ski school pro: Einar Aas.

Few entrepreneurs can realize their business dreams in their own backyards. Ski-resort developer Channing Murdoch, who lives at the foot of Warner Mountain, in between Great Barrington and Monterey, is one such lucky man.

Murdoch designed and built Butternut Basin Ski Area right there on a site that has become one of the Berkshires' premier winter recreation meccas. At Butternut there are challenging downhill runs, a separate beginner's slope, and extensive cross-country ski trails. The area offers ideal options for every kind of skier — from first-timer to serious racer.

But Butternut is more than terrific trails and the welcoming charm of its two lovely lodges. From the top of Warner Mountain, there are extraordinary views of the distant Catskills in the west and of Mt. Greylock at the northern end of Berkshire County. The mountain's timed slalom course is open to everyone, making a potential Olympic-

Choosing an alpine trail, at Butternut.

Jonathan Sternfield

class racer — at least in fantasy — out of even a beginner. Whether you're an advanced skier or on the slopes for your debut, you'll find just the guidance you need from Butternut's personable ski pro, Einar Aas, and his team of expert ski instructors. And should you want the latest in skiwear and equipment, you'll find that, too, at Butternut's ski shop, one of the most extensive and stylish at any Berkshire mountain.

The big news at Butternut is their quadruple, fixed-grip lift, which replaces their base-to-summit double chairlift. New food facilities at the base include an area exclusively devoted to their Ski Wee kid's program, and their outside "Cruiser" barbecue deck.

From the mogul fields of the expert run, Downspout, to the meandering path of the novice Pied Piper's Trail, Butternut is a delight to the eye as well as a refreshing test of athletic skill.

CATAMOUNT
413-528-1262, 518-325-3200.
Rte. 23, S. Egremont, MA 01258.
On New York State border.
Trails: 24 Downhill (Novice to Expert); No XC.
Lifts: 4 Chairlifts; 1 T-Bar; 1 J-Bar.
Vertical drop: 1,000 ft.
Snowmaking: 95% of area.
Tickets: 1994 Wkdays, $29

On the cutting edge of Berkshire ski country," as *Skiing Magazine* put it, Catamount straddles two states and offers magnificent views of four: Massachusetts, New York, Connecticut, and Vermont. The slopes are primarily novice and intermediate, but seasoned skiers can find quite a bit of challenge through the glades near the summit, and down on through the Flipper and Dipper trails.

Called by some a vest-pocket Killington, Catamount is convenient, especially to New Yorkers.

Adults, $20 Junior/ Senior; Wkends/ Holidays, $37 Adults, $28 Junior/Senior; Night Skiing, Wed.–Sat., $21 Adults, $15 Junior. Open: 8:30–4 Wkends/ Holidays; Midwk./ Non-holidays, 9–4; Night Skiing, Wed.–Sat., 5–10. Ski school pro: Shy Reeves.

Not your trendiest, competition-minded ski resort, there's a pleasant quaintness here, right down to the Swiss Hutte restaurant at the mountain's base. Snowmaking equipment at Catamount has just been overhauled and expanded, and they're now firing state-of-the-art equipment onto 95% of their 24 trails and slopes. Furthermore, the area has added several new grooming vehicles to its fleet. Night skiing is also an attraction at Catamount.

A new 1,200-foot extension of Ridge Run, one of the region's more splendid trails, now connects Esplanade to Promenade. Two additional groomers have been added to Catamount's fleet, and they've installed an additional 22 airless snow makers mounted on towers. For borderline skiing in the Berkshires, there's no better.

Central County

The thrill of downhill.

Jonathan Sternfield

OTIS RIDGE

Otis Ridge is the molehill among the mountains, but few slopes do so much to cater to beginners and youngsters. Famous for its winter ski camp, the area takes on a special character on frosty weekends and holiday periods when camp's in session. Snowmaking covers 90% of the 11 trails at Otis, and their lift system consists of a double-chair, T bar, J Bar, a pony tow, excellent for beginning skiers and an old-fashioned rope.
Otis Ridge 413-269-4444; Rte. 23, Otis, MA 01253.

BOUSQUET
413-442-8316.
Dan Fox Dr., Pittsfield, MA 01201.
Access off South St. (Rte. 7)

It was 1932 when a group of winter enthusiasts first approached Clarence Bousquet about using the slopes of Bousquet Farm for some skiing. Three years later, the fledgling Bousquet Ski Area put

Trails: 21 Downhill (Novice to Expert); No XC.
Lifts: 2 Chairlifts; 3 Rope tows; Snowboarding half-pipe.
Vertical drop: 750 ft.
Snowmaking: 98% of area.
Tickets: $15 Wkdays, Wkends; $10 Night.
Open: 10–10 Wkdays; 9–10 Wkends; 9–4 Sun.; Night Skiing, Mon.–Sat. 4–0.
Ski school pro: Court McDermott.

together one of the Berkshires' greatest travel promotions ever: ski trains from New York to Pittsfield (with bus connector to Bousquet) for $2 round trip.

Now, over 50 years later, the Berkshires' oldest ski area continues to provide friendly slopes, primarily for novice and intermediate skiers. There are, however, several very demanding runs, and from the summit of Bousquet, there's a fine view of Mt. Greylock's whalelike profile (nearly the same view that so inspired Melville; see "Arrowhead" in Chapter Four, *Culture*). Bousquet is well known for its effective ski school, a corps of some 50 teachers under the direction of Court McDermott.

EASTOVER

For its guests only, Eastover, a resort hotel in a converted mansion, offers alpine ski runs suitable for beginners and intermediates. Because of the convenience of Eastover's lodging-dining-recreation facilities, learning to ski can be a pleasure at this Lenox resort. The vertical drop is gentle; the longest run about 3/4 mi. Besides skiing, Eastover offers tobogganing, and on a warmer note, indoor swimming and sauna.
Eastover 413-637-0625; 430 East St., Lenox, MA 01240.

JIMINY PEAK
413-738-5500.
Corey Rd., Hancock, MA 01237.
Access from Rte. 7, Lanesborough, or Rte. 43, Hancock, via Brodie Mt. Rd.
Trails: 28 Downhill (Novice to Expert); No XC.
Lifts: 7 Chairlifts; 1 J-Bar.
Vertical drop: 1,140 ft.
Snowmaking: 95% of area.
Tickets: 1994 Wkdays, $30 Adult, $20 Junior/Senior; Wkends/Holidays, $37 Adults; $26 Junior/Senior; Night Skiing: $20, 6–10:30 p.m.
Open: Wkdays, 9–10:30; Wkends, 8:30–10:30.
Ski school pro: Jay Barranger.

Jiminy is committed to long seasons of well-groomed slopes, and to that end, they go to extraordinary lengths. Frequently opening early in November and staying open well into March, Jiminy not only utilizes advanced snowmaking equipment but also lays out what they call a Sno-Coat, essentially a giant tarp to protect vulnerable areas from rainy washouts.

This is one of the area's most demanding mountains, with 40% of its trails being suitable for advanced skiers only. Those with such talents will greatly enjoy the North Glade, Upper Lift Line and Whirlaway. For intermediates, there's the 360, the West Way and the Ace of Spades. From these last two trails, you can see a magnificent vista of the Jericho Valley, northwards toward Vermont.

In addition to a full calendar of ski events (races, clinics and demonstrations), Jiminy also runs a race team just for children, a more serious tri-state

15.50 PER PERSON

CRC

CATERING
1994 TANGLEWO[OD]

DATES	PICNIC SELECTION # 1
WEEK 1 JULY 1,2,3,4	TARRAGON CHICKEN SALAD PASTA PRIMA VERA DILL CUCUMBER VINAIGRETTE
WEEK 2 JULY 7,8,9,10	THAI BEEF SALAD ORIENTAL SESAME NOODLES CARROTS, ZUCCHINI AND GINGER
WEEK 3 JULY 13,15,16,17	CROSBY'S FAMOUS OVEN FRIED CHICKEN MEDLEY OF PICKLED VEGETABLES CREAMY POTATO SALAD
WEEK 4 JULY 20,21,22, 23,24	RASPBERRY CHICKEN SALAD BLUE LAKE GREEN &YELLOW BEAN SALAD PASTA PRIMA VERA
WEEK 5 JULY 27,28,29, 30,31	GRILLED CHICKEN & PASTA SALAD MEDLEY OF PICKLED VEGETABLES POTATO VINAIGRETTE
WEEK 6 AUGUST 2,3,5,6,7	FUSSILI, SMOKED CHICKEN & SUN DRIED TOMAT[O] BLUE LAKE GREEN & YELLOW BEAN SAL[AD] RASPBERRY DIJON CARROTS
WEEK 7 AUGUST 11,12,13,14	THAI BEEF SALAD ORIENTAL SESAME NOODLES CARROTS, ZUCCHINI & GINGER
WEEK 8 AUGUST 17,19,20,21	CROSBY'S FAMOUS OVEN FRIED CHICKE[N] MEDLEY OF PICKLED VEGETABLES CREAMY POTATO SALAD
WEEK 9 AUGUST 22,24,26,27, 28,29,31	GRILLED CHICKEN & PASTA SALAD MEDLEY OF PICKLED VEGETABLES POTATO VINAIGRETTE

all picnics include: c[

WE ALSO HAVE A FUL[L

PICNICS MUST BE ORDERED BY

	PICNIC SELECTION #2
	TORTELLINI SALAD POTATO VINAIGRETTE RASPBERRY DIJON CARROTS
	CURRIED CHICKEN SALAD COUS-COUS SALAD LEMON, CUCUMBER & TOMATO
	GRILLED TOFU SESAME SALAD CARROTS, ZUCCHINI & GINGER COLD SUMMER RICE
	TORTELLINI SALAD POTATO VINAIGRETTE RASPBERRY DIJON CARROTS
	GRILLED TOFU SESAME SALAD CARROTS, ZUCHINI & GINGER COLD SUMMER RICE
AD	RASPBERRY CHICKEN SALAD BLUE LAKE GREEN & YELLOW BEAN SALAD PASTA PRIMA VERA
	TORTELLINI SALAD POTATO VINAIGRETTE RASPBERRY DIJON CARROTS
	CURRIED CHICKEN SALAD COUS-COUS SALAD LEMON, CUCUMBER & TOMATO
	TORTELLINI SALAD POTATO VINAIGRETTE RASPBERRY DIJON SALAD

se, bread, and a brownie

'INE AND BEER SELECTION

)F THE DAY PREVIOUS TO PICK UP

race team, a freestyle team, a night adult program and a ski school. When you go to ski at Jiminy, you'll spend most of your time skiing: lift lines are carefully monitored so that you'll rarely have to wait more than 12 minutes. And, they close the parking lots when the area nears its capacity of 3,500 skiers.

Jiminy has cut a new trail, Winding Brook, for novices; they've widened the Left Bank trail, making it safer and less icy in heavy use; and they've laid out a new kid's area, called Chipmunk. The upper part of the West Way Trail has been widened, creating a new snowboard park. Jiminy's Ski-Wee program for kids has been expanded, as has their Jiminy Cricket kid's center. Adding to the fun, a natural ice rink has been created on one of their base lodge tennis courts, offering "no frills" skating. In a very controlled, playful way, Jiminy keeps things jumpin'.

North County

BERKSHIRE EAST

Billing itself as "Southern New England's most challenging ski area," Berkshire East's steep terrain lives up to that claim. With only 20% of its trails suited to novice skiers, this mountain is demanding, especially down the steep Flying Cloud and Lift Line trails, both of which are over 4,000 feet long. For beginners, three separate open slopes around the west lodge provide plenty of room to learn the basics.

From the summit of Berkshire East, amid the pines, you can get a fine view of the Deerfield River valley (to the east) with mountains all around it. The area offers day and night skiing, and it has a rustic lodge with a bar upstairs.
Berkshire East 339-6617; Rte. 2 (near Savoy town line), Charlemont, Franklin County, MA 01339.

BRODIE MOUNTAIN
413-443-4752.
Rte. 7, New Ashford, MA 01237.
Trails: 28 Downhill (Novice to Expert); XC (25 km.).
Lifts: 4 Chairlifts; 2 Rope Tows.
Vertical drop: 1,250 ft.
Snowmaking: 95% of area.
Tickets: 1994 Wkdays, $30 Adult, $25 Junior/Senior.; Wkends, $35 adult; $30 Junior/ Senior. Night Skiing, $25 3–11 p.m., $18 7–11 p.m.

One of the oldest ski areas in the Berkshires, Brodie Mountain started out under the direction of Gregory Makeroff, and now has quite a different flavor under the guidance of the Kelly clan. "Kelly's Irish Alps," they call Brodie, and a more Irish slope you could not imagine, right down to the occasional staff leprechaun dressed in green and shushing downhill. Brodie is a fun area, and has always had tremendous appeal to singles and younger skiers.

Three-quarters of Brodie's 20-odd trails and slopes are geared to novice and intermediate skiers, and one slope (Tipperary) offers a not-too-demanding 2.25-mi. glide. For experts, there's

Open: 9–11; Twilight Skiing,
3–11; Night Skiing, 7–11.
Ski school pro: John Koch.

Mickie's Chute, Gilhooley's Glade, and Danny Boy's Trail. Brodie is committed to its snowmaking, pioneering large-scale snowmaking in 1965 and now covering 95% of its slopes. They utilize state-of-the-art equipment, employing various systems and a super arsenal of Hedco Snow Cannons. In addition, Brodie invented its own "Master Blaster" snowgun and now has the capability to be the first area open in all of New England, a feat once accomplished in late October. Brodie has recently added 50 new snow guns that can be moved to top any of their 75 new towers, as well as two new grooming machines.

At sundown especially, the views from Brodie across the valley are stunning, and of particular note is the view northward to Mt. Greylock's whalelike silhouette. But the skiing doesn't stop at sundown at Brodie; for Kelly's Irish Alps is one of the largest night skiing areas anywhere, with over 17 mi. of trails and four chairlifts fully illuminated.

And after skiing, off the slopes, Brodie keeps the fun going, with five indoor tennis courts, five racquetball courts (racquets and sneakers can be rented for both), and a sauna. After sports, there's the Blarney Room and Kelly's Irish Pub.

Brodie has widened its Catwalk Trail, making this access way safer and less prone to icing in heavy traffic. Two new Hedco snow cannons have been added to the snowmaking arsenal, giving Brodie greater depth, underski, where it counts.

Snowboarders on Berkshire Slopes

Another creature has been with us on Berkshire mountainsides for some years now, this one vaguely resembling the now-thriving downhill skier, but zipping down the snowy slopes on just one wide ski. Combining skateboarding, surfing, and skiing, snowboarding is attracting more and more enthusiasts, and most Berkshire ski areas can rent or sell you a board and follow up with instruction.

Some areas offer special trails for snowboarders; all urge caution and courtesy for snowboarders and skiers alike, for easier coexistence. And for the most part, Berkshire snowboarders and skiers do share the slopes in harmony.

SKIING — CROSS-COUNTRY

Berkshire is made to order for cross-country skiers — from flat runs along the Housatonic to steep trails up Mt. Greylock, from tours in town, such as Kennedy Park in Lenox and Heritage Park in North Adams, to wilderness paths like the one around North Pond in Savoy Mountain State Forest.

John MacGruer

There are no lines, no chair lifts, and most of Berkshire's ski touring is free, dependent only on the whims of the weather. Since Nordic skiing has gained in popularity, private touring centers have multiplied in the Berkshires, and if you prefer your trails groomed, your warming and waxing huts warm, there are now half a dozen such places to cross-country ski.

It's best never to ski alone, especially in a wilderness area. If you're planning to ski in a state forest, check in at forest headquarters first. They usually have a map and some helpful hints; besides, it's a good precaution to let someone know you're out there. Be sure to carry a compass and extra clothes. Snacks and drinks are also nearly required equipment on the trail, and the really well-prepared also carry a first-aid kit, knife, whistle, flashlight, and space blanket.

Dozens of public trails are described below, most with sufficient directions for a short tour. More detailed descriptions for some of these tours, including maps, can be found in the excellent and compact *Skiing in the Berkshire Hills* by Lauren Stevens.

South County

Southern Berkshire ski touring is a bit more benign than in the other parts. The wilderness down south is a trifle less rugged, the snowmobilers fewer in number, the variety of groomed trails much higher. Yet there's plenty of challenge, exciting views, and several long downhill runs that are pure pleasure.

PUBLIC SKI-TOURING

Many trails in the *Mt. Washington State Forest* offer quintessential Berkshire ski touring. No snowmobiles are allowed, so the whistle of the wind will be the loudest noise you hear all day. From the forest headquarters (East St.), the Ashley Hill Brook Trail runs south along the brook towards New York State, a four-mile, slightly uphill trip suitable for intermediate skiers. Nearby, from the parking lot just outside the Mt. Everett Reservation, you can ski up that 2,600-foot-tall mountain, the Dome of the Taconics. The climb up is gentle, passing Guilder Pond; the run down, long and exhilarating without being unduly dangerous.

Bartholomew's Cobble in Ashley Falls (Sheffield) has an interesting system of trails, with the runs on the far side of Weatogue Rd. being the best. A map is posted in the parking lot. Donation box — $3 per person.

Beartown State Forest in Monterey has some lovely trails, starting at Benedict Pond and circling through the 14,000 acres of forest preserve. Maps are available at the *State Forest Headquarters* (413-528-0904; Blue Hill Rd., off Rte. 23). Triangular red blazes or wooden markers designate the ski-touring trail in Beartown, with a blue-blazed trail circling Benedict Pond, the white-blazed Appalachian Trail passing through, and the orange-blazed trails for snowmobilers.

The West Lake area of the *Sandisfield State Forest* is a fine site for Nordic skiing. No snowmobiles are allowed on the Abbey Hill Foot Trail (marked with blue blazes), and from the state forest headquarters and parking area, just off West St., a beautiful tour of about two hours will circle you around Abbey Lake, up Abbey Hill (1,810 ft.) and then down past West Lake. The area around York Lake in the forest also has some good trails.

You can ski the Knox Trail in the *Otis State Forest* if you take Rte. 23 to Nash Rd. in Otis. Where Nash joins Webb Rd. is a good place to wax up, and as you ski, watch for red K's and red blazes marking the trail.

PRIVATE TOURING CENTERS

In Gt. Barrington, *Butternut Basin* (413-528-2000; Rte. 23) has seven km. of groomed novice and intermediate trails. In addition to their lovely lodges, to comfort you they also offer a pondside warming hut. *Otis Ridge* (413-269-4444; Rte. 23, Otis) has over six km. of packed, but not tracked, trails. And *Oak n' Spruce Resort* (413-243-3500; off Rte. 102, South Lee) has six km. of Nordic trails.

Central County

Central Berkshire ski trails are generally gentle with moderate slopes and climbs. Several "Nature Preserves" (see that section) maintain trails, and these are excellent and beautiful places to gain Nordic experience. And Bucksteep Manor maintains private, groomed trails.

PUBLIC SKI-TOURING

Lenox is graced with beautiful ski-touring areas, the most popular of which is *Kennedy Park.* Its 500 acres were once the site of the grand old Aspinwall Hotel (which burned to the ground in 1931). Now its long, rising driveway and its bridle paths are used for ski-touring. The Main Trail (white blazes) is the widest and simplest, with Lookout Trail (red blazes) being more of a challenge. Stately oaks dot this very pretty highland, and you gain access either at the Church on the Hill (Main St., Rte. 7A) or behind the Lenox House Restaurant (north of town on Rte. 7), where you can rent equipment from the Arcadian Shop..

Pleasant Valley Wildlife Sanctuary (see "Nature Preserves"), also in Lenox, has a trail system laid out by the Massachusetts Audubon Society. For $3 ($2 for kids), you can ski, going out on the trail marked with blue blazes and back on the one marked in yellow. There's also Yokun Brook Trail, Nature Trail, and others. Maps are free at the office next to the parking area (Closed: Mon.). The *Woods Pond* area in Lee and Lenox has a pretty, mostly flat trail running along the southern shore of Woods Pond, then north along the eastern bank of the Housatonic River for just over two mi. Enter via Woodland St. in Lee. The trail is best skied on weekdays due to weekend snowmobile traffic. *Canoe Meadows* (see "Nature Preserves") is another Massachusetts Audubon Society area, and it too has some lovely trails, open on weekends only. There is a $2 fee, which includes a map.

For more advanced Nordic skiers, the *Honwee Mtn.-Turner Trail* circuit is a challenge for the best skills. Park just off Cascade Rd. in Pittsfield State Forest. Check in at forest headquarters, get oriented, then start up the Mountain Trail, initially marked in orange, then in white. This trail has some great views, tough climbs, and steep descents. Closer to the center of the city, in *Sackett Brook Park* (Williams St.), there are four mi. of marked trails.

Northeast of Pittsfield on Rte. 9 is the *Notchview Reservation,* in the town of Windsor. Trails are well marked and maintained, and there is a modest $6 charge for touring. (Free to members of TTOR.) Maps are available for 50 cents. The Budd Visitor Center is open daily as a warming and waxing shelter. Notchview is owned by The Trustees of Reservations.

PRIVATE TOURING CENTERS

South of Lenox on Rte. 20, *Cranwell,* (413-637-1364; 55 Lee Rd.) has a network of trails, crisscrossing their golf course. And at the *Canyon Ranch* (413-637-4100; Kemble St.) closer to town, ski touring and instruction are available for spa guests, the trails sweeping across the majesty of the Bellefontaine estate.

In the hilltown of Washington, east of Pittsfield, *Bucksteep Manor* (413-623-5535; Washington Mt. Rd.) operates a long ski-touring season. Set on over 250 acres, at 1,900 ft., Bucksteep has 25 km. of looped, interconnecting trails.

There's a waxing room, a ski shop which sells and rents, as well as on-site lodging and dining. Nearby in Becket, *Canterbury Farm* (413-623-8765; Fred Snow Rd.) grooms 11 mi. of trails for its inn guests and daily cross-country ski guests. There is a ski shop for rentals, lessons are available, and the ski fee is $7.

PUBLIC SKI-TOURING

Up at 2,000 ft., where the snows come early and stay late, *Savoy State Forest* has miles of cross-country trails, best navigated with a map obtainable at *State Forest Headquarters* (413-663-8469). Enter the forest from Rte. 2 (Florida) or Rte. 116 (Savoy). A 2.5-mi.-long trail (blue blazes) makes a challenging circuit around North Pond and then South Pond. In North Adams itself, *Historic Valley Park* offers ski touring quite close to downtown. The trail starts at the parking area next to Windsor Lake and is well marked by blue blazes and signs which even describe the degree of difficulty of the next stretch of trail.

On *Mt. Greylock*, many opportunities for fine ski touring exist. Here again though, it's best to ski during the week, because weekends tend to draw much snowmobile traffic. Depending on your skills and fitness, you can ski part or all the way to the summit. It's an 8-mi. round trip up Rockwell Rd. to Jones Nose and back, 15-mi. round trip to Stony Ledge, or 17-mi. round trip to the summit. The views are breathtaking, the skiing sometimes testy, and the weather ever-fickle. With this last factor in mind and given the height of your ascent, be sure to take warm clothing and some snacks. Check in at the Visitor Center on Rockwell Rd., off Rte. 7, Lanesborough.

The area in and around *Williamstown* is striped with trails, most of them novice or intermediate, but at least one, Brooks Trail, is quite demanding. Brooks, and the Berlin Mtn. Trail near it, get heavy use from Williams College skiers. The trails begin off Berlin Rd., west of Rte. 2. The 4-mi. Stone Hill Loop in Williamstown is probably the area's most popular: it's relatively easy and offers all the splendor of the best ski touring. The trail starts and finishes in the *Clark Art Museum* parking lot (South St.), and it circles the 1,100-ft. Stone Hill, with its wonderful views. Finally, in *Hopkins Forest*, Williams College maintains a network of trails just off Northwest Hill Rd. Although the trails are groomed and maps are available at the forest "Carriage House," facilities are minimal. All the best cross-country ski trails in the area are described in the *Williams Outing Club's Trail Guide*. And further information might possibly be had by calling the club itself (413-597-2317; Baxter Hall, Williams College).

PRIVATE TOURING CENTERS

In New Ashford, *Brodie Mountain Ski Area* (Rte. 7) maintains a 25-km. trail network, of which 10 km. are groomed daily. Training site of the Williams College Cross-Country Ski Team, Brodie's trails were laid out by ski coach Bud

Fisher. Many of the trails are double-tracked and wind through field and wood. If you're adventurous enough for a guided ski tour to the summit of Mt. Greylock, Brodie can arrange it (413-443-4752; call well in advance).

SOARING

Soaring skyhigh over Great Barrington.

Jonathan Sternfield

Your attitude controls your speed, which is ideally 51 mph. In this unearthly quiet, half a mile high, the Berkshires seem like a Swiss landscape, all rolling patterns of farm and woodland.

You can try the **Berkshire Soaring Society**, out of the Pittsfield Municipal Airport (413-443-6700; Tamarack Rd.), or the **Mohawk Soaring Club** out of Harriman West Airport, North Adams (413-458-8650). If you wish to soar, it's best to hang out with the glider pilots at the far edge of the airstrip on weekends. Watch, ask a few questions. You could end up floating on air.

Should you feel an aircraft to be an awful encumbrance, but still want to soar, people are regularly jumping off the top of Mt. Greylock in Adams, and just as often off a steep slope of the Taconic Range, on Rte. 2, west of Williamstown — with only lightweight *hang gliders* to support their flight. We recommend watching only.

A LUXURY SPA

Toning up at Canyon Ranch.

CANYON RANCH AT BELLEFONTAINE 413-637-4100; 91 Kemble St., Lenox

Several years ago, health entrepreneurs Mel and Enid Zuckerman took their highly successful Tucson, Arizona, Canyon Ranch formula and transferred it to the sculpted hills of Lenox. There they transformed and built upon Giraud Foster's splendid "cottage," Bellefontaine — itself an exact replica of the French Le Petit Trianon — to create a world-class spa.

This is a spectacular facility, smoothly run by a group of skilled and friendly professionals. Whether you come for a short cool-out, a vacation, a chance to drop a few pounds and tone up, or an invigorating change of pace, Canyon Ranch lives up to its self-proclaimed billing as "The Spa that never leaves you." With over 50 fitness classes to choose from daily, swimming, racquet sports of all kinds and a state-of-the-art gymnasium, the three-level spa complex offers a physical workout that you can custom tailor to your needs. Add to that, hiking, mountain biking, and cross-country skiing in winter, and you have indoor/outdoor fitness possibilities unimaginable in your average spa.

Besides sumptuous Jacuzzis, steam rooms, and saunas, Canyon Ranch offers inhalation rooms (combining steam and eucalyptus) and a range of personal services to pamper yourself as never before. Want a massage to soothe tired muscles? Choose from Swedish, shiatsu, Reflexology, cranial, Jin Shin Jyutsu,

Trager, and Reiki. How about a herbal wrap, an aroma wrap, clay or salt treatment, or some hydrotherapy? Each of these ancient, exotic treatments is performed by experts, leaving you revitalized inside and out. The healthful opportunities go on and on, from skin and beauty treatments to dietary education and stop-smoking hypnosis. And speaking of diets, you're automatically on one when you stay at Canyon Ranch, a low-fat, low-cholesterol regime that's as delicious as it is healthy.

While Canyon Ranch is sensational for many, it's not for everybody. Prices vary seasonally but are always substantial. Access to the facility is limited to guests only, and should you wish to tour the spa, special arrangements must be made.

Getting in shape is good clean fun at Canyon Ranch. Fine by design, fine in maintenance, and fine in staffing, that's the Canyon Ranch system at Lenox. Says *Vogue* magazine: "Not a fitness factory or fat farm . . . you go to Canyon Ranch anticipating short-term results . . . and return with a long-term resolve." "A cross between boot camp and heaven," says *Self*. Said Berkshire humorist Roy Blount, in a report to *Gentlemen's Quarterly*: "Made me feel like a jackrabbit!"

SPELUNKING

For you cave men and women out there, Berkshire is like stumbling onto the Mother Lode. The hills are riddled with caves, each of which has a colorful name and legend to go with it. *French's Cave,* west of Williamsville in West Stockbridge, is 450 ft. deep, the longest cave in the whole of Massachusetts. Other Berkshire caves of note include *Radium Springs Cave* in Pittsfield; *Bat's Den Cave* in Egremont; *Cat Hole Caves* in New Marlborough; *Pittibone Falls Cave* in Cheshire; *Belcher's Cave* in Gt. Barrington; *Tory Cave* in Lenox; *Peter's Cave* in Lee; and the caves of western Lanesborough.

The *Williams College Outing Club,* Williamstown (413-597-2317) occasionally goes a-caving. Notable Berkshire cavemen of the Present Age include *Berkshire Eagle* ace photographer Joel Librizzi and Stockbridge Chief of Police Rick Wilcox.

Caving is great adventure, but it is also dangerous and should *not* be attempted alone or without an experienced guide.

SPORTS CAR RACING

Drivers, start your engines!

On the edge of Berkshire is the renowned *Lime Rock Race Track*, and an outfit even closer, the *Skip Barber Racing School* based in Canaan, CT, can teach you how to drive safely at very high speeds. Barber operates two schools actually, the *BMW Advanced Driving School* as well as the Skip Barber Racing School, both of which utilize the Lime Rock, CT, track as their training course. The Advanced Driving School uses BMWs and takes you through accident evasion, performance braking, controlled slides, and the limits of lateral acceleration. The Racing School seats you in specially prepared, low-slung Formula I cars, teaching you to drive at speeds you'd never consider on the highway. With either course, your driving skills are greatly enhanced, making you safer and more effective out on the road.

If you've been yearning to put the pedal to the metal, step on it and get on over to *Skip Barber Racing School* (203-824-0771; Rte 7, Canaan, CT).

SWIMMING

Berkshire swimming in full swing.

Paul Rocheleau, courtesy
the Berkshire Hills Conference

Berkshire is blessed with countless magical swimming spots, some secluded and known only to the likes of otter, and some quite public. There are sizable lakes and ponds, rushing green rivers, and deep, chilly quarries. For wintertime, and for those who prefer their water sport in a more controlled setting, there are numerous swimming pools, both indoor and out.

South County

Benedict Pond, Beartown State Forest, 413-528-0904; Gt. Barrington; Follow signs from Rte. 23 or from Rte. 102 in South Lee.

Eden Hill Recreation Center 413-298-5222; Congregation of the Marians, Prospect Hill, Stockbridge; Olympic-size heated indoor pool: Hours: Mon–Fri, 6 a.m.–6 p.m.; Sat, 12:30 p.m.–5 p.m.; Sun., 10:30 a.m.– 2 p.m.

Berkshire Motor Inn 413-528-3150; Main St., Gt. Barrington; Indoor pool and sauna.

Egremont Country Club 413-528-4222; Rte. 23, S. Egremont; outdoor pool.

Green River Off Rte. 23, 1 mi. west of Gt. Barrington; and off Hurlburt Rd., between Alford Rd. and Rte. 71; Clearest of the clear, greenest of the green, purest of the pure — a summer treat not to be missed.

Lake Garfield, Kinne's Grove, Rte. 23, Monterey.

Lake Mansfield 413-528-6080; off Christian Hill Rd., Gt. Barrington.

Oak n' Spruce Resort 413-243-3500; Off Rte. 102, S. Lee; Heated outdoor and indoor pools, saunas, whirlpool bath, physical fitness room; memberships available.

Otis Reservoir, Tolland State Forest, 413-269-6002 or 413-269-7268; Off Rte. 23, Otis; camping, fishing, picnicking, boating.

Prospect Lake 413-528-4158; Prospect Lake Rd. (0.75 mi. west, off Rte. 71), N. Egremont; Camping, day picnics, adult lounge; open to 6 p.m. daily.

Spectacle Pond Cold Spring Rd., Sandisfield.

York Lake, Sandisfield State Forest, 413-258-4774 or 413-229-8212; Off Rte. 57, New Marlborough; Picnicking, fishing, hiking.

Central County

Ashmere Lake Ashmere Beach, Rte. 143, Hinsdale.

Berkshire West 413-499-4600; Dan Fox Drive, Pittsfield; Outdoor pool open June–Sept. Bath house, snack bar, showers; Memberships available.

Boy's Club 448-8258; 16 Melville St., Pittsfield. (Under 18) Indoor pool open to members only; memberships available. Free swimming early eves. wkdays; Sat. 1–3 p.m..

Onota Lake Onota Blvd., Pittsfield; Free municipal beaches, supervised, 12–8 p.m. daily.

Pontoosuc Lake Rte. 7, Pittsfield; Free municipal beach.

Pittsfield Girls' Club 413-442-5174; 165 East St., Pittsfield; Indoor pool open for recreational swimming eves., Mon.–Fri.; Sat. 1–2:15.

Pittsfield State Forest 413-442-8992; Cascade St., Pittsfield; Swimming (lifeguards on duty 10 a.m. to 6 p.m.), picnicking, hiking and nature trails.

Pittsfield YMCA 413-499-7650; 292 North St., Pittsfield.

Plunkett Lake Lion's Club Beach, Church St., Hinsdale.

Ponterril 413-499-0647; Pontoosuc Lake, Rte. 7, north of Pittsfield; Operated by the Pittsfield YMCA (pool open to members only); Season memberships available.

Wahconah Falls State Park Off Rte. 9, Dalton.

North County

Clarksburg State Park Rte. 8, Clarksburg, near Vermont line; Camping, picnicking.

Hoosic Valley High School 413-743-5200; Rte 116, Cheshire; indoor pool open Sept. through June.

Jiminy Peak 413-738-5500; Corey Rd., off Rte. 7, Hancock; outdoor pool.

Margaret Lindley Park Rte. 2, Williamstown; swimming pond. $10 season pass.

North Pond, Savoy Mountain State Forest, Florida; Follow signs from Rte. 2 (in Florida) or Rte. 116 (in Savoy); $5 day-use, $30 season pass.

Northern Berkshire YMCA 413-663-6529; Brickyard Ct., N. Adams.

Sand Springs Pool and Spa 413-458-5205; off Rte. 7, near Vermont line, Williamstown; 50x75-ft. mineral pool (year-round temperature of the spring, 74); 2 mineral whirlpools (temperature of 102), mineral showers, sauna, shuffleboard, picnic area, beach. Pavilion for private party use.

Windsor Lake 413-662-3047; North Adams. Access via Bradley St. from North Adams State College or via Kemp Ave. from E. Main St.; Municipal swimming area; Supervised daily; Residents, $3 with car sticker, non-residents, $15 with car sticker; One-time use, $2.00.

Windsor Jambs State Forest 413-684-0948; Windsor; Follow signs from Rte. 9 in West Cummington or Rte. 116 in Savoy.

YMCAS

PITTSFIELD YMCA 413-499-7650; 292 North St., Pittsfield.

With its North St. facility and Ponterril Outdoor Recreation Center (see below), Pittsfield's YMCA undoubtedly serves more public recreational needs than any other complex in the county. At the *North St. Y,* the range of fitness and sports programs is staggering, if not revitalizing. Here you can enjoy aerobics, Aeroreflex (musical aerobics with hand-held weights); here, too, you can swim and scuba dive, both with instruction if you wish, and play racquetball, handball, and squash. The racquetball program is particularly fine, being led by top teaching-pro Mary McGinnis, who even offers a videotaped analysis of your game. There are Nautilus machines and programs; special classes for kids, in basketball, gymnastics, swimming, and Indian lore. To smooth things out, the Y has a sauna, a steam room, sunlamps, and a lounge with color TV.

From Memorial Day through Labor Day, the Pittsfield Y's *Ponterril Outdoor Recreation Center* (413-499-0640; Rte. 7 at Pontoosuc Lake) really comes to life, and here, too, the facilities are inviting, the programs enriching. There's an Olympic-sized pool, a wading pool, and a tot's spray pool; swim lessons are also offered. Down at the lake, the Y has a marina with moorings for 50 boats; they offer canoe, rowboat, and sailboat rentals, also sailing lessons. There's a tennis camp and a soccer camp, a day camp, and a preschool camp. And up at Ponterril's six fast-dry clay courts, some of the best tennis in the county is played.

NORTHERN BERKSHIRE YMCA 413-663-6529; 22 Brickyard Ct., North Adams.

North County's Y is another center of vitality in Berkshire, a facility that has continued to improve and upgrade its sports complex. There's a six-lane pool, a full gymnasium, a weight room and Nautilus, a new gymnastics room for children, and two new handball/racquetball courts, all with programs to match. As with the Pittsfield Y, other Y memberships are honored (with a slight surcharge), and special short-term guest passes can be arranged.

A YOGA RETREAT

KRIPALU CENTER FOR YOGA AND HEALTH 413-448-3400; Rte. 183 (just south of Tanglewood and actually in Stockbridge); Mailing address: Lenox, MA 01240.

One of the grandest of Berkshire's summer "cottages" was Shadowbrook, a 100-room Tudor house with a one-acre floor plan. Built by Anson Phelps Stokes, the gargantuan house passed to Andrew Carnegie in 1917 and burned to the ground in 1956. The view southwards from Shadowbrook was and still is among the Berkshires' most inspiring: a panoramic sweep of the sky, the lake (Mahkeenac, or Stockbridge Bowl) and the mountains (including Monument Mtn., off to the right). Though the red-brick structure built to replace Shadowbrook is modern and functional, the estate nevertheless feels like hallowed ground and continues to have a deeply moving effect on many who visit. It was a Jesuit monastery for several years.

Practicing the postures, at Kripalu.

Jonathan Sternfield

How appropriate, then, that such a facility be turned into a residential center for yoga and health with a staff of more than 300. Under the leadership of the ever-youthful Yogi Amrit Desai, Kripalu ("compassionate one") has emerged as a holistic health retreat of substantial importance. This center for yoga offers a comprehensive program of physically and spiritually rejuvenating practices. Facilities include spacious aerobic dance and yoga studios; saunas and whirlpools; 300 acres of forests, meadows, meditation gardens, and miles of woodland trails; private beach on the Bowl; bookstore and gift shop; special health services, including body and foot massage and skin care; and a natural foods kitchen serving quite tasty, well-balanced vegetarian meals.

Kripalu's Center's environment is itself nurturing. From the front terrace and the rolling meadow before it, one can see the green hills, trees, mountains, and lake. The well-equipped building has many more than the original Shadowbrook's 100 rooms, and, increasingly, people who come to Kripalu sign on for short-term room and board combined with the programs. Local day-visitors are welcome seven days a week; call for further information. With its healthy ways, Kripalu enhances the hills, and may well enhance you, too.

FOR KIDS ONLY

As far as most kids are concerned, Berkshire is one neat county. Besides the dozens of children's camps here (see "Camps" in this chapter), most of the ski slopes operate children's ski schools. In between the summer camping and winter skiing, dozens of little events are happening on a small scale all

A pumpkin face in progress, at the Berkshire Harvest Festival, Berkshire Botanical Garden.

Jonathan Sternfield

over the county. Most local libraries have story hours, most of the museums and playgrounds have kids' programs, and many of the local theaters have innovative children's productions. If you're serious about having a full calendar for the kids, *Adventures In Berkshire County — Places to Go with the Kids*, by Patti Silver and Becky Spencer, is highly recommended reading. This $7.95 paperback, available at some bookstores or through the publisher (Berkshire House), is chockful of fun things to do.

South County

In Great Barrington, the **Barrington Ballet** (413-528-4963) runs ballet classes for children Tues. through Sat. **Dos Amigos** Mexican Restaurant (413-528-0084; Stockbridge Rd.) often hosts David Grover, who sings and invites you to sing along, captivating kids of all ages. Across the way, at the Cove Bowling Lanes on Rte. 7, is the **Rainbow's End Miniature Golf Course** (413-528-1220), an indoor extravaganza to test even the deftest little putter. In West Stockbridge, **Clay Forms Studio** (413-232-4349; Austerlitz Rd., Rtes. 102W & 41) offers classes, workshops and other activities for kids eight and up who like to work in clay. Out in New Marlboro, **Four Colors Company** presents theater workshops for kids of all ages at the Flying Cloud Summer Camp (413-528-5614).

The **Stockbridge Library** (413-298-5501; Main St., Stockbridge) has a large and cozy children's section, and story hours are a regular event. During the summer, the **Berkshire Theatre Festival** (413-298-5536; Rte. 102, just east of the junction of Rte. 7, Stockbridge) gives Children's Theatre performances of plays written by local kids. They also offer an acting class for students, twelve to fourteen. The **Norman Rockwell Museum** (413-298-4100) offers a variety of activities geared to kids, one the best being their Family Day on the last Sunday of every month. Admission prices are lowered, and special guides are provided to inform both parents and kids. The **Berkshire Botanical Garden** (413-298-3926) holds a wonder-filled day camp for kids in summer, offering children in Grades One through Six the opportunity to explore the world of nature. Their early October Harvest Festival has lots of kids' activities, too. Art classes are a part of the *Interlaken School of Arts* (413-298-5252) program, with special courses for kids eight through seventeen.

Central County

The *Lenox Library* (413-637-0197; 18 Main St.) has a terrific children's room, which always seems to be brimming with kid energy. *Pleasant Valley Wildlife Sanctuary* (413-637-0320; 472 W. Mountain Rd.) runs a History Day Camp, one- and two-week sessions, featuring exciting educational outdoor activities for boys and girls, Grades One through Twelve.

Central County's other Massachusetts Audubon Society property, *Canoe Meadows Wildlife Sanctuary* (413-637-0320; Holmes Rd., Pittsfield), in conjunction with the Berkshire Museum, runs a one-week Native American camp for boys and girls, ages three, four, and five. During the summer, *Hancock Shaker Village* (413-443-0188; Rte. 20, Hancock) offers a hands-on experience in their "Discovery Room," where children may try on Shaker-style clothes and participate in such facets of 19th-century life as spinning wool, weaving, or writing with a quill pen at a Shaker desk. Outside, children can see the farm animals and demonstrations of sheepshearing or sheep-herding trials. Hancock Shaker Village also conducts "School Vacation Crafts Workshops" in basketmaking, cooking, and textiles in February and April. *Jacob's Pillow* (413-243-0745), offers programs for children out in the New Studio Theater, Becket.

The *Robbins-Zust Family Marionettes* often perform a full range of "classic tales for children of all ages." Bringing out the heavyweight dramas such as "Three Little Pigs," "Rumpelstiltskin" and "The Emperor's New Clothes," the Robbins-Zust troupe often performs in Lenox and Pittsfield. For more information, call the Marionettes themselves (413-698-2591). They are "the smallest, established, permanent, floating repertory company in America."

In downtown Pittsfield, the *Berkshire Athenaeum*'s (413-499-9483; Wendell Ave. at East St.) children's library has a wide range of programs, from story hours to films. The *Berkshire Museum* (413-443-7171; South St.) also has an extensive series of educational children's events — theater, dance, and storytelling for the whole family.

In town at the *Berkshire Public Theatre* (413-445-4631; Union St.), it's those miniature magicians again, the Robbins-Zust Marionettes doing their little thing anew for little ones of all ages. Jack was there, and so was his beanstalk; and Hansel was recently seen there with Gretel. The Public Theatre also has a Youth Ensemble, which now develops plays by children for children. *Either/Or Bookstore* (413-499-1705; 122 North St.) pays lots of attention to the little ones, with a regular children's series featuring authors, illustrators, and musicians. Their series brings to Berkshire some of the world's top talent in children's literature, a real opportunity for both kids and parents. At *Dalton Community House* (413-684-0260; 400 Main St., Dalton), kids will find a positive plethora of fun activities. There's miniature golf in Lanesborough to keep little hands busy at *Baker's Driving Range & Miniature Golf* (413-442-6102; Rte. 7) and the *Par 4 Family Fun Center* (413-499-0051; Rte. 7). Up-county a ways, at *Jiminy Peak* (413-738-5500; Rte. 43, Hancock), the fun goes right into summer with the *Alpine Slide*, a scenic 15-minute ride up, and an exhilarating 5-minute slide down. Jiminy also has a miniature golf course, trout fishing, and a separate tennis program.

North County

Over in North Adams, at the *Heritage Gateway State Park* (413-663-6312; Furnace St.) a recent feature was a "Kid's Korner" craft workshop. In Williamstown, there's an extensive summer playground program at the public schools, along with swimming lessons at *Margaret Lindley Park.* Information can be had by calling the program's operators, the *Youth Center* (413-458-5925; Cole Ave.). Winter recreational programs are also offered through the Youth Center. And treasure hunts, along with children's workshops on various artists, are a few of the *Clark Art Institute*'s (413-458-8109; South St.) offerings for kids.

CHAPTER SEVEN
Fancy Goods
SHOPPING

Helen Selzer at the helm of Farshaw's Books, one of many used and rare bookshops now thriving in Berkshire.

Even the shops that were closed offered, through wide expanses of plate-glass, hints of hidden riches. In some, waves of silk and ribbon broke over shores of imitation moss from which ravishing hats rose like tropical orchids. In others, the pink throats of gramophones opened their giant convolutions in a soundless chorus; or bicycles shining in neat ranks seemed to await the signal of an invisible starter; or tiers of fancy-goods in leatherette and paste dangled their insidious graces; and, in one vast bay that seemed to project them into exciting contact with the public, wax ladies in daring dresses chatted elegantly, or, with gestures intimate yet blameless, pointed to their pink corsets and transparent hosiery.

A description of shop windows on the main street of "Nettleton,"
the fictional name for Pittsfield in *Summer*, by Edith Wharton, 1917.

Antiques, books, clothing, handcrafts, home furnishings — shopping for the necessities and the accessories of life will find ample scope in the Berkshires, on still-vital downtown streets and at a variety of retail destinations. You'll find an ever-changing mix of the latest trends and styles, the genuinely old, and the timeless — sometimes all in one shop. You'll also find imaginative wares designed and made in the Berkshires, as well as goods from the farthest corners of the world. There are some chain stores, and outlets and discount centers, too. Note: many Berkshire shops have been in place for generations; others sprang up last week and will have moved on by next Monday; it's helpful to call ahead before making a special trip.

Recordings, Classical and Jazz

Compact discs, cassette tapes, and even those dinosaurs, records, are available throughout the county, in various chain stores and other retail outlets. Most places here with CDs and tapes have a small classical music selection, but if you're looking for more than the Three Tenors or the Four Seasons, visit the *Tanglewood Music Store*, at Tanglewood in Lenox, open for Tanglewood audiences, and featuring the music and performing artists of that week, plus much more. The *Berkshire Record Outlet* (413-243-4080; Rte. 102, Lee) has classical remainders listed in a catalog — send for one for $2 — from which you can select from thousands of classical CDs, tapes, and LPs, at closeout prices. On Saturdays, you can also browse through an eclectic selection of recordings in the small retail room, and you will be sure to turn up something you always wanted.

Jazz enthusiasts in particular will enjoy *Toonerville Trolley Records* (413-458-5229; 131 Water St., Williamstown) and its array of CDs, tapes, and LPs, out of print and current. In addition to jazz, there's rock, folk, and reggae.

ANTIQUES

From formal 18th-century furniture to bold Art Deco tableware, with country primitive carvings and High Victorian accessories in between, antiques in the Berkshires are varied and abundant. Whether you hanker after museum-quality pieces of a specific style and period or whether you simply enjoy exploring for unique home furnishings, you'll find plenty to choose from. The antiques scene here includes furniture large and small; vintage clothing, textiles, and jewelry; prints, paper, and other ephemera; trunks and lamps, kitchenalia and militaria, clocks and rugs, baskets and wicker. European and Asian antiques specialists have also found their way to the Berkshires. And a number of antiques shops also include new furnishings and accent pieces that complement their antiques, and custom decorating services, too.

South County in particular is an antiques center, with Rte. 7 the main artery for an array of multidealer shops, specialists, and generalists. They know their merchandise, and their prices reflect their knowledge. In Central and North County, prices are more flexible, but finding a bargain takes some looking.

Portraits on the block under a Berkshire big top.

Jonathan Sternfield

If you extend your antiques hunting to auctions or — the sign of the true diehard — to yard sales and flea markets, check the *Berkshire Eagle,* the largest daily paper in the county, for classified listings for antiques, tag sales, and auctions. A list of auctioneers is also given below. The weekly free shoppers stacked up at supermarket entrances also list yard sales, auctions, shows, and markets.

The annual brochure of the *Berkshire County Antique Dealer's Association* also lists dealers and locations, with business hours, telephone numbers, and a brief description of what they offer. Members of this association "take pride in their merchandise and guarantee its authenticity." Their brochure is available in member shops or by mail (send a SASE to BCADA Directory, PO Box 594, Great Barrington MA 01230).

Several rare book specialists also make their home here; they're listed in the following section, "Books."

South County

GREAT BARRINGTON

Asian Antiques (413-528-5091, phone/fax; Jenifer House Commons, Stockbridge Rd.) High quality Sri Lankan and Indonesian antiques, handcrafts, and art, along with gifts, clothing, jewelry. If you've always wanted an opium bed or a temple gong, this is the place to find it.

Blackbird Antiques and Collectibles (413-528-5862; 152 Main St.) American collectibles, 1850–1950; the nostalgia accessories here include tins, dishware, medicine bottles, rugs, quilts, lighting, and furniture, recently featuring two charming small-scale Adirondack chairs. Fri.–Mon. or by chance.

Bygone Days (413-528-1870; 969 S. Main St., Rte. 7) Country and formal furniture, large and small; tables and chairs, armoires, night stands, hutches, china closets.

Carriage House Antiques (413-528-6045; 389 Stockbridge Rd.) Tables, chairs, furniture, even a set of doors. Antique furniture restoration, repair, stripping, refinishing.

Coffmans' Country Antiques Market (413-528-9282; Jenifer House Commons, Stockbridge Rd.) Three floors of high-quality wares, pre-1949, from 75 New England and regional dealers, in the yellow house with two green doors. The large assortment is appealingly arranged in cases and room settings, and includes ephemera and prints, kitchenware, primitives, wood, pottery, furniture, tools, quilts, rugs, baskets, folk art, stoneware, glassware, and tin, brass, and copper. Books on antiques and collectibles are also sold here, and there's a lounge with coffee, tea, hot chocolate for customers and dealers.

Corashire Antiques (413-528-0014; Rte. 7 & 23, at Belcher Square) In the red barn: American country furniture and accessories.

Country Dining Room and Tea Garden Antiques (413-528-5050; 178 Main St., Rte. 7) Complete accouterments for dining in style, formal or country. In lavishly coordinated rooms, dining tables boast elaborate place settings of china, silver, glass, crystal, porcelain — down to the matching damask napkins with silk rose napkin rings. Chairs, rugs, paintings, and other furnishings and accessories complete the look. For a less formal but still elegant approach, Tea Garden Antiques, upstairs, offers more place settings, linens, and other accents. Country Dining Room's own Sheila Chefetz wrote the stunning book that shows you how to put it all together, *Antiques for the Table*.

Elise Abrams Antiques (413-528-3201; 11 Stockbridge Rd.) Glassware, tableware, and accessories, including art glass, crystal, china, porcelain. 18th- to early 20th-century decorative arts, and furniture.

Emporium Antique Center (413-528-2731; 319 Main St.) A variety of dealers here offer estate and costume jewelry, crystal, silver, accessories, furniture, furnishings, linens. You'll find the largest selection of salt-and-pepper shakers in the Berkshires here, it's safe to say. Open daily; Jan.–Apr. closed Tues., Weds.

The Kahns' Antique and Estate Jewelry (413-528-9550; 38 Railroad St.) Antique jewelry is their specialty; appraisals, diamond grading, gem identification, repairs, and custom work.

The Lion, The Witch, and The Wardrobe (413-528-6313; 173 Main St.) A small place with a hodgepodge of oddments awaiting an imaginative use: architectural elements, outdoor and garden items, including a weathered green metal lattice door.

Madison Upstairs (413-274-6361; 11 Railroad St.) A mixed bag of antiques, art objects, fine arts; from small collectibles to large-scale architectural elements.

Donald McGrory Oriental Rugs (413-528-9594; 12 Castle St.) Antique and decorative Oriental rugs. Tues.–Sat.

Artifacts from a slower time, at Memories, Great Barrington.

Jonathan Sternfield

Memories (413-528-6380; 310 Main St.) A well-chosen and decidedly eclectic array of antiques, collectibles, primitives, old cameras, furniture, lighting, nostalgia, old toys, musical instruments, and more. Many of these items — such as lamps and radios — have been carefully restored and are in working order. Their collection is "ideal for authentic theatrical props and restaurant decorations," the owners suggest, although most of us will just want to take it all home.

Mullin-Jones Antiquities (413-528-4871; 525 S. Main St., Rte. 7) The fragrance of lavender pervades this importer of 18th- and 19th-century country French furniture and accessories, including large-scale farmhouse pieces, garden accents, and fabrics. Restoration services. Closed Tues.; call ahead in winter.

Olde — An Antiques Market (413-528-1840; Jenifer House Commons, Stockbridge Rd.) Jam-packed with potential treasures. Over 65 dealers in a two-story red barn, offering collectibles, dishes, china, glass, porcelain, silver, games, books, jewelry, decorative items.

Once Upon a Table (413-442-6244, 413-443-6622; 42 Railroad St. at Drygoods; and at Coffman's Antiques, Jenifer House Commons) Recreate the moderne '30s, '40s, and '50s in your home, with these bold and bright creations for the kitchen and table, by top designers of the period: dishware, glassware, small appliances, clocks.

Red Horse Antiques (413-528-2637; 117 State Rd.) "Whatever I like, I buy; and, like the peddlers of old, I sell," says proprietress April. That includes furniture, paper, glass, and catch-as-catch-can.

Saturday Sweets (413-528-6661; 507 S. Main St.) Specialists in 20th-century decorative arts, including furniture, accessories, fashion prints, and vintage costume jewelry. A refreshing alternative when the previous two centuries begin to seem, well, old. Open most days except Tuesday.

Susan and Paul Kleinwald, Inc. (413-528-4252; 578 S. Main St.) 18th- and 19th-century American and English antique furniture, fine art, accessories; appraisals. Closed Tues.

Snyder's Store (413-528-1441; 945 Main St.) The pink flamingoes in the flower gardens by the door are a clue to what's inside: funky furniture and accessories, with rustic pieces, wicker, tramp art, jewelry, linens, garden accents, and architectural elements. Open most weekends 12–5; weekdays by whim.

LEE

Aardenburg Antiques (413-243-0001; 144 W. Park St.) Early 19th-century furniture and accessories; restoration and refinishing. Weekends by chance; any time by appointment.

Henry B. Holt (413-243-3184; PO Box 699) Specialist in 19th- and early 20th-century American paintings. Call for appointment regarding appraisal, purchase, sale, or restoration.

The Powder House Shop (413-243-0477, 800-499-0477; 195 Laurel St.) Furniture, china, silver, glass.

SHEFFIELD/ASHLEY FALLS

Note: The following antique shops are in the township of Sheffield where there are two villages — Ashley Falls and Sheffield proper.

Ashley Falls

Don Abarbanel (413-229-3330; E. Main St., at Lewis & Wilson) Formal furniture of the 17th through 19th centuries, and needlework, brass and other metalwork, English pottery, English and Dutch delft, Chinese export porcelain. In winter call ahead.

Ashley Falls Antiques (413-229-8759; Rte. 7A) American country and formal furniture, accessories, and authenticated antique jewelry.

Circa (413-229-2990; Rte. 7A) Good collections of Majolica and Canton; 18th- and 19th-century furniture, accessories, and "sophisticated oddments."

Europa (413-229-3148; Rte. 7A) Mirrors, lamps, and paintings are the specialties here; also a selection of European and American furniture, accessories, and decorative objects.

Lewis & Wilson (413-229-3330; E. Main St.) English, American, and Continental 18th- and 19th-century furniture and accessories; Oriental porcelains. Call ahead in winter.

Robert Thayer American Antiques (413-229-2965; E. Main St.) 18th- and early 19th-century country antique furniture and decorative arts, and folk art. By chance or appointment.

The Vollmers (413-229-3463; Rte. 7A) 18th- and 19th-century furniture, formal and country, firearms and militaria, accessories, and tools. Open daily; Tues. by chance or appointment.

Sheffield

Anthony's Antiques (413-229-8208; Rte. 7) English furniture from the 18th and 19th centuries, accessorized by ceramics, paintings and fine arts, and Chinese porcelain and furniture.

Carriage Trade Antiques (413-229-2870; 276 S. Undermountain Rd.) Country looks in a country setting, including furniture, blanket chests, kitchen items, jewelry, out-of-the-ordinary collectibles.

Centuryhurst Berkshire Antique Gallery (413-229-8131, 3277; Main St., Rte. 7.) Scores of ticking clocks sound like rainfall at this multidealer also specializing in Wedgwood; with country and formal furniture, glass, paintings, prints, and accessories.

Corner House Antiques (413-229-6627; corner of Rte. 7 & Old Mill Pond Rd.) Specialists in antique wicker furniture, including whole sets; with a variety of styles and finishes. A well-chosen selection of American country furnishings and accessories as well.

Cupboards & Roses Antiques (413-229-3070; Rte. 7) Beautifully displayed antique and reproduction paint-decorated 18th- and 19th-century furniture, featuring capacious armoires and chests. Decorative accessories, old and new, include baskets, boxes, textiles, and ceramics. Closed Tues.

Darr Antiques and Interiors (413-229-7773; S. Main St., Rte. 7) Two buildings of elegant room settings displaying formal 18th- and 19th-century American, English, Continental, and Oriental furniture and accessories, with a focus on dining room furnishings. May–Oct., open daily; Nov.–Apr., open Thurs.–Mon.

Dovetail Antiques (413-229-2628; Rte. 7) A select collection of American clocks, country furniture, including pieces with original paint or finish, and spongeware, stoneware, and redware. Open daily; Tues. by chance.

Falcon Antiques (413-229-7745; 176 S. Undermountain Rd., Rte. 41) Country furniture and accessories, with a good selection of brass, copper, pewter, woodworking tools, and treen (small wooden pieces).

Frederick Hatfield Antiques (413-229-7986; S. Main St., Rte. 7) Antiques and collectibles from the 18th through 20th centuries, with country and formal furniture, paintings, silver, paper items, jewelry, architectural elements, and other treasures from New England homes.

Good & Hutchinson Associates, Inc. (413-229-8832, -4555; Main St., Rte. 7, on the Green) Specialists in fine antiques and decorative arts from the 18th and 19th century, with American, English, and Continental furniture, Chinese export porcelain, paintings, brass, lamps; for collectors and antiquarians. Summer: Mon.–Sat., 10–5; Sun. 1–5. Open Oct.–May by chance.

Kuttner Antiques (413-229-2955; N. Main St., Rte. 7) American and English furniture and decorative accessories from the 18th and 19th centuries. Formal and high country. Closed Tues.

David J. LeBeau Fine Antiques (413-229-3445; S. Main St./Rte. 7) Fine American and English 19th-century antiques, including furniture and porcelain. Selected Asian pieces. Weds.–Mon; Jan.–Mar., Thurs.–Sun or by appointment.

Le Périgord Antiques (413-229-0250; Rte. 7) Antiques with a French accent: French country furniture and accessories, along with European and American pieces, 18th century through Art Deco. You'll find iron, pottery, garden accents, and architectural elements. Open weekends; weekdays by chance or appointment.

Lois W. Spring Antiques (413-229-2542; Ashley Falls Rd., Rte. 7A) 18th- and 19th-century furniture and accessories, country and formal. Open weekends; weekdays by chance or appointment.

Ole T.J.'s Antique Barn (413-229-8382; Rte. 7) Antiques and collectibles on two floors from all over, some of it gathered by the owners on their travels in the Far East and Africa, and some of it early American and European furniture, jewelry, paintings, rugs, lamps, and other accessories. Thurs.–Mon. or by chance or appointment.

1750 House Antiques (413-229-6635; S. Main St., Rte. 7) Specialists in the sale and repair of American, French, and European clocks. Also offering music boxes, phonographs, glass, china, and other accessories, and furniture.

Sheffield Plains Antiques (413-229-0113; Rte. 7, 1 mi. S. of center) A special feature here is Federal looking-glasses; a variety of other furnishings and accessories is offered too, from a range of periods. Gilding and design services are also offered.

Susan Silver Antiques (413-229-8169; N. Main St., Rte. 7/PO Box 621) English and American formal furnishings from the 18th and 19th centuries. Closed Tues.

Twin Fires Antiques (413-229-8307; Berkshire School Rd. & Rte. 41) Handmade imported country pine furniture, stained and painted, antique and reproduction. Armoires, cupboards, dressers, tables, beds from the British Isles and Europe — all attractively and abundantly displayed, along with other furniture and home accessories. Closed Tues.

Vincent and Barbara Beaver Antiques and Interiors (413-229-0113; at Sheffield Plains Antiques) Four centuries of furniture, accessories, paintings, textiles; interior design.

David M. Weiss Antiques (413-229-2716; N. Main St., Rte. 7) 18th- and 19th-century formal and country furniture, china, accessories. Open weekends or by appointment. Also at Weiss Antiques, items from **Kettering Fine 18th- and 19th-century Antiques**, of Main St., Southfield (413-229-6647).

SOUTH EGREMONT

Bird Cage Antiques (413-528-3556; Main St., Rte. 23, next to post office) An unusual variety of smalls and collectibles, including toys, dolls, fountain pens, silver, and jewelry; also clothes, linens, paintings.

Country Cat Antiques (413-528-4551; Rte. 23) Decoys and other sporting memorabilia; folk art, textiles, jewelry, paintings, prints, books, and collectibles.

Douglas Antiques (413-528-1810; Rte. 23 at the Weathervane Inn, PO Box 571) Victorian and turn-of-the-century furniture in oak and walnut, with tables, chairs, desks, bookcases, dressers, and chests, and accessories, including lamps and quilts. Open 10—5:30 daily; Tues. by chance.

Geffner/Schatzky Antiques and Varieties (413-528-0057; Rte. 23, at the sign of the Juggler) 19th century to '50s furniture and accessories, jewelry, architectural elements. Open May–Aug., daily 10:30–5; Sept.–Apr., Fri.–Sun. 10:30–5, during the week by chance or appointment.

Howard's Antiques (413-528-1232; Rte. 23/PO Box 472) Specialists in American country furniture and lighting. Antique lighting fixtures from the late 1890s to the 1930s have been wired for the 1990s. 19th-century dining room tables and chairs are also offered, as well as other country-style antique furniture. Closed Tues.

Barbara Moran Fine and Decorative Arts (413-528-0749; Main St., Rte. 23) Mostly contemporary artwork (see "Galleries" under *Culture*), but also offers antique country-style furnishings and accent pieces.

Red Barn Antiques (413-528-3230; Main St., Rte. 23/PO Box 25) Restored antique lighting from the early 19th century and onward, including kerosene, gas, and early electric fixtures. Repair and restoration of antique lamps on site; refinished furniture.

Elliot and Grace Snyder (413-528-3581; Undermountain Rd., Rte. 41, 0.5 mi. south of Rte. 23) By appointment. 18th- and 19th-century American furniture and decorative arts, with a selection of folk art and garden pieces.

The Splendid Peasant (413-528-5755; Rte. 23 and Old Sheffield Rd.) 18th- and 19th-century country furniture and accessories, and folk art, all stunningly displayed in a fascinating series of galleries and niches. Original paint a specialty.

SOUTHFIELD

Southfield Antiques Market (413-229-3576, Main St./Rte. 272; downstairs at the Buggy Whip Factory) Wares of a variety of dealers, with antique and estate jewelry, glassware, silver, china. Closed Tues. & Wed. off season.

Whip Shop Antiques (413-229-3576; Main St./Rte. 272; downstairs at the Buggy Whip Factory) Housewares, furniture, toys — everything you need for the country look from a variety of dealers. Closed Tues. & Wed. off season.

STOCKBRIDGE

Tom Carey's Place (413-298-4893; Sergeant St., off Main St.) American clocks, lamps, glass, and other accessories to complement the country furniture from the 18th to the 19th century. By appointment.

Reuss Antique & Art Center (413-298-4074; Pine & Shamrock Sts.) One block up from the Red Lion Inn, this 1880s house is stocked with art, antiques, and jewelry, on two floors. Art offerings include Audubon and other prints, contemporary and antique, and Berkshire-related paintings. The antiques are fine country pieces in walnut, pine, and cherry. Jewelry includes Victorian, heirloom, and Southwest items.

WEST STOCKBRIDGE

Sawyer Antiques (413-232-7062; Depot St.) In a Shaker-built grist mill, early American furniture and accessories, in a variety of styles: formal, Shaker, country. Open Fri.–Sun; otherwise call ahead.

Central County

LANESBOROUGH

Amber Springs Antiques (413-442-1237; 29 S. Main St./Rte. 7) Country American furnishings "from as early as we can find to as late as we can stand." That description includes tools, pottery, country store items, trivia. The alternate motto, according to owner Gae Elfenbein, is "we have it but we can't find it." Open daily; weekends in winter, or call ahead.

Walden's Antiques and Books (413-442-5346; Main St./Rte. 7) Bottles, baskets, books — along with furniture, jewelry, toys, china, paintings. Call ahead.

LENOX

Chelsea Downs (413-637-3580; Brushwood Farm) A bounty of old and new items for imaginative country decorating and living: furniture, linens, pillows, folk art, jewelry, glass, pottery, clothing both vintage and modern. It's all in a big downstairs room with an exposed beam ceiling. Custom woven-seat repair.

Country Home (413-637-9977; 79 Church St.) Antique, primitive, and country furniture, painted furniture, accessories, jewelry, and gifts, in a range of styles and prices. Old kitchen gadgets, baskets, and more make ideal decorator pieces.

Charles L. Flint Antiques Inc. (413-637-1634, -1242; 2 Kemble St./PO Box 971) Furniture, painting, accessories, folk art, Shaker items.

Mad Dogs and Englishmen (413-637-0667; 24 Walker St.) Worth going out to in the noonday sun, or any other time. Charming Victorian and Edwardian antiques, along with complementary collectibles, gifts, lingerie. Winter hours Weds.–Sun.

Stone's Throw Antiques (413-637-2733; 57 Church St.) American, French, English, and Oriental 19th- and early 20th-century furniture, accessories, and collector's items, including china, glass, silver, prints,

Unique Antique (413-637-3662; 36 Church St.) Estate and antique jewelry, sterling, pewter, and other small collectibles. Closed late fall and winter.

PITTSFIELD

Bargain Shop (413-499-0927; 1 Reed St., off South St.) Unprepossessing though it may seem, there are treasures here: recent finds include a 7-foot-long bench with weathered green paint, perfect for plants in a sunroom; maple bedsteads, twin and full; an expandable enamel-top kitchen table with four chairs, a cream-and-maroon hatbox, and a small bust of Dante. Also vintage clothes and fabrics. Closed Tues. & Sun.

Memory Lane Antiques (413-499-2718; 446 Tyler St.) A recommended source for useful and decorative pieces: furniture, rugs, mirrors, lamps, accessories, china and glass, ephemera, other collectibles. Owner Bev Martin is helpful, friendly, and enthusiastic about her merchandise. Look for the mannequin in a vintage dress on the sidewalk outside. Closed Tues., Sun.

RICHMOND

Wynn A. Sayman (413-698-2272) A by-appointment-only specialist in English pottery of the 18th and early 19th century, for collectors and museums; including saltglaze, redware, tortoiseshell ware, cream ware, pearl ware, and Staffordshire bocage figures.

North County

CHESHIRE

Cheshire Antiques (413-743-7703; 116 Church St.) An eclectic offering of china and glassware.

WILLIAMSTOWN

Collector's Warehouse (413-458-9686; 105 North St./Rte. 7) Antiques; collectibles, including glassware, jewelry, frames, dolls, linen, furniture. Weds.–Sat., 12:30–5. In the McClelland Press Building.

The Library Antiques (413-458-3436; 70 Spring St.) Old and new items in a series of rooms, artfully displayed, including jewelry, furniture, writing supplies, housewares, pillows, prints, books, international decor pieces, silver, dishes, pottery, fabrics and textiles. They say they welcome browsers. A great place for gifts or for yourself.

Saddleback Antiques (413-458-5852; 1395 Cold Spring Rd./Rte. 7) Furniture, glass, pottery, prints, posters. A group shop with five dealers, and more to come, in an old schoolhouse with a bell tower. Closed Weds.

Auctioneers

William Bradford Auction Galleries (413-229-6667 or 8737 evenings; Rte. 7, Sheffield) .

Caropreso Auction Gallery (413-528-8280; Jenifer House Commons, Stockbridge Rd., Great Barrington) .

John and Dina Fontaine (413-448-8922, Pittsfield) .

T.A. Gage (413-528-0076, 413-528-4771; Rte. 23, South Egremont) .

BOOKS

The Berkshires' literary traditions are upheld by several excellent book stores, new and used, each with its own distinct character. Specialists, rare-book, and antique-book dealers are also listed.

South County

GREAT BARRINGTON

Hugh Black Books (413-528-4902; 10 Dresser Ave., off Main St.) The classic second-hand bookstore for serious bibliophiles; an hour or so of browsing will discover the titles that you always look for but can't find — except, finally, here. Overflowing with books; a little musty, a little dusty; highlighted by unique memorabilia, and by the presence of Hugh Black himself.

Hunting literature, in the kingdom of the Bookloft, Great Barrington.

Jonathan Sternfield

The Bookloft (413-528-1521; Rte. 7/Barrington Plaza) A thoughtfully chosen selection of books, mostly new and some used, and tapes. It's also a good source for Berkshire-related titles. With its wooden bookcases and pleasant atmosphere, one of the nicest places in South County for browsing and consulting with fellow book-lovers, particularly owner Eric Wilska and assistant Debby Reed.

Farshaw's Books (413-528-1890; 13 Railroad St.) A select offering of antique and used or out-of-print titles, for the reader, collector, and bibliophile, in a well-organized, browser-friendly shop (with nice background music choices). In addition to Helen and Michael Selzer's own stock — they operate the antiquarian book firm of Selzer & Selzer — there are shelves of books from other dealers, with a predominance of literary and fine arts titles. The Selzers also recently established **Berkshire Book Auction, Inc.**, a rare book auction house (PO Box 746, Sheffield).

Yellow House Books (413-528-8227; 252 Main St.) Nearly new books include out-of-the-ordinary sections such as holistic health, metaphysical subjects, folklore; also literature, children's, art, music, cooking.

LEE

Apple Tree Books (413-243-2012; 87 Main St.) Books, magazines, Berkshire cards, stationery, gifts, audio, puzzles.

SHEFFIELD

Berkshire Used Books (413-229-0122, 800-828-5565; 510 S. Main St./Rte. 7) The ideal used-book store for the reader, with an extensive and well-organized collection. Co-proprietor Esther Kininmonth truly knows and loves her stock and its authors, and it's a pleasure to consult with her about various writers and editions. Categories include literature, travel, biography, and children's.

SOUTH EGREMONT

B&S Gventer Books (413-528-2327; Tyrrell Rd. & Rte. 23/PO Box 298) "Tons of books" from the 15th century to the 19th. Medieval manuscript pages on vellum, and various pages from books published from 1300 to 1600; 19th-century hand-colored engravings. Knowledgeable owner Bruce Gventer can tell you their stories. Weds.–Sun.; Jan. & Feb., Sat. & Sun.

Central County

LANESBOROUGH

Lauriat's (413-445-5191; Berkshire Mall) Big illustrated books, publishers' overstocks, current magazines of every persuasion — all the latest and brightest in print. Strong travel section.

Waldenbooks (413-499-0115; Berkshire Mall) The chain has the most recent books in the store the fastest; and often has titles others don't.

LENOX

The Book Maze and Audio (413-637-1701, fax 413-637-4604; Lenox House Country Shops, Pittsfield-Lenox Rd.) Cards, puzzles, rubber stamps, tapes, CDs, gemstones, T-shirts, craft supplies, gift wrapping paper, fax service — and even books.

The Bookstore (413-637-3390; 9 Housatonic St.) A literate and imaginative selection of new fiction, old fiction, and nonfiction. There are collections of small-press titles and books by local and regional authors, and well-chosen children's and young-adult titles. The Bookstore is a community center, too, presided over by owner Matt Tannenbaum with grace and humor. Matt and his assistants know their books and are happy to converse with you about them; they organize book-signing parties and special events, too. "The world's oldest, permanent literary establishment, serving the community since last Tuesday."

PITTSFIELD

Berkshire Book Shop (413-442-0165; 164 North St.) Headquarters for best-sellers and paperback fiction; stock up here for backyard and beach reading. How-to and self-help titles, too, and lots of magazines. Also in North Adams (413-664-4986; 67 Main St.).

Either/Or Bookstore (413-499-1705; 122 North St.) From the "Buck-A-Book" cart outside the entrance to a complete children's room upstairs (not to mention the video collection featuring classic films), the Either/Or is top-notch. In addition to the best of contemporary publishing and a good selection of classic fiction and literature, Either/Or features travel, women's issues, Berkshire titles, humor, reference, gardening, and culinary titles. Owner Steve Satullo also hosts book signings and other happenings, with special events for children: authors, stories, book parties. The Bonus Book Club is a great idea: for every $100 you spend on books, you get $20 toward book purchases.

A Novel Idea (413-448-2688; Williams St. Shopping Plaza) Recycled paperbacks ideal for vacation reading, plus new books; children's books.

North County

ADAMS

Adams News (413-743-7774; 57 Park St.) A great selection of magazines, including 15 or so foreign language periodicals and other specialty titles. And if by some chance the magazine you want isn't there, they'll try to find it for you. Other classic newsstand features include newspapers, candy, office and school supplies, local pastries, and other local specialties like Squeeze soda and cider. And it's next to the Miss Adams Diner. Ownership is currently planning to change hands, so stay tuned.

NORTH ADAMS

Crystal Unicorn Bookstore (413-664-7377; Rte. 8/Heritage State Park) Half-price paperbacks and hardcovers; gifts, handmade jewelry, and a small selection of old and rare books.

WILLIAMSTOWN

Village Book Store (413-458-4232; 48 Spring St., 2nd floor) "Books for All" is their motto, and that means a varied, thoughtfully selected collection of university and small press titles, plus the best from the mainstream publishers, in a pleasant upstairs space. There's a Berkshire-related section, and the children's books offer some especially good titles not often seen elsewhere.

Water Street Books (413-458-8071; 26 Water St.) A large selection in just about every category displayed on classy architectural shelving with murals behind them. The help is hip and friendly. There are sale books, children's books, and the Williams College bookstore is in the back. A booklover's paradise.

Farther afield, but a destination for a good browse: ***Librarium*** (518-392-5209; off Rte. 295, 1 mi. E. of East Chatham) More than 25,000 second-hand, out-of-print books "for all interests and ages." Sat. & Sun. 10–5; by chance or appointment otherwise.

Book Dealers

These specialist book dealers do business by catalog or appointment.

J&J Lubrano (413-528-5799; 39 Hollenbeck Ave., Great Barrington) Specialist in old and rare music books and autographs.

Howard S. Mott (413-229-2019; Rte. 7, Sheffield) First editions; books from the 16th to the 20th centuries, autographs.

John R. Sanderson Antiquarian Bookseller (413-298-5322; Box 844/Stockbridge) Rare and fine books.

Adler Children's Books (413-298-3559; Stockbridge) Out of print, old and rare children's books; search services.

CLOTHING & ACCESSORIES

You can outfit yourself in just about any style of your choice in the Berkshires: classic, traditional, designer, funky, all-natural, English country squire, buckaroo — it's all here. Some boutiques also feature designs and concepts created in the Berkshires, too. For clothing factory outlets, and there are a number of them, check the listings below plus the "Shopping Streets, Mews, & Malls" section.

South County

GREAT BARRINGTON

Berkshire Leather & Silver Outlet (413-528-4455; 34 Railroad St.) Native American-style jewelry, leather clothes, sandals, shoes, and accessories, especially some stylish bags. Also in Lenox (413-637-4363; 98 Main St.).

Byzantium (413-528-9496; 32 Railroad St.) A rainbow of stacked sweaters will catch your eye first, but don't stop there. Stylish and easy women's dresses, blouses, skirts, and ensembles, casual to dressy; lots of lovely lingerie and sleepwear; jewelry, throws, and other accessories.

Diva (413-528-1754; 179 Main St.) Women's large size clothes, contemporary looks, moderate prices.

Drygoods (413-528-2950; 42 Railroad St.) A '90s blend of contemporary and

---

Especially for Children

Berkshire Child (413-528-6430; Stockbridge Rd., Great Barrington) Clothing and accessories from infant to size 14. The labels you love for kids: Oshkosh, Spumoni, etc.

The Gifted Child (413-637-1191; 80 Church St., Lenox) Children's clothing, newborns to pre-teens, with a contemporary flair; high-quality toys and gifts. Camp care packages — what a great idea. And don't miss the sale barn.

Hey Diddle Diddle (413-458-2855; 96 Water St., Williamstown) Handcrafted children's clothes; unique and creative toys and games by American artisans and designers include rocking horses, rocking boats, and rocking dragons.

kids and . . . (413-528-1188; Rte. 23, South Egremont) Children's clothing and accessories. Open Fri.–Sat. Call to confirm hours.

The Nature of Things (413-637-4373; Brushwood Farm, Pittsfield-Lenox Rd., Lenox) A science and nature store with lots of hands-on fun in a two-story octagon barn. Bird houses, field guides, rockets, chemistry sets, and dinosaur gear share space with a live iguana, big puppets to play with on a little stage, and a place to crawl and play under it; and huge wooden sculptures, including a praying mantis larger than a kid.

Teddybears (413-458-9844; Colonial Shopping Center, Rte. 2, Williamstown) Children's clothing. Closed Mon.

Other spots for clothes, toys, and gifts for children include *Hodge Podge* in Stockbridge and *Mary Stuart* in Lenox (for exquisite clothes designed for grandmothers to give); for imaginative toys, Marsters in Stockbridge has a small, select display, and several area museums and galleries, particularly the *Berkshire Museum* in Pittsfield, have gift shops with sections devoted to educational items disguised as toys.

---

retro styling, as seen in women's clothes, hats, jewelry, accessories, and home decor items.

Gatsby's (413-528-9455; 25 Railroad St.) Useful and funky stuff, including cotton nightgowns, Doc Martins, Teva sandals, Birkenstocks, denim, socks and turtlenecks, and housewares. Gatsby's covers the territory with shops in Williamstown (413-458-5407; 31 Spring St.) and Lee (413-243-3412; 62 Main St.).

Hildi B (413-528-0331; 15 Railroad St.) Natural fiber clothes, including sweaters, skirts, blouses, dresses; handcrafted jewelry and other crafts, leather items, oils and soaps. A friendly atmosphere created by helpful sales people.

Jack's Country Squire (413-528-1390; 316 Main St., Gt. Barrington) *See description under Jack's Department Store, Lee.*

Main Street (413-528-1923; 280 Main St.) "City styles, country prices," they say, with women's designer items at discount prices. Clothes include dresses, separates, sportswear, suits; accessorized with jewelry, belts.

Reeves Leather (413-528-5877; Jenifer House Commons, Stockbridge Rd.) Unique and skillfully crafted leather goods of top-quality materials are made on the premises, and include bags, briefcases, and belts. The wood carriers and carpet bags made from antique rugs are especially wonderful. Antiques are for sale here, too, featuring trunks.

Tanglewool (413-528-6162; 296 Main St.) *See Tanglewool in Lenox.*

LEE

Ben's (413-243-0242; 68 Main St.) A friendly store packed with outdoor and work wear, shoes.

Jack's Dept. Store (413-243-0999; 53 Main St.) Family clothing and shoes, including Nike, Woolrich, Reebok, Levi. Also **Jack's Country Squire** (413-528-1390; 316 Main St., Gt. Barrington).

Zabian's Ltd. (413-243-0136; 19 Main St.) Traditional men's clothing, sportswear, and accessories; suits, coats, shirts, and shoes for men and young men; big and tall.

STOCKBRIDGE

The Coat Factory (413-298-4682; Elm St.) Casual women's clothes and accessories, cotton items from jackets to T-shirts, jewelry, bags.

Currier & i (413-298-4840; The Mews) Women's coordinated clothing, including dresses and separates; accessories and gifts; in a small, friendly shop.

1884 House (413-298-5159; Main St.) Fine clothes with a British Isles heritage.

Hodge Podge (413-298-4687; The Mews) Just that, with ladies and children's clothing, cotton lingerie, Rockwelliana, Rockwell signed prints, and various decor accessories — the floral-accented frames are especially appealing.

Katherine Meagher (413-298-3329; 10 Elm St.) Women's clothing, casual and dressy, classically fashionable; sportswear, separates, dresses, accessories, jewelry.

Sweaters Etc. (413-298-4287; South St./Rte 7) At the third house behind the Red Lion Inn is an outlet for South Wool, which designs and distributes women's handknit sweaters to stores and boutiques. Wool and cotton sweaters are discounted. Seasonal.

Vlada Boutique (413-298-3656; Elm St.) Creative clothes in natural fibers and delicious colors, and scarves, lingerie, hats, and jewelry. The clever ensembles of clothing, jewelry, and accessories displayed here are dangerously inspiring. Highlights are Vlada's own handbags, and elegant floral socks, tapestry belts, and imaginative cards and toys.

Central County

LANESBOROUGH

Camellia's (413-442-9233; S. Main St.) Shopping for women's clothes the way it used to be: a big mirror at one end of the store, fancy shoes to put on while modeling a potential outfit, and saleswomen who enjoy helping. Party, prom, and evening wear, mother-of-the-bride selections, and casual wear, too. Gifts and accessories. Look for the pink building.

Canedy's Pendleton Store (413-443-6822; Rte. 7 betw. Pittsfield and Williamstown) Classic wool clothes and accessories for the complete look. Men's sports shirts and sweaters, too, and a large selection of Indian trade blankets and robes.

Vivian's (413-499-0099; 61 N. Main St.) Women's fashions, accessories, and gifts — new and pre-owned. The consignment clothing is carefully selected and features designer fashions. Some craft work, too. Opens at noon; closed Sun.–Tues.

The Berkshire Mall (413-445-4400; Old State Rd./Rte 8) Comprises many and varied clothes-shopping options for men, women, teens, and children: the Gap, Barbara Moss, American Eagle Outfitters, Weathervane, Limited, Casual Corner, and their friends. Eddie Bauer and Filene's, as of this writing, are coming soon.

LENOX

African Magic (413-637-4242; 48 Church St.) Dramatic flowing clothing to accessorize with jewelry and beadwork. Crafts, musical instruments, gifts, and imaginative toys for kids.

Beba Sweaters (413-637-4550; 48 Church St.) A small space and a big selection of men's and women's sweaters, wool to cotton; handknits. Discount prices.

Casablanca (413-637-2680; 57 Church St.) Men's and women's contemporary clothes, stylishly displayed.

Chase Ballou (413-637-2133; 305 Pittsfield-Lenox Rd.) Women's clothing, dressy to casual; and shoes, lingerie, sleepwear, and accessories. A large selection, frequent sales, and personable salespeople, too. Smaller shop in Pittsfield, Allendale.

Chessa & Co. (413-637-3669; 28 Walker St.) Women's fashionable and good-quality footwear in varying widths, with selected clothes and accessories. The For Kids Only section includes Capezio, Mootsies Kids, Rachel.

Clothes Works (413-442-7782; Rte. 7) Discounted name brands like BD Baggies, casual clothing; gifts and wicker.

Jonathan Sternfield

Evviva (413-637-9875; 18 Walker St.) Sophisticated dresses, separates, and accessories by designers "well known and undiscovered."

Glad Rags (413-637-0088; 76 Church St.) Women's contemporary casual styles with a funky attitude. Lots of natural fibers and hats, scarves, and other accessories for that '90s neo-romantic look.

K's Coats (413-443-5358; 600 Pittsfield-Lenox Rd.) Ladies' coats, dress and casual, in a variety of styles, with designer labels like J.G. Hook and Jones of New York. Across from **Michael's Shoes** (413-442-3464), with footwear for men and women, handbags.

Leather Loft (413-637-1108; Lenox House Country Shops) Fine leather at discount prices, with briefcases, handbags, coats, luggage.

London Fog Factory Store (413-499-2779; 615 Pittsfield-Lenox Rd.) Jackets, sweaters, other clothes, not to mention raincoats.

Mary Posts Ltd. (413-637-4767; Lenox House Country Shops) Aerobic wear is their specialty.

Purple Plume (413-637-3442; 39 Church St.) A large selection of fun and stylish clothing, featuring the latest looks and natural fibers. The amazing array of accessories includes jewelry, headbands, and scarves. Gifts, too.

Talbot's (413-637-3576; 46 Walker St.) Classic women's clothing and accessories, and a special Petites section.

Tanglewool, Inc. (413-637-0900; 57 Church St.) Sophisticated clothing, jewelry, shoes, handknits for the fashion-conscious. Also in Great Barrington (413-528-6162; 296 Main St.)

The Knitting Store and Weaver's Fancy (413-637-2013; 69 Church St.) Unique hand-made clothing and accessories. Wearables include scarves and jack-

Cultural Shopping

Many Berkshire museums, and other institutions devoted to the arts and culture or to historical preservation, fund and publicize their operations with their own gift and book shops. They are excellent sources for unique Berkshire gifts, books about a wide range of historical subjects and the visual and performing arts, and fun and educational items for children. Institution members often get discounts at the shop.

Berkshire Museum Shop (413-443-7469; 39 South St., Pittsfield) An excellent array of items reflecting the scope of the museum's collections: books, prints, cards, plates and other home accessories, international crafts, and jewelry; and a treasure-trove of small and creative items for children, from the artistic to the scientific. Shop staff, mostly volunteers, are helpful and personable.

The Clark Museum Store is not only at the Clark Art Institute (413-458-9545; 225 South St., Williamstown) but also has an outpost at the Lenox House Country Shops (413-637-4022; Pittsfield-Lenox Rd., Lenox). The shop at the museum is larger, but both of them feature items based on the Clark's collection and those of museums and art galleries around the world: cards, posters, and prints, matted and framed; fine art books; jewelry; and great toys from basic to upscale.

Ex Libris: The Lenox Library Shop (413-637-0197; 18 Main St., Lenox) This pocket-sized shop offers cards, postcards, toys, T-shirts, bookplates, bookmarks, games, tote bags, sealing wax, and various Berkshire-related items.

Hancock Shaker Village Shop (413-443-0188; Rte. 20, Pittsfield) The spacious gift shop offers books, clocks, Shaker reproduction furniture and other items, in kits or assembled — even the Shaker cloak. Prints of drawings of the Hancock Shaker community and of Shaker "spirit drawings," too. Wonderful children's toys and kits. Open seasonally; and open for some weeks in Nov.—Dec.

The Norman Rockwell Museum (413-298-4100, Rte. 183, Stockbridge) A well-designed center for books, prints, and cards; the children's section has books and toys and art-related things to do. There are limited-edition artist's proofs signed by Rockwell; and there are even mugs and T-shirts.

Additional cultural shopping options include the shop at *Chesterwood*, particularly for their selection of National Trust publications; *Tanglewood*'s gift shop, with lots of Tanglewood-logo wearables and other items; the *Arrowhead Museum* shop, with books about Melville and county history, and cards, gifts; the *Garden Gift Shop* at the *Berkshire Botanical Garden; The Mount* (former home of Edith Wharton and current home of Shakespeare & Co.); the *Berkshire Theater Festival*; and even the *Berkshire Scenic Railway Museum* (books, toys, T-shirts).

ets knitted from rayon chenille in stunning colors — they feel like you're wearing a soft, warm rainbow. Stylish sweaters, too. Knitting supplies, patterns, all colors and kinds of yarns (alpaca, cashmere, wool, mohair, camel hair, angora, etc.).

PITTSFIELD

Champion Factory Outlet (413-442-1332; 454 W. Housatonic St./Pittsfield Plaza) Sweatshirts and turtlenecks at discount prices, and other athletic apparel.

Cosmetic Design & Color Accents (413-443-0872, 89 North St.) Designer scarves, hats, belts, jewelry, lingerie, and various accessories for the boudoir, including English toiletries and other cosmetics. Instruction in make-up; color analysis.

The Cottage (413-447-9643; 31 South St./Downtown Pittsfield) A popular shop where women's clothing shares space with home and gift items (see below). Styles range from Liz Claiborne to Putumayo; you'll find suits, dresses, separates, casual wear, partywear, and accessories. Also in Williamstown (413-458-4305; 24 Water St.).

Greystone Gardens (413-442-9291; 436 North St.) Victorian and vintage clothing, accessories, jewelry, and linens, for men and women. The long, high-ceilinged shop has floral carpeting, curtained dressing rooms with antique mirrors, stacks of hat boxes, swanky fashion prints, and vintage songs being crooned in the background — the perfect setting for '40s evening gowns, sporty rayon dresses, lacy camisoles, vintage tuxedos, top hats, tweed jackets and coats, bowling shirts, fringed scarves, and more, all eminently wearable. Owner Carla Lund, creator of this outpost of nostalgia, is a genius at putting it all together. Cards, soaps, and other niceties, too. Don't miss it.

Richard's Menswear (413-445-7704; Allendale Shopping Center) Woolrich items and a good selection of casual shirts.

The Stock Room (413-445-5500; 440 Merrill Rd.) Liquidators offer clothing from upscale department stores at a discount, from blue jeans to party dresses. You never know what you might find. For the whole family; some non-clothing items, too.

Steven Valenti (413-443-2569; 157 North St.) Menswear for the '90s in a well-appointed store, with up-to-date styles by Perry Ellis, Alexander Julian, and other contemporary designers. Shirts, sweaters, suits, jackets, and coats here feature fine fabrics and colors from subtle to wild. An outstanding collection of silk ties.

North County

WILLIAMSTOWN

House of Walsh (413-458-8088; 39 Spring St.) Classic clothes for men and women in a classic setting, with sportswear, accessories, gifts, and Williams College items, too.

Fabrics and Weavers

For your home or for yourself, two sources of special textiles and fabrics:

Skilled hands and tools of the trade, at Undermountain Weavers, Housatonic.

Jonathan Sternfield

Maplewood Fabrics (413-229-8767; Rte. 7A, Ashley Falls) Liberty of London, Scalamandre, Schumacher and other fine fabrics in a low-key setting.

Undermountain Weavers (413-274-6565; Rte. 41, West Stockbridge/RR1, Box 26, Housatonic) In a restored barn, on century-old hand looms, traditional Shetland Island patterns are taking shape. Purchase by the yard, or tailoring can be arranged.

Salvatore's (413-458-3625; 42 Spring St.) Women's and teen's fashions and accessories, with friendly help.

Zanna (413-458-9858; 41 Spring St.) Contemporary women's clothes and accessories, featuring natural fibers and up-to-the-minute looks. **Zanna Shoes** at 48 Spring St. (413-458-2161).

GIFT & SPECIALTY SHOPS

South County

GREAT BARRINGTON

Berkshire Cupboard (413-528-1880; 297 Main St.) The Berkshires in a store — regionally produced food items, books, prints, maps, cards, T-shirts, and more; a great source for a true Berkshire souvenir.

Church Street Trading Company (413-528-6120; 4 Railroad St.) A trendy mix of antiques, natural-fiber clothes, nature-oriented cosmetics, pottery, crafts, and various lifestyle accessories, attractively arranged.

Crystal Essence (413-528-2595; 39 Railroad St.) Geodes, jewelry, gemstones, ceramics, clothes, books, and other items for enhancing a New Age lifestyle.

Jillifer's Emporium (413-528-5277; Jenifer House Commons, Stockbridge Rd.) Gifts and treats such as fragrant soaps and candles, toys, country-American and gourmet-international treats, including cookies and candy.

Primrose Cottage (413-229-8401; Jenifer House Commons, Stockbridge Rd.) In this little enchanted cottage, there's a gravel floor, soft lighting, and lovely dried flowers everywhere: hanging in bunches from the beams overhead, and in swags, topiaries, and other imaginative arrangements. They're from local gardens and from the wild. Don't miss the signature potpourri, "Berkshire Woods." Special orders; workshops on arranging, wreath-making.

T.P. Saddle Blanket and Trading Co. (413-528-6500; 304 Main St.) An outpost for the Southwest look, from cowboy-motif pajamas to saddleblankets for your living room, with a colorful abundance of boots, belts, pillows, books, candles, bedding, dishware, shirts, vests, and furniture accents.

SOUTH EGREMONT

The Rookery (413-528-3323; Rte. 23) Concrete garden and lawn ornaments and accessories. Create an outdoor bench with two pedestals and a top with classical motifs, as a focal point in your garden. Or a cast pig or rabbit will also do nicely. Family-run for 65 years, and they're very helpful. It's a great place.

STOCKBRIDGE

Accents (413-298-3882; Main St./PO Box 178) Gifts, antiques, and art imaginatively chosen and displayed in a lofty, sunny room. Gourmet foods, kitchen gear, pillows, tapestries for your wall or table, and more. An excellent source for a house gift, or for yourself.

Pink Kitty (413-298-3134; at the Red Lion Inn) A lovely shop with gifts, cards, and accessories, featuring Berkshire items.

Seven Arts (413-298-5101; Main St.) Asian carvings share space with Rockwell T-shirts, funky jewelry, cotton clothes and throws, other natural fiber clothing options, nostalgic advertising plaques, Mexican-style glassware in lots of colors, moccasins, pillows, and quilts.

Williams & Son Country Store (413-298-3016; Main St.) A Stockbridge institution, with jams and jellies, soaps, candy, gourmet foods, glassware, gifts, cards, and various nostalgia items. You'll enjoy the old tins displayed behind the counter.

SOUTH LEE

Naomi's Herbs (413-243-3675; Rte. 102) *See description under Naomi's Herbs in Lenox.*

WEST STOCKBRIDGE

Hotchkiss Mobiles Gallery (413-232-0200; 8 Center St.) Open Sat., Sun.; or call for an appointment. Contemporary mobiles for your home or office.

Laughing Crow (413-232-0233; 127 State Line Rd./Rte. 102) This New Age general store stocks an eclectic array of vintage clothes, cards and tapes, organic and natural snack foods and tobacco, and Native American crafts. Also featured are jewelry items, some created by owner Khat; beads and beading supplies, and classes in beading and jewelry repair. A little off the beaten track, but worth a visit.

Central County

LENOX

Body & Soul (413-637-3014; 63 Church St.) Massages, facials, skin care, natural body care products, gifts. Aromatherapy and spa treatments, too. Also in Great Barrington at 34 Railroad St. (413-528-6465).

Celtic Origins (413-637-1296; Curtis Shops/Walker St.) Irish and Scottish clothes and accessories, for men, women, and children. Jewelry, cassette tapes.

Danaë Boudoir and Bath (413-637-2545; Curtis Shops/Walker St.) Pampering as an art form, with perfume bottles and other glass art, jewelry and accessories, fine towels, oils, all in an elegant setting.

Mah-Kee-Nac Trading Co. (413-637-0424; 2 Housatonic St.) Lenox goes West, with this tribute to Native American and buckaroo-inspired gear: clothing, jewelry, Stewart Boots, hats, belts, gourmet food, pottery, kachinas, and other home and fashion accessories.

Mary Stuart (413-637-0340; 81 Church St.) Accessories for gracious country living, including china, glassware, linen, needlepoint, antiques, and toiletries; lingerie and sleepwear; books and cards. Beautiful storybook-style clothing for infants and toddlers upstairs.

Naomi's Herbs (413-637-0616; 11 Housatonic St.) Dried herbs and flowers fill the rafters of this charming shop. There's an assortment of potpourri fragrances, and ingredients to make your own. Teas, bath blends, massage oil, and floral arrangements are also offered here as "resources for a healthy and beautiful life." Also in S. Lee (413-243-3675; Rte. 102).

Ormsby's (413-637-3591; 57 Church St.) A fabulous card selection, plus home accessories, T-shirts, sweatshirts, toys for all ages, and picnic ware.

Outpost Specialties (413-637-3001; Lenox House Country Shops) Sheepskin items here include slippers, hats, mittens, auto seat covers, and the sheepskins themselves. Deerskin, lambskin, and other leather items, too. Friendly and knowledgeable help.

Rice's Country Store (413-637-0883; Lenox House Country Shops) Something old and something new. Small antiques and collectibles, including prints, books, and an assortment of oil lamps, some one of a kind, share space with candles, home accessories, potpourri, tea, candy, snacks, ice cream, and cold drinks.

The Silver Sleigh (413-637-3522; Lenox House Country Shops, Pittsfield-Lenox Rd.) Complete and imaginative Christmas accessorizing, plus gifts for all seasons.

Villager Gifts (413-637-9866; 88 Main St.) A engaging variety of gifts and collectibles, featuring jewelry, pottery, stationery, candles, cards, and particularly cunning glass boxes.

Write-n-Style (413-637-0851, fax 413-637-8934; Lenox House Country Shops) Pens and pencils of every description, from fine to funky; cards, stationery, and other paper products; leather items, frames, and creative things for kids.

Yankee Candle (413-499-3626; 639 Pittsfield-Lenox Rd.) Candles, gifts, bath accessories. Dip your own candles, too.

PITTSFIELD

The Cottage (413-447-9643; 31 South St./Downtown Pittsfield) Stylish tableware, including glasses and goblets and vases and bottles, napkins and placemats, baskets, gourmet foods, frames, soaps, along with clothes and jewelry. A deservedly popular shop. Also in Williamstown (413-458-4305; 24 Water St.).

Pasko Frame & Gift Center (413-442-2680; 243 North St.) Berkshire landscapes by Walter Pasko, the Berkshire map, superb custom framing, prints and posters, and gifts and handcrafts from around the world.

North County

NORTH ADAMS

Heritage Country Store (413-664-4886; Western Gateway Heritage State Park) Country gifts and collectibles, such as candles, Christmas ornaments, even a Bear Boutique. Gift baskets of local food products and a Bake Shop.

The North Adams General Store (413-663-3907; Rte. 8) Ice cream, kitchenware, old-fashioned candy and gum, potpourri, candles, soap, and a fun variety of other little gifts and toys.

WILLIAMSTOWN

Berkshire Treasure House (413-458-2434; 20 Spring St.) Out-of-the-ordinary educational toys, handcrafted jewelry, unusual cards, soaps and accessories.

HANDCRAFTS

See Chapter Four, *Culture,* for additional listings of galleries with handcrafted art.

South County

GREAT BARRINGTON

Evergreen (413-528-0511; 291 Main St.) These contemporary American crafts include vases, tableware, floral-papered accessories, clocks, and handcrafted jewelry.

October Mountain Stained Glass (413-528-6681; 343 Main St.) A vivid array of lampshades, window panels, perfume bottles of etched glass, paperweights, and glass jewelry. Custom design work is a specialty, including commissions for home owners, builders, architects. Beveling, sandblasting, repairs, and supplies are also offered. Closed Mon.

Wonderful Things (413-528-2473; 232 Stockbridge Rd.) Handcrafted gifts, or make your own with yarn, needlework accessories, beads, feathers, stencils, paint, other craft supplies.

HOUSATONIC

The Great Barrington Pottery (413-274-6259; Rte. 41) Potter Richard Bennett uses a Japanese woodburning kiln for firing pottery designs that combine

Master potter, Richard Bennett, working the clay at his Great Barrington Pottery.

Jonathan Sternfield

East and West. In a beautiful garden setting, visit the pottery showroom or participate in an ancient tea ceremony. (See "Seasonal Events" in Chapter Four, *Culture.*)

MONTEREY

Joyous Spring Pottery (413-528-4115; Art School Rd.) Potter Michael Marcus fires his climbing kiln once a year for a 10-day period for his Japanese-inspired unglazed ceramics.

SHEFFIELD

Fellerman Glass Works (413-229-8533; 534 S. Main St./Rte. 7) Glass art here includes perfume bottles, jewelry, vases, and paperweights — try one of these on a small light-box for a glowing miniature universe. Large glass bowls in organic shapes and glass sculpture, too. Call to find out when you can watch glass artists at work. Closed Mon.

Hot Glass Studios (413-229-2788; 1592 County Rd./Rte. 7) Contemporary and traditional glass — fused, sandblasted, stained — in a new showroom with skylights and vaulted ceilings for dramatic display. Art glass, windows, mirrors, lamps, boxes, tables, glass beads, and jewelry; custom designs and Tiffany-type glass. Classes, supplies, tools.

Sheffield Pottery (413-229-7700; Rte. 7) New England potters' ware, including mugs, tea pots, platters, tureens; terra cotta items. Supplies and equipment.

SOUTHFIELD

Artisans Gallery (413-229-3223; Main St./Rte. 272 at the Buggy Whip Factory) Fine regional handcrafts that blend art with utility in the form of pottery, textiles, wood, and more.

STOCKBRIDGE

Barong Imports (413-298-4281; Stockbridge Industrial Park off Rte. 102) A warehouse of Asian art: sculpture, clothing, antique furniture, and exotic carvings, large and small, including temple doors, masks, Japanese stone garden pagodas, icons, and animal figures. Flying mermaids and other creatures that can be suspended from a ceiling will delight and possibly terrify. Associated with **Asian Antiques** at the Jenifer House Commons (see above).

Marsters Pottery (413-298-5240; Elm St.) A small shop with big ideas: salt-and-pepper shakers masquerading as lifelike ceramic fruit; teapots dancing with their creamers and sugar bowls. Owner Peter Marsters' stoneware and Raku pottery will also delight. Or how about a handcrafted glass "kiss" that looks like the chocolate kind? Many of these clever items are made locally in New England. And, a section of great toys.

WEST STOCKBRIDGE

Hoffman Pottery (413-232-4646; #103 Rte. 41/Gt. Barrington Rd.) Hand-thrown, hand-painted functional ware in bright colors.

New England Stained Glass Studios (413-232-7181; 5 Center St./PO Box 381) A specialist in Tiffany-style lamps. Admire the giant mushrooms and flowers in the windows next to the showroom, and a lion set in a door, on the way to the main entrance. Hundreds of lampshades; windows and other items, too. Custom work on a limited basis.

Central County

LENOX

Brushwood Studio Collection (413-637-2836; Brushwood Farm) This abundant collection of "cross-cultural art" includes high quality paintings, jewelry, primitives, rugs, icons, textiles, masks, pottery, carved wooden animals, and other sculpture.

Concepts of Art (413-637-4845; 67 Church St.) Fine crafts and local artisans, with lamps and other glass, wood sculpture, jewelry, throws.

Stevens & Conron Gallery (413-637-0739, 716-652-9424; Curtis Shops/5 Walker St.) Fine art and rugs, handhooked and handwoven.

Wall Quilts (413-637-2286; 26 Cliffwood St.) Contemporary and imaginative wall hangings, in a variety of techniques: quilted, appliqued, embroi-

The art and architecture of Brushwood Studio, Lenox.

Jonathan Sternfield

dered. Daily 1–5 in July, Aug.; closed Weds.; Sunday 10–2, and by appointment. Call to confirm hours.

PITTSFIELD

Potala (413-443-5568; 148 North St.) Asian arts and crafts, including rugs of all sizes, baskets, carvings large and small, clothes made from antique textiles, silk scarves, jewelry, lacquerware, arrayed bazaar-style on the hardwood floor and brick walls. Also in Great Barrington (413-528-2723; 285 Main St.).

North County

NORTH ADAMS

Up Country Artisans Craft Gallery (413-663-5802; Rte. 8/Heritage State Park) Once a coal storage building for the passenger and freight trains that stopped here, now a spacious showplace for pieces by New England artists and craftspeople: wood sculpture, pottery, stained glass, quilts, furniture, textiles. Daily May–Dec.; call to confirm hours Jan.–Apr.

WILLIAMSTOWN

Pottery Plus (413-458-2143; 25 Spring St.) Creative handcrafted jewelry, glass, wooden items, and, of course, pottery. Imaginative and sophisticated wares from craftspeople all over the U.S., including bird houses, goblets, and candles; all attractively displayed.

The Potter's Wheel (413-458-9523; 84 Water St.) A craft gallery with sensational stoneware, ironware, porcelain; gold, silver and cloisonné jewelry; and art objects by leading craftspeople throughout the US. The spacious showroom, perched above the Green River, is filled with the sound of the rushing water below.

HOME & KITCHEN

South County

GREAT BARRINGTON

Berkshire Cottage (413-528-0135; 290 Main St.) Cooking and dining ware for the country chef, featuring innovative kitchen equipment and imported tableware. Recently noted were clever contemporary tea kettles, thermal stainless steel espresso cups, and lots of other accessories for Euro-style coffee lovers. They also offer gift packages of Berkshire gourmet products and accessories, named after, not surprisingly, Berkshire "cottages."

DeWoolfson Down (413-528-1200, 800-554-3693; Jenifer House Commons, Stockbridge Rd.) Fine bed linens and accessories, such as down comforters, pillows, sheets, duvet covers, throws. Featherbeds, too. Fabrics include Egyptian cotton, cotton damask from Germany, and other European imports.

Gatsby's (413-528-9455; 25 Railroad St.) In addition to wearables, you'll find futons, wicker and other furniture, bedclothes, and housewares.

Out Of Hand (413-528-3791; 81 Main St.) Every size, shape, and color of basket you could ever need or imagine — one upstairs room is full of them — plus rugs, throws, pillows, glassware in a rainbow of colors, toys, candlesticks, clothing. A great place for accessorizing your kitchen or sun porch. Or dining room or bedroom. Or . . . .

Resources (413-528-4002; 312 Main St.) Contemporary kitchen and dining room gear, cookbooks, gourmet foods.

The Lamplighter (413-528-3448; 162 Main St.) An exceptional lighting store with a wide selection and knowledgeable staff. Chandeliers, floor and table lamps, and outdoor lighting in all shapes, sizes, and styles, from Colonial to Art Deco to contemporary. Shades and other accessories.

Vajra Carpets (413-528-0656; 8 Lake Buel Rd.) A gallery and studio for handmade woolen carpets, designed in the Berkshires and handknotted in the Himalayas. Custom design, or design one yourself. Open Sat., Sun., Mon., or by appointment.

STOCKBRIDGE

Country Curtains (413-298-5565; at the Red Lion Inn) Curtains and matching bedding are displayed in a series of bountifully accessorized room settings. You can select from a variety of styles and fabrics. This Stockbridge shop (originally located in a building down the street) is the one where this nationally known store began.

WEST STOCKBRIDGE

Anderson & Sons' Shaker Tree (413-232-7072; Rte. 41 in downtown West Stockbridge) Exquisite Shaker reproduction furniture, with quilts, herbs, and other wares. The craftsmanship is so highly regarded that the Andersons were entrusted with permission to measure the Shaker pieces in the noted Andrews' collection at the Metropolitan Museum of Art. The showroom is not always open; call ahead.

Central County

HANCOCK

Hancock Union Store (413-738-5072; Main St./Box 1009) Fine reproductions of American cabinet furniture, and tables, chairs, sofas, beds, in Queen Anne, Shaker, Federal, and Chippendale styles. Michael Boulay, cabinet maker.

LENOX

Ali Baba's Tent (413-637-4363; 98 Main St., behind Berkshire Leather) Oriental rugs, Afghan and Turkish kilims, Pawley hammocks, Shaker-style rocking chairs, and other handmade items.

Different Drummer Kitchen (413-637-0606; 568 Pittsfield-Lenox Rd.) All manner of equipment and accessories for kitchen and table, from pasta pots to measuring spoons.

Kaoud Oriental Rugs (413-499-5405; 598 Pittsfield-Lenox Rd.) Antique and "semi-antique" rugs, hand-knotted 100% wool; "authentic village rugs."

Tassels (413-637-2400, fax 413-637-1836; Brushwood Farm) Fine furniture and accessories in room settings in a variety of styles. A division of Designers Furniture Showcase, Ltd.

PITTSFIELD

Haddad's Rug Company (413-443-4747; 32 Bank Row/Park Square) Specialists in Oriental and Oriental-style rugs, new and antique, plus carpeting and other types of rugs.

Linen Closet (413-499-4200; 137 North St.) Fine sheets of every size and description, down comforters, throws, pillows, towels, various accessories, presided over by helpful sales people.

Paul Rich & Sons Home Furnishings (413-443-6467, 800-723-7424; 242 North St.) A large and well-chosen selection of traditional, contemporary and country furniture, and accent pieces.

Your Kitchen (413-442-0602; 170 North St.) You'll wish it were, with gourmet pots and pans, coffee and coffee equipment, cookbooks, and tools and gadgets. For the gourmet and the everyday.

North County

ADAMS

Interior Alternative (413-743-1986; 5 Hoosac St.) A home furnishings center with seconds and discontinued famous-brand upholstery and curtain fabric, wallpaper, Oriental carpets, hooked rugs, area rugs, bedspreads, comforters, pillows. Two huge floors in this old mill.

Old Stone Mill (413-743-1042; Rte. 8) Factory outlet for famous brands of wallpaper, fabric for upholstery and drapes. Wallpaper is hand-printed and machine printed. Over-runs, seconds, close-outs up to 70% off.

NORTH ADAMS

International Outlet (413-664-4580; 192 State St./Rte. 8) Despite the small warehouse ambiance, a good source for crystal, glassware, dinnerware, kitchen utensils, wicker furniture, rugs, brass, table and kitchen linen, candles, pottery, cookware. Terra cotta pots.

JEWELRY

For additional jewelry options, check the listings in "Antiques" and "Gifts and Handcrafts."

Heirlooms Jewelry Classics (413-298-4436; The Mews, Stockbridge) A glittering treasure-box of a shop, with antique and estate jewelry, and museum reproduction pieces.

L'Artisanat (232-7187; Main St., West Stockbridge) Elegant one-of-a-kind custom jewelry pieces; artisan's shop on premises.

L&R Wise Goldsmiths (413-637-1589; 81 Church St., Lenox) Richard Wise finds gemstones from all over the world — traveling recently in Brazil, Africa, and Tahiti — and offers them superbly crafted in contemporary fine art jewelry. Imaginative and unique combinations of gems and precious metals. Custom design service. Closed Mon. in winter.

SHOPPING STREETS, MEWS, & MALLS

Shopping in style in Stockbridge, at the Mews.

Jonathan Sternfield

Many of the shops described in this chapter are, happily, on Berkshire downtown Main Streets, where real people actually walk along the sidewalks, go to the hardware store and post office, get books at the library, pick up a few groceries, run into friends, and stop for lunch or coffee or ice cream, against a backdrop of mostly 19th-century civic architecture, highlighted by a few notable historic buildings. For beyond-the-downtown shopping experiences, a short and usually scenic drive will take you to clusters of destination shops, some in genuinely venerable buildings, others where the quaintness is of more recent vintage. And yes, there's even a mall. Following is a roundup of where to find your favorite shops and shopping settings. More detailed listings of many of the establishments in these centers may be found in relevant sections of Chapters 4–7, *Culture, Restaurants & Food Purveyors, Recreation,* and *Shopping.*

South County

Southfield's Buggy Whip Factory (Main St./Rte. 272) The drive there takes you through classic New England scenery. The huge, two-century-old building houses two antiques centers, the work of a varied group of artisans and some of their studios, and factory outlets for sweaters, handbags, and children's clothing and bedding. You'll also find displays about buggy whip history, places for kids to play outside, and delicious dining options at the Cottage Café.

Downtown Great Barrington is a happening place, with a true Main Street atmosphere created by a combination of several shops and boutiques, antiques stores, bookstores, an outstanding selection of eateries, a first-rate coffee place, and the grand old Mahaiwe Theatre, for current movies and special live performances. The action centers around Railroad St. and Main St., and takes in other side streets, too. Great Barrington hosts downtown food and music events throughout the year.

Jenifer House Commons (Rte. 7, Stockbridge Rd., Gt. Barrington) is just north of Great Barrington's center. This cluster of multilevel barns and buildings — some old and some new — houses an extensive group of antiques dealers' wares, a vast assortment of collectibles, leather goods, dried flowers, Asian and contemporary art, fine linen and bedding, and countless other gifts and goodies. Do lunch there or nearby. Open every day.

Main St., Stockbridge still looks like — and is — Norman Rockwell territory, even though the Rockwell Museum has moved (but not far; see *Culture*). The welcoming expanse of the Red Lion Inn shares the scene with the gracious library, an excellent market, and several stores. Connected to Main St. is *The Mews*, a cozy cul-de-sac of shops offering clothes, jewelry, and gifts. Many Stockbridge shops offer Rockwelliana in one form or another, from T-shirts to signed prints. Also around the corner from Main St. is Elm St., with more shops, eateries, and the post office. Note: Main St. and The Mews can seem overrun on high season weekends; come during the week, then, if you can.

A side trip to the small downtown of *West Stockbridge* will reward you with several galleries, good restaurants and cafes, and antiques — not to mention a hardware store and a shop devoted to flavoring extracts. The gallery scene offers outdoor sculptures on display, hand-crafted jewelry, mobiles, stained glass, and reproduction Shaker furniture, and many other options for contemporary art and craft work. A vintage depot houses a cafe and studios; a Shaker mill building is home to antiques. A small concentration of excellent restaurants will please everybody from the hamburger-and-pizza crowd to the international gourmet.

Central County

Downtown Lenox still maintains a "real" downtown flavor, though the boutique and gallery contingent seems to be in the ascendancy. The appealing variety of architecture — neoclassic and Victorian-cottage predominate — is home to inns and taverns, several dining options, an exceptional library and bookstore, and those shops and galleries: a number of clothing shops, mostly for women, covers the style territory from fine to funky, from classic to casual; art and handcraft galleries offer Berkshire scenes and world-renowned jewelry and other creations. The *Curtis Shops* — in an imposing hotel building, the place to stay in the 19th century — also is home to a mix of fine shops and galleries.

Just north of Lenox on Rte. 7/Pittsfield-Lenox Rd. are the *Brushwood Farm Shops* and the *Lenox House Country Shops.* Brushwood Farm is a complex of barnlike buildings of specialty shops, with antiques, interior decorating and design, an educational toy store for kids of all ages, places to eat, and a craft and painting gallery featuring Asian pieces. *Lenox House Country Shops* (413-637-1341; Pittsfield-Lenox Rd./Rtes. 7 & 20) mix specialty shops and factory outlets; the latter include Bass, Corning/Revere, Harvé Benard, Izod, Van Heusen, L'Eggs/Hanes/Bali, Boston Traders, Jackeroos, and more. Specialty shops offer leather and sheepskin items, stationery and fine writing instruments, jewelry, outdoor gear, and Christmas accessories. A big destination for many visitors.

Downtown Pittsfield was once the commercial and civic hub of the Berkshires, and though the glory of its main thoroughfare, North Street, has somewhat faded, it still hosts a number of services and shops, including excellent sources for books, kitchen gear and housewares, Asian crafts, men's and women's clothing and shoes, fine bedding, vintage clothing, and sporting goods. The downtown area includes several large churches and buildings that will interest the architecture buff, plus the Berkshire Museum and the Berkshire Athenaeum (the public library). You might catch a free concert downtown in the summer.

Lanesborough's Berkshire Mall can supply your basic mall needs, with a multiscreen cinema complex, clothing and shoe stores, dozens of places to eat, two bookstores, and so forth.

North County

The *Western Gateway Heritage State Park* in *North Adams* (413-663-6312) is a former railyard for the Boston and Maine line, six buildings on the National Register of Historic Places. Once used for storing freight and coal, the buildings now house various shops, galleries, and eateries, and a Visitor Center with historic and tourist information. Off Rte. 8 between State and Furnace streets.

Spring Street and *Water Street* in *Williamstown* roughly parallel each other and are across from the main Williams College campus. Both easily walkable, they offer handcrafts, clothing, books, tapes and CDs, places to eat, antiques and accessories, sports gear, and all the Williams memorabilia you'll ever need. And don't miss *Phillips General Store* (413-458-3723; 16 Water St.) for bird feeders, baskets, teapots, plastic flamingoes, brass door knockers, pliers, and friendly help.

Near Berkshire County

A recommended destination just outside the county is *Chatham, New York.* Main Street shops include the *Dakota* for clothes; the *Chatham Bookstore; Pavanne* jewelry and gifts; the *Handcrafters* for fine crafts; and the fantastico *Italian Accent* for paper, glass, jewelry, pottery, dishware. The *White Linen* outlet store (2 Park Row) offers seconds or irregulars of beautiful upscale linens and fine fabrics.

CHAPTER EIGHT
Practical Matters
INFORMATION

Checking the way, at the Stockbridge Information Booth.

Jonathan Sternfield

We offer here a little encyclopedia of useful information to help facilitate everyday life for locals and vacation time for visitors in the Berkshires. This chapter provides information on the following topics.

AMBULANCE, FIRE, POLICE

The general emergency number for Pittsfield and a number of other Berkshire communities is **911**. This "enhanced-911" service is part of a statewide system being put in place. Consult an up-to-date phone book for a list of the communities that already have this service, as well as local emergency numbers for towns that are not yet linked to the service.

In an emergency situation anywhere in the county, dial "**0**" and the operator will connect you directly to the correct agency.

Another county-wide set of emergency numbers is:

Fire	413-445-4559
Poison Control	800-682-9211
Police	413-442-0512
Rape	413-443-3521

AREA CODES, TELEPHONE EXCHANGES, ZIP CODES, TOWN HALLS/LOCAL GOVERNMENT

AREA CODES

The Area Code for all of Berkshire County is 413. Area codes for adjacent counties are as follows.

Massachusetts

Franklin County (most towns), Hampshire, and Hampden Counties — 413.

Connecticut

Litchfield County and all of Connecticut — 203.

New York

Columbia and Rensselaer Counties — 518.

Vermont

Bennington County and all of Vermont — 802.

TOWN HALLS

Except for Adams, North Adams, and Pittsfield, each of which has a City Hall, all Berkshire communities have Town Halls as the seats of local government. Most townships are governed by Boards of Selectmen; a few have Town Managers. For general information, call the Town Offices at the following numbers or write to the Town Clerk, c/o Town Hall in the village in question.

Town	Telephone Exchange	Zip Code	Town Hall Office
Adams	743	01220	413-743-8300
Alford	528	01230	413-528-4536
Ashley Falls	229	01222	413-229-8752 (Sheffield)
Becket	623	01223	413-623-8934
Berkshire County Commissioners	Pittsfield	01201	413-448-8424
Cheshire	743	01225	413-743-1690
Clarksburg	663	01247	413-663-7940
Dalton	684	01226	413-684-6103
Egremont	528	01258	413-528-0182
Florida	662	01247	413-662-2448
Glendale	298	01229	413-298-4714 (Stockbridge)
Gt. Barrington	528	01230	413-528-3140
Hancock	738	01237	413-738-5225
Hinsdale	655	01235	413-655-2301
Housatonic	274	01236	413-528-3140 (Gt. Barrington)
Lanesborough	442, 443, 447, 499	01237	413-442-1167
Lee	243	01238	413-243-5505
Lenox	637	01240	413-637-5506
Lenoxdale	637	01242	413-637-5506 (Lenox)
Middlefield	623	01243 (Becket)	413-623-8934
Mill River	229	01244	413-229-8116 (New Marlborough)
Monterey	528	01245	413-528-1443
Mt. Washington	528	01258	413-528-2839
New Ashford	458	01267	413-458-9341 (Williamstown)
New Marlborough	229	01244	413-229-8116

N. Adams	662, 663, 664	01247	413-662-3015
N. Egremont	528	01252	413-528-0182 (Egremont)
Otis	269	01253	413-269-0100
Peru	655	01235	413-655-8027
Pittsfield	442, 443, 445 446, 447, 448 494, 499	01201 01202 (Post Office)	413-499-9361
Richmond	698	01254	413-698-3882
Sandisfield	258	01255	413-258-4506
Savoy	743	01256	413-743-4290
Sheffield	229	01257	413-229-8752
S. Egremont	528	01258	413-528-0182 (Egremont)
S. Lee	243	01260 (Lee)	413-243-5505
Southfield	229	01259	413-229-8116 (New Marlborough)
Stockbridge	298	01262	413-298-4714
Tyringham	243	01264	413-243-1749
Washington	623	01223	413-623-8878
W. Stockbridge	232	01266	413-232-0301
Williamstown	458, 597	01267	413-458-9341
Windsor	684	01270	413-684-3878

BANKS

Several Berkshire County banks are linked electronically to banking systems elsewhere in the United States. If you are visiting here, you may find these options quite helpful — especially if you need extra cash or traveler's checks. It's best to inquire with your home bank to see which system you can use and which Berkshire bank can serve you.

Adams Co-operative Bank
   93 Park St., Adams; 413-743-0001. Branch: N. Adams.
Berkshire County Savings Bank
   Park Square, Pittsfield: 413-443-5601. Branches: Gt. Barrington, N. Adams.
City Savings Bank
   116 North St., Pittsfield; 413-443-4421; 800-292-6634. Branch: Gt. Barrington.

Jonathan Sternfield

First Agricultural Bank
  99 West St., Pittsfield. 413-499-3000; Branches: N. Adams, Adams, Dalton, Gt. Barrington, Sheffield, Williamstown.
First National Bank of the Berkshires
  76 Park St., Lee; 413-243-0115; Branches: Gt. Barrington, Otis.
Fleet Bank
  66 West St., Pittsfield; 413-447-6149. Branches: Gt. Barrington, N. Adams, Stockbridge.
Great Barrington Savings Bank
  Main St., Gt. Barrington; 413-528-1190. Branches: Lee, Sheffield, W. Stockbridge.
Lee Bank
  75 Park St., Lee; 413-243-0117. Branch: Stockbridge.
Lenox National Bank
  7 Main St., Lenox; 413-637-0017. Branch: Lenox-Pittsfield Rd., Lenox
Lenox Savings Bank
  35 Main St., Lenox; 413-637-0147. Branch: Holmes Rd.-Rte.7, Lenox
North Adams-Hoosac Savings Bank
  93 Main St., N. Adams; 413-663-5353.
Northeast Savings Bank
  5 North St., Pittsfield; 413-447-8400.
Pittsfield Co-operative Bank
  70 South St., Pittsfield; 413-447-7304. Branches: Dalton, Gt. Barrington.
South Adams Savings Bank
  2 Center St., Adams; 413-743-0040. Branches: Williamstown, Cheshire.

Williamstown Savings Bank
795 Main St., Williamstown; 413-458-8191.

BIBLIOGRAPHY

Here are two lists of books about the Berkshires, many of which we used in researching this book.

"Books You Can Buy" shows titles available either through Berkshire bookshops, bookstores elsewhere or from the publishers. For information on Berkshire booksellers, see "Bookstores" in Chapter Seven, *Shopping.*

"Books You Can Borrow" suggests a wealth of other reading in earlier publications now no longer for sale. Some of the more rarefied material on this list does not circulate outside the libraries, and its use may be restricted to those with professional credentials. Several popular items here will especially interest history buffs. The best sources for book borrowing are described under "Libraries" in Chapter Four, *Culture.*

Books You Can Buy

COOKBOOKS

Chase, Suzi Forbes. *The Red Lion Inn Cookbook.* Stockbridge: Berkshire House Publishers, 1992. 224 pp., photos, $24.95; pap., $14.95.

Cook, Janet, ed. *Berkshire Victuals.* Stockbridge: Berkshire County Historical Society, 1993. 208 pages, illus., $19.95. Historical and contemporary recipes.

Jacobs, Miriam. *Best Recipes of Berkshire Chefs.* Stockbridge: Berkshire House Publishers. 208 pp., illus., $12.95.

Williamstown Theatre Festival. *As You Like It.* Williamstown: Williamstown Theatre Festival Guild, 1993. 222 pp., illus, $15.00. Recipes from the festival's stars, directors, writers, and associates.

LITERARY WORKS

Howard, Walter. *Sisyphus in the Hayfield — Views of A Berkshire Farmer.* Cobble Press, 1988. 128 pp., photos, $14.

Melville, Herman. *Great Short Works of Herman Melville.* NY: Harper & Row, 1969. 507 pp., bibliog. $18.50.

Metcalf, Paul, ed. *October Mountain: An Anthology of Berkshire Writers.* Williamstown, MA: Mountain Press, 1992. 163 pp., $11.95, pap.

Nunley, Richard, ed. *The Berkshire Reader.* Stockbridge: Berkshire House Publishers, 1992. 544 pp., illus., $29.95.

Wharton, Edith. *A Backward Glance.* NY: Charles Scribner's Sons, 1985 reprint. 379 pp., index, $13.95, pap.

Wharton, Edith. *Ethan Frome.* NY: Scribner's, 1988 reprint. $5.95.

LOCAL HISTORIES

Burns, Deborah E. and Lauren R. Stevens. *Most Excellent Majesty: A History of Mount Greylock.* Stockbridge: Berkshire House Publishers, 128 pp., photos, $8.95.

Chapman, Gerard. *Eminent Berkshire Women.* Gt. Barrington: Attic Revivals Press, 1988. 32 pp., $5.00.

———. *A History of the Red Lion Inn in Stockbridge, Massachusetts.* Stockbridge: Red Lion Inn, 1987. 54 pp., illus., $12.00.

Drew, Bernard A. *A Berkshire Further Off the Trail.* Attic Revivals Press, 1992. 56 pp., illus., pap. $7.50.

———. *A History of Notchview Reservation: The Arthur D. Budd Estate in Windsor, Massachusetts.* Gt. Barrington: Attic Revivals Press, 1986, 48 pp., illus., maps, $5.00.

———. *History of The Mahaiwe Theatre in Great Barrington, Massachusetts.* Gt. Barrington: Attic Revivals Press, 1989, 48 pp., illus., $5.00.

———. *Spanning Berkshire Waterways.* Gt. Barrington: Attic Revivals Press, 1990. 32 pp., photos, maps, $5.00.

———. *William Cullen Bryant's "A Border Tradition."* Gt. Barrington: Attic Revivals Press, 1988, 32 pp., bibliog., $6.50.

Drew, Bernard A. and Donna M. *Mapping the Berkshires.* Gt. Barrington: Attic Revivals Press, 1985. 48 pp., illus. maps, $5.00.

Miller, Amy Bess. *Hancock Shaker Village/The City of Peace: An Effort to Restore a Vision 1960–1985.* Hancock: Hancock Shaker Village, 1984. 170 pp., illus., photos, appendices, bibliog., index, $19.95; pap., $12.00.

Murray, Stuart and James McCabe. *Norman Rockwell's Four Freedoms.* Stockbridge: Berkshire House Publishers, 1993. 176 pp., illus., $24.95; pap. $14.95.

Owens, Carole. *The Berkshire Cottages: A Vanishing Era.* Stockbridge: Berkshire House Publishers, 1984. 240 pp., photos, illus., index, $29.95, pap.

Pincus, Andrew L. *Scenes from Tanglewood.* Boston: Northeastern University Press, 1989. 287 pp., photos, $14.95, pap.

The Stockbridge Story: 1739–1989. Stockbridge: Town of Stockbridge, 1989. 209 pp., illus., photos, index, $25.00.

PHOTOGRAPHIC STUDIES

Bazan, John. *Rails Across the Berkshire Hills. Railroad Photography, 1890–1984.* Pittsfield: The Author, 1984. Photos, $9.95, pap.

Binzen, Bill. *The Berkshires.* Chester, CT: Globe-Pequot Press, 1986. 90 color photos, $19.95.

Chefetz, Sheila. *Antiques for the Table*. New York: Viking-Penguin, 1993. 232 pp., 275 color photos, bibliog., Berkshire resource directory, index. Many photographs of Berkshire summer cottages.

Gilder, Cornelia Brooke. *Views of the Valley-Tyringham 1739–1989*. Tyringham: the Hopbrook Community Club, 1989. 142 pp., photos, $15, pap.

Scott, Walter. *The Norman Rockwell Bicycle Tours of Stockbridge*. Stockbridge: SnO Publications, 1980. 32 post cards, $10.95.

RECREATION

A Canoe Guide to the Housatonic River, Berkshire County. Pittsfield: Berkshire County Regional Planning Commission. Illus., maps. This guide being updated for summer 1994.

Appalachian Trail Guide to Massachusetts-Connecticut. Harpers Ferry, WV: Appalachian Trail Conference, 1990. 189 pp., maps, $18.95.

Cuyler, Lewis C. *Bike Rides in the Berkshire Hills*. Gt. Barrington: Berkshire House Publishers, 1990. 200 pp., illus., maps, $8.95, pap.

Laubach, René. *A Guide to Natural Places in the Berkshire Hills*. Stockbridge: Berkshire House Publishers, 1992. 288 pp., illus.,maps, $9.95.

Lyon, Steve. *Bicyclist's Guide to the Southern Berkshires*. Lenox, MA: Freewheel Publications, 1993. 256 pp., pap., $16.95.

Silver, Patti, and Spencer Becky. *Adventures in Berkshire County: Places to Go With Children*. Stockbridge: Berkshire House Publishers, 1992. 144 pp., illus., maps, $7.95, pap.

Stevens, Lauren. *Hikes & Walks in the Berkshire Hills*. Stockbridge: Berkshire House Publishers, 1990. 224 pp., maps, $9.95, pap.

Stevens, Lauren. *Skiing in the Berkshire Hills*. Stockbridge: Berkshire House Publishers, 1991. 232 pp., maps, $8.95, pap.

TRAVEL

The Berkshire Hills-A WPA Guide, with a new foreword by Roger Linscott. Boston: Northeastern University Press, 1987. 390 pp., illus., photos, maps, lore, history, $14.95, pap.

Bryan, Clark, W. *The Book of Berkshire*. N. Egremont: Past Perfect Books, 1993 reprint. 304 pp., engravings, index, large color map of county, $24.95. A splendid reprint of the first guide to the Berkshires.

Davenport, John. *Berkshire-Bennington Locator*. Madison, WI: First Impressions, 1988. 112 pp., maps, $10.95, pap.

Whitman, Herbert S. *Exploring the Berkshires*. NY: Hippocrene, 1991. 240 pp., illus., $9.95, pap.

Books You Can Borrow

Annin, Katherine Huntington. *Richmond, Massachusetts: The Story of a Berkshire Town and Its People, 1765–1965.* Richmond: Richmond Civic Association, 1964. 214 pp., photos, illus., index. Only complete readable history of town.

Birdsall, Richard. *Berkshire County, A Cultural History.* NY: Greenwood Press, 1978 reprint. 401 pp., notes, bibliog., index. Only cultural study of region; emphasis on first half of the 19th century. Chapters cover development of law, newspapers, education, religion. Special attention to the literary heritage.

Bittman, Sam, and Steven A. Satullo, eds. *Berkshire: Seasons of Celebration.* Pittsfield: Either/Or Press, 1982. 112 pp., photos.

Boltwood, Edward. *The History of Pittsfield, Massachusetts from the Year 1876 to the Year 1916.* Pittsfield: The City, 1916. Covers history of most important county communities to early 20th century.

Bulkeley, Morgan. *Mountain Farm: Poems From the Berkshire Hills.* Chester: Hollow Springs Press, 1984. 95 pp., illus.

Collections of the Berkshire Historical and Scientific Society. Pittsfield: Sun Printing Co., 1892–1899. Papers on historical topics read at Society meetings. Often composed by local authorities, subjects range from Berkshire geology to glass manufacture in Berkshire. Often unique and usually reliable.

Consolati, Florence. *See All the People: Or, Life in Lee.* Lee: The Author, 1978. Colorful, quaint history of the town and its citizens. 442 pp., photos, bibliog., index.

Coxey, Willard D. *Ghosts of Old Berkshire.* Gt. Barrington: The Berkshire Courier, 1934. Legends and folktales of Berkshire people and places.

Drew, Bernard A. *Berkshire Between Covers: A Literary History.* Gt. Barrington: Attic Revivals Press, 1985. 32 pp., illus., bibliog. Brief biographical sketches of deceased fiction writers with significant connections to the Berkshires.

―――. *Berkshire Off the Trail.* Gt. Barrington: Attic Revivals Press, 1982. 96 pp., illus., index. Informal history of less traditional subjects.

Emblidge, David, ed. *The Third Berkshire Anthology: A Collection of Literature and Art.* Lenox: Berkshire Writers, Inc., 1982. 185 pp., illus.

Field, Stephen, ed. *A History of the County of Berkshire, Massachusetts.* Pittsfield: Samuel W. Bush, 1829. Perhaps the first history of the Berkshires, sponsored by the Berkshire Association of Congregational Ministers. A general history of the county, followed by accounts of individual towns, each written by its minister.

Jones, Electa F. *Stockbridge, Past and Present: Or, Records of an Old Mission Sta-*

tion. Springfield: Samuel Bowles & Co., 1854. History of early Stockbridge (early Indian mission and Stockbridge Indians).

Kupferberg, Herbert. *Tanglewood.* NY: McGraw-Hill, 1976. 280 pp., photos, bibliog., index. Most thorough history of the Berkshire Music Festival.

Lewis, Joseph W. Berkshire *Men of Worth.* 4 Vols. Scrapbook of newspaper articles. From 1933 until well after Lewis' death in 1938, over 300 columns on Berkshire notables were published in the *Berkshire Evening Eagle.* Series featured penetrating biographical sketches of men whom Lewis regarded as important historical figures. Perhaps the most comprehensive biographical treatment of historical Berkshire figures.

Oakes, Donald, ed. *A Pride of Palaces: Lenox Summer Cottages, 1883–1933.* Lenox: Lenox Library, 1981. 83 pp., illus., photos.

Perry, Arthur L. *Origins in Williamstown.* NY: Charles Scribner's Sons, 1896. Detailed, well-researched history of early Williamstown and other segments of northern Berkshire.

Preiss, Lillian E. Sheffield, *Frontier Town.* Sheffield: Sheffield Bicentennial Comm., 1976. 188 pp., photos, illus., bibliog., index. Good, traditional town history.

Resch, Tyler, ed. *Berkshire, The First Three Hundred Years 1676–1976.* Pittsfield: Eagle Pub. Co., 1976. 163 pp., photos, illus., maps, bibliog., index. Photographs and illustrations of significant and interesting historical events and people, with concise captions.

Sedgwick, Sarah Cabot & Christina Sedgwick Marquand. *Stockbridge, 1739–1939: A Chronicle.* Stockbridge: The Authors, 1939. 306 pp., photos, illus., bibliog. Popular, readable history.

Smith, J.E.A., ed. *History of Berkshire County, Massachusetts, With Biographical Sketches of Its Prominent Men.* 2 Vols. NY: J.B. Beers & Co., 1885. Wideranging history covering every aspect of Berkshire life. Nine chapters on individual towns. Most comprehensive, reliable history of the first 200 years of Berkshire development.

Smith, J.E.A. *The History of Pittsfield (Berkshire County), Massachusetts, From the Year 1734 to the Year 1800.* Boston: Lee, Shepard, 1869. *The History of Pittsfield (Berkshire County), Massachusetts, From the Year 1800 to the Year 1876.* Springfield: C.W. Bryan & Co., 1876. The most detailed, thorough town histories for the county. Smith had access to much material since lost; covers surrounding communities as well.

Taylor, Charles J. *History of Great Barrington (Berkshire), Massachusetts 1676–1882. Part II, Extension 1882–1922* by George Edwin MacLean. Gt. Barrington: 1928. Detailed, accurate history of town, particularly the Taylor segment.

Wood, David H. *Lenox, Massachusetts Shire Town.* Lenox: 1968. Similar to Sedgwick history of Stockbridge but more detailed.

CLIMATE AND WEATHER REPORTS

CLIMATE

If you don't like the weather in New England, wait five minutes. . . . That was Mark Twain's opinion (he summered in Tyringham), and there are plenty of days when his exaggeration seems pretty close to reality. How the Berkshire climate strikes you depends on what you're used to. People visiting from outside the region may be helped by the following information.

In general, while summers are blessedly mild due to the elevation of the Berkshire hills, winters can be fiercely cold and snowy with tricky driving conditions. Of course, what one person (who doesn't ski) finds annoying in a New England winter, another (who does ski) will praise to the skies. Summer visitors should remember that nights can be quite cool; bring sweaters. And those in search of great snow should note that spring comes to South County well before it does up north and up higher. One day, we went cross-country skiing in the morning on good snow at Notchview in Windsor and then ran the rototiller in the garden at home in Great Barrington that same afternoon!

TEMPERATURE AND PRECIPITATION

Average Temperature	October	48.4°
	January	20.4°
	April	43.4°
	July	68.3°

Average Annual Total Precipitation

Rainfall plus water content of snow		44.15"
	Snow	75.7"

For people who are really into statistics or are interested for business or investment purposes, the source for this information and a great deal more, *The Berkshire Data Book*, is available (for $100) from the Central Berkshire Chamber of Commerce (413-499-4000; 66 West St., Pittsfield, MA 01201).

WEATHER REPORTS

Great Barrington	413-528-1118
Lee/Stockbridge	413-298-5556
Pittsfield	413-499-2627
Adams/Cheshire	413-743-3313
North Adams	413-662-2221
Williamstown	413-458-2222

GUIDED TOURS

If you want to be bused directly to Berkshire's high spots by an informed guide, there are hosts of possibilities, some based here in the hills, some coming from New York and Boston. From the big cities, there are fall-foliage tours, Tanglewood tours, and ski tours, all of which provide transport, tickets, meals, and lodging plus background on the sites. For an individual, these tours offer a taste of the area's delights in a perfectly packaged form. For groups, the tours turn a possible logistical nightmare into a fun-filled holiday.

Should you be coming from New York or Boston, a travel agent may be very helpful in choosing the right tour. The best of the commercial tour companies belong to the National Tour Association. The best of the charter bus companies belong to the American Bus Association. Here are a few of the most experienced Berkshire guided-tour companies operating from New York and Boston.

NEW YORK

Parker Tours 718-428-7800, 800-833-9600; 218-14 Northern Blvd., Bayside, NY.
Tauck Tours 800-468-2825; 11 Wilton Rd., Westport, CT.

BOSTON

Collette Tours 401-728-3805; 162 Middle St., Pawtucket, R.I.

WITHIN THE BERKSHIRES

Within Berkshire, there are also a number of guided tour options. For something relatively brief and informal, a local cab driver can usually be persuaded to drive you around, adding colorful histories that only a cabbie might know. For more organized, detailed tours, consider the following.

Berkshire Cottage Tours (413-637-1899; The Mount, Plunkett St., Lenox) This step-on guide service focuses on the mansions of the Gilded Age. Starting at the Mount, the tour takes you by your own group's tour bus through Lenox and Stockbridge, filling you in on the fabulous histories as you view more than 20 of the "cottages." Light refreshments served in the garden of Naumkeag are a highlight of this three-hour tour. Advance reservations are required.

Berkshire Tour Company (413-443-5017, 800-244-5017; Box 383, Pittsfield, 01202) Berkshire native Nancy C. Henriques provides a wide range of tour services, including group tours of Berkshire County sites (a favorite is the Berkshire Cottages tour), plus walking tours of the Main Streets of Stockbridge, Lenox, and Williamstown. She also provides customized tours including lunch or dinner at local restaurants, excursions to Tanglewood and other music and theater festivals, and combinations of tours for individuals or any size group. Phone for prices and schedules.

Berkshire Hiking Holidays — See the description under "Hiking" in Chapter Seven, *Recreation*.

HANDICAPPED SERVICES

Although Berkshire is a mountainous region with lots of rough terrain, handicapped people will find access quite easy to most cultural sites and events, to many lodgings and restaurants, and to most shops. In Chapter Three, *Lodging*, we specify those places where we know handicapped access is feasible. Elsewhere, to confirm the situation, use the phone numbers we provide to get information.

The Berkshire Visitors Bureau (413-443-9186; Berkshire Common, Pittsfield, MA 01201) publishes an annual guide listing many Berkshire services and attractions, in many cases, specifying access to handicapped people. The *AAA Tour Guide*, available through the Auto Club of Berkshire County (413-445-5635; 196 South St., Pittsfield) also designates restaurants, lodging, etc. with handicapped access.

As for transportation, the *Berkshire Regional Transit Authority* (413-499-2782 or 800-292-2782) runs the public bus system throughout the major towns in the county and has buses equipped with wheelchair lifts. See Chapter Two, *Transportation*, "Getting Around the Berkshires" for more information.

HOSPITALS

South County

GREAT BARRINGTON

Fairview Hospital 413-528-0790; 29 Lewis Ave.

Central County

PITTSFIELD

Berkshire Medical Center 413-447-2000; 725 North St.
Hillcrest Hospital 413-443-4761; 165 Tor Court.

North County

NORTH ADAMS

North Adams Regional Hospital 413-663-3701; Hospital Ave.

LATE NIGHT FOOD AND FUEL

Berkshire Truck Plaza (food and fuel); open all night: Rte. 102, W. Stockbridge, 413-232-4233.

Convenience Plus (food and fuel); open all night: 84 Tyler St., Pittsfield, 413-499-1741; 241 Main St., Lee, 413-243-2724; open till 11 p.m.: South St., Stockbridge, 413-298-4036.

Cumberland Farms (food and fuel); open all night: 885 Dalton Ave., Pittsfield, 413-447-9532; Main St., Gt. Barrington, 413-528-9852.

Dakota Restaurant (food); open till 11 p.m., Fri.–Sat: Pittsfield-Lenox Rd., Pittsfield, 413-499-7900.

Depot 22 (food and fuel): Rte. 22, Canaan, NY, 518-781-4400.

Diesel Dan's (food and fuel); restaurant open all night Mon.–Thurs., Fri. till 11 p.m.; pumps open all night, exc. Fri. till midnight: Rte. 102, Lee, 413-243-4432.

Dunkin' Donuts (food); open all night: 5 Union St., N. Adams, 413-662-2274; 18 First St., Pittsfield, 413-499-0371; Main St, Lee, 413-243-1696.

Grampy's Convenience Store (food and fuel); open all night: 223 Columbia St., N. Adams, 413-743-0322; 41 Housatonic St., Lee, 413-243-2088.

Jimmy's (food); open till midnight Fri.–Sat.: 112 W. Housatonic, Pittsfield, 413-499-1288.

Joe's Diner (food); open all night except Sat. and Sun.: Main St., Lee, 413-243-9756.

Luau Hale (food); open till midnight Fri.–Sat.: Pittsfield-Lenox Rd., Lenox, 413-443-4745.

P.J.'s Convenience Store (food); open till 11:30 p.m. Mon.–Sat.: S. Main, Sheffield, 413-229-6610

Papa Joe's (food); open till 11 p.m. Fri.–Sat.: 107 Newell St., Pittsfield, 413-442-1472.

Price Chopper Supermarkets (food); open all night, Mon.–Fri., Sat. till midnight: Pittsfield Rd., Rte. 7, Lenox, 413-443-5449 and Merrill Rd., Pittsfield, 413-442-6440; open till midnight, Mon.–Sat., till 7 p.m., Sun: Stockbridge Rd., Rte. 7, Gt. Barrington, 413-528-9262, and Park St., Lee, 413-243-2238.

Salt & Pepper North (food); open all night from 11:30 p.m. till 3 p.m.: 641 North St., Pittsfield, 413-499-3306.

Stop & Shop Supermarket (food); open all night Mon.–Fri.; Sat. till midnight: Merrill Rd., Pittsfield, 413-499-0745.

MEDIA: MAGAZINES AND NEWSPAPERS; TV/RADIO STATIONS

MAGAZINES AND NEWSPAPERS

The Advocate (413-458-9000; 36 Spring St., Williamstown; every Wednesday) Highly readable, well-researched articles, mostly on community-related topics for northern Berkshire and southern Vermont.

Berkshire Business Journal (413-499-3400; 74 North St., Pittsfield; monthly freebie) Berkshire's answer to the *Wall Street Journal.* Lively up-to-date news of Berkshire business doings.

The Berkshire Courier (413-528-3020; 620 S. Main St., Gt. Barrington; every Thursday) An oldie but goodie among town newspapers, with informative articles on all local topics.

The Berkshire Eagle

The Berkshire Eagle (413-447-7311; 75 S. Church St., Pittsfield; daily) The county's newspaper of record, a Pulitzer Prize–winning publication with extensive world, national, state, and local news, plus features and comics ("Doonesbury"!). The *Eagle*'s Sunday edition, added several years ago, is chockful of interesting features of global, national, and local significance. During the summer the *Eagle* also publishes *Berkshires Week,* a supplementary magazine-in-newsprint containing colorful articles, a calendar of events, and lots of ads from local dining and entertainment places.

Berkshire Magazine (413-298-3791; Box 617, Stockbridge; bimonthly) Graphically exciting, regional. Feature stories and information calendar in a glossy, full-color format.

The Berkshire Record (413-528-5380; 271 Main St., Gt. Barrington; weekly) Newest Southern Berkshire weekly features current affairs and articles of historic note.

Berkshire Senior (413-499-1353; 66 Wendell Ave., Pittsfield; monthly) Articles by and about Berkshire senior citizens.

Country Journal (667-3211; 25 Main St., Huntington, Hampshire County; Thursday) Covers the central hill towns.

New Visions (413-443-4817; P.O.Box 2336, Pittsfield; quarterly) Articles, announcements and ads about alternative healing, psychological growth and spiritual transformation.

The Paper (518-392-2674; P.O.Box 336, Chatham, NY; monthly, first Thursday).

The Penny Saver (413-243-2341; 14 Park Pl., Box 300, Lee; Tuesday) Central County's shopping guide, including classifieds, TV listings, nightlife, comprehensive business service listings.

The Pittsfield Gazette (413-443-2010; 141 North St., Pittsfield; Thursday) Local Pittsfield news.

Shopper's Guide (413-528-0095; Bridge St., Box 89, Gt. Barrington; weekly) Southern Berkshire's shopping guide, including enticing sections on real estate and automobiles.

The South Advocate (413-637-2225; 25 Housatonic St., Lenox; weekly).

The Transcript (413-663-3741; American Legion Dr., N. Adams; weekday afternoons, Saturday morning) Local, some state and national news; covers northern Berkshire County and southern Vermont.

Yankee Shopper (413-684-1373; 839 Main St., Box 96, Dalton; weekly) Central and Northern Berkshire's shopping guide, including scads of used cars, rototillers, computers, vacuum cleaners, baby bunnies as well as a business/professional services directory.

RADIO STATIONS

National Public Radio. There are four stations receivable in the Berkshires:
   WAMC-FM, 90.3; 800-323-9262; Albany, NY.
   WAMQ-FM, 105.1; 800-323-9262; Albany, NY
   WFCR-FM, 88.5; 413-545-0100; Amherst, MA.
   WMHT-FM, 89.1; 518-356-1700; Schenectady, NY.

Other Local Radio Stations:
   WBEC-AM, 1420; 413-499-3333; Pittsfield. General.
   WBEC-FM, 105.5; 413-499-3333; Pittsfield. Rock music.
   WBRK-FM, 101; 413-442-1553; Pittsfield. General.
   WMNB-FM, 100.1; 413-663-6567; N. Adams. General.
   WNAW-AM, 1230; 413-663-6567; N. Adams. General
   WSBS-AM, 860; 413-528-0860; Gt. Barrington. General.
   WTBR-FM, 89.7; 413-499-1483; Pittsfield. General.
   WUHN-AM, 1110; 413-499-1100; Pittsfield. General.
   WUPE-FM, 96; 413-499-1100; Pittsfield. Rock and other music.

TELEVISION

A recent phenomenon in the Berkshires is the growing popularity of community-based television on cable channels. Particularly in southern Berkshire, weekly selectmen's meetings have attracted a burgeoning collection of viewers.

In addition to taping town meetings, city council meetings, and other events of civil and local interest, the three locally run stations in each region generate

such programs as "Adopt-a-Pet," live viewer call-ins, self-help and religious programs, along with musical and dramatic entertainments by local performers.
Community-based television channels:

Community Television for the Southern Berkshires (CTSB): Century Berkshire Cable Channel 11 (413-243-0676)
Pittsfield Community Television: Warner Cable Channel 5 (413-443-4755).
Adelphia Cable: Channel 15 (413-664-4011)

Consult the *Berkshire Eagle* for schedules.

REAL ESTATE

Window shopping for a dream house in the Berkshires.

Jonathan Sternfield

What's your dream house? An isolated cabin, deep in the woods? A late 20th-century split-level, suburban tract house? A lakeside condo for time-sharing? Or a 40-room Gilded Age mansion that just needs a couple-of-hundred grand in handyman repairs? Berkshire County has them all.

If you are shopping for Berkshire real estate, you can obtain information as follows.

Lists of realtors: Consult the Yellow Pages of the telephone book or, if you're far away, contact any of the three Chambers of Commerce: *Southern Berkshire*

Chamber of Commerce (413-528-1510; 362 Main St., Gt. Barrington, MA 01230); *Central Berkshire Chamber of Commerce* (413-499-4000; 66 West St., Pittsfield, MA 01201); *Northern Berkshire Chamber of Commerce* (413-663-3735; 69-1/2 Main St., N. Adams, MA 01247). All three organizations will send a list of their realtor members. The seasonal tourist information brochures from the *Berkshire Hills Conference* (413-443-9186; 50 South St., Pittsfield, MA 01201) also list numerous realtors.

Once you're into the process of buying land or a house, it is essential to check with the local town government about zoning laws, building permits, etc. Such regulations vary widely from town to town. See "Area Codes," in this chapter, for town hall telephone numbers.

You can also follow the real estate market in the newspapers; see "Media," in this chapter. *The Berkshire Home Buyers Guide* is a free monthly publication, distributed in local shops or available from 413-528-5829; P.O. Box 422, Monterey, MA 01245.

RELIGIOUS SERVICES AND ORGANIZATIONS

Berkshire County has an active and unusually diverse religious community. The best source for information about church and synagogue services is the Saturday edition of the *Berkshire Eagle*. The Berkshire County Telephone Directory has a comprehensive list of all mainstream religious organizations, under the headings "Churches" and "Synagogues." For nontraditional groups, a helpful publication to consult is *New Visions*, published seasonally and distributed through various shops. Also, keep an eye on community bulletin boards at the area's colleges and in towns such as Great Barrington, Stockbridge, Lenox, Pittsfield, and Williamstown.

ROAD SERVICE

Emergency road service from *AAA*, anywhere in the county, can be obtained by calling 413-443-1635, Pittsfield. For non-AAA drivers, the following is a listing of some 24-hour emergency towing services throughout the county.

South County

Decker's Auto Body, Gt. Barrington	413-528-1432
's Garage, Gt. Barrington	413-528-1234

R W's Inc., Lee   413-243-0946
Steve's Auto Repair, Gt. Barrington   413-528-9833

Central County

Sayers' Auto, Pittsfield   413-443-1635
Southgate Motors, Pittsfield   413-445-5971
Wetherell's, Hinsdale   413-655-2575

North County

West End Auto Body & Glass, N. Adams   413-664-6708

SCHOOLS

PUBLIC SCHOOL DISTRICTS

South County

Berkshire Hills Regional School District, Stockbridge; 413-298-3711
Lee Public Schools; 413-243-0276
Southern Berkshire Regional School District, Sheffield; 413-229-8778

Central County

Central Berkshire Regional School District, Dalton; 413-684-1330
Lenox Public Schools; 413-637-5550
Richmond Consolidated Schools; 413-698-2207
Pittsfield Public Schools; 413-499-9512

North County

Adams-Cheshire Regional School District; 413-743-2939
Town of Clarksburg School Department; 413-664-8735
Town of Florida School Department; 413-664-6023
Town of Lanesborough Schools; 413-442-2229
Town of New Ashford School Department; 413-458-5461
City of North Adams Public Schools; 413-662-3225
Town of Savoy School Department; 413-743-1992
Town of Williamstown School Department; 413-458-5707

PRIVATE AND RELIGIOUS SCHOOLS

South County

Berkshire School, Sheffield; 413-229-8511
De Sisto School, Stockbridge; 413-298-3776
Great Barrington Rudolf Steiner School, Gt. Barrington; 413-528-4015
St. Mary's School, Lee; 413-243-1074

Central County

Berkshire Country Day School, Lenox; 413-637-0755
Berkshire County Christian School, Pittsfield; 413-442-4014
Miss Hall's School, Pittsfield; 413-443-6401
Sacred Heart School, Pittsfield; 413-443-6379
St. Agnes School, Dalton; 413-684-3143
St. Joseph's Central High School, Pittsfield; 413-447-9121
St. Mark's School, Pittsfield; 413-445-4506

North County

Buxton School, Williamstown; 413-458-3919
The Highcroft School, Williamstown; 413-458-8136
Pine Cobble School, Williamstown; 413-458-4680
St. Stanislaus, N. Adams; 413-743-1091

COLLEGES

South County

Simon's Rock College of Bard, Gt. Barrington; 413-528-0771

Central County

Berkshire Community College, Pittsfield; 413-499-4660. In Gt. Barrington: 413-528-4521.

North County

North Adams State College, N. Adams; 413-663-9231
Williams College, Williamstown; 413-597-3131

Index

LODGING BY PRICE

Price Categories:

Inexpensive	Up to $65
Moderate	$65 to $100
Expensive	$100 to $175
Very Expensive	Over $175

SOUTH COUNTY

Inexpensive
Daffer's Mountain Inn
Grouse House
Prospect Hill House

Inexpensive–Moderate
Centuryhurst Antiques B&B
The Depot
Elling's B&B
Stagecoach Hill Inn
Woodside B&B

Inexpensive–Expensive
Arbor Rose B&B
Card Lake Country Inn
Mountain Trails B&B
Parsonage on the Green

Moderate
Baldwin Hill Farm B&B
Bread & Roses
Brook Cove
Coffing-Bostwick House
The Donahoes
Elm Court Inn
Greenmeadows
Hidden Acres B&B
Ivanhoe Country House
Kasindorf's
Littlejohn Manor
New Boston Inn
Race Brook Lodge B&B
Seekonk Pines Inn B&B

Staveleigh House
Stonewood Inn
Trail's End Guests

Moderate–Expensive
Aunti M's
Berkshire Thistle
The Egremont Inn
The Federal House
The Golden Goose
Marble Inn
The Morgan House Inn
Oak n' Spruce Lodge
Orchard Shade
Ramblewood Inn
Red Bird Inn
Round Hill Harm B&B
Thornewood Inn
Turning Point Inn

Moderate–Very Expensive
Best Western Black Swan Inn
Chambéry Inn
Inn on Laurel Lake
Old Inn on the Green, The and
    Gedney Farm

Expensive
Christine's Guest House B&B
Merrell Tavern Inn
Weathervane Inn
The Williamsville Inn
Windflower Inn

Expensive–Very Expensive
Applegate
Haus Andreas
Inn at Shaker Mill Tavern
The Inn at Stockbridge
Joyous Garde B&B
The Red Lion Inn
The Roeder House
Taggart House B&B

Moderate–Expensive
The Mill House Inn
The Sedgwick Inn
Swiss Hutte Country Inn

Expensive–Very Expensive
Swift River Inn
The Undermountain Inn
The White Hart Inn

RESTAURANTS BY PRICE

Price Codes:

Inexpensive	Up to $10
Moderate	$10 to $20
Expensive	$20 to $35
Very Expensive	Over $35

SOUTH COUNTY

Inexpensive
Berkshire Place
The Cafe
The Deli
Dos Amigos
The Gaslight Cafe
Great Wall Chinese Restaurant
Hickory Bill's Bar-B-Que
Hill's
Hoplands
Joe's Diner
Martin's
Midge's
Mom's
Naji's
Ruby's Diner
20 Railroad Street
Wildflower Bakery & Cafe

Inexpensive–Moderate
The Back Porch
Cactus Cafe
Castle Street Cafe
Jodi's Country Cookery
Oh Calcutta!
Panda West

Sullivan Station

Inexpensive–Expensive
Caffe Pomo d'Oro

Moderate
Bronze Dog Cafe
Cygnet's at the Black Swan Inn
The Hillside
Kintaro
La Tomate
The Painted Lady
Shaker Mill Tavern
Stagecoach Hill Inn

Moderate–Expensive
Egremont Inn
Michael's
Morgan House Inn
The Old Mill
Shogun
Spencer's Restaurant
Truc Orient Express

Moderate–Very Expensive
Old Inn on the Green & Gedney
  Farm

Expensive
Boiler Room Cafe
Elm Court Inn
Federal House
John Andrew's
La Bruschetta Ristorante
Red Lion Inn
Williamsville Inn

RESTAURANTS BY CUISINE

SOUTH COUNTY

American/Regional
Boiler Room Cafe
Bronze Dog Cafe
The Cafe
Castle Street Cafe
The Deli
Egremont Inn
The Gaslight Cafe
Hickory Bill's Bar-B-Que
Hill's
Hoplands
Joe's Diner
John Andrew's
Martin's
Michael's
Midge's
Mom's
Morgan House Inn
Old Inn on the Green & Gedney Farm
The Old Mill
Red Lion Inn
Ruby's Diner
Shaker Mill Tavern
Sullivan Station
20 Railroad Street
Wildflower Bakery & Cafe

Chinese
Great Wall Chinese Restaurant
Panda West

Continental
Boiler Room Cafe
Cygnet's at the Black Swan Inn
Elm Court Inn
Federal House
The Hillside
The Painted Lady
Spencer's Restaurant

Eclectic
John Andrew's
Windflower Inn

English
Stagecoach Hill Inn

French
Castle Street Cafe
La Tomate
Old Inn on the Green & Gedney
Farm
Williamsville Inn

Greek, Lebanese
Naji's

Indian
Oh Calcutta!

International
The Back Porch
Berkshire Place

Italian
Caffe Pomo d'Oro
Castle Street Cafe
Jodi's Country Cookery
La Bruschetta Ristorante
Michael's
Mom's
The Painted Lady
Shaker Mill Tavern
Stagecoach Hill Inn

Japanese
Kintaro
Shogun

Macrobiotic
Shogun

Mexican
Cactus Cafe
Dos Amigos

Middle Eastern
Hill's

SHOPPING BY AREA

SOUTH COUNTY

Antiques
Aardenburg Antiques
Don Abarbanel
Elise Abrams Antiques
Anthony's Antiques
Ashley Falls Antiques
Asian Antiques
Vincent and Barbara Beaver Antiques
    and Interiors
Bird Cage Antiques
Blackbird Antiques and Collectibles
Bygone Days
Carriage House Antiques
Carriage Trade Antiques
Centuryhurst Berkshire Antique
    Gallery
Coffman's Country Antiques Market
Corashire Antiques
Corner House Antiques
Country Cat Antiques
Country Dining Room and Tea Gar-
    den Antiques
Cupboards & Roses Antiques
Darr Antiques and Interiors
Douglas Antiques
Dovetail Antiques
Emporium Antique Center
Europa
Falcon Antiques
Geffner/Schatzky Antiques and Vari-
    eties
Good & Hutchinson Associates, Inc.
Frederick Hatfield Antiques
Henry B. Holt
Howard's Antiques
Susan and Paul Kleinwald, Inc.
Kuttner Antiques
David J. LeBeau Fine Antiques
The Kahns' Antique and Estate Jew-
    elry
Le Périgord Antiques
Lewis & Wilson

The Lion, The Witch, and The
    Wardrobe
Madison Upstairs
Donald McGrory Oriental Rugs
Memories
Barbara Moran Fine and Decorative
    Arts
Mullin-Jones Antiquities
Olde-Antiques Market
Ole T.J.'s Antique Barn
Once Upon a Table
The Powder House Shop
Red Barn Antiques
Red Horse Antiques
Reuss Antique & Art Center
Saturday Sweets
Sawyer Antiques
1750 House Antiques
Sheffield Plains Antiques
Susan Silver Antiques
Elliot and Grace Snyder
Snyder's Store
Southfield Antiques Market
The Splendid Peasant
Lois W. Spring Antiques
Robert Thayer American Antiques
Tom Carey's Place
Twin Fire Antiques
The Vollmers
David M. Weiss Antiques
Whip Shop Antiques

Book Stores
Apple Tree Books
Berkshire Used Books
Hugh Black Books
The Bookloft
Farshaw's Books
Gventer B&S Gventer Books
Yellow House Books

Clothing and Accessories
1884 House
Ben's

Berkshire Town Maps

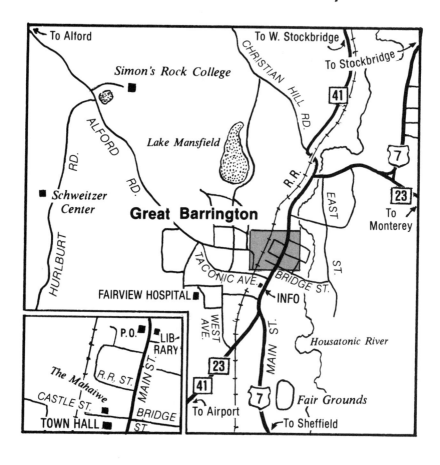

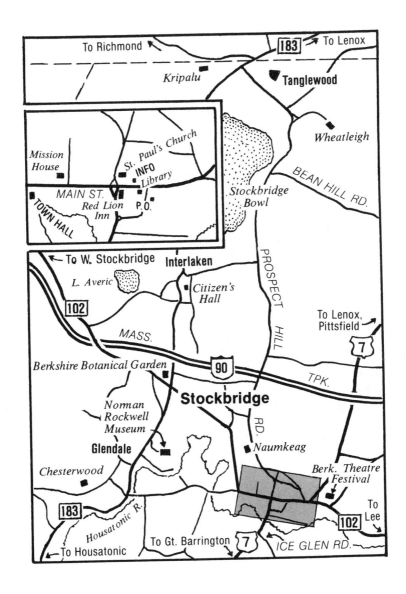

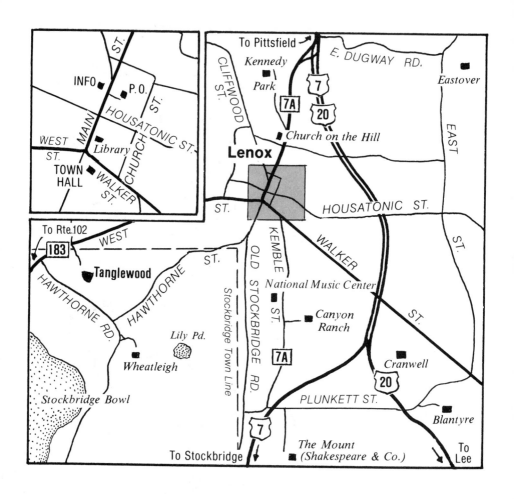

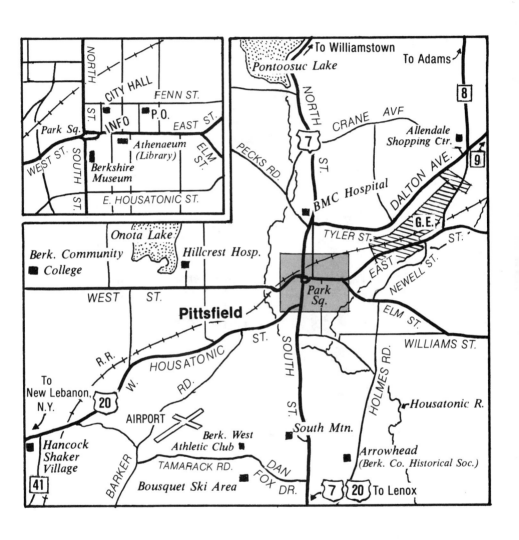

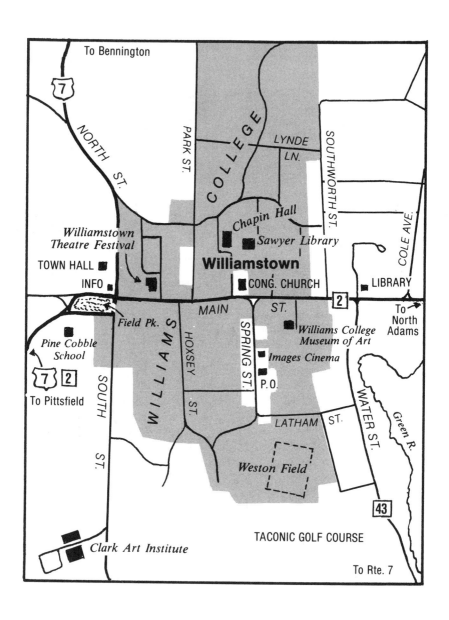

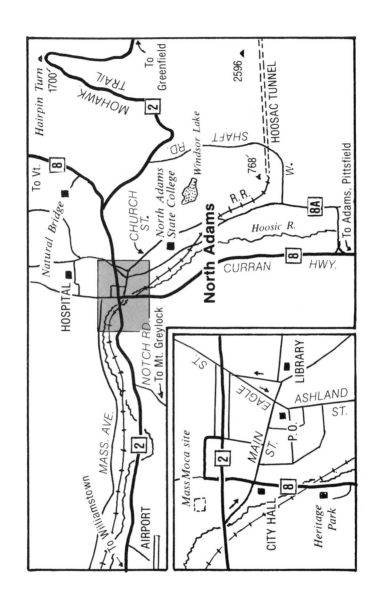

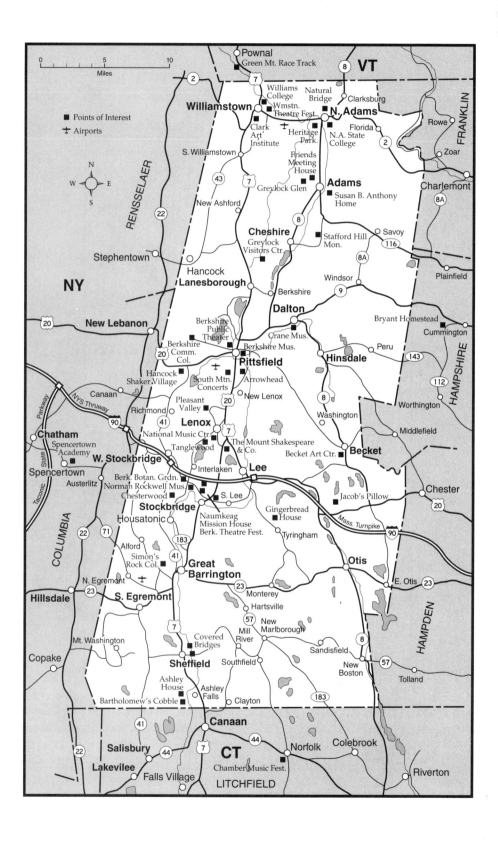

About the Principal Author and Photographer

Mark Sternfield

Jonathan Sternfield is a writer, photographer, inventor, publisher, and tennis pro. Born in New York City, he has lived in the Berkshires since shortly after graduating from the University of Pennsylvania in 1969. Residing in and around Great Barrington, he has also traveled extensively in Europe, living for periods in England and France. As a writer he has worked in Hollywood, developing screenplays for feature films, as well as for the "College Bowl" television show, Rockefeller Center, and General Electric, among other clients. His published works include *The Complete book of Mopeds* (Funk and Wagnalls), *Starring Your Love Life* (Lynx), *The Look of Horror* (Running Press), and numerous articles for *Berkshire Magazine* as well as pieces on electric cars and solar energy for other publications. His nonfiction exploration, *Firewalk*, was published by Berkshire House in 1992. As a photographer, he has created images for advertising, for actors, for book illustration, and for rock videos. His book of color views of New Yorkers, *Apple of My Eye*, is awaiting publication. As publisher of Past Perfect Books, he has produced facsimile editions of *The Book of Berkshire* (1887) and *Nature Studies in Berkshire* (1899), with Wallace Bruce's *The Hudson* (1882) soon to be released. When he's not writing, photographing, inventing, or publishing, Jonathan Sternfield is a tennis pro at Canyon Ranch in Lenox.